SPECULATIVE GRAMMARS OF THE MIDDLE AGES

APPROACHES
TO
SEMIOTICS

edited by

THOMAS A. SEBEOK

assisted by

DONNA JEAN UMIKER

11

1971

MOUTON

THE HAGUE · PARIS

SPECULATIVE GRAMMARS
OF THE
MIDDLE AGES

THE DOCTRINE OF *PARTES ORATIONIS*
OF THE MODISTAE

by

G. L. BURSILL-HALL

1971

MOUTON

THE HAGUE · PARIS

LIBRARY OF CONGRESS CATALOG CARD NUMBER: 70-151246

Printed in The Netherlands by Mouton & Co., Printers, The Hague.

*To my Mother and
the memory of my Father*

ACKNOWLEDGEMENTS

I take much pleasure in acknowledging the great amount of help I have received while preparing this study. I would make particular mention of two scholars.

My debt to Professor R. H. Robins of the University of London is very great indeed. I owe to him the choice of subject which introduced me to a whole new field of scholarly interest; more important still, he has been throughout a constant source of patient and friendly criticism, warm encouragement, and scholarly stimulus.

I owe also a very real debt to Father F. P. Dinneen, S. J. of Georgetown University with whom I have over the years enjoyed many fruitful and profitable discussions on subjects as widely separated as mediaeval grammatical theory, classical logic, mediaeval metaphysics, and modern linguistic theory.

My thanks for the great amount of material aid I received in the course of the preparation of this book go: to the President and Board of Governors of the University of British Columbia for the extended leave of absence of two academic years from my post which enabled me to undertake and complete the research as well as the writing of the original thesis; to the Canada Council, the British Council, the Leon and Thea Koerner Foundation for their financial awards; to the Central Research Fund of the University of London and the President's Research Fund of Simon Fraser University for grants which have enabled me to obtain copies of the Grammatica Speculativa of Thomas of Erfurt and the Summa de arte grammatica of Peter Helias and other texts; to Dr. R. W. Hunt of the Bodleian Library, and to the Librarians and Staffs of the Library of the British Museum and of the Library of Cornell University for their unfailing kindness and help.

My very real thanks go to Professors R. H. Robins, E. W. Roberts, and D. H. Hymes who were kind enough to read part or all of the manuscript; they were prolific in their suggestions which I have tried to incorporate in this book. I am also most grateful to Professor L. M. de Rijk who made many valuable criticisms; his very scholarly book did not become available to me until after I had completed this study and I have not been able to incorporate the results of his researches as fully as I would have liked. More important still, at least as far as I am concerned, is that they have saved me from numerous inaccuracies, careless errors, and factual mistakes. The errors and inaccuracies that remain result entirely from my own inadequacies or my obstinacy. I also wish to express my thanks to Professor T. A. Sebeok; his constant counsel and kindness are very much appreciated.

Lastly, my thanks to my wife, my most demanding critic, not only for the material help in preparing the index and the typescript, but more particularly for her constant encouragement, for without that this book would most surely never have been completed.

North Vancouver, 1968   G. L. Bursill-Hall

CONTENTS

INTRODUCTION

This study was approved in substantially its present form for the Ph.D. degree in the University of London in 1959.

The work represents a somewhat new departure for studies in General Linguistics. The speculative grammarians of the Middle Ages are quite well known to most students of the Middle Ages but are almost unknown to the majority of modern linguists. This book attempts to make a critical examination of some of these mediaeval grammarians,[1] *not,* however, by a mediaevalist but by a modern linguist; the aim has been to examine and describe the grammatical theories, in particular the theories of the partes orationis, of a group of speculative grammarians now known as the Modistae, who were active in the later 13th and 14th centuries.

Grammatical theory and study in Europe can look back on an unbroken past of some 2000 years but little is known, however, by modern linguists about this long and illustrious past. Professor R. H. Robins has shown [2] the broad lines of progress in grammatical study from the ancient Greeks to the close of the Middle Ages and has more recently given us a general history of linguistics; [3] we have, however, no detailed history of linguistics which takes us up to the present era, but, as Professor H. Hoenigswald has pointed out,[4] it is not yet possible to write the full history of grammatical theory, since so much of the original material remains to be edited and interpreted. Robins, indeed,

---

[1]   This work is based to a very great extent on the grammars of Siger de Courtrai and Thomas of Erfurt; constant reference is made throughout to the grammars of Martin of Dacia and Michel de Marbais. A separate study of Martin is in preparation; his work would appear to be of particular interest since he was probably the first of the Modistae, *viz.* H. Roos, "Die erste Gruppe, deren vorzüglichster und vielleicht erster Vertreter der Traktat des Martinus de Dacia ist ..." (*Die Modi Significandi des Martinus de Dacia,* 1952, p. 132).

[2]   R. H. Robins, *Ancient and Mediaeval Grammatical Theory in Europe* (London, 1951).

[3]   R. H. Robins, *A Short History of Linguistics* (London, 1967).

[4]   H. M. Hoenigswald, Review of: "R. H. Robins, Ancient and Mediaeval Grammatical Theory in Europe", *Language* 29 (1953), 180-182.

has also provided us with a more detailed examination of the grammatical theories of Dionysius Thrax,[5] and the present book is similarly a critical examination of the theories of a group of grammarians of the Middle Ages, i.e. the Modistae, and is in effect a study *in depth* of this group of grammarians.

The Modistae are of particular interest to the modern linguist in that they represent a stage in the development of grammatical theory in the Middle Ages not unlike the present position in modern linguistics. Professor W. O. Dingwall has pointed out[6] that sciences tend to pass from classification to the establishment of theory; it is reasonable to say that such a progression may be observed between Priscian and the Modistae who were concerned with the construction of an over-all theory in terms of Latin just as scholars such as N. A. Chomsky, C. F. Hockett, and M. A. K. Halliday have as their object the formalisation of a linguistic theory, almost it would seem, to the exclusion of descriptive matters. Professor Hockett, in his Presidential address,[7] referred to 'break-throughs' in his account of the development of modern linguistics and we may similarly refer to 'break-throughs' in the development of mediaeval linguistics;[8] the Modistae attempted an 'accountability hypothesis', though it would be foolhardy to develop the analogy any further.

In recent years, a great deal of interest in the history of linguistics has been aroused; many graduate schools and the Summer Institutes of the Linguistic Society of America now offer courses in the history of linguistics.[9] This interest has tended to be limited to post-Saussurean linguistics or at best to linguistics, since Humboldt, but along with the researches of individual scholars this has done much to awaken

---

[5] R. H. Robins, "Dionysius Thrax and the Western Grammatical Tradition", *TPS* (1957), 67-106.

[6] W. O. Dingwall, "Transformational Grammar: Form and Theory", *Lingua* 12 (1963), 233-275.

[7] C. F. Hockett, "Sound Change", *Language* 41 (1965), 185-204.

[8] Peter Helias: "Species cuiuslibet artis qualitates sunt quas artifex per artem attribuit materie. Cum enim species pluribus modis accipiatur, hic pro forma vel pro qualitate ponitur. Sunt ergo species artis grammatice genera linguarum in quibus ars gramatica tractata est et composita". (Ch. Thurot, pp. 126-127.) Robert Kilwardby: "Cum scientia maneat eadem apud omnes, et subiectum eius idem manet. Quare subiectum gramatice debet manere idem omnibus." (Ch. Thurot, p. 127.)

Roger Bacon: "grammatica una et eadem est secundum substantiam in omnibus linguis, licet accidentaliter varietur." (*Gram. Graec.* Oxford MS, ed. Charles, p. 278.) *Cf.* also R. H. Robins, *Op. cit.*, p. 77.

[9] It is perhaps not without significance that at the Seventeenth Annual Round Table Meeting of the Institute of Languages and Linguistics of Georgetown University a whole session should have been devoted to the history of linguistics.

a lively interest in this aspect of linguistic science. More recently still, the work of Professor Chomsky [10] has prompted a great expansion in studies in the linguistic theories of our predecessors.

The significance of Chomsky's contribution has been to demonstrate that the forefathers of modern linguistics – and by that is meant the students of grammar *prior* to the 19th century – were far from being linguistically naive, and that they discussed problems concerning the nature of language which are of the greatest relevance to the *speculations* of the modern linguist.[11] Furthermore, as Chomsky implies, and this is one of the principal underlying themes of the present work, these ideas were developed in an intellectual context quite different from that of today. We reject much of the work of these earlier linguists because we reject the intellectual tradition that nurtured them;[12] nevertheless, the earlier grammarians were studying aspects of the nature of language which are of perennial interest,[13] and it is surely one of the functions of the historian of linguistics to examine the 'capital of ideas' of our predecessors and to suggest their exploitation in the further study of language.[14] We achieve nothing, however, if we insist on viewing them through the filter of our own intellectual environment; they must be seen in terms of a very different situation and it is therefore imperative that the student of the history of linguistics become a participant in the situation.[15]

It is a good thing for the modern linguist to begin to realise that his predecessors did have considerable insights into general linguistic theory and the problems of linguistic description[16] and that they had much to say on these fascinating subjects.[17] It is important that the modern linguist become aware of the history of his science and thereby obtain a more appropriate sense of his own place in a long and honoured

---

[10]   N. A. Chomsky, *Current Issues in Linguistic Theory* (*Janua Linguarum*, Series Minor XXXVIII), 1964. N. A. Chomsky, *Cartesian Linguistics* (New York, 1966).
[11]   N. A. Chomsky, *Cartesian Linguistics*, p. 1.
[12]   G. L. Bursill-Hall, "Notes on the Semantics of Linguistic Description", *In Memory of J. R. Firth* (London, 1966), 40-51.
[13]   R. G. Godfrey, "Late Mediaeval Linguistic Meta-Theory and Chomsky's Syntactic Structures", *Word* 21 (1965), 251-256. N. A. Chomsky, *Cartesian Linguistics*, pp. 72-73. R. H. Robins, "The Development of the Word Class System of the European Grammatical Tradition", *Foundations of Language* 2 (1966), 3-19. D. T. Langendoen, "A Note on the Linguistic Theory of M. Terentius Varro", *Foundations of Language* 2 (1966), 33-36.
[14]   N. A. Chomsky, *Cartesian Linguistics*, p. 3.
[15]   G. L. Bursill-Hall, *Op. cit.*, pp. 41-42.
[16]   N. A. Chomsky, *Current Issues*, pp. 15-16.
[17]   *Cf.* D. Abercrombie, "Our Antecedents are Older and Better than we Think." "Forgotten Phoneticians", *Studies in Phonetics and Linguistics* (Oxford, 1965), p. 75.

tradition. It is probably true to say that the revival of interest in the ancient and mediaeval grammatical traditions derives in great part from the shift in emphasis in modern linguistics. Prior to the fifties, linguistics was concerned essentially with phonology and morphology with only a peripheral interest in syntax (what Dingwall has called the 'classification of observable properties and relations'),[18] whereas there is no question that linguistics in the late fifties and sixties has become grammar oriented. One result of the earlier emphasis on phonology had been the proper recognition of the excellence of Indian work in phonetics and an almost total disregard of the Graeco-Roman tradition, whereas the contemporary shift in emphasis to grammar has produced a rehabilitation of the achievements of the ancient, mediaeval, and early modern grammatical traditions;[19] as Robins points out,[20] the linguistic achievement of grammarians prior to the 19th century was in grammar.

There is, however, a great deal more still to be done before linguists will be in a position to write the history of their science. In the last few years, critical editions of the Danish 'Modistae' have appeared,[21] but if, for example, we consider the period of the later Middle Ages, beginning with the rediscovery of Aristotle, we find that there are a larger number of grammarians, prior to the Modistae, scholars of real importance in their day whose work has never been interpreted by the modern linguist – I refer to the work of scholars such as Peter Helias, John of Salisbury, Petrus Hispanus,[22] Robert Kilwardby, Roger Bacon; unfortunately, much of their work still remains unedited. This is one field at least where there can be genuine and fruitful cooperation between the philologist and the structural linguist.

[18] W. O. Dingwall, *Op. cit.*, p. 256.
[19] N. A. Chomsky, *Current Issues*, p. 16.
[20] R. H. Robins, *A. and M.*, p. 4.
[21] A. Otto (ed.), *Johannis Daci Opera. (Corpus Philosophorum Danicorum Medii Aevi,* I) (Copenhagen, 1955). H. Roos (ed.), *Martini de Daci Opera. (Corpus Philosophorum Danicorum Medii Aevi*, II) (Copenhagen, 1961). A. Otto (ed.), *Simonis Daci Opera (Corpus Philosophorum Danicorum Medii Aevi,* III) (Copenhagen, 1961). J. Pinborg and H. Roos (eds.), *Boethii Daci Opera (Corpus Philosophorum Danicorum Medii Aevi,* IV) (Copenhagen, 1969). This last work was in fact published after this study was completed.
[22] Petrus Hispanus was not in fact a grammarian. There are editions available of his so-called "Summulae", viz. J. P. Mullally (ed.), *The "Summulae Logicales" of Peter of Spain (Publications in Medieval Studies,* VIII) (Notre Dame, 1945); this is not a complete version, and I. M. Bochenski (ed.), *Petri Hispani Summulae Logicales* (Rome, 1947). Professor de Rijk is preparing the first critical edition.

I

A SHORT HISTORY OF GRAMMAR IN ANCIENT AND MEDIAEVAL EUROPE

A. GENERAL OUTLINE

The study of grammar in Europe has a long and fruitful history[1] and linguistics is now recognised in most universities as an autonomous academic discipline. It has not always enjoyed such a privileged position although there have been occasional periods when the study of grammar achieved quasi-autonomy; for the most part, however, linguistic speculation in the past was carried on by men who were not primarily grammarians. An examination of the theories of these grammarians of the past has its own intrinsic worth but another service that such study does is to stress the degree of interpenetration that must obtain between linguistics and various associated disciplines, and in the past theories and terminologies from associated disciplines, e.g. logic, metaphysics, etc.[2] have been introduced to support and explain the speculations on the nature of grammar.

One such period when grammar achieved a position of prominence was the later Middle Ages; theirs was a grammatical heritage of considerable wealth and can be traced back to a number of sources. The Greeks were pioneers in grammatical theory as in so many other fields, and the mediaeval grammarians derived many of their ideas from them. Mediaeval grammarians were also logicians and influenced obviously by Plato and Aristotle, but prior to the rediscovery of Aristotle, the mediaeval schoolmen had to rely on the translations of Boethius for their knowledge of Aristotle.[3] Peter Helias and scholars such as Robert Kilwardby who (particularly the former) were the creators of the mediaeval grammatical tradition achieved, it would seem, a remarkable

---

[1] J. R. Firth, "The Technique of Semantics", *Papers in Linguistics*, p. 139.
[2] G. L. Bursill-Hall, "Notes on the Semantics of Linguistic Description", *In Memoriam J. R. Firth*, pp. 40-51.
[3] H. M. Barrett, *Boethius. Some Aspects of his Times and Work* (Cambridge, 1940); H. O. Taylor, *The Mediaeval Mind* (New York, 1925).

synthesis of these lines of descent from Aristotle, Plato, the Stoics, and the Alexandrian grammarians, via (i) the new discoveries of the later works of Aristotle, (ii) the Aristotelian tradition through the translations of Boethius who is himself a scholar of importance in the history of grammatical thought during the early Middle ages, and (iii) the Greek grammatical tradition of Thrax and Apollonius as they had been transmitted to the Middle Ages by Donatus, Priscian, and their commentators.[4] It remained for the Modistae to confirm this tradition in their own work which reveals the culmination of the grammatical and logical theories of the Greeks expressed in the language of the schoolmen but using the organisation of the Latin grammarians.

We can point to three important sources on which the Modistae were able to draw in the construction of their theories. The first is the pioneering work of the Greek philosophers. Thrax and Apollonius had themselves derived their grammatical theories from Aristotle, the Stoics, and other philosophers of language in the sense that these philosophers were the great pioneers of grammatical writing in ancient Greece, and without their work the theories of the Alexandrian school would not really have been possible. This is the second source, though it can be considered an indirect one, dormant through the history of grammar from the Alexandrians onward, until it appears once more as a positive factor in the great synthesis of grammarians of the 12th and 13th centuries, such as Peter Helias and Robert Kilwardby who wrote commentaries on Priscian's grammar using the terminology and critical processes that they had acquired from ancient Greek logical and philosophical works which had recently been discovered by the West.

The third source is through the influence of Peter Helias and other commentators of Priscian; there seems to be some doubt about Peter's exact status in the academic world of the 12th century[5] but it seems safe to say that he was the first in the mediaeval world to make a *systematic* attempt to relate the ideas of the new philosophy (i.e. Aristotle's rediscovered philosophy) to the study of grammar. Peter Helias thus represents one of the first attempts to make a fusion of the two schools of Greek grammatical theory, *i.e.* Aristotle, the Stoics, and other philosophical schools on the one hand, and on the other the grammatical theories of Thrax and Apollonius transmitted to the Middle Ages by Priscian – two schools which had for so long remained separate.

[4]   R. H. Robins, "Dionysius Thrax and the Western Grammatical Tradition", *TPS* (1957), 67-106.
[5]   R. W. Hunt, "Studies on Priscian in the 11th and 12th Centuries", *Mediaeval and Renaissance Studies* 2 (1950), p. 39.

B. GREEK GRAMMARIANS

The contributions of the linguistic scholarship of the Ancient Greek world have long been known to European scholarship and it is regrettable that this contribution has been misjudged by those scholars who have tended to view linguistics in terms of phonetics and phonology and who therefore have prized the work of the earliest Indian linguists at the expense of the Greeks. In recent years, there has been an increasing recognition of the importance of the Greek contribution, and this too has been coincidental with a shift in emphasis in modern linguistics. The Greek achievement was in grammar and with them we can see the burgeoning of a tradition which has continued with little interruption to the present day.[6]

The relevance of Greek grammatical scholarship in the present context is directed to its contribution to mediaeval grammatical thought[7] and we shall see that its influence, though in no real sense a direct one, was nonetheless enormous. In a sense the mediaeval grammarian represents the culmination of the three great traditions of ancient linguistic scholarship, *i.e.* the philosophical tradition which began with the Pre-Socratics, the grammatical tradition of the Alexandrians, and the adaptation of the Greek descriptive scheme to Latin, especially in the work of the late Latin grammarians Donatus and Priscian. Professor R. H. Robins, who has done more than any other modern linguist to make us aware of the extent and value of Greek grammatical scholarship,[8] points out that their basic procedure was classification of the word-classes and grammatical categories and that this classification was done by means of definitions in basically Aristotelian form. It is very suggestive to think that mediaeval grammatical theory which was in fact based in terms of its classificatory procedures on the unbroken Aristotelian tradition should come to its full fruition after the re-discovery of the Aristotelian logical tradition. Professor T. Langendoen has shown[9] that classical, especially Greek linguistic scholarship, was amongst other things concerned with levels of theoretical adequacy.[10]

---

[6] R. H. Robins, "The Development of the Word Class System of the European Grammatical Tradition", *Foundations of Language* 2 (1966), 3-19.

[7] R. H. Robins, *Ancient and Mediaeval Grammatical Theory in Europe* (London, 1951). This work will be referred to frequently and will be abbreviated as *A and M.*

[8] R. H. Robins, *cf.* the items already mentioned.

[9] T. Langendoen, "A Note on the Linguistic Theory of M. Teventius Varro", *Foundations of Language* 2 (1966), 33-36.

[10] Langendoen points out that Greek scholarship referred to what we might call four levels of adequacy. He points out also that Greek linguistic scholarship never

The interesting fact is that the mediaeval grammarians married success-
fully the Aristotelian grammatical and logical traditions and that the
Modistae in particular welded this with their own philosophical tradition
to produce of Latin grammar a very different interpretation which
required explanatory adequacy rather than descriptive adequacy.[11] And
although the Modistae worked entirely within the framework for Latin
which had been settled by Priscian, it is nonetheless possible to trace
the origins of this framework back beyond the Stoic and Alexandrian
schools to the speculations of Plato and Aristotle.

The details of Greek (and Latin) grammatical theory are well known
and it is unnecessary to spell them out once more in this essay.[12] The
earliest records in Europe of grammatical writing go back to the Pre-
Socratic philosophers and Rhetoricians but the first grammatical thinker
of significance was undoubtedly Plato, and it can be said of him
that he 'first considered the potentialities of grammar'.[13] It was Plato
who justified, on logical or philosophical grounds however, the separation of the noun and verb. Grammatical theory was further developed
by Aristotle, but at no stage in the work of these thinkers do we find
specific grammatical treatises; philosophical and grammatical studies
were accepted as parts of the general body of knowledge, but statements of grammatical reference have to be abstracted from a body of
treatise which were not grammatical in tone or intent.

It is not until we reach the Stoics that we find that grammar is
accorded a separate place, but even so it is not an autonomous place;
grammar was accorded a place in their philosophical system. With the
Stoics, grammar made important advances and although grammar is
continually influenced by philosophy, it was studied by them as a
separate branch of learning. They gave to grammar a definite place
in a wider scheme of general linguistic scholarship and for the first time
we find scholars attempting to frame a general theory of language.[14]

The importance and originality of the contributions of Greek philosophers to a general theory of grammar are beyond dispute, but the
next stage in Greek grammatical work is in many ways the most
significant for its intrinsic value and for the influence it had on sub-

---

sought to go beyond descriptive adequacy; it is also reasonable to say that Priscian
was content with observational adequacy.

[11] N. Chomsky, *Current Issues in Linguistic Theory* (*Janua Linguarum*, Series
Minor XXXVIII) (The Hague, 1964), Chapter 2.

[12] R. H. Robins, *A. and M.*, and other items already listed.

[13] R. H. Robins, *A. and M.*, p. 17.

[14] R. H. Robins, *A. and M.*, p. 25.

sequent grammatical theory in that it provided a framework which has to all intents and purposes survived to the present day. The Alexandrian school[15] should be considered much more as a group of specialist grammarians than as philosophers of language; they also introduced a new factor into grammatical study, *i.e.* a consciousness of their literary past and the divergence between the spoken Greek of their day and classical literary Greek. Priscian took the Alexandrian grammarians as his model and 'literary' grammarians basing their own work on the language of literature became the mode for the transmission of grammatical theory into the Latin speaking world; as such, they became the model for grammatical teaching in the mediaeval world and indeed the later speculative grammarians continued to accept the Priscianic framework even if their premises and criteria differed quite radically.

The key figures of the Alexandrian school were Dionysius Thrax and Apollonius Dyscolus;[16] Thrax formalised the word-class system which became the basis of the syntactic works of Apollonius and it was this combined system which was passed on to Priscian. Thrax is very typical of this new style of grammarian. For him, grammar had the practical purpose of preserving the Greek language from decay; this definition of grammar was to place an emphasis on literature in contrast to colloquial speech. This too is the starting point of a tradition in grammatical work which has to a great extent survived to the present. The value of the work of Thrax is that he was much more linguistic than any of his predecessors; his word-classes were defined to a very large extent in formal terms of morphology and syntax. None of his successors in the Greek or Latin worlds achieved the same degree of formal descriptive rigour.

It is far too facile for us to reject the work of the Greek grammarians; wholesale rejection of the work of our predecessors has no more place in scholarship than the indiscriminate acceptance of modern ideas. The Greeks began their grammatical theorising and practice from nothing and we should honour them for their awareness of the world about them. To disparage them would be to lose sight of the importance and extent of their achievements; instead, we must be grateful for the intellectual curiosity which led them to speculate on the nature of language and to build up a framework of grammatical study which became the basis of almost all subsequent grammatical work, an inheritance we enjoy today.

[15]   R. H. Robins, *Thrax*, p. 36.
[16]   Thrax lived in the first century B.C. and Apollonius some 200 years later.

C. LATIN GRAMMARIANS

The contributions of Latin grammarians to general grammatical theory are pale in comparison to those of the Greeks. The Romans admired the achievements of the Greeks in original thought and it was the Roman genius for organisation that protected these Greek achievements. As far as grammar is concerned, the Romans were faced with a different task since they had to hand a systematic approach to the problem of the organisation and description of linguistic form-classes. The Latin grammarians were, however, content to apply the Greek grammatical system to a description of Latin word-classes and grammatical categories rather than set up a grammatical system for Latin in terms of Latin.[17] It is for this reason that it is difficult to ascribe any degree of originality to their work, since, with one notable exception, they confined themselves in the construction of their models to observational adequacy, though it must be conceded that there are what we might call 'flashes' of descriptive adequacy in Priscian's work.

There are three Latin grammarians of note who must be mentioned in this brief account of the contributions of Rome to grammatical theory, *i.e.* Varro, Donatus, and Priscian. There is no doubt that Varro[18] was a grammarian of originality, and indeed, as Langendoen has suggested, Varro was the only grammarian of the ancient classical world

---

[17] R. H. Robins, *A. and M.*, p. 48.

[18] Varro established a distinction between VOLUNTARY and NATURAL derivation on lines which in a way anticipated the Modistic distinction of ABSOLUTE and RESPECTIVE within the modes of signifying. He described VOLUNTARY DERIVATION as something which is not conditioned by external factors, *i.e. declinationum ... voluntarium est, quo ut cuisque tulit voluntas declinavit* (*De Lingua Latina*, VIII. 21); this would today be called derivation which does not involve the word in syntactic relations with other sentence constituents. He described NATURAL DERIVATION as something which is conditioned by external factors, *i.e. naturalem declinationem dico, quae non a singulorum oritur voluntate, sed a communi consensu* (*De Lingua Latina*, VIII. 22). This would today be called inflection – Varro in fact referred to case-forms — and this does have a specific syntactic function.

The Modistae divided the modes of signifying into absolute and respective, *cf.* pp. 106-107. The absolute is internal to the modes of signifying and excludes all reference to other word-classes; accidental modes such as *species* and *figura* (in the *nomen*), which describe the derivational features of the *nomen*, are absolute modes and as such have no syntactic function. The respective mode is considered in terms of the mutual relations which can be established between the word-classes, so that the respective mode must be syntactically functional; accidental modes such as *casus* and *declinatio* (in the *nomen*), which describe the inflectional features of the nomen, are relative modes and as such do have a syntactic function.

There is no evidence, however, that the Modistae were directly influenced by Varro in setting up their distinction of absolute and relative.

to deal with the problem of explanatory adequacy.[19] It is, however, impossible to make any real judgment of Varro's contribution to grammatical theory since his work has come down to us far from complete; in any case, a consideration of his work is not germane to this study, since he does not appear to have had any influence at all on mediaeval grammatical theory.

It is not until we reach the time of the Late Latin grammarians, especially Donatus and Priscian,[20] that we find significant contributions in the context of mediaeval grammatical theory. Their intellectual climate was not unlike that of the Alexandrian grammarians; they were conscious of their literary past and they were intent on the preservation of the literary language. They were not innovators of linguistic and grammatical theories, and were content to follow on the lines of their Greek predecessors.[21]

Their most significant task was their massive compilation of the facts of the Latin Language; their importance is further enhanced by their influence on the grammarians of the Middle Ages, as their works became the accepted textbooks of the Middle Ages. Of the two, Priscian is the more prominent and his grammar has survived in more than a thousand manuscripts which is striking testimony of its popularity. It is reasonable to state that his work remains the most complete statement of the facts of Latin. He made meaning his main criterion in grammar,[22] although in actual fact he kept to the more formal classification developed by the Alexandrians. He did not, however, make his definitions according to any consistent principle since we find, alongside meaning, criteria such as formal structure and philosophical abstractions; in precision and consistency of theory, it does not compare to Thrax's work on which it is based, by Priscian's own admission. Its importance to us in the present study is that it was the source on which the mediaeval grammarians drew so extensively; this will account for the sparseness of illustration to be found in so many mediaeval grammatical writings, since they were almost always commentaries in their own terms of Priscian's grammar of Latin.

---

[19] Varro lived in the 1st century B.C.; he may not have been the first Roman grammarian, but it is with Varro that the study of grammar by the Romans really begins.

[20] Donatus taught in Rome during the 4th century A.D.; Priscian taught in Constantinople during the 6th century A.D.

[21] R. H. Robins, *A. and M.*, p. 62.

[22] Priscian (II, 16-7): *non aliter possunt discerni a se partes orationis, nisi uniuscuiusque proprietates significationem attendamus.*

It would be quite wrong to belittle and disparage the work of the Late Latin grammarians. Their achievements were great and lasting; they built the foundations on which mediaeval scholars could know, develop, and criticise classical grammar. It was this knowledge which enabled Western scholars to keep alive, during the early Middle Ages, the study of literature and other scholarly pursuits.

D. MEDIAEVAL GRAMMARIANS

1

There are wide and serious gaps in our knowledge of the development of grammatical theory between the 6th and 11th centuries. We know little if anything of the works of e.g. Boethius, Cassiodorus, Isidore of Seville, Aelfric, to mention but a few. What is beyond dispute is that grammar came to hold a position of considerable privilege in the programme of university studies in the Middle Ages; it achieved this not only because of its intrinsic importance, but because it became the key to what the mediaeval schoolmen considered higher forms of learning, i.e. dialectic and theology.[23] The curriculum of the mediaeval university was built around the Liberal Arts which were divided into the Trivium and Quadrivium;[24] grammar was the first subject of the Trivium and naturally assumed the position of pre-requisite to all the Liberal Arts, being the necessary study for the reading and writing of the 'universal'[25] language of learning, i.e. Latin. Thus grammar came to be studied for its own sake as part of human culture and for the study of classical authors, particularly of the Latin Bible.[26]

The year 1000 can be said to mark the transition from one of the darkest periods to a period of progress culminating in the intellectual

---

[23] R. W. Hunt, "Studies in Priscian in the 11th and 12th Centuries", *Mediaeval and Renaissance Studies* I and II (1941-43: 1950), 194-231: 1-56, cf. 194: "If we neglect grammatical theory, we are cutting ourselves off from an important source for understanding the thought of the 11th and 12th centuries. At that time everyone had to study grammar, and it was regarded as the 'foundation and root' of all teaching. Its influence is as pervasive as that of logic and may be seen in unexpected places, in theology and even more in logic itself; no study of the logical doctrines of the early 12th century would be adequate which did not take account of Priscian and the glossators of his work". Cf. also J. P. Mullally, *The "Summulae Logicales" of Peter of Spain (Publications in Mediaeval Studies VIII)* (Notre Dame, 1945), especially Introduction, XI-XCVII.

[24] These terms are attributed to Boethius.

[25] In the mediaeval sense of the term.

[26] R. H. Robins, *A. and M.*, p. 70.

revival of the 12th century.[27] This period coincided with the encouragement given to learning by Charlemagne, one of his greatest services being the encouragement of the study of grammar.[28] Prior to this period, however, grammar as a science appears to have made no progress; grammar was defined and practised as the art of speaking and writing correctly and the art of interpreting the poets,[29] the text-books used being the grammars of Donatus and Priscian.

The second period of learning in the Middle Ages, the so-called 'Renaissance of the 12th century',[30] during which time grammar came to be regarded as a pre-requisite for all scholarship, dates from the middle of the 11th century and can be thought of as continuing up to the end of the 13th century,[31] a period in the history of grammar which culminated in the complete philosophy of language of the Modistae.[32] Four important and closely connected facts characterise the intellectual history of this period insofar as grammar is concerned: (a) the discovery of Aristotle and the concomitant introduction of logic into grammar; (b) the influence of William of Conches and Peter Helias; (c) the triumph of the grammarians over the humanistic schools of the 'authors', *i.e.* the struggle between Orleans and Chartres, the home of the study of classical literature, against the rising influence of logic in the schools of Paris;[33] (d) the constitution of speculative grammar embodying the new knowledge which followed upon the rediscovery of Aristotle's philosophical works and which culminated in the treatises on the modes of signifying (Summa modorum significandi) of the Modistae. A more detailed statement is to be found in Pinborg's excellent account (Pinborg 1967: 55-6).

2

The Middle Ages are often divided into two periods, the first going up to the 12th century and the second to the Renaissance. Such a division

---

[27]   J. E. Sandys, *A History of Classical Scholarship*, Vol. I (Cambridge, 1921), p. 514.
[28]   G. Wallerand, *Les Œuvres de Siger de Courtrai* (*Les Philosophes belges* VIII) (Louvain, 1913), p. 34.
[29]   Quintilian: recte loquendi scientiam et poetarum enarrationem (*De institutione oratoria*, I. IV. 2).
[30]   C. H. Haskins, *The Renaissance of the 12th Century* (Cambridge, Mass., 1927).
[31]   The Modistae span a period of at least 100 years, *i.e.* ca. 1250-ca. 1350, *cf.* J. Pinborg, *Die Entwicklung der Sprachtheorie im Mittelalter*.
[32]   G. Wallerand, *Op. cit.*, p. 34.
[33]   This is well described in Henri d'Andeli's allegorical poem "La Bataille des Sept Arts", published by L. J. Paetow, *The Battle of the Seven Arts* (*Memoirs of the University of California* IV) (Berkeley, 1914).

is of course artificial, but well before the 12th century certain influences were experienced which were to have a profound effect on
mediaeval grammatical theories. The first period was formative and
contains little of interest in the history of grammar; it merely uses
theories and methods already well established and which derive directly
from Donatus and Priscian. Latin was the only classical language in
use since Greek was, to all intents and purposes, unknown; indeed, the
only Greek works known to the early Middle Ages were those that
had survived in Latin translations.[34]

In the earlier mediaeval period, the study of grammar was carried
on as preparation for the serious study of literature; Latin literary
studies in northern France in the first half of the 12th century gave
every promise of leading to a great revival of classical literary studies,[35]
and the work of John of Salisbury suggests that the 12th century was
well on the way to a real comprehension of classical civilisation. This
was cut short by the growing interest in dialectical and theological
studies which followed upon the rediscovery of ancient Greek philosophy; the decline in the study of the classics and other literary
pursuits can be attributed directly to the rise of dialectic to a position
of undisputed eminence in the arts.[36]

By 1215, classical authors were absent from the Arts course in the
University of Paris and by 1255, only Donatus and Priscian remained
of the ancient Latin authors; the plain fact is that the classical literary
tradition which had been so superbly fostered by the cathedral schools
of Chartres and Orleans died of sheer starvation, because the ideas
which the study of Aristotle produced became too absorbing to allow
the study of the classical authors to remain important.[37] Grammar, the
weathervane of intellectual change, turned from the study of literature
to a logical science, a speculative philosophical discipline, and its
problems were no longer solved by reference to the best Latin literature

---

[34] Thomas Aquinas, however, is known to have used translations made directly
from the Greek, whereas most mediaeval schoolmen of this period knew Greek
philosophy only through the translations and commentaries of Arab and Jewish
scholars which came to Europe via Spain. Robert Grosseteste and Roger Bacon
both knew Greek and the former particularly made many translations into Latin
from Greek and not only of Aristotle.

[35] F. B. Artz, *The Mind of the Middle Ages* (New York, 1953), p. 433.

[36] L. J. Paetow, *The Arts Course at Mediaeval Universities with Special Reference
to Grammar and Rhetoric* (*The University of Illinois Studies*, III, 7) (Urbana,
1909), p. 29.

[37] L. J. Paetow, *The Arts Course at Mediaeval Universities*, p. 29.

but by logic.[38] The liberation of grammar from philological restraints, the influence of Aristotle, and the commentaries of Arab scholars produced a new orientation in grammatical studies; from being a pedagogical, normative subject, it became philosophical, theoretical, and speculative, and the introduction of logic made grammar the 'handmaid of the philosopher'.[39]

In the 12th and 13th centuries the study of logic and its pervasion of grammar spread throughout northern Europe, and the digestion of Aristotle's logic became the greatest intellectual task of the period.[40] The progressive invasion of the University of Paris by the doctrine of Aristotle is a well known fact, but we are still far from knowing the details with any precision.[41]

There is a great difference, however, between grammar in northern Europe, and in France south of the Loire, *i.e.* Orleans, Italy and Spain; in northern Europe, particularly in Paris where humanistic tendencies had once been strongest, the reign of Aristotle became absolute[42] and by the 13th century dialectic and theology had become the exclusive intellectual pursuits with grammar as a purely speculative science. In southern Europe, however, the pursuit and study of grammar and logic were subordinate to law, and the student cultivated them in order to speak and write Latin elegantly.[43] The principal reason for the decline in classical studies can be attributed to the change in the nature of grammatical studies which became more and more speculative and deductive.

The stimulus given to dialectic by Abelard reinforced by the knowledge of Aristotle's logic produced a marked change in the Trivium;[44] the earlier Trivium had preserved a balance between logic on the one hand, and grammar and rhetoric on the other, but this was destroyed by the addition of new material to be mastered, so that there was less time and inclination left for the more leisurely study of grammar and literature;[45] rhetoric virtually disappeared and grammar became no

---

[38] L. J. Paetow, *The Arts Course at Mediaeval Universities*, p. 35.
[39] R. H. Robins, *A. and M.*, p. 89.
[40] R. W. Southern, *The Making of the Middle Ages* (London, 1953), p. 181.
[41] E. Gilson, *History of Christian Philosophy in the Middle Ages* (London, 1955).
[42] L. J. Paetow, *The Arts Course at Mediaeval Universities*, p. 29.
[43] J. E. Sandys, *A History of Classical Scholarship*, Vol. I, p. 666. H. O. Taylor, *The Mediaeval Mind*, Vol. I (New York, 1925), p. 251.
[44] G. Leff, *Mediaeval Thought from Saint Augustine to Ockham* (London, 1958), p. 169.
[45] C. H. Haskins, *Op. cit.*, p. 355.

longer the guide to literary expression, but was instead governed by its logical aspects and absorbed in philosophy, devoted to the language of logic.[46]

To the Parisian masters of the early 13th century, the discovery of Aristotle's philosophy meant a new and universally applicable method,[47] and the whole field of intellectual endeavour, from grammar to theology, was invaded by the notion of science, *i.e.* a necessary knowledge justified by strict demonstration together with the notion of 'art', *i.e.* a systematic body of principles and consequences.

3

The period from the 11th century to the Renaissance is significant in the history of grammar, in terms of both grammatical theory and grammatical method.[48] The effect of this development was to bring grammar

[46] . C. H. Haskins, *Op. cit.*, pp. 135-137.

[47] E. Gilson, *Op. cit.*, p. 312.

[48] It is possible to discern two lines of grammatical thought in the Middle Ages, and these two trends continue the philosophical and literary traditions of the ancient world. The literary tradition, however, comes to an end in the 13th century, and from then on to the Renaissance, philosophical grammar becomes the dominant trend. Grammar prior to the 13th century might be considered an equivalent term to 'philology'; after this period, grammar comes closer to its modern equivalent, *i.e.* as a part of linguistic science. The struggle between literature and logic in the universities of the 13th century has been well reported in Henri d'Andeli's poem "La bataille des sept arts". We have seen that in ancient Greece, Alexandrian grammarians based their grammatical theory and method on the study of literature; in the time of the Late Latin grammarians we found a similar insistence on the study of literature as the model for the grammarian. This use of literature as a model for grammar was bequeathed to the Middle Ages by Priscian, the last of the 'literary' grammarians of the ancient world, so that the mediaeval schools based their grammatical teachings on the literary grammars of Priscian and other grammarians of a similar type – *e.g.* Alexander de Villa-Dei, "Doctrinale" – until literary grammar came to be superseded by philosophical grammar in the late 12th century and onwards. This must not be interpreted that Priscian disappeared from mediaeval schools; he may have been superseded in the later Middle Ages by Alexander's "Doctrinale" as a students' teaching manual, but he remained the principal source for all the philosophical and speculative grammarians of the 13th and 14th centuries.

There are two grammars which merit mention at this stage: they are the "Doctrinale" of Alexander de Villa-Dei and the "Graecismus" of Eberhardus Bethuniensis, which were typical of the type of literary grammar introduced in this period; Alexander's work achieved an enormous popularity, and eventually succeeded in superseding the grammars of Donatus and Priscian as a teaching manual. Written in verse, its purpose was didactic and was designed for students whose mother tongue was not Latin: it retained its popularity throughout the later Middle Ages, but makes no attempt to justify grammatical rules nor does it contain any theorising about grammatical doctrine. Its interest lies purely in the part it played as a teaching manual and its value in the history of grammatical writing can be largely ignored.

under the control of logic and metaphysics, and rules of grammar were now derived and justified by recourse to logic and metaphysical theories of reality.

The great achievements in mediaeval grammatical work are often said to date from the rediscovery of Aristotle's logical and philosophical works but recent research[49] allows us to be more specific. During the 11th century a noticeable change took place in grammatical teaching when dialectic began to infiltrate the domain of grammar. From the middle of the century grammarians borrowed from dialectic a number of doctrinal data as well as methodological procedures in order to provide grammar with the scientific basis which the contemporary intellectual paradigm demanded. This infiltration of dialectic, dating from the middle of the 11th century, marks the first change in the development of mediaeval grammatical theory and the period saw a great revival of grammatical teaching; indeed the degree of infiltration was such that it presented a real danger to the scope and purpose of grammar. It must, therefore, be made quite clear that it is no longer correct to view the infiltration of logic into grammar as dating from the middle of the 12th century under the influence of Peter Helias.

The effect of this logicisation of grammar (not to mention other concomitant changes in the scholarly life of the Middle Ages) was to produce an entirely different approach to grammar, one which lasted until well into the 14th century and one which continued to have a considerable impact on certain aspects of grammatical thought in the Renaissance and Early Modern period. Instead of grammar being studied as a key to knowledge of classical literature and the Bible, it became a branch of speculative philosophy,[50] and grammar was now justified, not by illustration from classical literature, but by systems of logic and metaphysical theories of reality. Grammar, *i.e.* normative grammar, continued to be taught, hence the popularity of Alexander's 'Doctrinale' as a teaching manual, but throughout the period there is an increasing rift between pedagogical grammar and philosophical treatises on grammatical theory, until normative grammar is entirely superseded by philosophical grammar.[51]

Inevitably there was a reaction against the predominance of dialectic

---

[49] *Cf.* R. W. Hunt, "Studies on Priscian", and L. M. de Rijk, *Logica Modernorum*.
[50] R. H. Robins, *A. and M.*, p. 75.
[51] Modistic attitude to grammar is not unlike Chomsky's *viz.* N. Chomsky, *Syntactic Structures* (*Janua Linguarum* IV) (The Hague, 1957).

over grammar but it is safe to say that a close association between logic and grammar had become a fact of life, and from the 12th century, it is possible to suggest three stages in the logicisation of grammar, though it must not be imagined that these stages can be fitted into neatly separated compartments.

The first stage is associated with three masters, William of Conches, Peter Helias, and Ralph of Beauvais. William taught grammar at Chartres from c. 1120 to c. 1154; he was Peter Helias's teacher and a scholar of real significance in the history of grammar although it is difficult at present to make a completely valid assessment of him as a grammarian and it is doubtful whether this will be possible until we possess a fully commented edition of his work; once this has been done it should also be possible to see Peter Helias's work in its proper perspective. However, it can be said that William did set out to build up grammatical theory out of its own inspiration; furthermore, he merits the position of importance that even our present meagre knowledge of his work can properly assign to him by virtue of his criticisms of Priscian. There is a modern ring about these criticisms of Priscian and his lack of explanatory power.[52]

The matter of causes of invention (cause inventionis) is a notable achievement on the part of William and was of great importance for mediaeval grammar, since the mediaeval grammarians believed that the cause inventionis would provide them with the most profound knowledge about the parts of speech, i.e. once these were found, it would then be possible to examine the parts of speech and thereafter to determine the proper grammatical function of a word.[53]

It is quite wrong to claim that Peter Helias was the first to introduce dialectic into grammar, but this should not be allowed to minimise his achievement – he was the most famous master of grammar in the 12th century.[54] Under the influence of William of Conches, Peter, aware as he was of the domination of grammar by dialectic, made a considerable effort to disentangle them, his aim being to free grammar from questions that seemed unrelated to its purpose. He realised that grammar could not dispense with the methods of dialectic since the latter provided the basis for the scientific approach. He therefore sought to

[52] This is an excellent example of a scientific revolution of the past in linguistics of the type discussed by Kuhn, cf. T. S. Kuhn, *The Structure of Scientific Revolutions* (Chicago, 1962).
[53] R. W. Hunt, "Studies on Priscian", pp. 211-212.
[54] L. M. de Rijk, *Op. cit. II*, p. 229.

achieve his aim by restricting the use of logical distinctions in grammatical discourse to certain areas and undertook a thorough systematisation of the grammatical theories of his predecessors. It is not without some significance that he was the first to write a Summa in Priscianum, *i.e.* an orderly comment on Priscian's grammar; it was not however designed to be a continuous commentary, much less an original exposition, but rather a systematic account of the discussions of his day on Priscian. It seems reasonable to say, therefore, that his teaching along with the impetus given to speculative scholarship in logic and philosophy provided not only the spur to the study of a subject already established as part of the Arts curriculum, but in fact it encouraged speculation with a new bias on the nature of language and grammar.

The generation of grammarians following Peter Helias achieved a synthesis between logic in grammar and the study of classical authors; such a synthesis was achieved in the study of syntax, and it is from this time that the first independent treatises on syntax date. As early as the second half of the 12th century we find separate treatises on syntax and this became the outlet for the grammarian's interest in logical analysis. In this respect the work of Ralph of Beauvais[55] is significant, since it is in his work that the development of syntactic theory and the renewal of the study of classical authors appear; however, grammar did not develop along the lines that Ralph marked out. Nevertheless, the attention paid to syntax by the grammarians of the later 12th century laid the basis for the continued close association between logic and grammar, a relationship fruitful enough to create a logical grammar within the domain of grammar and which culminated in the speculative grammars of the Modistae; this was not a development from the work of Ralph but the result of the full assimilation of the 'new' Aristotle and the works of the Arab logicians.[56]

There is a gap in our knowledge of the development of grammatical theory between the time of Ralph of Beauvais and the Modistae some 100 years later. The second stage, the period between William of Conches, Peter Helias, Ralph of Beauvais and the Modistae, can be thought of as a period of consolidation; this period is, of course, the golden age of mediaeval scholasticism, and is the period when leading philosophers such as Thomas Aquinas, Robert Grosseteste, Albertus Magnus, logicians such as William of Sherwood, Petrus Hispanus and Lambert of Auxerre, and grammarians such as Robert Kilwardby,

[55] *Cf.* R. W. Hunt, "Studies on Priscian", p. 39.
[56] *Cf.* R. W. Hunt, "Studies on Priscian", p. 39.

Jordan of Saxony, Nicholas de Paris (all of whom wrote commentaries on Priscian), and Roger Bacon,[57] were active in creating and developing their theories in the light of the new knowledge.

Of this period of grammatical history, it is possible only to make general statements about trends and developments; it is known that by the 13th century, lectures on grammar with a logico-philosophical bent were part of the teaching programme in the Faculty of Arts in Paris, the texts used, according to Grabmann,[58] being the commentaries on Priscian of Jordan of Saxony, Nicholas de Paris, and Robert Kilwardby and in addition Kilwardby's grammatical Sophismata.[59] It will be possible to say more of these personalities and to draw more positive conclusions about the development of grammatical theory during this period when the philology of the period is better known.[60] Broadly speaking, it seems that this period brought about a refinement in theory and terminology by the application of logical and philosophical criteria to grammatical description, and that it became the task, so to speak, of the third stage, to bring to fruition this preparatory work, in the shape of the theories of the speculative grammarians of the late 13th -14th centuries, *i.e.* the Modistae.

The effect of these changes on grammatical writing can be seen with unmistakable clarity in Roger Bacon, who can be considered the starting point of the third stage, marked by the evolution of a new approach to grammar.[61] Bacon observed that in every language there are two sorts of problems, some proper to the language in question and others

[57]   Roger Bacon (and indeed Robert Kilwardby too) were much more than grammarians, but have been included in this context because of their grammatical activities. Roger Bacon, considered by Grabmann to be the author of the first of the speculative grammars, is mentioned at this stage since he cannot be thought of as one of the Modistae but rather as one of their immediate precursors.

[58]   M. Grabmann, *Mittelalterliches Geistesleben* I (Munich, 1926), p. 118.

[59]   Kilwardby was a scholar and grammarian of considerable stature, but as his grammatical work remains unedited, it is not possible for the historian of grammar to make a proper assessment of his contribution to grammatical theory. Roos reports (*Die Modi Significandi*, p. 123) that Martin of Dacia knew and used Kilwardby's commentaries on Priscian; there is no overt suggestion, *i.e.* no textual reference, in either Siger or Thomas that either of them used Kilwardby's work, unless some of the references to the 'grammatici antiqui' are in fact references to Kilwardby. Presumably, however, they knew his work which was written during the first half of the 13th century.

[60]   A most serious gap is the fact that Kilwardby's Priscian commentaries and grammatical Sophismata are as yet unedited: in addition, there are no critical editions of Peter Helias's commentaries on Priscian, or Jordan of Saxony's and Nicholas de Paris's commentaries on Priscian. Furthermore, there is, of course, a complete dearth of comparative studies on their grammatical theories.

[61]   E. Gilson, *Op. cit.*, p. 312.

common to all language, *e.g.* what is a noun, verb, *etc.* The first sort
could not become the object of scientific study, but the second could
become a science and be taught as true learning because its object
was universal. Bacon therefore conceived the possibility of a general
grammar, *i.e.* the general grammar of human language.[62] This change
of attitude to grammar led to a renewal of interest in grammatical study,
which had seemed at one time to be in danger of being relegated to
the position of just one of the seven liberal arts confined to its elementary task of teaching the Latin language for literary purposes.[63] Men
now sought to derive rules of grammar from logic and metaphysical
theories of reality,[64] and a concominant of this increase in interest was
an increase in output of grammatical writing culminating in the speculative grammars of the Modistae. Grammar remained fundamentally
what it always had been in the Middle Ages, a grammatical statement
of Latin, but the Modistae made of their grammars a study of the
word-classes (partes orationis) and syntax of the idealised, perfect
language, *i.e.* Latin, but their methods had by now evolved in a speculative sense – speculative being used by the Modistae in the sense that
language mirrors the 'reality' which, according to mediaeval metaphysics, underlies the phenomena of the physical world.

E. THE MODISTAE

1

For the first time, in the second half of the 13th century, a new type
of grammatical literature appeared, setting out in a very systematic
manner the philosophy and logic of language which Scholastic philosophers had been developing in terms of the new spirit following upon
the rediscovery of Aristotelian and other Greek philosophy. These
grammarians, who were at their height during the 13th-14th centuries,
stated their theories in the form of treatises on the modes of signifying
(Summa Modorum Significandi).

These writers of speculative grammars have come to be known as
'Modistae'[65] but our knowledge of them is slight.[66] Grabmann men-

---

[62] E. Gilson, *Op. cit.*, p. 313.
[63] C. H. Haskins, *Op. cit.*, p. 135.
[64] R. H. Robins, *A. and M.*, p. 75.
[65] Grabmann states that the first modern use of the term 'Modistae' was by
J. Müller in an article published in the "Anzeiger für deutsches Altertum".

tions by name some twelve or thirteen grammarians,[67] Lehmann lists some ninety manuscripts [68] of the writings of this group and Pinborg some two hundred and sixty manuscripts (most of them of the Modistae), which suggests that they constitute quite an important group of grammarians. Roger Bacon, described by Grabmann as the first author of a speculative grammar, produced his *Summa Grammatica* about 1245;[69] he was not one of the Modistae but his work does represent a valuable startingpoint for dating the work of the Modistae.[70] Martin of Dacia probably wrote his grammatical treatise about 1270,[71] and John of Dacia produced his grammar in 1280,[72] but Siger de Courtrai and Thomas of Erfurt did not write their grammars until the first half of the 14th century.[73] Little seems to be known about Michel de Marbais; Leclerc[74] offers a tentative date, *i.e.* ca 1300, for his death which would place him among the earlier Modistae. It is not possible, in view of the paucity of material, to say anything substantive about a coherent doctrine but if we take Martin of Dacia as one of the earliest and Thomas of Erfurt as one of the last of the Modistae, it is easy to point to certain refine-

---

[66] M. Grabmann, *Thomas von Erfurt und die Sprachlogik des mittelalterlichen Aristotelismus. Sitzungsberichte der Bayerischen Akademie der Wissenschaften* (Munich, 1943). Cf. also J. Pinborg, *Op. cit.* This important work should be consulted for more details of the development of grammatical theory in the Middle Ages.

[67] *E.g.* Siger de Courtrai, Thomas of Erfurt, Michel de Marbais, Jean Josse de Marvilla, Martin of Dacia, John of Dacia, Simon of Dacia, Boethius of Dacia, Johannes Aurifaber, John Avicula of Lotharingia, Matthew of Bononia, Radulfus Brito, Erhardus Knab von Zwiefalten. This list obviously does not include the large number of anonymous treatises on speculative grammar. J. Pinborg, *Op. cit.* discusses these in more detail and it would appear that Johannes Aurifaber should be regarded as anti-Modista and one of the earliest of the Nominalist grammarians; the theoretical position of other grammarians in Grabmann's list will also have to be examined more carefully.

[68] P. Lehmann, "Mitteilungen aus Handschriften VIII", *Sitzungsberichte der Bayerischen Akademie der Wissenschaften* (Munich, 1944), 3-34. Cf. J. Pinborg, *Op. cit.*, pp. 309-337.

[69] There is a possibility that Martin of Dacia may have known Roger Bacon in Paris, but it seems most unlikely that either Siger or Thomas knew him.

[70] H. Roos, *Die Modi Significandi*, p. 129.

[71] H. Roos, *Die Modi Significandi*, p. 134.

[72] A. Otto (ed.), *Johannis Daci Opera (Corpus Philosophorum Danicorum Medii Aevi)* (Copenhagen, 1955), p. XVIII.

[73] Siger took his Master of Arts in 1309, and presumably wrote his treatise some time after he had begun to teach, probably between 1309 and 1320. Grabmann suggests that the adult portion of his life was spent in the 14th century, and he probably died about 1350.

[74] V. Leclerc, "Michel de Roubaix ou de Brabant, Grammairien" *Histoire Littéraire de la France* XXI (1847), 267-271.

ments absent from Martin's work but which do appear in Thomas's, *e.g.* the clearly labelled divisions of Etymologia and Diasynthetica, and much more revealing of the improvements in presentation is the use made by Thomas of the clearly defined progression of generalissimus, subalternus, and specialissimus modes to describe the essential mode of any pars orationis.

Since most of their work remains unedited, it is difficult to say whether they can be considered a group or circle in the sense that one finds in the 20th century groups of linguists, *e.g.* Prague, Copenhagen. If we cannot point to documentary evidence in order to suggest that the Modistae were anything so cohesive as a linguistic circle, there is no doubt, if the grammarians to be referred to in this book are reliable witnesses, that they do present a doctrine which in essentials is much the same, although their actual presentations do vary a great deal. It is possible to see, even in the few edited works available to us, the effect of time on their work; time may indeed have refined the presentation and organisation of their work but it did not affect their doctrine.

Of the thirteen grammarians listed by Grabmann, the work of four or five only are available in a fairly modern form and few of them are to be found in critical editions. This dearth of a modern critical apparatus is, of course, a serious handicap to any investigation of the grammatical theories of the Modistae and of the history of linguistics during the mediaeval period. The edition of Martin of Dacia[75] is the most complete modern version of a Modistic grammar and indeed it remains the only critical edition of any mediaeval grammarian. John of Dacia's *Summa Grammatica* was recently published but his work is incomplete and contains only his preamble and the section on the nomen; the work of Simon of Dacia has also been published.[76] The work of John and Simon is, however, pale in comparison to the work of Martin and Boethius, who must be considered grammarians of first importance, especially among the Modistae. There is no modern critical edition available of Thomas of Erfurt's *Grammatica Speculativa;*[77] the edition

---

[75] H. Roos (ed.), *Martini de Dacia Opera* (*Corpus Philosophorum Danicorum Medii Aevi II*) (Copenhagen, 1961). An edition of the works of Boethius of Dacia, edited by H. Roos and J. Pinborg, for the series *Corpus Philosophorum Danicorum Medii Aevi* was published after this study was completed.

[76] A. Otto (ed.), *Simonis de Dacia Opera* (*Corpus Philosophorum Danicorum Medii Aevi III*) (Copenhagen, 1963).

[77] A modern edition of Thomas of Erfurt's, *Grammatica Speculativa* is in preparation, to appear in the series *Classics in Linguistics* published by Longmans, Green and Co. Ltd.

used for this study was published in 1902[78] but is attributed to Duns Scotus – the editor was clearly unaware of the extant MS which Grabmann and Lehmann have listed and bases his version of the text on Wadding's edition of the collected works of Duns Scotus published in 1639.[79] There is no edition at all of Michel de Marbais; extracts only are to be found in Thurot's monumental work.[80] Wallerand, in his edition of Siger de Courtrai,[81] refers to eight manuscripts but only one of these contains his grammatical treatise which is furthermore incomplete;[82] Grabmann and Lehmann do not list any other manuscript of Siger. The remainder of the works of the Modistae remain unpublished.

[78] J. Duns Scotus, *Grammaticae Speculativae*, ed. Fr. Mariani Fernandez Garcia (Quaracchi, 1902). The quotations from Thomas in the body of this study are taken from the Garcia edition and the quotations from Siger de Courtrai from the Wallerand edition. Quotations from Martin of Dacia are from Roos's edition, and the quotations from other Modistae as well as Peter Helias and Robert Kilwardby are taken from Thurot.

[79] The 'grammatica speculativa', which was for so long attributed to Duns Scotus and which has also been thought to be the work of Thomas Aquinas and Albertus Magnus is now generally accepted to be the work of Thomas of Erfurt; Grabmann has explained at great length his argument for assigning this work to Thomas of Erfurt, *cf.*: M. Grabmann, "De Thoma Erfordiensi auctore Grammaticae quae Joanni Duns Scoto adscribitur speculativae", *Archivum Fr. Hist.* (1922), 273-277; M. Grabmann, *Mittelalterliches Geistesleben*, Vol I, 118-125; M. Grabmann, *Thomas von Erfurt und die Sprachlogik des mittelalterlichen Aristotelismus, SB* (Munich, 1943). There is also an edition of Thomas of Erfurt, *Grammatica Speculativa* published by M. Doyon, Quebec in 1962, but this cannot be considered in any sense a critical edition.

[80] Ch. Thurot, *Notices et extraits de divers manuscrits latins pour servir à l'histoire des doctrines grammaticales au moyen âge* (*Notices et extraits des manuscrits de la Bibliothèque Impériale* XXII) (Paris, 1868). Reprinted *Minerva G.m.b.H.* (Frankfurt am Main, 1964).

[81] G. Wallerand, *Les Œuvres de Siger de Courtrai* (*Les Philosophes belges* VIII) (Louvain, 1913).

[82] Scholars writing on Siger de Courtrai, *e.g.* Thurot, have stated that his work is incomplete; Wallerand disputes this, and referring to Thurot's statement, that "le copiste n'a pas continué, il ne donne pas la suite du pronom, non plus, que l'adverbe, la préposition et l'interjection, mais il a ajouté le complément des traités de Siger, les discussions que Siger appelle 'sophismata' " (*Notices et extraits*, p. 41); Wallerand argues that the author, *i.e.* Thurot "ne nous semble pas avoir saisi le plan de l'œuvre de Siger", and continues: "dans la partie suivie de son traité 'De modis significandi', Siger ne traite que des parties déclinables du discours. Dans le 'sophisma': 'O Magister', la discussion montre sur le vif la nécessité des parties indéclinables ... Cette incident ne prouve-t-elle pas que Siger réservait, pour la traiter à propos de ce 'sophisma', cette partie de la grammaire dont il n'a encore rien dit" (p. 31). The inescapable fact is that Siger's treatment of the pronomen is incomplete, that his discussion of the indeclinable partes is not nearly so detailed as Thomas's, and that he lacks a section on syntax, though he does refer at the end of his discussion of the nomen to a projected section on syntax.

2

The Modistae can be thought of as the second generation of speculative grammarians who sought to codify and refine the pioneer work of scholars such as William of Conches, Peter Helias, Robert Kilwardby, *etc.* The Modistae and their immediate precursors represent a great synthesis of two lines of thought which can be traced back to ancient Greece and which had passed down unbroken to the Middle Ages.

The philosophical background of the Modistae led them to believe that grammar had its basis outside language itself; they claimed therefore that there was one universal grammar dependent on the structure of reality,[83] and that the rules of grammar were quite independent of the language in which they were expressed.[84] There was one grammatical system fixed and valid for all languages but which the philosopher of language alone is able to discover.[85] In the process of creating their own grammatical theory, the Modistae kept the grammatical system of Donatus and Priscian more or less intact but restated the parts of speech and their accidents in semantic terms,[86] using a terminology which they derived from the metaphysical and logical theories of their contemporaries. It would be quite unfair to suggest that the Modistae considered this to be sufficient to constitute a new theory; they were not linguistically naïve and they recognized that a new theory represents a new system[87] of thought, so that restatements of Priscian by means of their 'new' terminology were conditioned by the demands of their epistemology. What they seem to have been unaware of is the fact that their theories were in fact a projection into reality of the basic patterns of the language in which they were expressed.[88]

The Modistae did not add a great deal to grammatical theory, although their work does reflect a remarkable degree of sophistication

---

[83] This is a rather different position from the one taken by Peter Helias; he had stated that there are as many grammatical systems as there are languages.

[84] *Cf.* L. Hjelmslev, *Principes de grammaire générale*, p. 268; the great difference of course between Modistic theory of a general grammar and Hjelmslev's theory is that the Modistae constructed their theory on extra-linguistic facts based on the structure of reality, whereas Hjelmslev sought to found his theory on formal linguistic criteria, *i.e.* "une théorie du système morphologique du langage", L. Hjelmslev, *Principes*, p. 3.

[85] R. H. Robins, *A. and M.*, p. 79.

[86] It must be understood that the Modistic use of 'meaning' was in no sense notional.

[87] 'System' is used here in the every day sense of the term.

[88] R. H. Robins, *A. and M.*, p. 87.

and as such is a worthy representative of the golden age of mediaeval scholasticism;[89] in all fairness to the Modistae, however, it must be pointed out that they did make a definite advance in their definition and description of the preposition by basing their definition solely on its syntactic function.[90] The Modistae also recognised the syntactic relations of *regimen*,[91] though this had already been noted by Peter Helias and the didactic grammarians, *e.g.* Alexander de Villa-Dei. The modern linguist will reject their theories because he rejects the whole system of thought that they reveal. But for the historian of grammar, the great interest of the Modistae is not only their contribution (such as it is) to general grammatical theory but the evidence they give of the tenor of the thought of their day.[92] A grammatical theory must be considered not only in terms of its own intrinsic value but also as an expression of the intellectual climate which produced it. In this sense the Modistae are admirable representatives of certain aspects of mediaeval achievement.

[89] We must remember that the Modistae were teachers of grammar as well as creators of a grammatical theory, and it is therefore important to see something of the position of grammar in the general pedagogy of the 12th and 13th centuries.
[90] *Cf.* pp. 276-279. The fact that the Modistae stated their definitions in semantic terms should not be allowed to minimise the importance of this new analysis of the preposition.
[91] *Cf.* pp. 63-64.
[92] G. L. Bursill-Hall, "Mediaeval Grammatical Theories", *The Canadian Journal of Linguistics* 9 (1963), 40-54.

II

THE GRAMMATICAL THEORIES AND TECHNIQUES
OF THE MODISTAE

A. THE GRAMMATICAL THEORIES OF THE MODISTAE

The theoretician of language is the creation of the associated disciplines
of his intellectual background; this is manifestly true of most modern
linguists, *e.g.* Ferdinand de Saussure who came to his theory of linguistics under the influence of the sociological theories of Durkheim.[1]
Despite their non-linguistic backgrounds, these linguists have all for-
mulated theories of language which must be considered in and of themselves without interference from the disciplines which formed their
creators or which are akin to them by virtue of the similarity of their
subject-matter.

The Modistae too were the spiritual children of their age and were
clearly influenced by the philosophical theories on which they were
nurtured. This is quite clear from the terminology used in their grammatical treatises; but the Modistae did more than retain the language
of the disciplines closely associated in the Middle Ages to the study of
grammar since they were, of course, more than grammarians and applied to the study of grammar not only the technical language of
contemporary metaphysics and logic but also the theories of this metaphysics and logic.

In the earlier Middle Ages, grammar had tended to be almost synonymous with literary studies like Priscian's grammar which sought
to provide the key to the understanding of a literary text.[2] From the 11th
century onwards, the incorporation of Aristotle's logic began to play a
very important role in the logicisation of grammar, part of the logica
vetus having been available from the 10th century (the remainder

---

[1] J. R. Firth, "Personality and Language in Society", *Papers in Linguistics 1934-
1951* (1957), pp. 177-189.
[2] This is the implication in Paetow's important study; *cf.* L. J. Paetow, *The Arts
Course at Mediaeval Universities, The University of Illinois Studies*, III. 7 (1910).

becoming available from the middle of the 12th century), and as a result of this and the concomitant revival of learning the study of literature was overshadowed by the study of logic and as a result of this change in emphasis, grammar came to be associated with the formulation of concepts of reality and their expression by language – the Modistae were, however, very insistent on the discreteness of logic and grammar.[3] Nevertheless, this association with logic and other non-linguistic disciplines had a profound effect on Modistic grammatical theories. Their conception of reality and of human reason led them to maintain that grammar must be 'one',[4] and therefore Robert Kilwardby, one of the immediate predecessors of the Modistae, could argue that grammar can only be a science if it is one for all men;[5] as a result of the intimacy between the reality of things and their conceptualisation by the mind, grammar becomes the study of the formulation of these concepts, their actual expression being accidental, and therefore incidental to Modistic grammatical theory. Furthermore, this theory of grammar had the effect of creating the belief that the universality of things as conceived and understood by the universality of human reason could be expressed in the universal language, Latin, which was thus raised to the status of a metalanguage. Minor matters such as the vernaculars had perhaps the effect of attesting differences in vocabulary, but these could be dismissed since they could not affect structure.

The result of this new approach to grammar was that the Modistae restated the semi-formal[6] definitions of Priscian of Latin grammar in terms suitable to the new spirit. This new descriptive procedure for grammar can be described as semantic, but it must be made quite clear that semantic in this context of situation should not be interpreted as notional or translational. For this reason, it would seem that Nehring's

[3]   Siger de Courtrai, p. 135: "sicut logica defendit animam nostram a falso in speculativis et a malo in practicis, sic grammatica defendit virtutem nostram interpretativam ab expressione conceptus mentis incongrua in omnibus scientiis."
[4]   Roger Bacon: "grammatica una et eadem est secundum substantiam in omnibus linguis, licet accidentaliter varietur." (*Gram. Graec.*), Oxford MS, p. 278, quoted by Wallerand, *Op. cit.*, p. 43 and by Robins, *A. and M.*, p. 77.
[5]   Robert Kilwardby: "cum scientia maneat eadem apud omnes, et subiectum eius idem manet, quare subiectum grammaticae debet manere idem in omnibus. Sed oratio constructa vel vox literata ordinabilis propter congruum non idem manet apud omnes; quare non erit subiectum grammaticae". (Quoted by Wallerand, p. 44.
[6]   I have used the term 'semi-formal' to account for the variety of criteria, *e.g.* meaning, formal structure, *etc.* which Priscian used to distinguish the parts of speech, *cf.* Robins, *A. and M.*, p. 67.

term of 'functional linguistics'[7] is much more suitable than logical grammar[8] or Sprachlogik[9] which have been used by scholars to describe Modistic theory; the Modistae, in using 'significatio' and 'consignificatio', merely aimed at a statement of the functional nature of the formal categories which Priscian had described, the criteria for these categories being however stated in terms of the correlates of reality to which they correspond. This, apart from anything else, underlines the dubious value of 'signify' when applied to the indeclinable partes orationis unless it is understood that 'signify' in such a context has no notional value but must be interpreted as 'function'. Mediaeval grammarians, i.e. the Modistae, in context with their philosophical theories, now established the partes orationis as the correlates of reality; the metaphysician had established within the world of things two primary elements, that of permanence and that of becoming (habitus and fieri), the expression of which became the province of the grammarian. The partes orationis which express permanence and stability are the nomen and pronomen, while the verbum and participium express the concept of becoming; the metaphysical device of the contrast of matter and form is introduced to distinguish the nomen and pronomen, and the verbum and participium. This is, however, a terminological distinction which is not to be correlated with reality and it would therefore be a mistake to identify matter with 'materia prima' and then apply this contrast of matter and form with its metaphysical implications and associations with substance directly to an analysis of the binary oppositions which serve to distinguish some of the partes orationis, viz. nomen/pronomen, verbum/participium; clearly the Modistae, influenced as they were by the metaphysical theory of reality, would naturally resort to a similar terminology to describe those words and more particularly those partes orationis which they had come to regard as the linguistic correlates of this reality.

It is almost a commonplace, therefore, to say that philosophical theories had a tight hold on Modistic grammatical theories; the great controversy of nominalism and realism had by their day lost much of its virulence and prominence but was, however, still vital enough to influence their philosophical outlook. The Modistae were not nominalists, nor were they extreme realists, which would have been to imply that a word became merely an imitation of reality;[10] in keeping with many

---

[7] A. Nehring, "A Note on Functional Linguistics in the Middle Ages", *Traditio* IX (1953), 430-434.

[8] G. Wallerand, *Op. cit.*, p. 73.

[9] This is the term used by (inter alia) Roos and Grabmann.

[10] Priscian's definition of the noun, i.e. signifying substance with quality, was

of their contemporaries, they took up a mid-way position and can perhaps be best described as moderate realists since they do accept the existence of the universal in the individuals; this permitted them to set up word-classes for the individual words and yet they insist on the necessary function of the intelligence to be the necessary connection, albeit indirect, between the reality and its functional signification in a grammatical system. The word, in the Modistic scheme, is not just the imitation of a piece of reality but must pass through a 'filter of intellectual apprehension'[11] which will impart to the word something of the subjective ideas of the creator of the word. On the other hand, the word, which will however not be entirely a figment of the mind but must have some correlate in the world of things outside the mind,[12] will therefore be defined in terms of the properties of the thing meant; this amounts to a subjective evaluation of the being and its properties which the intelligence has perceived and is now seeking to signify.

The danger is to classify the whole of a grammatical theory in terms of certain features employed in the description of these categories. It is quite true that the Modistae not only used technical terms which were borrowed from current philosophical language but also set up a grammatical theory which was based *in theory* on non-linguistic criteria (but in fact based on Donatus and Priscian), and then resorted to metaphysical values in order to define certain partes orationis which are, as a result, unequally classified in terms of the metaphysical values they do or do not possess.[13] This does not mean that all their terms and all their grammatical features can be so described; indeed their definition of the nomen substantivum as signifying by means of the modus per se stantis is more in the way of being a functional definition rather than either a metaphysical or a logical one.

The semantics of Modistic grammatical theory are discussed in more detail in the following sections of this chapter and in the following chapter. It is sufficient to state at this stage that Modistic grammatical

---

generally accepted; substance simply means the individual thing and quality the universal nature in which the thing participates, *cf.* de Rijk, *Op. cit. II*, p. 521.

[11] A. Nehring, *Op. cit.*, p. 433.

[12] Thomas of Erfurt, #6: "modi significandi activi non sunt figmenta, oportet omnem modum significandi activum ab aliqua rei proprietate radicaliter oriri ... cuilibet modo significandi activo correspondet aliqua proprietas rei seu modus essendi rei".

[13] The difference between the indeclinable and the declinable partes can be described very simply, that the declinable partes represent certain metaphysical qualities and the indeclinables (which are therefore described in syntactic terms) do not.

theory rests on the study of words and the properties of these words as the 'signs of things' which are, however, capable of signification;[14] the mind seizes upon the properties of the thing, there being a mode of understanding for each property to be understood.[15] The mind is not satisfied with the mere understanding of the thing but seeks to give it linguistic formulation by means of the mode of signifying – this meaning is not a possession of the thing itself but is bestowed on it by the mind[16] and the process therefore continues until the word has the ability not only to signify, *i.e.* to denote, but also to signify functionally, *i.e.* syntactically, by means of the modus consignificandi.

There is complete interdependence in such a theory between the structure of reality and the operations of the mind; but the active mode of signifying, such as the Modistae used it, never goes beyond the conceptual (which will to some extent at least account for the total exclusion of phonetic criteria in their grammatical theory), so that the partes orationis become the formulation of these concepts and are validated by their modes of signifying the things and the properties of the things that the mind has perceived.[17] Grammar, therefore, becomes the study of these formulations of a mental concept, but this must not be confused with the function of logic which is to distinguish right from wrong.

The grammarian, whatever his theoretical standpoint may be, studies the same data as other grammarians with different theoretical backgrounds; the test of his theory will obviously not be his data, which must by definition always be the same but his interpretation of his data. Hjelmslev has postulated three requirements for the examination of a theory, *i.e.* self-consistency, exhaustiveness and simplicity. If we apply these requirements to Modistic theory, we find a remarkable degree of consistency in their grammatical theories, but we cannot claim a similar degree of exhaustiveness of their account, since so many of their criteria were taken from extra-linguistic matters, *e.g.* the syllogism of formal logic had the effect of dismissing the subordinate clause from the type of constructions which the Modistic

[14] Thomas of Erfurt, #19: "grammatica est de signis rerum".
[15] Siger de Courtrai, p. 94: "modus intelligendi activus est modus quo intellectus comprehendit modum essendi seu proprietatem ipsius rei".
[16] Siger de Courtrai, p. 135: "grammatica est de modis significandi qui sunt operati ab anima".
[17] Siger de Courtrai, p. 94: "modi significandi activi sunt quidam conceptus ipsius intellectus; nunc conceptus intellectus manent in intellectu et sunt in eo et non transeunt extra".

grammarian would include in his inventory.[18] The Modistae retained practically the whole of the Priscianic grammatical system but omitted or restated those features which did not fit into their 'a priori' grammatical system, e.g. they omitted altogether the subordinating conjunction from their inventory of the conjunctions. The principle of simplicity can also be said to apply to the grammatical theory of the Modistae, since the number of their premises and the terms involved are fairly few, so that the inventory of the operations necessary to their grammatical procedure is relatively simple and economical.

If, on the other hand, we accept Wallerand's definition[19] of the grammarian-philosopher, i.e. 'étudier les formes de pensée correspondant aux choses et à leurs propriétés, déduire de ces formes de pensée, afin de les exprimer, les parties du discours et les justifier par elles jusque dans leurs détails, en un mot, faire correspondre parfaitement les formes logiques et les formes grammaticales, tel est le travail du grammairien philosophe',[20] then we can say that the grammatico-metaphysical schemes of the Modistae were eminently suitable, though the modern grammarian cannot begin to contemplate such a method of grammatical description as an efficient framework on which to build his analysis of linguistic structure.

B. MODISTIC DESCRIPTIVE TECHNIQUE

There is a considerable degree of agreement among the Modistae on their grammatical doctrine, but there tends to be more divergence in their actual presentation of this doctrine. It would, however, be a mistake to exaggerate the degree of divergence among them because it is possible to equate the definitions of the various categories used by the Modistae and the different elements used in the creation and description of the pars orationis.

The broad line of their procedure was a tri-partite statement, made progressively but in unequal divisions, of a dualist view of grammar. The first part consists of a description of their metalanguage[21] which

---

[18] Thomas does mention once the use of a subordinating conjunction when discussing the criteria for a complete construction, so that this cannot be dismissed altogether.

[19] G. Wallerand, Op. cit., p. (71).

[20] 'les formes logiques' must be understood as traditional logical forms; this must not, in any sense, be understood in terms of modern formal logic.

[21] This is my term for a section which is variously called by the Modistae.

is followed by their descriptions of the partes orationis (called the 'Etymologia' by Thomas of Erfurt) and then of the syntax of these partes orationis (called the 'Diasynthetica' by Thomas of Erfurt).

The preamble or the Metalanguage is used not only to describe their technical language, but also, and more particularly, the elements and categories[22] required in a descriptive process beginning with the speech act[23] and culminating in the word. In reality this preamble becomes an introduction to the type of analysis required for the description of any pars orationis, from its conception to its inception, and consists of two inter-related procedures, *viz.* vox to pars orationis and modus essendi to modus significandi.

The preamble, therefore, explains the development from the sound to the word, from the thought to the expression and from the thing to be signified to the thing as it is signified; the sound – it must be remembered that the Modistae excluded phonetics altogether from grammatical theory[24] – will also be a sign and can therefore designate something which has been understood by the mind. The sign acquires the capability of signifying (ratio significandi) as a result of which the sign (signum) becomes a dictio. The process does not cease at this stage; the dictio acquires from the mind the mode of signifying (modus significandi) which turns it into a pars orationis which is a grammatical unit with the capability of consignifying (ratio consignificandi), *i.e.* of signifying syntactically; this is the Modistic way of saying that it is usable syntactically, and it acquires thereby its mode of consignification (modus consignificandi) which is its syntactic mode of signifying.[25] Similarly, every thing – and the Modistae do not restrict this term 'thing' (res) to material objects – has a mode of being (modus essendi) which can be conceived by the mind by means of the mode of understanding (modus intelligendi) and once this stage has been reached, it is now capable of being signified by means of the mode of signifying (modus significandi). A pars orationis is, therefore, a creation of (i) the thing (res), (ii) the understanding of the thing (modus intelligendi), (iii) the

---

[22] These and other technical terms are discussed in detail in Chapter 3.
[23] Vox is used here in the sense of 'expression'; it must not be associated with the 'voice' or 'phoneme' of modern linguistics.
[24] Frequent reference will be made to this fact.
[25] *Ratio* is a complex term implying a basis or cause for doing something; in this instance, it can be said that the mode of signalling implies a basis for signifying and that the mode of signifying implies a basis for consignifying, *i.e.,* functioning (signifying) syntactically, *cf.* also pp. 53-55.

expression of the thing (vox), and (iv) the signifying of the thing (modus significandi).

The real tools in Modistic description of the partes orationis are the modes of signifying divided into essential and accidental. The essential mode was divided, by Siger into general and specific, and by Thomas into the modus generalissimus, the modus subalternus, and modus specialissimus; the modus generalissimus is, in effect, the same in doctrine as Siger's essential mode, but aims at distinguishing the partes orationis which may be related in terms of their essence, e.g. the nomen and pronoun, the verb and the participle, and does so by means of the matter-form contrast.[26] Siger in fact starts one stage 'prior' to Thomas's modus generalissimus by using the modus generalis to indicate those partes orationis which share the same essence; he uses the specific mode to indicate the essential feature by means of which the pars in question is discrete from all the others. Thomas completes his essential mode by means of subaltern modes and modi specialissimi, which are in fact detailed descriptions and inventories of the type of word which make up a particular pars orationis. Both Siger and Thomas then describe each pars orationis in terms of its accidental modes which represent variations of the essence of the pars in question; it can be said that these accidental modes, in the Modistic scheme, correspond to a large extent to the traditional 'accident' of grammar, but it would be quite mistaken to equate these terms entirely in view of the philosophical term 'accidentia' which featured prominently in mediaeval metaphysics. The difference between the Modistae and their predecessors on the matter of accident and accidental modes will be dealt with later, but it can also be easily seen[27] in their different conceptions of certain features, e.g. 'potestas' in the conjunction,[28] and by the introduction of certain accidental modes, e.g. Thomas's use of compositio[29] as an accidental mode of the verb, which is entirely absent from Donatus and Priscian.[30]

The Modistae, once the partes orationis have been described, proceed to a description of the syntax of these partes orationis. This is done in

---

[26] Cf. below, pp. 48-52, where the use of this contrast is discussed in much greater detail; cf. also the list of grammatical oppositions which the Modistae describe by means of the matter-form contrast, p. 296, fn. 57.

[27] Cf. the diagram in Appendix D, p. 391, which shows the different treatments of various accidents or accidental modes.

[28] Cf. pp. 268-269.

[29] Cf. pp. 217-219.

[30] Thomas of Erfurt, #128: "verbum habet quemdam modum significandi qui vocatur compositio, de quo antiqui grammatici mentionem expresse non fecerunt".

three stages, *i.e.* (i) *constructio,* the combination of the constructibles or members of the construction, (ii) *congruitas,* the *proper* combination of these constructibles, and (iii) *perfectio* which is the proper expression of a complete construction, by means of which a compound concept of the mind can be expressed and understood.

The Modistae derived their grammatical data from Donatus and Priscian and from Peter Helias's commentaries on Priscian;[31] the absence of exemplification in Thomas's and Siger's treatises can in most instances be explained by the fact that Siger and Thomas taught students who would already be familiar with Donatus and Priscian and who would refer to Donatus and Priscian for examples to illustrate the theories of the Modistae. Modistic grammatical procedure is largely a semanticisation of the more formal categories of Priscian and a restatement of these formal categories by means of the various modes of signifying. The diagram in Appendix D[32] shows at a glance that both Siger and Thomas turned most of the accidents described by Donatus and Priscian into accidental modes, except that any accident of Donatus's, which is in fact a means of stating in more detail those words or types of words which constitute the pars in question, is assigned by Thomas to a subaltern essential mode; *e.g.* qualitas in the nomen, which Donatus describes as an accident of the nomen, is described by Thomas in the form of the subaltern modes and the modi specialissimi of the nomen. This may well be a refinement introduced by Thomas, since he comes after Siger who included this feature, *i.e.* qualitas as an accidental mode of the nomen; if more works of the Modistae were available in print, it would be interesting to note the improvements made by the later Modistae to

---

[31] Siger de Courtrai, p. 102: "ideo dicit Priscianus, V Minoris, capitulo de figura dictionis: in quantitate comprehenditur, et Commentatur quod figura est qualitas quantitatis dictionis". Peter Helias is often called Commentator in relation to Priscian; this quotation is used here as a typical example of their occurrence together in Siger's text.

[32] *Cf.* below, p. 391. The blanks in the different columns indicate that this particular feature is not found in the pars in question in a particular grammarian's work, *e.g.* Thomas does not describe 'gradus' as an accidental mode of the nomen. Siger's section on the pronomen is incomplete which will in his case account for the blanks. His Sophismata "O Magister" contains a brief account of the indeclinables; though he does not say so specifically, it is quite clear that he would have described 'significatio' in the adverbium, 'potestas' in the coniunctio, and 'casus' in the praepositio as part of their essential modes. It is interesting to note that Martin of Dacia does not use the term 'modus accidentalis' with reference to the indeclinables but rather uses the expression, 'modi significandi posteriores modo significandi essentiali'.

the work of their immediate predecessors[33] – Roos has pointed out[34] a number of refinements, albeit terminological ones, absent from Martin of Dacia, one of the earliest of the Modistae, but which are to be found in the later Modistae, e.g. the terms 'Etymologia' and 'Diasynthetica' are not found in Martin (nor in Siger for that matter) but are found in Thomas.

We find, then, that Siger follows Priscian and Donatus very closely in the organisation of his material, though his exposition, by virtue of his different theoretical approach, is often quite different; Thomas too follows them closely, but does however introduce features not found in his predecessors[35] and in addition assigns material taken from Donatus to a different part of his exposition.[36]

C. TECHNICAL TERMINOLOGY

The technical vocabulary used by the Modistae in their grammatical descriptions has been described as formidable;[37] it is indeed, not only in its complexity and occasional obscurity, but there is in addition the danger of confusion with certain terms familiar by other use to the modern or traditional linguist, e.g. demonstratio which is used by Thomas of Erfurt to include 'presence' (praesentia) as an aspect of the feature of concreteness in the pronoun, i.e. presence in the concrete physical world – this is clearly different from the usual grammatical conception of demonstration. This complicated grammatical terminology becomes more understandable, however, when we realise that the

---

[33]   The Modistae as a group constitute the second generation of grammarians who benefited from the rediscovery of Aristotle in order to restate much of traditional grammatical theory, and can be considered the successors of people like Peter Helias, Petrus Hispanus, Robert Kilwardby, etc.; the Modistae often improve and refine the work of their pioneer predecessors, rather like linguists of today who follow on from scholars like de Saussure, Trubetzkoy, Jones, Bloomfield, and Firth, etc. However, even within the second generation which the Modistae constituted there appear to have been two 'age-groups', so that we find Thomas making refinements which are absent from Siger.

[34]   H. Roos, Op. cit., pp. 139-141.

[35]   E.g. compositio in the verb and persona in the nomen; he also uses 'significatio' in the verb quite differently from his predecessors including Siger.

[36]   E.g. qualitas in the noun and pronoun, significatio in the adverb and interjection, casus in the preposition and potestas in the conjunction, all of which were accidents in Donatus's account but become subaltern modes in Thomas's account, but significatio in the interjection becomes the modus specialissimus, since Thomas does not include a subaltern mode for this particular pars orationis.

[37]   R. H. Robins, A. and M., p. 80.

Modistae were not 'pure' grammarians – (the word 'pure' is used here in the sense that scholars of linguistics such as Bloomfield in America or Hjelmslev in Denmark can be termed 'pure' in that they devote their scholarly energies to the study of linguistics and have sought to create a technical vocabulary which is free from association with other disciplines) – for the Modistae were also logicians and philosophers[38] which will perhaps account, at least to a certain extent, for the intricacy and wealth of this grammatical terminology.

Certain items in Modistic terminology occur with great frequency, whereas others are found either much less frequently or in much more easily definable contexts; some terms have been included for discussion in this chapter, not because there is any intrinsic problem in their definition, but because they are used by the Modistae in more than one sense, *e.g.* genus in the nomen[39] and verb, modus in the verb and as a general descriptive term for any mode of signifying, and forma which is used as a general term in contrast to materia and also by Thomas as an accidental mode of the verb equivalent to 'species' in the nomen, – Siger in fact uses 'species' to describe this feature in the verb, – while 'species' is also used in Modistic non-technical language to indicate the different types of any word or pars orationis, *etc.* It is inevitable that certain words acquire a technical value in certain contexts which they do not possess elsewhere; this only accentuates the inadequacy of language, particularly when talking about language,[40] and one of the aims of this section will be to separate the technical and non-technical usage of many of these terms, since the Modistae too must surely have been aware of such a difference.[41] Apart from anything else, the exami-

---

[38] Wallerand's edition of Siger de Courtrai's work contains his "Ars Priorum", and his "Fallaciae".

[39] Nomen is used throughout to refer to both substantive and adjective, since noun is usually taken to refer to substantive only: the terms substantivum and adjectivum are occasionally used to refer obviously to substantive and adjective.

[40] J. R. Firth, "The Semantics of Linguistic Science", *Papers in Linguistics*, p. 140: "Let it be borne in mind that language is often not very apt when used about itself, even in technical linguistic studies ... The technical language for the systematic statement of the facts of language cannot, any more than for mathematics, be the language of every day common sense."

[41] F. C. Copleston, *Aquinas*, p. 66: "It is also a mistake to assume that the mediaevals, because they lived centuries ago, must all have been linguistically naïve. They were aware, for example, that the same word may have different senses in common usage, that the meaning of a word when used as a technical term in philosophy may not be exactly the same as the meaning or meanings which it bears in non-philosophical language, and that the meaning of a word in its philosophical use needs to be precisely stated."

nation and interpretation of these terms becomes a valuable exercise in the application of J.R. Firth's theory of meaning by collocation and context of situation[42] to the understanding and definition of such terms.

The presentation of this technical vocabulary is divided into three parts; the first contains those terms which refer more to the metalanguage of the Modistae, the second to those terms which are found in the analyses of the different partes orationis – certain of the accidental modes are included since they are quite different from the usual vocabulary of description of modern grammarians, e.g. species, figura, compositio, etc., whereas others, e.g. casus, numerus, coniugatio, tempus, persona,[43] are used approximately as any grammarian today would use them, and require no special explanation; the third part contains technical terms found in Modistic syntactic theory, and which, apart from certain terms incorporated from contemporary philosophical and metaphysical theory, e.g. actus, potentia, represent the greatest innovation and divergence from traditional grammatical vocabulary.

D. TERMINOLOGY OF THE METALANGUAGE

The linguist who studies the Modistae is faced with the problem of a technical terminology which is intrinsically difficult, since the Modistae were typical of the mediaeval schoolmen, i.e. in the intricacy of their terminology and in the subtlety of their argument, but the linguist – who may not, moreover, be familiar with mediaeval philosophical metalanguage – has also to cope with a technical grammatical vocabulary which in many cases has been borrowed from philosophy and, to complicate matters further, has retained a marked undertone from its philosophical or logical origin.

The theory of hylomorphism and its adaptation by the Modistae has already been referred to, and the terms associated with it, i.e. materia, forma, substantia and accidentia, were used by the Modistae in their general descriptive processes as the terms for describing a number of binary oppositions, especially between the four declinable partes orati-

---

[42] The terms are discussed by Firth in his "Modes of Meaning", "The Technique of Semantics", "General Linguistics and Descriptive Grammar" in *Papers in Linguistics, 1934-1951,* and also in his "A Synopsis of Linguistic Theory, 1930-1955" in *Studies in Linguistic Analysis* (special volume of the Philological Society), 1957.
[43] Thomas of Erfurt, and Martin of Dacia do actually use 'persona' as an accidental mode of the nomen, as well as an accidental mode of the verb.

onis and also between members of the same pars orationis.[44] The
Modistae do not, however, make extensive use of substantia or accidentia as technical terms; Siger uses substantia, in a more everyday
sense, as one of the features which the general essential modes of the
nomen and pronoun signify. Thomas, in his description of the nomen
(and by implication of the pronoun),[45] deliberately substitutes 'modus
entis' for substantia as one of the criteria for the general mode; he does
this presumably in view of the problem which the use of the term 'substantia' would create in the description of items such as 'negatio',
'privatio' and 'figmentum'.[46]

It is, however, difficult to draw any absolute conclusion from the way
that both Siger and Thomas use these terms. Siger, as has just been
pointed out, uses substantia as a feature of the nomen and pronoun, but such usage does not carry with it any metaphysical
implications; on the other hand, Siger does use on two occasions the
analogy of substantia-accidentia as a means of suggesting the difference
between the substantive and adjective, and between the nomen and
verb.[47] The Modistae use 'accidentia' considerably less frequently than
their predecessors, since they have 'created', to fit their general descriptive scheme, the term 'modus accidentalis' to describe most of the
features traditionally considered 'accidents', and it is often difficult to
decide whether the use is in the conventional grammatical or the contemporary metaphysical sense. It seems, however, reasonable to suggest,
that in view of their creation of the term 'modus accidentalis', the term
'accidentia', when used, is to be considered more as a counterpart to
'substantia' rather than in the more formal[48] grammatical sense.[49] It
is difficult and rash, however, to assume that this will always be so;

---

[44]   Siger de Courtrai, p. 102: "adiectiva dependent inesse a suis substantivus sicut
accidentia a substantiis".

[45]   Thomas of Erfurt, #25: "intelligere per significare substantiam modum substantiae, qui est modus entis sumptus a proprietate rei, quae est proprietas habitus
et permanentis".

[46]   Thomas of Erfurt, #26: "licet privationes et negationes non sint entia positiva
extra animam posita: sunt tamen entia positiva secundum animam". This suggests
considerable alertness on the part of Thomas in that, having appreciated the inadequacy of the term 'substantia' as the criterion for the nomen, he is at least
better able to justify on philosophical grounds his new term 'ens'.

[47]   Siger de Courtrai, p. 140: "nomen dignius est verbo quia substantia dignior
est accidente".

[48]   'Formal' is here used in the modern grammatical sense of the term.

[49]   Thomas of Erfurt, #131: "modus, ut est accidens verbi . . ."; Siger de Courtrai,
p. 123: "a nomine, scilicet, substantiam et per consequens accidentia eius, scilicet,
genus et casum".

Siger uses substantia and qualitas in his description of the nomen[50] but negatively so in the pronoun, *i.e.* the pronoun signifies substance but without quality; in this sense it might be argued that Siger is using substantia and qualitas as associated terms for materia and forma in his analysis of the nomen and pronomen and this is particularly true of the pronoun.[51] We shall see that one great difference between the nomen and pronoun is the absence of form in the pronoun, so that the pronoun has the similar function in grammar to that of matter in substance, that of being informable, *i.e.* capable of bearing a qualification.

The Modistae, especially Thomas, made deliberate and extensive use of the materia-forma contrast to produce a number of binary oppositions at various levels. Thomas uses matter (materia) as a means of stating a feature which the pars shares in common with other partes,[52] while form (forma) is used to indicate the quality which distinguishes it, *i.e.* which marks it off from other partes,[53] *e.g.* the nomen and pronoun have the same matter (*i.e.* modus entis); but the nomen, by reason of its form, is capable of designating distinctly[54] which the pronoun cannot, since it possesses no form.[55] A similar use of this contrast is made to distinguish the verb and the participle, except that in the case of the participle (in contrast to the pronoun) it does possess a form of its own, and the two, *i.e.* verb and participle, are distinguished by means of a formal element.[56] Siger also makes use of the opposition (without explicitly saying so) in the indeclinable partes, in that they all have the same matter, *i.e.* the modus disponentis, but a different form which distinguishes them from each other, *i.e.* the specific mode of each of the indeclinable partes. Thomas does not use 'matter-form' to describe and distinguish the indeclinables but resorts to more strictly syntactic

---

[50] Siger de Courtrai, p. 131: "modus significandi essentialis est qui ingreditur essentiam partis, sicut substantia et qualitas in nomine".

[51] Siger de Courtrai, p. 125: "in pronomine est substantia per se et quod pronomen substantiam solum non etiam qualitatem significat, ita quod consimili modo imaginandum in pronomine sicut materia prima".

[52] Thomas of Erfurt, #23: "modus entis habet rationem materiae, quae est facere convenire".

[53] Thomas of Erfurt, #23: "modus determinatae apprehensionis habet rationem formae, quae facit nomen ab aliis partibus orationis differre".

[54] Siger de Courtrai, p. 96: "qualitatis seu formae est distinguere"; Thomas of Erfurt, #24: "a proprietate formae et qualitatis, quae est proprietas determinantis quoniam forma determinat et distinguit".

[55] G. Wallerand, *Op. cit.*, p. (50): "la fonction du pronom en grammaire est celle de la matière première dans les substances".

[56] Distantia in the verb and indistantia in the participle represent the form by means of which they are discrete.

criteria; Siger, although he does set up by implication the contrast of matter and form also uses syntactic criteria to describe the indeclinables. Mention at this length is made, partly to illustrate Siger's tremendous consistency in his method of presentation, but more particularly to suggest that, if we do accept the materia-forma contrast as a device used in Siger's description of the indeclinable,[57] it reinforces the argument that grammatical as well as philosophical reasons governed the retention of these technical terms; it is quite possible to argue that there are philosophical grounds for the use of the materia-forma opposition in the declinable partes, but it requires a real effort of the imagination to conceive of the metaphysics of substance playing a part in the definitions of the indeclinable partes.

Thomas makes extensive use of matter and form in his preamble, and this applies to both the elements and categories, which form his metalanguage. A dictio and pars orationis have one feature in common, *i.e.* vox which constitutes their matter; a dictio is a signum which possesses the ability[58] to signify (ratio significandi), while the pars is distinct from the dictio since it possesses the ability to consignify (ratio consignificandi), and the formal differences here are achieved by means of the two 'rationes'.[59] The contrast of matter and form is used by Thomas to distinguish the categories,[60] though not perhaps in quite so simple or obvious a manner as in the case of dictio and pars orationis. There is distinction of form between the three levels of being, understanding and signifying, but similarity of matter between the passive modes;[61] at the levels of understanding and signifying, there is in both cases a difference of matter and a similarity of form between the active

---

[57] In the declinable partes, Siger uses the general and specific modes as the matter-form contrast: similarly, therefore, the general and specific modes in the indeclinables represent the same *grammatical* opposition.

[58] Michel de Marbais: "dictio unde dictio est, includit in se vocem tanquam sibi materiam et rationem significandi tanquam sibi formam" (quoted by Thurot, p. 156).

[59] *Cf.* above, pp. 53-54, for a discussion of the term 'ratio' and its different uses as a technical term in Modistic metalanguage.

[60] Thomas of Erfurt, #14: "modus intelligendi activus et modus intelligendi passivus differunt materialiter, et conveniunt formaliter ... eadem est ratio intelligendi, per quam intellectus proprietatem rei intelligit active, et per quam rei proprietas intelligitur passive".

[61] Cf. Thomas of Erfurt, #12-13: "modi essendi, et modi intelligendi passivi, et modi significandi, sunt idem materialiter et realiter, sed differunt formaliter ... modus essendi, et modus intelligendi activus, et modus significandi activus differunt formaliter et materialiter".

and the passive.[62] The following diagram shows the matter and form of the three levels of the metalanguage:

	materialiter	formaliter
modus essendi	proprietas rei	ratio essentiae
modus intelligendi activus	proprietas intellectus	ratio intelligendi
modus intelligendi passivus	proprietas rei	ratio intelligendi
modus significandi activus	proprietas vocis	ratio significandi
modus significandi passivus	proprietas rei	ratio significandi

This suggests the grammatical application of the close relationship between matter and form and another mediaeval metaphysical distinction, *i.e.* act and potentiality, which, however, the Modistae do not use to any great extent in their grammatical writings; the form can be said to actualise the matter.[63]

The relationship of matter and form and act and potentiality explain another problematical item of Modistic metalanguage. A dictio possesses a mode of designating (modus signandi) as its matter and an ability to signify (ratio significandi) as its form which actualises its matter to become a pars orationis; in turn a pars orationis has as its matter an active mode of signifying (modus significandi activus) which is actualised by its form (ratio consignificandi) *i.e.* its ability to consignify to become a mode of consignification (modus consignificandi) which represents its function at the syntactic level.

This matter and form distinction is indeed taken by Thomas to the syntactic level, where he maintains that the relationship and combination of the dependent and terminant constructibles can be compared to the relationship of matter and form, and act and potentiality;[64] matter and form combine to form a whole, and similarly dependent and terminant constructibles combine to form a construction. The contrast is further applied by Thomas to the principles of construing; the principium *materiale*, the matter of the construction refers to the constructibles, which

[62]   Thomas of Erfurt, #15: "modus significandi activus et passivus differunt materialiter et sunt idem formaliter; quia modus significandi passivus dicit proprietatem rei sub ratione consignificandi passiva; sed modus significandi activus dicit proprietatem vocis, quae est ratio consignificandi activa; sed eadem est ratio, per quam vox est significans active, et per quam proprietas rei significatur passive".

[63]   F. C. Copleston, *Op. cit.*, p. 93: "first matter, considered in abstraction, is pure potentiality for successive actualisation by substantial forms, each of which stands to its matter as act to potentiality, actualising the matter's potentiality".

[64]   Thomas of Erfurt, #191: "sicut ex materia et forma, quorum unum est in actu, alterum vero potentia, fit per se compositum in natura; sic ex ratione dependendi et terminandi fit per se constructio in sermone".

are capable of being actualised by the form, *i.e.* by the principium *formale,* into a construction.

Thomas and Siger use the term qualitas in the essential mode of the nomen almost as an equivalent to 'forma'; its use here is clearly different from 'qualitas' which Siger describes as an accidental mode of the nomen. Thomas, although he too, like Siger, takes qualitas from Donatus, makes of it however the subaltern mode of the nomen to create the proper names, substantives and adjectives. Thomas also makes of *qualitas* an accidental mode of the verb; this too he takes from Donatus and divides it into mood (modus) and forma (which represents in this instance [65] a similar feature in the verb to 'species' in the nomen), – indeed, Siger also calls it 'species' in the verb as well. There are other uses of qualitas, *i.e.* as a type of adjective and adverb; qualitas is also used to describe the relationship between mood and compositio, and genus and significatio, but these different uses can be clearly observed by their collocations within different contexts of grammatical description.

There are, in addition, two other terms requiring mention here, which are encountered in Modistic metalanguage, *i.e. ratio* and *consignificatio;* they have no semantic relationship but in association they suggest explanations of other terms included in this chapter. Ratio can be found collocated with a number of technical terms, and there seem to be three basic types of these collocations; furthermore, ratio occurs very frequently in various other collocations and situations which suggest that it is in such instances a word (rather than a technical term) used to express the means of doing or achieving something.[66]

In collocation with terms of the metalanguage, *e.g.* intelligendi, significandi, consignificandi, ratio suggests the capability of doing something,[67] so that the dictio possesses the mode of designating which is the basis for its ability to signify, and the pars orationis possesses the mode of signifying which is the basis for its ability to consignify.

The second collocation occurs with syntactic terms such as princi-

---

[65]   Thomas of Erfurt, #134: "forma, quae est accidens verbi, idem est, quod species in nomine, et ab eadem proprietate sumpta, scilicet a modo essendi primarie vel secundarie".

[66]   Siger de Courtrai, p. 130: "si ista oratio est congrua: 'amo est verbum', aut hoc est *ratione* significati, aut *ratione* modi significandi, aut *ratione* vocis" (my emphasis).

[67]   In these collocations with significandi and consignificandi etc., modus may be regarded as the exponent of *ratio, cf.* Boethius of Dacia, Quaestio 14: "quod quia modi significandi diversarum partium in specie differunt, ideo rationes, quas illi modi significandi circa significata dictionis denotant, sunt diversae."

pium, terminus, suppositum and appositum, and in such instances ratio implies potential syntactic function; for instance, in discussing the cases of the nomen Thomas clearly suggests that word-order is a relevant factor, and ascribes a different value, in some instances to a case-form in terms of its relevant position in the construction.[68] Similarly, an equally relevant position is ascribed to the suppositum or appositum, and by this means Thomas is able to produce a very formal analysis,[69] despite its semantic description,[70] of a sentence such as 'ens est'[71] which otherwise requires a lengthy explanation if we are to be satisfied with a conventional Modistic explanation of modus entis and modus esse as the means of differentiating between 'ens' and 'est' in this sentence.[72] Thomas states, in effect, that this is not done by means of the meaning of the suppositum but by means of the relevant position of the suppositum (ratio suppositi).

The third collocation of 'ratio' is used by Thomas on two occasions with materia and forma in discussing the general modes of the nomen and verbum; it seems almost as if Thomas is describing the two parts of each mode by analogy with matter and form, *i.e.* that the modus entis corresponds to matter and determinata apprehensio to form, *etc.* rather than that they actually represent matter and form.[73]

Reference has been made to the collocation of 'ratio consignificandi' and once more it would seem relevant to contrast the occurrence of 'consignificare' in such a collocation with its use in other contexts. Scholars, discussing this feature,[74] have used the words 'dolor' and 'doleo', and also 'donum' and 'datum' to illustrate the significance of the term 'consignificare', and it would appear that they use it both alike and with two widely different implications. The first is found in collocation with 'modus' or 'ratio' and in such instances suggests syntactic meaning.

---

[68] Thomas of Erfurt, #88: "iste genitivus Socratis significat rem in ratione principii, respectu huius verbi interest".

[69] This is the modern use of the term.

[70] On many occasions the Modistae present us with a 'formal' explanation despite their attempts to hide it under their semanticisation, *cf.* the discussion of the essential mode of the adverb, pp. 260-261.

[71] Thomas of Erfurt, #116: "in ista propositione significatum verbi non differat essentialiter et secundum rem a significato supposici, differt tamen ab eo secundum rationem, et hoc sufficit ad distantiam et diversitatem verbi a supposito, quae sunt entia secundum rationem".

[72] Thomas even tries the matter-form contrast to explain the difference between 'ens' and 'est' in "ens est".

[73] This is mentioned to support the argument that matter and form were as much grammatical devices as metaphysical distinctions in the hands of the Modistae.

[74] Ch. Thurot, *Op. cit.*, pp. 155-156; H. Roos, *Op. cit.*, pp. 143-144.

A word (dictio) has the potential capability of signifying (ratio significandi) which is actualised by means of the 'vox significativa'[75] to become a pars orationis which is such by means of the active mode of signifying;[76] a pars orationis is functionally useless, unless it can combine with another pars orationis in order to consignify or signify syntactically.[77] Thomas tells us that the 'ratio consignificandi' refers to the principium materiale,[78] i.e. the potential constructible, and the 'ratio consignificandi activa' refers to the principium formale,[79] i.e. the actualised combination of constructibles into a construction; this last is very similar to Siger's mode of consignification which implies that the *pars* is ready to signify functionally, i.e. syntactically, since it presupposes the capability to signify, the *vox* and the significatio, i.e. the primary or referential meaning.[80] Consignificatio in such a collocation suggests syntactic meaning, which results from its functional combination with other partes orationis.

In other contexts and collocations, consignificatio seems to imply connotation, secondary or semantic meaning; there are not many instances of such usage, and Thomas applies it to a description of certain accidental modes,[81] thereby implying that the mode in question, e.g. tempus in the verb,[82] is a means used by the pars in question to describe semantic features in addition to those features which are described by means of the primary of its essential mode, e.g. modus entis in the nomen.

---

[75] Thomas of Erfurt, #4: "rationem significandi, quae vocatur significatio, per quam efficitur signum vel significans; et sic formaliter est dictio"; Thomas of Erfurt, #18: "dictio est vox significativa".

[76] Thomas of Erfurt, #18: "pars orationis formaliter est per modum significandi activum, dictioni superadditam, quia pars orationis est dictio, ut habet modum significandi activum".

[77] Cf. Firth's definition of 'meaning by usage'.

[78] Thomas of Erfurt, #4: "pars est pars secundum se per hanc rationem consignificandi, seu modum significandi activum, tanquam per principium formale ... rationem consignificandi, quae vocatur modus significandi activus, per quam vox significans fit consignum, vel consignificans; et sic *formaliter* est pars orationis" (my emphasis).

[79] Thomas of Erfurt, #4: "sed est pars relata ad aliam per eamdem rationem consignificandi activam, tanquam per principium efficiens intrinsecum".

[80] Siger de Courtrai, p. 95: "modus consignificandi per quem pars est pars praesupponit rationem significandi, vocem et significatum".

[81] I.e. case, person, tense, etc.

[82] Thomas of Erfurt, #147: "tempus est modus significandi accidentalis verbi, quo mediante verbum, citra rem, modum temporis consignificat".

E. TERMINOLOGY OF THE ETYMOLOGIA

This group of terms refers to the language of description particularly of the partes orationis: *modus,* though not difficult in itself to explain, must be included on three counts, (a) by virtue of its relationship with ratio and consignificare which were discussed in the preceding section, (b) by reason of its use as a generic term in the whole Modistic scheme of presenting a semantic dress for every grammatical feature, and (c) since it is used with an entirely different meaning to describe an accidental mode of the verb, a category known to traditional and modern grammarians alike as 'mood' and which has a very close connection with three other terms to be discussed in this section, *i.e. compositio, significatio,* and *genus.*

Modus and ratio are found, especially in Thomas, in the similar collocations of signandi, intelligendi, significandi and consignificandi, the difference between them being similar to that of act and potentiality, modus representing act and ratio potentiality, *i.e.* the actualisation of the potentiality of something; thus the modus signandi is the act of the dictio which has also the potential ability to signify (ratio significandi). Thomas states, therefore, that a *pars orationis* is such by means of the ratio consignificandi or the modus significandi activus, *i.e.* the pars possesses the active mode of signifying, *i.e.* the means of signifying which makes it a grammatical functive and also the potentiality of consignifying (ratio consignificandi), *i.e.* of having meaning at the syntactic level in addition to its primary referential meaning.

Modus is also used by the Modistae to designate the various grammatical and pre-grammatical categories, since *every* grammatical feature must be described in terms of some mode or other; every grammatical feature must possess actuality rather than mere potentiality before it can be considered a perfect complete feature.[83]

Thus each stage, *i.e.* essendi, intelligendi, significandi, becomes complete and self-contained by means of its particular mode, and so we have, even at the pre-grammatical level, the complete stages of modus essendi and modus intelligendi, leading to the modus significandi; each in turn is made up of a number of complete, self-contained components. Thus a pars orationis will be described in terms of its various modes of signifying, none of which overlap but all of which are necessary for a

---

[83]   If we consider 'modus' as act and 'ratio' as potentiality, only 'modus' can be used to complete the description of the feature, since a form must be actualised before it can be considered complete and perfect.

complete description of the pars, and it might even be argued that the mode of consignification (modus consignificandi) should also be added since this describes the pars by means of its syntactic meaning (and connotations).

Mention was made of the third meaning of modus, *i.e.* mood which by itself presents no great problem of interpretation to the grammarian; however, in conjunction with compositio, significatio and genus, it presents an interesting theoretical approach to the problem of defining the relationship between the nomen suppositum and the verb and the verb and nominal oblique in constructions such as 'Socrates currit' and 'lego librum'. This theory is found in Thomas only and demonstrates an approach which would not be unfamiliar to many modern linguists.[84] For reasons such as the structure of the favourite sentence-types of Latin, and the requirements of formal logic, Thomas considered only two types of construction, *i.e.* intransitive and transitive, the first being made up of nomen and verb (NV) and the second of verb and nominal object,[85] and Thomas introduces, therefore, the accidental mode of *compositio* to restore the relationship between the nominal subject and verb. Mood (modus) becomes, as a result, the quality of this compositio, *i.e.* the relationship or predication of NV remains basically constant but it can be expressed by means of different qualities and will do so by means of mood. *Significatio* provides the balance to compositio, since significatio expresses the relationship between the verb and the post-posed nominal oblique found in all transitive constructions; just as the basic relationship of NV remains constant, so the basic relationship of VN remains constant but can employ different qualities in the expression of this relationship, and the accidental mode of voice (genus) is created to describe these different relational qualities. Compositio and significatio can thus be said to control the colligations[86] of NV and VN respectively in the primary favourite sentence-type of Latin.

The term *genus* is used by the Modistae in three senses; the first, *i.e.* voice, has just been discussed and the second, *i.e.* gender, can be classi-

---

[84]   *I.e.* Thomas's constructions can be considered a primitive form of endocentric and exocentric constructions, and his analytical procedure a rudimentary form of Immediate Constituent analysis.

[85]   He does not list the subordinating conjunctions nor does he mention subordinate clauses, except to draw attention to the subordinate clause and its incompleteness by virtue of its dependence on something outside the clause, and completion of dependences is one of the criteria for a constructio perfecta.

[86]   *Cf.* J. R. Firth, "A Synopsis of Linguistic Theory (1930-1955)", *Studies in Linguistic Analysis.*

fied, like the first, as a well-known grammatical category and requires no further explanation. The third usage, albeit very sparing, might be classified as a logical term adapted to grammatical description; it is used in conjunction with species [87] and specific differences (differentia specifica) since a species is made up of genus and differentia specifica which can correspond in this particular case to the contrast of matter and form, genus representing the matter and differentia specifica the form, and combining to produce the species. This of course represents the general mode, *i.e.* genus and the specific mode, *i.e.* differentia specifica, which combine to produce the essential mode of signifying of the pars orationis in question though neither mode can exist without the other. [88]

Species in this sense can be taken to mean 'type', so that Thomas can use the term, when discussing compositio as a feature of the verb, to say that compositio is not an essential mode since it does not constitute any particular type (species) of verb. [89] *Species* is, however, used by the Modistae in a much more technical sense, and along with *figura*, [90] they are accidental modes of the nomen and verb; they are both absolute modes, and as such have no syntactic function, though this does not of course affect the syntactical operations as a result of the other accidental modes of the pars to which they belong. Both species and figura are derivational items – the term 'derivational' is here used in its synchronic, not its diachronic sense; species might be said to represent type and *figura* the 'skhema' [91] as used by Dionysius Thrax, but they were clearly not set up by means of the formal [92] criteria which such categories would be given in a modern structural description. Species is divided into simple (primitiva) and derived (determinativa, or derivativa in the case of Thomas) and figura is divided into simple (simplex), compound (composita), and double-compound, *i.e.*

---

[87]   Siger de Courtrai, p. 95: "sicut ad constitutionem speciei concurrent genus et differentia specifica, sic ad constitutionem partis concurrent modus significandi generalis et specificus".

[88]   This is clearly implied in Siger's argument that an indeclinable pars must possess an essential mode made up of the general and specific modes.

[89]   Thomas of Erfurt, #128: "nec est essentialis specialis, cum non constituat aliquam speciam verbi".

[90]   (a) Thomas of Erfurt, #68: "species est modus significandi accidentalis nominis, mediante quo modum significandi primarium vel secundarium significat"; (b) Thomas of Erfurt, #82: "figura est modus significandi accidentalis nominis, mediante quo, nomen proprietatem simplicis, compositi, vel decompositi significat".

[91]   *Cf*. R. H. Robins, *Thrax*, p. 99.

[92]   This is the modern sense of the term.

derived from a compound word (decomposita). Species is described by criteria which could not be regarded as remotely formal; species is defined, in effect, in terms of primary and derived or secondary meaning. This produces a reasonable explanation for 'montanus' as a species derived from 'mons'[93] but on the other hand, this non-formal procedure will produce monstrosities such as 'albus' being derived from 'albedo',[94] since for the Modistae the property of 'whiteness' must exist before the quality of 'white' can be obtained.

The Modistae described 'figura' in rather more formal terms than they did 'species', and it is possible to equate their description of this feature to a more modern morphological description of stem plus derivational affix. Thomas goes so far as to argue that figura is *not* derived from the property of the vox, but from the property of the thing to be expressed;[95] a simple form, *e.g.* pauper cannot be divided into component parts,[96] a compound form, *e.g.* equiferus, is divisible into its component parts, even if the components have different meanings when treated separably than when in combination[97] (as in the well-known example of 'green house' and 'green-house'). Siger does not consider the double- compound form to be a separate category but merely a form derived (determinata) from a compound form,[98] *e.g.* magnanimitas, and it cannot therefore be broken down into meaningful component parts.[99] Figura is thus a descriptive category for a word, but this is not

---

[93]   Thomas of Erfurt, #68: "mons primitivae speciei est, quia significat rem sub essentia primaria ...: sed montanus derivativae speciei est, quia significat rem sub esse secundario, quae est essentia comparata".

[94]   Thomas of Erfurt, #67: "albus descendit ab albedine".

[95]   Thomas of Erfurt, #79: "figura ... non accipitur a proprietate vocis ... figura sumitur a proprietate rei".

[96]   Siger de Courtrai, p. 102: "figura simplex est figura designans circa rem modum essendi individionis intelligendo individionem non solum quantum ad rem sed quantum ad intellectum ut apparet in 'n' et 'x' et huius modi, cuius partes separatae nihil significant nec valent significare".

[97]   Siger de Courtrai, p. 103: "licet partes nominis compositae figurae, ut partes, propinque, sunt et in actu talis nominis nihil significant separate, quia sunt partes incompositae, ... tamen partes nominis compositione figurae remote, in potentia, partes secundum se consideratae, bene aliquid significant separatae et idem quod in composito vel non penitus idem".

[98]   Siger de Courtrai, p. 103: "figura decomposita non designat circa rem aliquem modum essendi distinctum a praedictis ... sola determinatio ex composito est figura decompositae figurae".

[99]   Siger de Courtrai, p. 103: "non potest esse simplicis figurae et a composita, quia id non potest esse composite quod non potest dividi in partes intelligibiles; nunc magnanimitas est huius modi quia 'animitas' per se non divitur, ideo non potest esse compositae figurae; est ergo decompositae pro tanto quia a composito determinatur".

done in morphological terms (in the modern sense of morphology), but in terms of the meaning or lack of meaning of the component parts.

F. TERMINOLOGY OF THE DIASYNTHETICA

The greatest wealth and complexity of terminology is found in the section dealing with Modistic syntactic theories. Reference, however, will be made, and frequently so, to the degree of interpenetration between the levels of etymologia and diasynthetica, and many of the ideas of the Modistae on the partes orationis can be clarified by a 'forward' reference to their syntax. Furthermore, the Modistae viewed the partes orationis as something more than isolated words, and their conception of the major partes orationis was conditioned by factors other than the metaphysics of a reality, factors such as the structure of the favourite sentence-types of Latin; the partes orationis, especially the declinable partes, were conceived, even if they were not formally so defined, with their syntactic functions included as a latent factor. It is impossible to make any assessment of Modistic grammatical theories and their treatment of the partes orationis without some consideration of their technical language used in describing grammatical features which are not immediately connected with their word-class theories.

A construction (*constructio*)[100] at least for Thomas, is made up of two constructibles, one of which will be the *dependent* constructible and the other will be the *terminant* constructible, and the nature of the dependence will decide the type of construction. If the first member is the dependent constructible, the construction is described as a *transitive* construction; the other fundamental type of construction is the *intransitive* but the intransitive construction requires the second constructible to be the dependent constructible. In a construction such as "Socrates currit", the verb or appositum 'currit' is dependent on the nomen subject or suppositum 'Socrates'. In the case of a construction in which a constructible depends on the pre-posed suppositum as in "Socrates currit", this member, *i.e.* Socrates, will be the principium, and in the case of a construction in which the dependent constructible is the first member, as in "lego librum", the constructible 'librum' will be the terminus.

The terms transitivus and intransitivus, as used by the Modistae,

---

[100] Thomas of Erfurt, #185: "unius constructionis non sunt plura, vel pauciora duobus; quia ... constructio causatur ex dependentia unius constructibilis ad alterum".

should not be confused with these terms in traditional or structural use; in traditional grammar, the term 'transitive' or 'intransitive' is applied to verbs which can or cannot take an object, whereas the Modistae apply these terms to explain the relationships and positions of the two members of a construction. A sentence such as "Socrates percutit Platonem" consists of two constructions, *i.e.* the intransitive "Socrates percutit" and the transitive 'percutit Platonem',[101] since in every construction, the subject, as either in the above construction or in "lego librum', is automatically subsumed.[102] The terms 'suppositum' and appositum' were used to express the SP relationship of the favourite sentence type; the suppositum is in fact the substantive element, although it may possess a determinant, and the appositum clearly refers to a verb only – its definition is almost exactly the same as the definition of the verb.[103] It must be stressed that 'appositum', as used by the Modistae, is not synonymous with the predicate as used in traditional or modern grammar – the appositum refers to the verb only,[104] and indeed the term seems to refer only to the verb used in the constructio intransitiva of the NV type.

The terms 'principium' and 'terminus' are applied to the substantival element in the two types of constructions just outlined, *i.e.* principium refers to the suppositum in the NV type of construction[105] and terminus to the oblique nominal form in the VN type of construction.[106] These terms are also used by Thomas in his analysis of the case-system of the nomen; it is clear that Thomas considered word-order to be a criterion of syntactic function, so that principium and terminus, when he describes for instance the genitive case, become the criteria for differentiating the functional value of the genitive in instances such as "Socratis accidit" in which the genitive form is the principium, and in "misereor Socratis" in which the genitive is the terminus. There is, of course, a

---

[101] Thomas of Erfurt, #185: "Socrates percutit Platonem; hic propter diversas dependentias verbi ad suppositum ante se, et ad obliquum post se, non potest esse una constructio".
[102] Thomas of Erfurt, #195: "omne verbum requirit suppositum, sive sit personale, sive impersonale, sive finitum, sive infinitum".
[103] Thomas of Erfurt, #195: "cum appositum significet per modum distantis a supposito secundum situm."
[104] Thomas of Erfurt, #225: "haec distantia est inter suppositum et appositum, ex hoc quod solum verbum est appositum, quod per modum distantis se habet". Contrast C. F. Hockett, *A Course in Modern Linguistics*, p. 204.
[105] Thomas of Erfurt, #191: "quod ante se dependet ad suppositum dependet ad ipsum ut ad principium et ad primum".
[106] Thomas of Erfurt, #191: "quod post se dependet ad obliquum, dependet ad ipsum ut ad terminum et ultimum".

close link between the various case-forms and their criteria of principium and terminus, and between principium and terminus as equivalent terms for the suppositum and the oblique nominal form of the transitive construction;[107] Thomas states that only a case-form can be a suppositum[108] which, by definition, is the principium, and he also argues that case-forms are required in the oblique terminus.[109]

Another use of 'principium' by certain Modistae, *e.g.* Michel de Marbais and Siger de Courtrai, is the concept of *principium constructionis,* by means of which Siger and Michel included as criteria for the partes orationis the fact that the pars in question was capable of becoming a member of a construction by virtue of this particular feature. The definition of principium especially, but also of terminus, can be realised largely as a result of their collocations, *e.g.* ratio principii in supposito, ratio termini in obliquo, principium constructionis, *etc.* Principium thus represents the nominal element of a primary exocentric construction of Latin and terminus the nominal element of a primary endocentric construction.

Dependentia[110] and *determinatio,*[111] dependence and determination, express the basic relationships between the members of any construction, dependentia representing the general relationships, and determinatio a specific relationship. Whether the construction be intransitive or transitive, one member must always be the dependent member,[112] and will in fact be the verb[113] in the NV and the VN constructions. The constructio intransitiva personarum, *i.e.* the NN type of construction,[114] while still possessing the basic relationship of terminant and dependent, represents also the specific relationship of determinant and determinable and the determinant serves to determine either member of the basic NV construction; the determinant constructible can be either

---

[107] Compare Thomas's analysis of case as a feature of the nomen and his analysis of the suppositum and obliquum.
[108] Thomas of Erfurt, #195: "nihil supponat, nisi casus, vel habens casum".
[109] Thomas of Erfurt, #214: "cui correspondet in obliquo modus significandi per modum termini absolute modo conformi casuum contrahibilis".
[110] Thomas of Erfurt, #185: "una dependentia non est nisi duorum, scilicet: dependentis, et determinantis".
[111] Thomas of Erfurt, #195: "constructio intransitiva personarum sit determinabilis cum determinatione".
[112] Thomas of Erfurt, #191: constructibilium unum sit dependens, alterum dependentiam terminans".
[113] Siger de Courtrai, p. 108: "omne verbum significat rem suam per modum significandi dependentis".
[114] N = Nomen; V = Verb: NN is used to symbolise the constructio intransitiva personarum.

a declinable or indeclinable pars,[115] so that we can have a complex intransitive construction, in which the suppositum will be determined by an adjective, and the appositum by an adverb, *e.g.*

In such a construction *homo* is the substantive determined by *albus* and *currit* the appositum determined by *bene*, but the adjective depends on the substantive, the adverb depends on the verb, and furthermore the verb depends on the suppositum.

The second stage of Modistic syntax was *congruitas*[116] which is roughly equivalent to 'congruence', but seems in fact to represent not only the agreements of government and concord but also the proper collocations of the constructibles in their contexts of situation;[117] indeed congruitas would seem to be the controlling factor in the creation of any construction since it is responsible for the mutual appropriateness of the modes of signifying and ensures that one constructible will show the same features as the other.

Thurot states[118] that the term 'regere' to express 'government' was well established by the time of Peter Helias, and that by the 13th century there was a tendency to distinguish between 'regere', 'servire' and 'determinare'; the Modistae make little if any use of these terms – Thomas does not use 'regere' at all, nor do Thomas or Siger use 'determinare' in the sense of government, and 'determinare' as a syntactic term has already been discussed. Siger and Thomas do not use 'servire' although Thomas and Siger use 'deservire' in discussing the preposition and the cases that the prepositions govern but offer no discussion of the use of this term.[119] Siger makes some use of the terms 'regere' and 'regimen', though it is not easy to establish with any certainty, in view of the fact that the term occurs only in his Sophismata,

---

[115] Thomas of Erfurt, #202: "si determinatio addatur supposito, hoc est duplicitur: vel haec determinatio est declinabilis, vel indeclinabilis".

[116] Thomas of Erfurt, #221: "congruitas ... est ... partium sermonis debita unio, ex modorum significandi conformitate ad aliquam speciem constructionis requisitorum derelicta".

[117] *Cf.* J. R. Firth, *Papers in Linguistics*, for the use of these terms.

[118] Ch. Thurot, *Op. cit.*, pp. 239-243.

[119] Thomas of Erfurt, #178: "sic praepositio simpliciter sumpta dividitur in praepositiones deservientes accusativo tantum, et in praepositiones deservientes ablativo tantum, et in praepositiones deservientes utrique". This is quoted as a typical instance of Thomas's use of the term 'deservire' which he uses in the preposition only.

whether and how he would have made consistent use of the term to express the syntactic device of government; Siger likened *regimen* to the state of affairs in natural things, *i.e.* in the animal kingdom we find one animal, *e.g.* man, who is fit to govern all the other animals, and similarly in the human body, there is one member, *i.e.* the heart, which governs all the other members. Therefore, there will be among the partes orationis one pars which will properly govern the other partes but will itself not be governed, *i.e.* the verb,[120] which acts therefore as a pivot as in a complex construction such as "Socrates percutit Platonem".

Thomas used the terms *similitudo*[121] and *proportio*[122] to describe the different relationships between the members of any construction, and although similitudo may be equated, to a large extent with concord, the relative similarity of proportio to government is not nearly so close. Siger too uses the term proportio, but in a more general sense of concord and government, *e.g.* he describes as proportionality the requirement for the mode of becoming (modus fieri) in the appositum by association with the mode of permanence (modus entis et habitus) of the suppositum,[123] and he also describes as proportionality the concord of gender;[124] furthermore, he states that a 'concordant' construction (constructio congrua) is achieved by means of proportionality.[125]

Thomas uses similitudo and proportio to describe the basic types of syntactic relationships: similitudo can therefore be equated to concord, *e.g.* of gender, since in a dependent relationship of substantive and adjective or suppositum and verb, the dependent constructible will acquire certain properties from the terminant constructible and not

---

[120] Siger de Courtrai, p. 139: "ad similitudinem huius sumitur regimen inter partes orationis, ita quod est devenire ad aliquam partem orationis dignissimam respectu talis multidudinis, quia multitudinem et orationem complet, quae proprie regit omnes alias partes et a nulla alia regitur, videlicet verbum".

[121] Thomas of Erfurt, #220: "quandoque constructibile dependens habet aliquod modos significandi, non ex proprietatibus suae rei per se, sed ex proprietatibus rei constructibilis terminantis; et tunc illos modos significandi exigitur similitudo".

[122] Thomas of Erfurt, #220: "si constructibile dependens habet aliquod modos significandi ex proprietatibus suae rei per se et non ex proprietatibus rei constructibilis terminantis, tunc exigitur in illos modos significandi proportio".

[123] Siger de Courtrai, p. 96: "modus significandi per modum fieri seu motus seu esse in apposito proportionatur modo significandi per modum substantiae, permanentis habitus seu entis".

[124] Siger de Courtrai, p. 101: "genus est principium constructionis cum genere proportionali, scilicet, masculini cum masculino etc. cuius ratio est tum quia in re masculus et femella proportionem non habet ad invicem".

[125] Siger de Courtrai, p. 153: "omnis constructio congrua est per modos significandi proportionales".

from itself, *i.e.* the adjective acquires gender, number and person from the nomen, and the verb acquires number and person from the substantive suppositum. Such a relationship is similitudo. Proportio expresses a relationship which we shall call 'government', though it implies more than the conventional idea of government, *i.e.* the different case-forms in the substantive oblique which are governed by the verb,[126] but does not imply the government of the case-form by the preposition. Proportio is used to express in combination with compositio and significatio, the relationships between the suppositum and the verb or the nominal oblique and the verb,[127] compositio and significatio set up these relationships but proportio is required for two purposes, to ensure the appropriateness of the case-forms in the suppositum and oblique[128] and also to ensure the proportionality of the modus entis in the suppositum or oblique with the modus esse in the verb;[129] proportio is also used to ensure the proportionality of the mode of adjectivality (modus adiacentis) in the adjective and the mode of substantivisation (modus per se stantis) in the substantive.[130] Proportio might therefore be described as a syntactic linkage and complementation; it also functions in combination with compositio and significatio to express the government of the suppositum and verb, and verb and nominal oblique.

---

[126] *Cf.* L. Bloomfield, *Language*, p. 192.

[127] Thomas of Erfurt, #144: "sicut verbum per modum compositionis exigit modum entis per se stantis in ratione principii in supposito, sic per modum generis exiget modum entis per se stantis in ratione termini in obliquo".

[128] Thomas of Erfurt, #144: "sicut verbum per modos proportionalis casibus modo verbi superadditos, exigit in supposito rationem principii, aliter et aliter coniunctam; sic etiam verbum per modos proportionales casibus generi verbi superadditis exigit in obliquo rationem termini, aliter et aliter coniunctam, et ex consequenti alium et alium obliquum".

[129] Thomas of Erfurt, #113: "huic modo verbi, qui est modus esse et successionis, proportionatur in supposito et in obliquo modus entis, id est, modus habitus permanentis".

[130] Thomas of Erfurt, #220: "quia adiectivum habet modum adiacentis proprie et de proprietatibus suae rei, ideo per huiusmodi modum adiacentis requirit in subiecto modum per se stantis qui est sibi proportionabilis".

III

METALANGUAGE

In the previous chapter we said something of Modistic procedure, but before we consider in greater detail their whole descriptive process, it will clearly be necessary to describe their technical language which reveals, as one may well expect, the structure of their descriptive system and also much of the system of thought which created it.[1] The treatment adopted follows roughly the procedure used by the Modistae, which was to divide their analysis into three parts: (a) the preamble, which is the more immediate concern of this chapter;[2] (b) the modi significandi of the eight partes orationis, and (c) the 'passiones sermonis', *i.e.* the mutual relationship of the modes of signifying (modi significandi) of the partes orationis, which are thereby discussed in terms of their constructions, the congruities of such constructions and the perfection of these constructions. No more will be said about (b) and (c) at this stage, since they do in fact constitute the material of the next chapters.

A. ORDER OF ANALYSIS

The consideration of the preamble of each Modistic treatise has been somewhat arbitrarily divided into two parts: any such arbitrary division will of course entail a certain degree of overlap. The first part is called 'elements', and the second part 'categories'. There is a necessary rela-

[1] G. L. Bursill-Hall, "Notes on the Semantics of Linguistic Description", *In Memory of J. R. Firth*, p. 41.
[2] Martin of Dacia calls this the 'pars prohemialis', while John of Dacia calls it 'Proemium', which he divided into (i) Principia gramatice in communi, and (ii) Principia gramatice in speciali. Thomas of Erfurt calls his introduction "Prooemium Auctoris"; Siger de Courtrai does not give his introductory section any title, but they all use the introduction for more or less the same purpose. Thomas, moreover, is much more detailed than Siger in his analysis of the modus significandi, though less so in his description of the process leading up to the modus significandi; he is also very similar in this to Martin of Dacia.

tionship between the two systems, but in the following discussion they will in the first place be kept discrete, the object of so doing being to show the sequence within them from vox to pars orationis on the one hand, and from modus essendi to modus significandi essentialis and accidentalis on the other.

Although the Modistae excluded phonetic material from their descriptive process, their conception of linguistic description nevertheless required 'vox' despite the fact that at the outset 'vox' appears to be somewhat isolated and excluded from their linguistic system. One might indeed ask what the semantic value of *vox* can be in any Modistic grammatical system; however, combined with meaning, 'vox' becomes an integral part of the system[3] which culminates in the pars orationis, the keystone of their grammatical system. It is their picture of the pars orationis and its component parts and combinations which inspires their theories of connected discourse, even of grammar itself.

The second part, called 'categories', outlines the procedures which the description and analysis of a pars orationis as a grammatical unit entail. This requires another type of description which is the very heart of Modistic descriptive technique and which depends on their linguistic theory; their whole system and conception of grammar depended on this analysis, and even syntax has to be considered in the light of this metalanguage. This is then the high-point of Modistic methodology, and from there to a consideration of the various partes orationis in course is a necessary and logical step.

There is a further methodological item which has already been briefly mentioned and which must now be discussed in more detail. Siger and Thomas, we have said, were roughly alike in the treatment of their preambles, but Thomas was more detailed in his presentation. This is perhaps an overstatement.

Siger begins with a brief discussion of grammar, which is the proper expression of concepts of the mind;[4] the concept can be either uncompounded, in which case it will be expressed by means of a dictio or pars orationis, or compounded, in which case it will be expressed by a sentence.[5] The mind perceives 'ens', *i.e.* things which exist, and the

[3] Siger de Courtrai, p. 94: "vox, mediante modo significandi, significat ipsam rem, sic, mediante modo significandi activo significat modum essendi seu proprietatem rei".

[4] Siger de Courtrai, p. 134: "grammatica ... est propter expressionem conceptus mentis per sermonem congruum".

[5] Siger de Courtrai, p. 93: "conceptus mentis duplex est: unus est simplex et indivisibilis, scilicet, conceptus dictionum seu partium quae per simplicem sermonem exprimuntur: ... alius est conceptus mentis compositus seu constitutus,

partes orationis are distinguished by the properties of the things observed by the mind, therefore we cannot distinguish the partes orationis unless we have first established the properties of the things which are to be signified in the form of partes orationis. Siger thus asserts and establishes the necessary link between the modus essendi and the modus significandi on the one hand, and the thing with its properties and the pars orationis which expresses it in the form of significant speech on the other.[6] From the modus essendi Siger proceeds to the modus intelligendi which he divides into activus and passivus; the modus intelligendi leads to the modus signandi, which too he divides into activus and passivus.[7] It is at this stage that he introduces the term 'dictio', since the vox now becomes a dictio 'formaliter' by means of this modus signandi.[8] The modus signandi is followed by the modus significandi which also divides into activus and passivus; it is at this stage that the vox becomes a pars orationis.[9] He then describes the modus significandi in terms of its absolute, respective, essential, and accidental modes, ending in the modes of consignifying (modus consignificandi), by virtue of which a pars is 'really' a pars orationis in that it now acquires syntactic meaning. The pars orationis consists, Siger tells us, of (a) the mode of consignifying (modus consignificandi) which presupposes the modus essendi – this presupposition represents the nexus of the extremes of the metalanguage beginning with the modus essendi and culminating in the modus consignificandi, (b) the ability to signify (ratio significandi) which presupposes the meaning,[10] and (c) the vox which presupposes the thing which is to be signified.[11]

---

scilicet orationum quae per sermonem compositum exprimuntur". Siger also refers to a similar division in Priscian, *i.e.* into Volumen Maior and Volumen Minor.

[6] Siger de Courtrai, p. 94: "vox, mediante modo significandi, significat ipsam rem".

[7] Siger de Courtrai, p. 94: "modum intelligendi sequitur modus seu ratio signandi quia prius intelligitur res et etiam concipitur antequam per vocem signetur quia voces sunt signa passionum ... Modus seu ratio signandi duplex est".

[8] Siger de Courtrai, p. 94: "per quam rationem signandi vox formaliter dicitur dictio".

[9] Siger de Courtrai, p. 94: "vox formaliter dicitur pars orationis per modum significandi activum".

[10] Siger de Courtrai uses 'significatus' whereas Thomas of Erfurt uses 'significatio'.

[11] Siger de Courtrai, p. 95: "pars est dictio et vox, ideo modus consignificandi per quem pars est pars praesupponit rationem significandi, vocem et significatum, quia modus consignificandi non potest esse vocis non significativae et ita ad partem concurrunt modus consignificandi praesupponens modum essendi et ratio significandi praesupponens significatum, et vox praesupponens rem natam per eam significari".

Thomas's use of the preamble is in many ways quite different from Siger's and is much more grammatical (*i.e.* as opposed to ontological), in that he pays much less attention to the *modus essendi* and *modus intelligendi*. He makes no use of the modus signandi, a mode which may be linguistic though it is certainly not grammatical; unfortunately many linguists today would query its pertinence to linguistic theory.

Roos tells us[12] that Martin of Dacia, like Thomas, leads in with the modus significandi, and since the modus significandi is the principle, *i.e.* the starting point (principium) of grammar, they use the preamble to discuss the hypotheses of this principle. Thomas begins by asking six questions: [13]

(i)   how is the modus significandi divided and described;

(ii) from what does the modus significandi originate;

(iii) on what is the modus significandi dependent;

(iv) in what way are the modus essendi, modus intelligendi, and modus significandi differentiated;

(v)   how is the modus significandi ascertainable;

(vi) what is the mutual relationship between the terms, *signum, dictio, pars orationis, terminus*.

It should be noted that Thomas does not include *vox* in this last question; he does in fact discuss *vox* to this extent, that it is not to be considered by the grammarian except in so far as it is a *signum*, since grammar deals with 'signa rerum'. Therefore *vox* in the sense of 'phonetics'[14] is not considered by the grammarian except 'per accidens'.[15] It is interesting to note that at no time during the preamble does Thomas provide a definition of modus intelligendi or modus significandi, but their active and passive forms are defined, and the combination of the definitions of the active and passive will, as a result, con-

---

[12]   H. Roos, *Op. cit.*, p. 141.

[13]   Thomas of Erfurt, #2: (i) "quomodo modus significandi partiatur et describatur"; (ii) "a quo modus significandi radicaliter oratur"; (iii) "a quo modus significandi immediate sumatur"; (iv) "quomodo modus significandi a modo intelligendi et a modo essendi distinguatur"; (v) "in quo modus significandi tanquam in subiecto inveniatur"; (vi) "qualem ordinem habeant ad invicem isti termini, signum, dictio, pars orationis, et terminus".

[14]   The fact that the Modistae do not consider '*vox*' in the sense of phonetics to be a matter for the grammarian does not prevent '*vox*' from being a unit in the expression; for this reason, it is maintained that *vox* can be considered to have a phonological function.

[15]   Thomas of Erfurt, #19: "vox, inquantum vox, non consideratur a grammatico, sed inquantum signum, quia grammatica est de signis rerum ... ideo grammaticus considerans vocem, considerat eam per accidens".

stitute the definition of the whole mode, *i.e.* of understanding or signifying.

The definitions of Siger and Thomas of the modus intelligendi activus et passivus and the modus significandi activus et passivus have little if anything to choose between them, and their conclusions are essentially the same, *i.e.* that the vox becomes a pars orationis by means of the modus significandi activus.[16]

It would be useful, however, to compare briefly the one stage where there is an apparent discrepancy between them, *i.e.* their analysis of the origin of the dictio.[17] Siger had used the modus or ratio signandi activus as the means whereby the vox becomes a dictio 'formaliter', *i.e.* it is the ability (ratio or ens rationis) bestowed on the vox by the mind by means of which the vox can indicate the thing.[18] Thomas states that the mind bestows on the vox a double ability (ratio), that of signifying and consignifying, and the first he calls signification (significatio) by means of which the vox becomes a signum, and this is 'formaliter' a dictio.[19] We have, however, seen that 'ratio' in collocation with 'significandi' or 'consignificandi' represents the potentiality of the mode, *i.e.* in this instance, the 'ratio significandi' represents the potentiality of the mode of signifying which will make a dictio into a pars orationis. The difference between Siger and Thomas is more apparent than real; it amounts to the fact that Thomas describes in much more detail the different categories and the relationships of the elements to these categories by exploiting the features of 'ratio' and 'modus' which can be considered the two members of a grammatical opposition that corresponds to the metaphysical contrast of act and potentiality.

The second ratio, *i.e.* of consignifying, which is the potentiality of the mode of signifying, Thomas discusses along with the modus significandi activus, and by virtue of this combination of vox and ratio consignificandi, we derive the pars orationis 'formaliter'.[20] Thomas confirms this by saying that the *pars* is also related to other partes by

---

[16] Siger de Courtrai, p. 94: "vox formaliter dicitur pars orationis per modum significandi activum".

[17] *Cf.* pp. 82-83 for a further discussion of *dictio*.

[18] Siger de Courtrai, p. 94: "modus seu ratio signandi activus est ratio quaedam seu ens rationis concessum voci ab intellectu secundum quod talis vox talem rem signat".

[19] Thomas of Erfurt, #4: "rationem significandi, quae vocatur significatio, per quam efficitur signum, vel significandi; et sic formaliter est dictio".

[20] Thomas of Erfurt, #4: "et rationem consignificandi, quae vocatur modus significandi activus, per quam vox significans fit consignum, vel consignificans; et sic formaliter est pars orationis".

means of this same ratio consignificandi which he describes as a 'principium efficiens intrinsecum', which is made up of modi significandi respectivi which are used to create a construction;[21] the ratio consignificandi is thus the potential *syntactic* meaning of the pars, and by reason of this, the pars can function in combination with other partes orationis.

Siger, at the end of his preamble, tells us that the pars is made up of vox and dictio;[22] this is not the end of the process, since this merely means that such a combination is the actualisation of the ratio significandi and both Siger and Thomas clearly had in mind the fact that the pars orationis possesses a syntactic meaning. Siger completes his statement by describing the mode of consignification (modus consignificandi) which is the syntactic meaning of the pars in question,[23] and by means of which the pars orationis becomes functional.

Siger's modus consignificandi can be considered the realisation or actualisation of Thomas's ratio consignificandi.[24] Since, however, the modus consignificandi cannot exist alongside the '*vox non significativa*', the pars orationis will consist of the mode of consignification (modus consignificandi) which must presuppose the modus essendi, the potentiality of signifying (ratio significandi) presupposing the meaning and the vox presupposing the thing which is to be signified by it.[25] This is in fact one step further than Thomas's description of the 'pars secundum se',[26] but everything fits into place, if we look upon Thomas's account of the 'pars relata ad aliam'[27] and Siger's pars created by the modus

[21] Thomas of Erfurt, #187: "principium efficiens intrinsecum constructionis sunt modi significandi respectivi, ratione quorum vel unum constructibile est ad alterum dependens, vel alterius dependentiam determinans ... hi modi significandi dicuntur efficere constructionem".

[22] Siger de Courtrai, p. 94: "pars est dictio et vox".

[23] Siger de Courtrai, p. 95: "modus consignificandi per quem pars est pars praesupponit rationem consignificandi, vocem et significatum".

[24] Siger does not use the term 'ratio consignificandi' at all, nor does Thomas use the term 'modus consignificandi'; this statement therefore represents a deduction from a synthesis of the descriptions made by Siger and Thomas and the use of the contrast of modus and ratio.

[25] Siger de Courtrai, p. 95: "ad partem concurrunt modus consignificandi praesupponens modum essendi et ratio significandi praesupponens significatum, et tertio, vox praesupponens rem natam per eam significari".

[26] Thomas of Erfurt, #4: "rationem consignificandi, quae vocatur modus significandi activus, per quam vox significans fit consignum, vel consignificans; et sic formaliter est pars orationis; ita quod pars est pars secundum se per hanc rationem consignificandi, seu modum significandi activum, tanquam per principium formale".

[27] Thomas of Erfurt, #4: "sed est pars relata ad aliam per eamdem rationem consignificandi activam, tanquam per principium efficiens intrinsecum".

consignificandi as the same. Thomas's 'second' pars is the pars orationis, not considered per se, but ready to function, *i.e.* with the potentiality of meaning, *i.e.* functioning syntactically, and so is Siger's; 'consignification', which can be taken as syntactically functional, is necessary before a pars orationis can function syntactically, *i.e.* a pars orationis must possess the mode of consignification, which necessarily entails the ratio consignificandi, in order to be able to function with other partes orationis in the sentence.

Finally, we have to appreciate that Thomas describes his elements *i.e.* signum, dictio and pars orationis, discretely, though he does, as has already been stated, mention them en passant when analysing the rationes significandi and consignificandi. He tells us that they can occur together in the same subject for the very reason that they can be discerned in that same subject,[28] just like the sign and that which is designated. They differ, however, as regards their potentiality (ratio). The signum becomes such by means of the ratio signandi though it remains an absolute element: the dictio becomes such 'formaliter' by means of the ratio signandi with the addition of vox, because a dictio is a 'vox significativa': but the pars orationis is such 'formaliter' by means of the modus significandi activus added to the dictio, because the pars is the dictio which has acquired a modus significandi activus. If, therefore, we accept that vox is the same as signum, we have a process which can be stated in the following manner:

vox + ratio signandi > dictio
vox + modus significandi activus > pars orationis,

which is the same as saying, as Thomas does,[29]

vox + ratio significandi > dictio
vox + ratio consignificandi > pars orationis.

The whole pattern showing the inter-relationship between the various processes and modes can be expressed in the form of an equation as above.

B. ELEMENTS

In keeping with the philosophical theories of their day the Modistae stated that things possess various properties or modes of being (modi

---

[28] Thomas of Erfurt, #18: "conveniunt in subiecto, et in obiecto; quia in eodem subiecto reperiri possunt, sicut signum et signatum".
[29] *Cf*. fn. 18 and 19.

essendi). The mind apprehends these properties by means of the active modes of understanding (modi intelligendi activi) and they thus become the qualities of things as apprehended by the mind (modi intelligendi passivi); the mind imposes on noises (voces) certain active modes of meaning (modi significandi activi) which become the qualities of things as signified by words (modi significandi passivi), thus completing the scale beginning with the thing and ending with its expression. As a result of this addition of signification, *i.e.* the potentiality of signifying and consignifying (rationes significandi et consignificandi), the vox becomes a word (dictio) and then a pars orationis. There is a complete interdependence between language on the one hand and the structure of things on the other; this is central to Modistic grammatical theory, with the human mind, with its ability to perceive, signify and interpret these things in language, acting as the link. In language, these things are stated by means of partes orationis, while the modes of signification provide the means of distinguishing the qualities and properties of the things which the partes orationis designate.

The progression of being, understanding, and signification can be labelled a metaphysical series; alongside this we have the linguistic sequence of vox, dictio, and pars orationis. The partes orationis are established by means of the dictio and the meaning which the dictio qua pars will convey; this is expressed by means of the vox. This is, however, neither a purely functional nor a formal approach. This has an immediate implication, the reasons for which cannot be stated here in detail [30] without introducing extra-linguistic matters; the implication, however, is that we should not look for any definition of 'sonus' or for that matter of 'vox' in phonetic terminology. In all the texts of the Modistae which are available (with the exception of the *Summa Gramatica* of John of Dacia), the term 'sonus' is not used at all, and vox,[31] though used quite deliberately by the Modistae as a technical term, is given no definition except to repeat Priscian.[32]

The Modistae excluded any physiological-auditory approach to linguistic analysis, phonetics being outside the province of the gram-

[30] Although Latin was in the Middle Ages the language of the Church and of scholarship, it possessed no spoken norm but would be pronounced according to the local vernacular; this may explain, to some extent at least, the lack of interest shown by the Modistae in spoken language.
[31] The operating effect of vox is to set up a series of levels rather reminiscent of Firth's 'spectrum analysis', *cf.* J. R. Firth, "Atlantic Linguistics", *Papers in Linguistics*, pp. 170-171. We have as a result a sequence of symbolisation which changes as a result of the addition of vox which has in itself no individual function.
[32] Priscian: "vocem esse aerem tenuissimum ictum" (I, i).

marian, a matter more for the natural philosopher;[33] this will account for the absence of any discussion of vox in articulatory-motor terminology. The discreteness between vox and sonus is clearly portrayed in John of Dacia[34] and also in William of Sherwood's *Introductiones in Logicam* (quoted by Roos).[35] It is interesting to note that we have here in the statement, "vox . . . non significativa, que nil significat ut buba blictrix", a similar idea to that of the Stoic theory and of modern practice, *i.e.* the use of 'nonsense' words in phonetics.[36]

The word, which must express a reality, is a sign (signum). Human intelligence indicates with the help of a word a particular reality, a definite 'ens' or thing; these words, which can be considered grammatical expressions, *i.e.* partes orationis, must, if they are to function realistically, be taken as correlatives of things in the world of reality.[37] The 'word' can therefore be considered as (a) a physical sound produced by the vox, (b) a sign which expresses one or other reality and is therefore a dictio, and (c) as a particular word-class or grammatical category or pars orationis.

Our faculty of understanding bestows on the sound a meaning, and thereby the vox becomes a dictio; but our understanding has another more positive function, *i.e.* to give to every word, to every dictio, a precise meaning, a 'geformte Bedeutung', and thereby assigns every

[33] Michel de Marbais; *Summa modorum significandi*: "grammaticus unde grammaticus vocem, unde vox est, non debet diffinire sed ipse naturalis ipsam secundum se et secundum suo principia considerans" (quoted by Wallerand, p. 46).
[34] John of Dacia, *Summa grammatica*, p. 101: "omnis vox est sonus, non tamen econuersa". A cursory reading of John's theory of the vox suggests that a closer study would be very profitable, *e.g.* statements such as, "vox est qualitas et aer est substantia", are suggestive of the mentalist approach to phonological theory which has been characteristic of certain linguistic 'schools' of today.
[35] William of Sherwood, *Introductiones in Logicam*: "est autem sonus proprium sensibile aurium et dividitur sic. Sonus unus vox, alius non vox. Sonus vox est ut quod fit ab ore animalis. Sonus non vox ut strepitus pedum, fragor arborum et similia. Vox sic dividitur: alia significativa, alia non significativa. Vox significativa est, quo aliquid significat, non significativa, que nil significat ut buba blictrix. Vox significativa quedam significat naturaliter, quedam ad placitum. Naturaliter, que natura agente aliquid significat ut gemitus infirmorum et similia. Ad placitum, que ex humana institutione significationem recipit" (quoted by H. Roos, p. 142).
[36] *Cf.* R. H. Robins, *A. and M.*, also J. R. Firth, "The Techniques of Semantics", *Papers in Linguistics*, p. 24.
[37] Thomas of Erfurt, #9: "licet privationes non sint entia positiva extra animam, sunt tamen entia positiva in anima, . . . et sunt entia secundum animam; et quia eorum intelligi est eorum esse, ideo eorum modi intelligendi erunt eorum modi essendi. Unde nomina privationum, per suos modos significandi activos, non erunt consignificativa falsa, quia cum modi intelligendi privationum reducantur ad modos intelligendi habitus (nam privatio non cognoscitur nisi per habitum), ideo modi essendi privationum tandem ad modos essendi habitus reducuntur".

word to a particular word-class; the dictio thus becomes a pars orationis. The intellect bestows upon the vox a double function; in the first place the vox acquires meaning (primary or referential meaning) as a result of which it becomes a dictio [38] and as such possesses a ratio significandi, *i.e.* the potential ability to signify. (Siger, however, attributes to the dictio the mode of designation (modus signandi), but this automatically implies the potential ability to signify).

This dictio not only has a significatio but also a consignificatio which can best be described as syntactic meaning (or functional meaning) and as a result of this, the word is not only a signum but a consignum, and therefore it is not only a dictio but a pars orationis. In other words, the word can have not only a notional or semantic meaning which will be linked to its essence and is thus its essential meaning, but also a syntactic meaning which enables it to function by means of a substantial, verbal or other meaning which will derive from its essence.[39]

This leads to a very important feature of the Modistic grammatical system, *i.e.* that the individual word or pars orationis *in isolation* is grammatically powerless, and it is only the potentiality and its realisation to become the act of consignification, *i.e.* the ratio and modus consignificandi, which permits the word to function at a different, *i.e.* syntactic level. This is something that they took no doubt from contemporary logic which is understandable in view of the intimacy between grammar and logic from the 12th century onwards; de Rijk calls this the "contextual approach" and points out (de Rijk II: 123-4) that the terminist logicians did at least recognise the dependence of a word on one kind of context. The difference in referential terms between substantivum and adiectivum, nomen and verbum, and between nomen and pronomen, etc. depends on the difference between their various modes of signifying, but they can be distinguished functionally, i.e. syntactically only by their consignification. Mediaeval grammarians may have failed to see the importance of the larger context, but it must be said to their credit that there was at least an awareness, albeit inchoate, of the necessary relationship between context and meaning which is the guarantee of linguistic meaning.

Consignification (consignificatio) is therefore the feature which functionally, *i.e.* syntactically, distinguishes those partes orationis which

[38] Thomas of Erfurt, #4: "intellectus vocem ad significandum, et consignificandum imponit, duplicem rationem tribuit, scilicet, rationem significandi, quae vocatur significatio, per quam efficitur signum vel significans; et sic formaliter est dictio".
[39] *Cf.* N. Chomsky, *Aspects of the Theory of Syntax*, p. 84.

have the same primary or referential meaning (significatio), and this is thus the *syntactic* meaning of each word-class.[40]

A second value to consignification, *i.e.* connotation, derives from the first usage of consignification since *this difference is marked by the functional i.e. syntactic meaning* as well as by the different essential modes of the partes orationis concerned.

When one investigates a grammatical expression, *i.e.* isolated words and their meaning, one must consider not only what they indicate but also how they indicate the object in question. It often happens that since this object may possess several properties which require therefore several modes of signifying for their expression,[41] the object is the same but the way of indicating it is different, *e.g.* 'dolor' and 'doleo' have the same primary meaning but the word 'doleo' has, in contrast to 'dolor', the consignification of the modus fluxus.[42] Every word signifies not only a definite reality but also possesses the consignification or connotation of a definite mode or property of being.

The matter is made more explicit if we consider the result when two different properties are signified and expressed by modes of signifying and voces which belong to the same pars orationis. In such an instance the difference is one of 'species' since 'species' is derived from the property of the thing and not from its expression (vox), so that 'albedo' and 'albus' are different 'species' of the same nomen, *i.e.* expressions of different properties of the same thing, *i.e.* they both represent, by means of different modes of signifying,[43] different aspects of the same

---

[40]   Thomas of Erfurt, #4: "pars est pars secundum se per hanc rationem consignificandi, seu modum significandi activum, tanquam per principium formale ... sed est pars relata ad aliam per eamdem rationem consignificandi activam, tanquam per principium efficiencs intrinsecum".

[41]   Thomas of Erfurt, #114: "in una et eadem re possunt reperiri diversae proprietates rei non repugnantes, a quibus sumi possunt diversi modi significandi activi licet una vox non imponatur ei, ut stat sub ombibus illis proprietatibus, sed quandoque imponatur una vox, ut stat sub una proprietate, quandoque alia vox, ut sub alia proprietate".

[42]   As was pointed out previously, Siger and Thomas do not use dolor/doleo or donum/datum at all when discussing consignification; these are terms quoted by Thurot (pp. 155-156) and Roos (pp. 143-144), though neither of them refers to a *Modistic* text to illustrate.

[43]   Thomas of Erfurt, #114: "haec res, albedo, habet diversas proprietates, sub quibus possunt ei imponi diversae voces, Nam si consideretur in ea modus entis, qui est modus habitus et permanentis, sic significatur per vocem nominis absolute. Si autem consideretur in ea modus entis, et cum hoc modus essentiae determinatae, sic significatur voce nominis substantivi, ut albedo. Si autem consideretur in ea modus entis et cum hoc modus inhaerentiae alteri secundum essentiam, sic significatur in voce nominis adiectivi, ut albus".

modus entis. It may well happen, however, that the different properties of the same things are signified by means of modes of signifying which represent different partes orationis, *e.g.* dolor/doleo, or albedo/dealbo;[44] by contrasting this with the two instances within the accidental mode of 'species' of the pars, we are able to see much more clearly the consignification involved. As dictiones, 'albedo/dealbo' possessed the same significatio, *i.e.* root meaning which might be crudely represented as /*alb-/, but they also possessed different potentialities (rationes) of consignification. They possess therefore different essential modes of signifying, *i.e.* modus entis et permanentis in the case of 'albedo' and modus esse et fluxus in the case of 'dealbo'; since an active respective mode of signifying implies an ability to consignify (ratio consignificandi), it follows that 'albedo' and 'dealbo' possess different consignifications because they signify different properties by means of modes of signifying which are essential to different partes orationis.

It follows from all this that the object of speculative grammar, *i.e.* the modi significandi, is to express ideas which are dependent on our understanding; this perhaps explains Roger Bacon's belief that there is only one grammar for all languages. It should be remembered that for the Modistae at least, grammar meant a categorial semasiology; the investigation of isolated linguistic expressions, *i.e.* the dictio or the pars orationis per se, which differ in every language, do not belong in themselves to the affair of universal grammar.

Vox

The Modistae make great use of 'vox' but not as an independent member of a linguistic system. In Modistic terminology, vox does not imply phonetic, *i.e.* auditory and articulatory, criteria, and indeed as we have already noted, phonetic material is rigorously excluded from their corpus;[45] the purely phonetic material is a matter for the physicist, not for the grammarian.[46] In this the Modistae seem to have been in com-

---

[44] Thomas of Erfurt, #114: "si consideretur in ea modus esse, qui est modus fluxus et successionis et cum hoc modus essentiae distinctae, sic significatur verbaliter, ut dealbo. Item si consideretur in ea modus inhaerentis secundum esse, sic significatur participaliter, ut dealbans".

[45] It is true that John of Dacia does discuss vox at some length, but quite differently from Priscian and other 'literary' grammarians who were in so many instances the models used by the Modistae; John of Dacia's position *vis-à-vis* the Modistae is discussed in Chapter I.

[46] G. L. Trager also suggests that phonetics may be pre-linguistic; *cf.* G. L. Trager, "The Field of Linguistics", pp. 2-4.

plete agreement. Michel de Marbais, for instance, denies any independent function to the vox because of its lack of signification or of any system of signifying;[47] on the other hand (and herein may lie some explanation of the importance which the Modistae did nevertheless attach to vox), he insists on the role that vox (*but it must be the vox significativa*), plays in the creation of the dictio and the pars orationis.

Both Siger and Thomas treat the relationship between the vox and signum, and from the intimate nature of their association, it becomes clear that the vox may be a signum and a signum may be a vox. For Thomas, it is in fact this very closeness that gives a definite function to the vox in a grammatical system, because grammar deals with 'signa rerum' and a vox is the most suitable of all 'signa'. It is because the vox belongs to the signum that the grammarian considers vox at all, but even so he does this 'per accidens'.

Siger is perhaps a little more positive than Thomas in attributing a positive function to the vox; it is true that he is content with Priscian's definition of vox, but at the same time he attaches to the vox a more meaningful function,[48] and it thereby becomes a dictio. Furthermore, by the addition of the modus significandi activus, it becomes a pars orationis. Thus the vox, by means of the modus signandi, signifies, *i.e.* designates, the thing and by means of the modus significandi, it signifies the properties of the thing, as a result of which it can become grammatically operable. The vox has thus a double function;[49] firstly, the result of the intellect's combining the vox with the modus signandi is the dictio, and secondly, the intellect's combining the vox with the modus significandi results in the pars orationis. The vox is thus a material form of realisation, but a contingent one.[50]

The vox then has no power of its own to signify; this alone would account for the speed with which the Modistae pass over all consideration of vox. The vox and the modus significandi have the power to signify the thing, but the vox and the modus significandi activus have the power to signify the modus essendi or the *property* of the thing;[51]

---

[47] Michel de Marbais: "vox, unde vox est, nullum in se includit significatum vel rationem significandi, nisi loquendo methaphorice" (Thurot, p. 156).

[48] Siger de Courtrai, p. 94: "vox ... est vox ex actu proferendi".

[49] Martin of Dacia, *Tractatus de modis significandi* 8: "vox significat rem et consignificat proprietates rei".

[50] Thomas of Erfurt, #19: "vox est habilissimum signum inter alia signa, ideo vox inquantum signum prius consideratur a grammatico, quam alia signa rerum. Sed quia esse signum accidit voci, ideo grammaticus considerans vocem, considerat per accidens".

[51] Siger de Courtrai, p. 94: "vox, mediante modo significandi, significat ipsam

vox is thus an integral part of the pars orationis. We might therefore say that the modus significandi represents the thought symbolism, but that the vox is required to give it linguistic symbolism. This is in fact suggested by Siger who tells us that the modus significandi activus is a concept of the mind (conceptus intellectus) and as such will always remain in the mind; the modus significandi and the vox must remain discrete, although the expression of the modus significandi will be by means of the vox.[52] This, however, serves to stress the secondary, or we might even call it the 'inferior', nature of vox in the eyes of the Modistae, since nothing can be signified by the vox unless it has first been conceived by the intellect. The whole theory of the modus significandi is based on the understanding of the *thing* and its properties, but it is the modus significandi, *not* the vox, which is the formulation of this concept of the mind.

Another reason for the dismissal by the Modistae of vox as a vital active element in grammar is that the Modistae are not at all concerned with the difference in the expression planes of various languages. Indeed the Modistae were not concerned at all with other languages or for that matter with any particular language, but with a theory of grammar, which, rightly or wrongly, they considered to be universal, *i.e.* a form of meta-grammar.

So far our consideration of vox has dealt almost entirely with its phonetic aspect, but if we consider vox from a linguistic[53] point of view, we shall find that vox is a much more vital part of the Modistic system than a superficial examination of their work implies or than is stated overtly in their writings.

It is quite clear that the Modistae quite deliberately excluded all physiological-acoustic considerations of vox, but can we also say that vox has no phonological functions? This can perhaps be stated more positively, *i.e.* what is the linguistic function of vox in the creation of a dictio and a pars orationis, and does its activity cease at that point? We cannot dismiss vox as a purely incidental feature of their system, even if it appears to be so as a result of their descriptions of vox, because it is the constant feature which is found among the features con-

---

rem sic, mediante modo significandi activo significat modum essendi seu proprietatem rei".
[52] Siger de Courtrai, pp. 94-95: "conceptus intellectus manent in intellectu et sunt in eo et non transeunt extra, tamen voces denominant et per eas invicem construuntur sicut universale existens in intellectu denominat rem extra".
[53] The term 'linguistic' is here used in the same sense as Hjelmslev uses it, *cf. Prolegomena*, p. 50.

stituting a dictio and a pars operationis. It seems possible, therefore, to argue that, even though vox is of no consideration in so far as articulatory and acoustic values are concerned, it does become a more positive feature at a phonological[54] level. It may not and does not imply phonic criteria, but it must, however, remain on the level of expression, and will refer to "la réalisation de l'image intérieure dans le discours".[55] But vox is not merely just a device for a look outside the intellectual confines of the modus significandi.

"Vox unde vox" was not a matter for the grammarian, but "vox unde signum" does have a functional significance in the Modistic grammatical system (although they never say with any preciseness just what it is). More recently, Trubetzkoy suggested that phonetics was almost outside the province of the linguist[56] and differentiated between "les sons de la parole", *i.e.* phonetics and "les sons de la langue", *i.e.* phonology;[57] we can perhaps equate "les sons de la parole" to "vox unde vox". Troubetzkoy also insisted on the functional and meaningful nature of phonology;[58] the Modistae clearly never envisaged 'vox' in such terms, but vox did become, (and this almost despite the Modistae themselves), a constant feature, *i.e.* the expression or manifestation of the changes of meaning, made by means of the inter-change of the various modes of signifying.

Signum

It seems safe to say that the vox significativa[59] was not conceived of as something which might be the equivalent of the phoneme of today; 'vox unde vox' is used really to indicate the articulation or the vocal expression of a mental concept. The Modistae appear to have sensed,

---

[54] Siger de Courtrai, p. 133: "Volumus facere sermonem de toto aggregato ex voce significato et modo significandi et non possumus nisi per vocem, ideo necesse fuit huic aggregato imponere vocem aliquam ad significandum totum aggregatum sub modis significandi qui dicti sunt".

[55] F. de Saussure, *Cours de linguistique*, p. 98.

[56] N. S. Troubetzkoy, *Principes de phonologie*, pp. 10-12.

[57] N. S. Troubetzkoy, *Op. cit.*, p. 10.

[58] N. S. Troubetzkoy, *Op. cit.*, pp. 11-12: "la phonologie doit rechercher quelles différences phoniques sont liées, dans la langue étudiée, à des différences de signification, comment les éléments de différenciation se comportent entre eux et selon quelles règles ils peuvent se combiner les uns avec les autres pour former des mots et des phrases".

[59] It might be possible to describe the 'vox articulata' as the equivalent of the phoneme, but this is not at all pertinent to this study, since none of the Modistae studied (with the exception of John of Dacia) make any use of this term or even of the term 'litera'.

almost intuitively, the relationship between the concept (conceptus intellectus) and its expression or, to be more exact, its signification (significatio), which is the function of the signum. The term 'intuitively' is used quite deliberately, for although all the Modistae seem to have used the term, they do not seem to have done so specifically, and certainly not with any definition attached to it; we have, therefore, to try to deduce its function. Indeed, much of the deduction about the nature of the signum depends on one's interpretation of 'vox'; 'vox unde vox' is not, according to the Modistae, a matter for the linguist, but 'vox unde signum' is. Siger tells us[60] that voces are the signs of the 'passiones', i.e. affections of the mind, and that grammar deals,[61] inter alia, with the sentence (sermo) and its various occurrences. Similarly, Thomas tells us[62] that vox is considered by the grammarian only in so far as it is a signum, since grammar deals with the signs of things. Therefore, by reason of this, vox can be considered as a part of Modistic sign theory.

Martin of Dacia describes a signum as something which has the ability to signify.[63] He sees the relationship between the signum and the dictio thus: they are alike in that they both possess the *ability* to signify,[64] but differ 'ex parte substantie'. He has furthermore seen that the signum is a much broader concept than the dictio, inasmuch that any dictio will be a signum, since it must refer to something, but not every signum will necessarily be a dictio.[65] This points to the fact that 'signum' is a super-class, and that a dictio, as a member of this class, is really nothing more than a signum manifested in vox.

Thomas makes a somewhat similar distinction between signum and dictio; he too does not attempt to define signum. The distinction between signum and dictio is that the latter, in addition to the ability to designate[66] makes use of vox significativa, which produces a term *capable* of signifying.

[60] Siger de Courtrai, p. 94: "voces sunt signa passionum".
[61] Siger de Courtrai, p. 93: "grammatica est sermocinalis scientia, sermonem et passiones eius in communi ad exprimendum principaliter mentis conceptus per sermonem coniugatum considerans".
[62] Thomas of Erfurt, #19: "vox, inquantum vox, non consideratur a grammatico, sed inquantum signum, quia grammatica est de signis rerum".
[63] Martin of Dacia, #13: "quod habet rationem aliquid significandi".
[64] Martin of Dacia, #13: "signum et dictio non differunt a parte eius quod significatur, sed a parte substantiae utriusque".
[65] Martin of Dacia, #13: "signum potest dici de nuptu corporeo de voce et de aliis; dictio autem tantum de voce dicitur".
[66] Thomas of Erfurt, #18: "dicitur dictio formaliter per rationem signandi voci superadditam, quia dictio est vox significativa".

Dictio

Peter Helias followed Priscian's definition of the dictio as the minimal pars orationis which can be constructed in a sequence;[67] every dictio is therefore a pars orationis, but it should not be imagined that every dictio will be the same pars orationis, for, as Peter points out, Priscian did not mean that the dictio would be any particular pars orationis, *e.g.* nomen, but just any pars.[68] (Peter adds that it is the modus significandi which serves to distinguish one pars from another – but then the dictio qua dictio does not have a modus significandi).

For the Modistae, the dictio was something more than a mere vocal noise. The dictio, according to Michel de Marbais, possesses, as its substantial element, vox, and acquires the ratio significandi as its form.[69] It is linked, however, to the thing which is to be signified by means of the modus intelligendi. The dictio is therefore a creature of the intellect, which is, so to speak, preparing to bestow signification on the thing under consideration, *i.e.* the thing has been marked by the vox as being capable of being signified.[70] Dictio is therefore a combination of vox (which will be its expression) and of ratio significandi, which marks it off as a special kind of 'signum'; since every dictio will be a signum, though not every signum will be a dictio, a dictio is thus a sub-class of 'signum'.[71] There is here what appears to be a minor divergence between Siger on the one hand and Thomas, Michel, etc. on the other. Siger tells us[72] that the modus signandi is the means by which the intellect uses the vox to designate the thing[73] – there is no question of any meaning being introduced, but it is by means of the 'ratio signandi' that the vox becomes a dictio. It would seem, therefore, that for Siger the dictio is still pre-grammatical. On the other hand, it may just be a matter of terminological variation between the ratio signandi of Siger and the ratio significandi of Thomas and Michel. It

[67] Peter Helias: "dictio est minima pars orationis constructa in ordine".
[68] Peter Helias: "dictio est pars orationis, pars integralis intelligitur, non quod dictio aliqua sit hec pars orationis nomen vel alia" (Thurot, p. 151).
[69] Michel de Marbais: "dictio, unde dictio est, includit in se vocem tanquam sibi materiam et rationem significandi tanquam sibi forman" (Thurot, p. 156).
[70] Michel de Marbais: "dictio est vox rei significativa mediante ratione significandi ab intellectu sibi concessa" (Thurot, p. 156).
[71] Martin of Dacia, #13: "signum in plus se habet quam dictio, quia omnis dictio potest dici signum, sed non e converso, quia signum potest dici de nuptu corporeo, de voce et de aliis; dictio autem de voce tantum".
[72] Siger de Courtrai, p. 94: "per rationem signandi vox formaliter dicitur dictio".
[73] Siger de Courtrai, p. 130: "ratio signandi apud intellectum existens est illud mediante quo vox signat rem".

would in fact seem that Siger includes the ratio signandi as an additional stage in the process, *i.e.* the vox has the potentiality of designating and thus becomes a dictio which in turn possesses the potential ability to signify.

If dictio is the vox significativa, as Thomas states,[74] then we have a state of affairs much closer to the Saussurean theory of the 'signe linguistique' than was the case with the signum.[75] The signum can represent anything[76] but will not become a dictio until vox significativa and potentiality of signifying (ratio significandi) have been added; therefore a dictio is a combination of the vox and the primary (or potential) signification, *i.e.* expression and content.

It is difficult to find something in modern linguistic theory which can really be compared to the dictio: Gray's definition, "the smallest thought unit vocally expressible"[77] comes very close, but we must not be beguiled by the common etymology of 'vox' and 'vocally'. It is of course not really correct to speak of 'word' in reference to 'dictio', since 'word' as a technical term implies a meaning and an utterance which dictio does not have.

Pars orationis

The pars orationis is a grammatical expression, and can be considered the correlative of things in the world of reality;[78] the mediaeval grammarians argued that anything or any being which the intelligence can grasp can also be *indicated* by language. The mediaeval metaphysicians observed in beings two primordial elements – stability and becoming; their expression is the object of study by the grammarian. The parts of speech which are to indicate the permanence of things, are the nouns and pronouns; becoming is expressed by the verb and participle. The other parts of speech act in concert with the declinable parts of speech, but their signification will be rather different.

It is not enough for the word to signify, – it must also consignify; the word must possess both these attributes before it can become a

---

[74] Thomas of Erfurt, #18: "dictio est vox significativa".
[75] It seems almost feasible to say that the Modistae might have served themselves better if they had dropped all consideration of 'signum'.
[76] Thomas of Erfurt, #18: "dicitur signum per rationem signandi, vel repraesentandi aliquid absolute".
[77] L. H. Gray, *Foundations of Language*, p. 146.
[78] Siger de Courtrai, p. 93: "rerum proprietatibus partes orationis invicem distinguuntur".

grammatical element. The dictio possesses only the potential ability to
signify, the pars possesses both the potentiality (ratio) and the modes
of signifying and consignifying; in other words, it signifies the thing
by means of the mode of signifying which can be thought of in this
context as a 'blanket' term, and the properties of the thing by means
of the different modes of signifying which correlate to these different
properties.[79] Siger illustrates by the analogy of the red cloth outside the
inn: the cloth indicates the wine, but 'red' indicates the redness of the
wine.[80]

The mind makes use of the vox both to signify and to consignify;
the dictio has the power *potentially* to signify by virtue of the ability
to signify (ratio significandi), and it becomes a pars orationis by the
addition of the modus significandi activus,[81] so that it realises its potential ability as a dictio to signify, and by virtue of the potential ability
to consignify (ratio consignificandi) it acquires its character of 'consignum',[82] which is its particular method of referring to the thing involved.

The pars orationis is thus a creature of three elements, the vox,
dictio and consignificatio.[83] The pars orationis has its status by virtue
of the modus significandi but in order to become a pars orationis it
really requires a mode of consignifying (modus consignificandi)[84] which
will consist of primary meaning and class-meaning, and also the thing
and its properties and the vox by means of which the thing will be
signified. We have thus completed the full logical progression, in which
one term presupposes the preceding term, though the contrary is not
the case; we end up with a pars orationis which is capable not only of
signifying, but by virtue of its consignification, of functioning syntactically.

[79] Siger de Courtrai, p. 94: "vox, mediante modo significandi, significat ipsam
rem, sic, mediante modo significandi activo significat modum essendi seu proprietatem rei".
[80] Siger de Courtrai, p. 94: "sicut pannus rubeus pendens ante tabernam; unde
pannus significat vinum, unde rubeus, rubedinem vini".
[81] Thomas of Erfurt, #18: "pars orationis formaliter est per modum significandi
activum, dictioni superadditum, quia pars orationis est dictio, ut habet modum
significandi activum".
[82] This term should be considered in conjunction with consignificatio; if vox as a
signum becomes a dictio by reason of its potential ability to signify, as a 'consignum' it becomes a pars orationis by reason of its potential ability to consignify.
[83] Michel de Marbais: "pars est vox significativa rei cum proprietatibus suis
mediante ratione significandi et consignificandi ab intellectu sibi concessa" (Thurot,
p. 157).
[84] Siger de Courtrai, p. 95: "modus consignificandi per quem pars est pars, praesupponit rationem significandi, vocem et significatum".

All the partes orationis, whether declinable or indeclinable, have two essential modes of signifying, *i.e.* the general and the special (at least in Siger's system), and by means of these sub-modes, the essence of each pars can be integrated into the system, for all the partes orationis are in fact distinguished by means of the properties of the things, *i.e.* the essence, they represent.[85] It is difficult to see how the indeclinable partes can possess any essence in the sense that the declinable partes express either 'ens' or 'esse', *i.e.* being or becoming. Siger in fact tries to side-step this issue by saying that such partes do not partake of the essence of language.[86]

The pars orationis is, therefore, made up, in Siger's scheme, of (a) the general mode of signifying which is derived from the essence of more than one pars orationis, *e.g.* substantia which belongs to the essence of both the nomen and the pronomen, and (b) the specific or special mode of signifying which is added to the general mode to complete the species of the pars orationis,[87] but also serves to distinguish or particularise one pars orationis from another.[88] This is particularly true of the indeclinable partes, all of which, in Siger's scheme, have the same modus significandi essentialis generalis, *i.e.* the mode of disposition (modus disponentis).

There is little, if any, disagreement between the Modistae on matters of grammatical doctrine, though their organisation and presentation is often at variance: we have an excellent example of this in the difference in organisation of the essential modes of the partes orationis, particularly of the declinable partes. In contrast to Siger, Thomas presents the essence of each pars in the form of the modus generalissimus which contains, to all intents and purposes, the same doctrine as Siger's, but Thomas is not concerned with the general/specific contrast which is so characteristic of Siger's presentation. Thomas is, however, as concerned as Siger in demonstrating the similarities and differences between the partes orationis, and to do this, Thomas makes use of the matter/form contrast. The pars orationis, therefore, is made up, in Thomas's scheme, of a modus generalissimus which states the essence of the pars (and contains the same content as Siger's general and

---

[85] Siger de Courtrai, p. 93: "non aliter possunt distingui partes orationis a se nisi uniuscuiusque proprietates significationum attendamus".

[86] Siger de Courtrai, p. 144: "sunt magis de bene esse orationis quam de esse". *Cf.* also R. H. Robins, *A. and M.*, p. 85.

[87] Siger de Courtrai, p. 95: "modus significandi specificus est modus significandi qui additus modo significandi generali constituit speciem".

[88] Siger de Courtrai, p. 145: "specificus qui est sicut differentia specifica in diffinitione speciei logicalis distinguens illam partem ab omnibus aliis speciebus".

specific modes), and the modus subalternus and the modus specialissimus (which are absent from Siger's work), which describe and individualise the various members of the word-class in question.

The similarity of the modus generalis leads one to suggest that Siger, unlike Thomas, had in mind a three-rank system of the partes orationis made up from the three features which constitute the essence of the eight partes orationis, *i.e.* (i) modus entis for the nomen/pronomen, (ii) modus esse for the verbum/participium, and (iii) modus disponentis for the indeclinable partes. This arrangement of the general mode of signifying suggests the idea of establishing a system of 'archipartes', which, though obviously based on entirely different criteria, would be reminiscent of the Prague theory of the 'archiphoneme'[89] and of the 'archimorpheme' as proposed by Saporta.[90]

There is also a very definite hierarchy in the system of partes orationis, which is structured in terms of the essence of the partes orationis; we have therefore a clear-cut division (which happens to coincide with the division between the declinable and the indeclinable partes), between those partes which have only a grammatical essence. Thomas has nothing specific to say on this point, but by implication he does deny the possession of essence *i.e.* metaphysical essence by the indeclinable partes; in the essential modes of the declinable partes, his definition can be split up into the material and formal elements, the material element referring to the essence of the pars and the formal element to the distinctive features of the essence of the pars, *e.g.* in the verb, the material element, *i.e.* its essence, is the modus esse and its formal element, *i.e.* its distinctive element is 'distantia', its separation from the suppositum.[91] In the indeclinable partes, Thomas no longer uses two-part definitions but describes the essential mode in syntactic terms which are equivalent to Siger's specific mode, *i.e.* he no longer makes use of a 'material' essential element but relies entirely on the formal element to define the pars in question.[92] He continues however to use the term 'essentialis', but it seems that this is more for the sake of symmetry of descriptive terminology rather than an attempt to attach a metaphysical origin to something which he obviously con-

[89]   N. S. Troubetzkoy, *Principes de phonologie*, p. 81. A. Martinet, "Neutralisation et archiphonème", *TCLP* VI, p. 46. A. Martinet, *La description phonologique*, p. 42.
[90]   Sol Saporta, "Morph, Morpheme, Archimorpheme", *Word* 12 (1956), pp. 9-14.
[91]   Thomas of Erfurt, #110: "modus significandi generalissimus essentialis verbi est modus significandi rem per modum esse, et distantis a supposito".
[92]   Thomas of Erfurt, #170: "modus significandi essentialis coniunctionis generalissimus est modus significandi per modum coniungentis".

siders, by virtue of his definition, to be a grammatical feature. Siger is more insistent and consistent in attributing a grammatical essence to the indeclinable partes, so that every indeclinable pars possesses the essential modes of general, *i.e.* modus disponentis, and specific.[93] (It might be possible to argue too that Siger's system of dividing the essential mode into general and specific created the need for the grammatical essence of the indeclinable partes in order to preserve the symmetry of his descriptive procedure). Siger never suggested that the indeclinable partes possessed an essence in the sense that the declinable partes do; his argument is that in every species there is a general and specific, the general being used to express those features which overlap and are also possessed by other species while the specific serves to distinguish this particular species from all other species.[94] An indeclinable pars has, therefore, the grammatical essence of syntactic relationship with other partes, and this, its general mode, it shares with the other indeclinable partes alike, but it has also the specific mode of having a particular type of syntactic relationship which distinguishes it from all the other partes orationis both declinable and indeclinable.

The highest places in the hierarchy are filled by those partes which express 'ens' or 'esse' in their general modes of signifying; these are the nomen and pronomen, verbum and participium, which are collectively referred to as 'magis principales'. These partes orationis will have many more modi significandi than the indeclinable partes, since possessing more than grammatical essence, *i.e.* metaphysical essence, will mean that 'accidents' will happen to this essence, which must be expressed by means of modi significandi. The minor or indeclinable partes cannot obviously possess the same number of modes of signifying, since their lack of metaphysical essence might presumably deprive them of any accidental mode of signifying.[95] Thomas does ascribe certain accidental modes to the indeclinable partes, but these are either absolute modes representing 'derivation', and therefore without any syntactic

[93] Siger de Courtrai, p. 152: "generalis est significare per modum disponentis ... specialis est significare per modum afficientis animam". This is his definition of the essential mode of the interjection.

[94] Siger de Courtrai, p. 145: "in speciebus consideratis a grammatico, videlicet in speciebus partium orationis, dicuntur poni in diffinitionibus illarum specierum duo modi significandi essentiales integrantes essentiam illius speciei, quorum est generalis quia in alia specie partis reperitur et similiter in omnibus illius partis, et alius specificus qui est sicut differentia specifica in diffinitione speciei logicalis distinguens illam partem ab omnibus aliis speciebus".

[95] Siger de Courtrai, p. 144: "aliae partes orationis sunt minus principales quia modi significandi ipsarum sumuntur a proprietatibus minus principalibus et sunt indeclinabiles quia carent illis accidentibus penes quae attenditur declinatio".

function, or modes, *e.g.* ordo in the conjunction, which refer to the syntactic meaning, *i.e.* function of the pars in question. It is interesting to note that 'comparatio', which Thomas included as a modus significandi essentialis specialissimus of the nomen but which Siger has included as an accidental mode of the nomen, becomes an *accidental* mode of the adverb in Thomas's account. The individual pars orationis will be considered major or minor according to whether its modes of signifying are derived from properties which are themselves considered major or minor, *i.e.* whether they express 'ens/esse' or not.

C. CATEGORIES

Mediaeval *Sprachlogik* rests on the following divisions: (i) mode of signifying (modus significandi), (ii) mode of understanding (modus intelligendi), (iii) mode of being (modus essendi); the different logical and grammatical modes of signification are postulated from our intellectual experience (modus intelligendi) which in turn delineate the different categories and properties of reality (modus essendi). Grammar viewed in this light, does it not become a part of logic? The Modistae said not. Logic for them is concerned with truth or untruth, grammar with correct or incorrect expression.[96] Therefore, according to Martin of Dacia, the task of the grammarian is to investigate the principles of his science, the principles of grammar being the modes of signification.

The modus essendi is the thing itself with its various properties, which is of no direct concern to the linguist, since he is not concerned with the thing, *i.e.* the referent. The thing is perceived by the mind; in Modistic terminology this stage is the modus intelligendi. So far, however, linguistic factors have not been introduced.

The grammarian must express in language his understanding of the reality he is considering; this he does by means of the mode of signifying (modus significandi), though to be quite true, it is not until we come to the active mode of signifying that the grammarian really begins to use language as his tool, his mode of expression. Just as a thing has many properties, so a pars orationis will have many modes of signifying, each with the task of signifying some aspect or property of the

[96]   Siger de Courtrai, p. 135: "logica defendit animam nostram a falso in speculativis et a malo in practicis, sic grammatica defendit virtutem nostram interpretativam ab expressione onceptus mentis incongrua in omnibus scientis". Nevertheless, we should remember that the Modistae were logicians as well as grammarians, which is quite evident in their grammatical writings.

thing in question, *i.e.* its essential mode will describe its essence, its accidental mode will describe[97] the variations which will occur to its essence and thus permit the pars to function at a higher, *i.e.* syntactical, level by virtue of the external variations in its essence. The grammarian's concern is with these various modes of signifying.

The modus significandi is divided into the active and the passive modes; the grammarian has no concern with the passive mode of signifying, and works only with the active mode of signifying, its dimensions of essential and accidental, absolute and respective, and their sub-divisions of general and special modes of signifying, *etc.* Thereafter the eight partes orationis are described in turn, in terms of these different modes of signifying; the essential modes are always described first, since the grammatical function of each pars is established by virtue of its essence, whereas the accidental modes are really variations of the essence of the pars and do not influence the original mode of signification.

Modus essendi

This is not a linguistic category at all but a philosophical one. Things possess properties, which, Siger tells us, serve to distinguish the partes orationis;[98] in themselves, they exist outside the mind and therefore outside the linguistic system.[99] Just as cause precedes effect, so the modus essendi, which represents the properties of these things, precedes the modus intelligendi which is the manner in which the mind perceives and understands these things.

Although the modus essendi is in itself not a grammatical category, it has a close relationship to all the accidental modes of signifying and will exercise a particular influence on the nature and function of certain of these accidental modes, *e.g.* the species primitiva of the nomen; Siger suggests that this grammatical[100] category serves to designate the modus

[97] Siger de Courtrai, p. 131: "modus significandi accidentalis est qui advenit parti post suum completum esse, sicut accidentia dicuntur accidentia quia adveniunt rei secundum suum completum esse".

[98] Siger de Courtrai, p. 93: "rerum proprietatibus partes orationis invicem distinguuntur".

[99] The views of the Modistae on language as a mirror of reality were no doubt influenced by their attitude to the 'nominalist-realist' controversy of the day. Compare, however, the ideas of Kant and Whorf in particular on this subject.

[100] The closeness between the modus essendi and the accidental mode has interesting syntactic implications in Modistic theory; species is, by its nature, an absolute mode, and can therefore not possess any syntactic function. Expressed in modern terms, the 'species' refers to the morphology of the nomen without having any morpho-syntactic function.

essendi of the thing in its stark pristine state,[101] a statement which Thomas echoes,[102] and the latter goes so far as to exclude the vox from the species[103] which is derived directly from the property of the thing. Similarly the various other accidental modes of the principal partes are so conceived as to express accidents of the modus essendi or the properties of the essence of the thing under consideration. It is noteworthy that Siger, for instance, makes no mention of the modes of being of the 'partes minus principales'; this immediately calls to mind Aristotle's theory of grammatical words,[104] and also Tesnière's theory of 'mots pleins' and 'mots vides'.[105] It should not be imagined that each thing will have only one modus essendi: a thing can have many properties and therefore modes of being, which can mean, among other things, that one and the same thing can be of one or another gender.[106]

The modus essendi is the property of the thing considered absolutely,[107] *i.e.* without any further consideration of anything except as it is in itself. The modus essendi refers just to the essence of the thing whereas the other modes introduce other considerations, and thereby establish other levels, which are without the absolute essence of being, *i.e.* the mode of understanding introduces the factor of 'intellectus' and the mode of signifying the factors of 'vox' and signification. It is this matter of external factors which produces the 'formal' difference, because at the material level they are all considering the same thing; it is the addition of the ratio intelligendi and the ratio significandi and con-

---

[101] Siger de Courtrai, p. 96: "designans modum essendi ut est primus et formalis et non ab alio descendens".

[102] Thomas of Erfurt, #67: "species sumitur a proprietate rei, quae est modus existendi primarie" (*i.e. absolute*).

[103] Thomas of Erfurt, #67: "species ... non attenditur ex parte vocis, ut quidam dicunt, ita quod illud nomen sit primitivae speciei, cuius vox est primo ad significandum imposita".

[104] *Cf.* R. H. Robins, *A. and M.*, pp. 19-20: 85.

[105] L. Tesnière, *Esquisse d'une syntaxe structurale*, p. 7: "il existe deux espèces de mots, les mots *pleins,* qui expriment une idée (fonction sémantique), et les mots *vides,* qui n'expriment par eux-mêmes aucune idée, mais servent seulement d'outils grammaticaux".

[106] Siger de Courtrai, p. 101: "eadem res bene potest habere plures modos essendi seu plures proprietates eo quod modi essendi seu proprietates accedunt rebus et unius rei bene sunt plura accidentia propria; propter quod una et eadem res, sub alio et alio modo essendi designata, bene potest esse alterius et alterius generis". This reinforces the conviction that we are in fact dealing with modes and sub-modes of being; the modus significandi refers to the modus essendi, *i.e. das Ding an sich,* whereas the modus significandi, and its sub-divisions and sub-dimensions refer to the properties, *i.e.* sub-modes of the thing.

[107] Thomas of Erfurt, #12: "modus essendi est rei proprietas absolute".

significandi, both of which are factors at the mental level, which creates the 'formal' element of difference.

The modi essendi, intelligendi passivus and significandi passivus are the same materially (materialiter) but differ formally (formaliter);[108] the modus essendi refers to the property of the thing absolutely, whereas the passive mode of understanding refers to this same property as understood by the mind[109] and the passive mode of signifying to the same property as signified by the vox.[110] Grammar operates by virtue of the meaning involved; everything has meaning, but to have meaning, there must first be something in existence. Every material thing possesses form and matter which is capable of being understood and of being designated and signified.

The modus essendi, the modi intelligendi activus and significandi activus differ both 'materialiter' and 'formaliter'. There cannot however be a direct link between the modus essendi and the modus significandi activus, since the property of the thing, which is its modus essendi, has to be perceived and understood, which is done at the level of the modus intelligendi, before it can be expressed by the modus significandi. Any other property of the thing in question, even if it is not to be understood and then expressed, will nonetheless belong to the modus essendi of the thing (but this is essentially static).[111]

The modi essendi, intelligendi passivus and significandi passivus, although they differ formally (formaliter), possess the same material properties, but when we move onto the active level, they differ materially (materialiter) as well. In the case of the active mode of understanding, the 'ratio intelligendi', *i.e.* the ability to understand, which is a property of the intellect,[112] has come into operation, but once the mind has perceived a thing, we move from an active mode to a passive

---

[108] Modistic use of 'formaliter' is the same as mediaeval scholastic usage, it should not be thought of in the same sense as modern linguistic usage. Modistic use of terms such as 'materialiter' and 'formaliter' stem from their philosophical background which has already been described as a modified realism or conceptualism, and can be looked upon as the equivalent of Abelard's theory. It may well be that Siger is more of a 'realist' than Thomas, *e.g.* he describes the possession of properties as the criterion for the pars orationis, whereas for Thomas, it is the modus significandi activus which is his criterion.

[109] Thomas of Erfurt, #12: "ipsa proprietas rei, prout ab intellctu apprehensa".

[110] Thomas of Erfurt, #12: "cuiusdem rei proprietas, prout per vocem significatur".

[111] Martin of Dacia, #4: "omnes autem istae proprietates rei extra intellectum existentes dicuntur modi essendi".

[112] Thomas of Erfurt, #13: "modus intelligendi activus dicit proprietatem intellectus, quae est ratio intelligendi, sive concipiendi".

state of the thing having been perceived by the mind – this is of course
a philosophical rather than a linguistic matter. Similarly, at the level of
the active mode of signifying, it is the ratio consignificandi, *i.e.* the
ability to signify functionally, according to Thomas,[113] a property of the
vox, which makes the difference.

Modus intelligendi

The next level is that of the mode of understanding (modus intelligendi)
which follows the level of being just as the perception and understanding of the thing follow the thing itself. The mind now perceives
and understands the thing and its qualities.[114]

This too is a philosophical stage and of little intrinsic interest to the
linguist. Now that we have left the level of crude being, we begin to
operate in terms of active and passive modes. The mind has to be in
the active mode in order to perceive and apprehend; the mind can only
apprehend the properties, *i.e.* the modus essendi of the thing which is to
be signified. The mind cannot itself signify, and so it is the passive
mode of understanding which becomes the vital link between understanding and signifying, and the modes of signifying are derived from
the modi essendi *as they have been understood* by the mind.[115]

The modus intelligendi is divided into the active and passive modes.
The active and passive modes of understanding agree formally but
differ materially; the act of understanding remains the same, and because of this, there is no formal difference between the active and passive modes. The form is "the principle or *source*[116] of the characteristic
qualities, activity and behaviour of a substance";[117] in this case the act
of understanding is the source of the qualities of both the active and
passive modes of understanding. Similarly, "first matter does not and
cannot exist by itself; it cannot as such be seen but its presence as a
component metaphysical factor in corporeal substances is manifested
by substantial change".[118] In the case of the modes of understanding,
the substantial change which distinguishes materially the passive from

---

[113]   Thomas of Erfurt, #13: "modus significandi activus dicit proprietatem vocis,
quae est ratio consignificandi".
[114]   Martin of Dacia, #3: "Modi intelligendi sunt eaedem proprietates rei secundum quod res est in intellctu et ut eaedem proprietates cum re sunt intellectae".
[115]   Thomas of Erfurt, #11: "modi significandi activi sumuntur a modis essendi,
mediantibus modis intelligendi passivis; et ideo immediate modi significandi a
modis intelligendi passivis sumuntur".
[116]   My emphasis.
[117]   F. C. Copleston, *Aquinas*, p. 88.
[118]   F. C. Copleston, *Op. cit.*, p. 88.

the active modes is that the passive mode tells us the property of the thing which has been passively understood, while the active mode tells us the attribute of the mind which is the action of understanding the property of the thing.

We find an interesting sequence in this system of applied semantics. The thing exists absolutely; it is apprehended by the mind which is an action of the mind; the process could very possibly cease there, and the perception would pass into a state of having been perceived. The intellect, which is not the same as the mode of understanding (modus intelligendi), has the power of conferring expression on this passive state of perception. This activates it and brings the sequence up to the level of expression, which is active, but once having been expressed, that too passes into a passive state.

Modus intelligendi activus

This is the mode by means of which the intellect comprehends the modus essendi or the property of the thing under consideration,[119] but we are not yet at the grammatical level, inasmuch as no expressive element, i.e. vox has been added. The mind apprehends the property, i.e. modus essendi[120] of the thing, and it is by means of this that the intellect can signify and comprehend the properties of the thing.[121] It is now potentially signifiable – it must be stressed that it is only *potentially* signifiable, since at this level the intellect can append signification or it can merely conceive and comprehend. The act of conceiving is still a pre-grammatical level; it is a statement about the property of understanding.

The modus essendi, the modus intelligendi activus and the modus significandi activus do not agree formally or materially, and so we find ourselves, so to speak, mid-way between the thing itself devoid of any further attribute and the act of expressing the thing meaningfully, which is the grammatical level.

The formal difference, as Copleston points out, is a matter of the 'source of the characteristic qualities';[122] in the case of the active mode,

[119] Thomas of Erfurt, #13: "modus intelligendi activus dicit proprietatem intellectus, quae est ratio intelligendi, sive concipiendi".
[120] Siger de Courtrai, p. 94: "intellectus comprehendit modum essendi seu proprietatem ipsius rei . . .".
[121] Thomas of Erfurt, #10: "intellectus rei proprietas significat, concipit vel apprehendit".
[122] F. C. Copleston, *Op. cit.*, p. 88.

the difference stems from the fact that we are dealing with the acts of being, understanding and signifying. The material difference is that of substantial change, and in this instance it is the difference of level, *i.e.* the factors of essence, intellectus and vox which produce the material difference. It should be stressed that the substance will always remain the same, since "it is only of the substance that we can properly say that it exists".[123] "Matter cannot be said to be: it is the substance itself which exists".[124] This is perhaps not so pertinent here, but the passive modes are affected in that they are the same materially and substantially but differ formally;[125] they are the same materially, since the matter in every case is the same property, *i.e.* modus essendi of the thing under consideration, and the matter is always 'informable' by an active mode either of understanding or signifying. They are also the same substantially (realiter) since they are all dealing with the same property of the thing.[126]

Modus intelligendi passivus

From the active mode of understanding we pass to the passive mode, so that the mental concept, *i.e.* the thing as understood by the mind, can receive the signification which will take it to yet another level. Although we are talking about an active and a passive mode, we are nevertheless dealing with the same act of understanding.[127] We have in fact to deal with three factors, *i.e.* the act of understanding, and the mode of understanding which may be active or passive. Therefore the difference between the active and passive modes of understanding will be purely material; it will not be formal, by virtue of the fact that they both stem from the same property of the intellect.

The modus essendi, intelligendi passivus, and significandi passivus are the same materially and substantially, but differ formally; substan-

---

[123]   F. C. Copleston, *Op. cit.*, p. 87.
[124]   St. Thomas Aquinas, *Summa contra Gentiles*, 2.54: quoted by Copleston, p. 87.
[125]   Thomas of Erfurt, #12: "sunt eadem materialiter et realiter, quia quod dicit modus essendi absolute, dicit modus intelligendi passivus, prout refertur ad intellectum; et quod dicit modus intelligendi passivus, dicit modus significandi passivus prout refertur ad vocem".
[126]   Thomas of Erfurt, #12: "conveniunt autem realiter; nam modus essendi dicit absolute proprietatem rei; et modus intelligendi passivus dicit proprietatem rei sub modo intelligendi; et modus significandi passivus dicit proprietatem rei sub ratione consignificandi".
[127]   Thomas of Erfurt, #14: "eadem est ratio intelligendi".

tially they are the same because they all deal with the same property of the thing, and materially they are the same,[128] since no substantial change is involved but merely one of level, which in fact creates the formal difference, since it is the acts of being, understanding and signifying which are the 'source of the characteristic qualities, activity and behaviour'[129] which represent this change. It is possible to illustrate the formal and material similarities and dissimilarities between the levels of modes in the form of a diagram:

		modus essendi	
	modus intelligendi activus	modus intelligendi passivus	materialiter
modus significandi activus		modus significandi passivus	
formaliter			

Although these modes of understanding may be passive, they appear to perform a vital function, in that they represent the link between one stage or level and the next, *e.g.* the intellect has understood the property of the thing and has done so actively, so it becomes the role of the passive mode to link this action with the previous mode, which is the modus essendi; it is also the link between the act of understanding and the act of signifying, since the modus significandi activus becomes the expression of the properties of the thing *as they have been understood by the mind*. The modus intelligendi passivus indicates the property of the thing, but as comprehended by the intellect (ab intellectu apprehensa),[130] and thereby the modus significandi activus takes over from the modus essendi, i.e. it becomes the expression of the thing or of its properties as conceived by the mind.

[128] Though they all deal with the property of the thing, there is in the passive mode of understanding the element of 'intellectus', which in Thomas's system can be considered as logically presupposed in contrast to Siger's 'temporal' statement.
[129] F. C. Copleston, *Op. cit.*, p. 88.
[130] Such a statement is very suggestive of the modified realism or conceptualism of the Modistae.

At the vital levels of understanding and signifying we have two channels whereby the energy created by the activity of the intellect can pass to the passive state and either remain there and be lost or else pass to a higher level, *e.g.* the movement from the modus intelligendi passivus (which has understood the property of the thing) to the modus significandi activus; similarly, though none of our authors say this, the modus significandi activus, or the level of expression, becomes the point at which vox and significatio are added. It is at this point that the grammarian enters, but presumably before the modi significandi can operate grammatically, the properties of the thing have to *have been signified*; only then can the various aspects, essential and accidental, of the thing be used and expressed grammatically. One might say that the words in a dictionary represent the repository for the modi significandi passivi; they do not assume the functions of the varied qualities of the active modes of signifying until they have, so to speak, been taken out of the dictionary and used actively in some form of connected discourse.

Modus signandi

Of the grammarians of the period whose work has been consulted, Siger de Courtrai is the only one [131] to insert between the modes of understanding and signification, the mode of designation (modus signandi). The modus intelligendi is followed by the modus signandi, since once the thing has been understood and comprehended, it must then be designated by the vox,[132] even though meaning or signification has still not been added. This stage is the one at which the modus essendi receives its first external expression; hitherto it has merely been understood, but now it is clearly marked and is ready to *receive* meaning which will give it grammatical status. The modus signandi marks therefore another important stage forward; hitherto, the vox had been an amorphous element without any positive function, but now it becomes a grammatical functive,[133] since the intellect has now bestowed upon the vox the power of designating something, and as a result the vox becomes a dictio.[134] Vox now becomes functional as a dictio, *i.e.* as

---

[131]   Siger describes it as 'modus seu ratio signandi'; he is the only one to make of it a mode, but Thomas, in describing the dictio, does on one occasion make use of the term 'ratio signandi'.
[132]   Siger de Courtrai, p. 94: "voces sunt signa passionum".
[133]   L. Hjelmslev, *Prolegomena*, p. 83 (Definition 9): (functive is) object that has function to other objects.
[134]   Siger de Courtrai, p. 94: "per rationem signandi vox formaliter dicitur dictio".

something capable of designating, though it will not become grammatically functional until it reaches the level of modus significandi.

Like the modus intelligendi it is divided into active and passive. Siger tells us that the modus signandi is the thing of reason (ens rationis) which is given to the vox by the intellect by means of which the vox designates the thing.[135] The mediaeval philosopher looked upon the 'ens rationis' as "that which has being in the understanding which considers it, and which can have no being outside the understanding".[136] Again the passive mode plays its part as store-house of the information acquired up to this level: it is the link between the active mode of designation and the thing itself, *i.e.* it refers to the thing which has been designated by the vox.[137]

These three modes of being, understanding and designating have brought us to the grammatical level; we have passed from the thing baldly considered which, combined with the vox and the modes of understanding and designating, has become a word. But before the word can become a grammatical functive, it must become a pars orationis, and to become a pars orationis it must acquire signification and consignification, and this will happen at the level of the modus significandi. It is, therefore, at this level that the grammarian enters on the scene, because it is his task to take the dictio, give it meaning (especially functional, *i.e.* grammatical, rather than notional) and thus turn it into a grammatical unit.[138] John of Dacia tells us[139] that the process is not even complete at the level of modus significandi; a pars orationis is useless unless it is made to combine and operate in conjunction with other partes orationis – this becomes the 'modus construendi',[140] the final object of grammar.

---

[135] Siger de Courtrai, p. 94: "modus seu ratio signandi activus est ratio quaedam seu ens rationis concessum voci ab intellectu secundum quod talis vox talem rem signat".

[136] R. McKeon, *Selections from Mediaeval Philosophers*, Pt. II., p. 451.

[137] Siger de Courtrai, p. 94: "modus seu ratio signandi passivus est ipsa res mediante ratione signandi passiva per vocem signata seu ratio signandi relata ad ipsam rem".

[138] *Cf.* de Saussure's theory of 'entité linguistique' and 'unité linguistique'; *Cours*, pp. 144-149.

[139] John of Dacia (p. 76): "modus construendi est subiectum in grammatica". This is, of course, implied in Siger's modus consignificandi and Thomas's Diasynthetica.

[140] This is a term not normally used by either Siger or Thomas.

Modus significandi

The preceding sections of the categories should really be considered a preamble to the grammatical element, and are not at all properly within the province or competence of the grammarian. Many linguists of today would rigorously exclude all such considerations from the scope of the grammarian.[141] All linguists are agreed, however, that meaning must play a part, indeed an important part, in all forms of linguistic analysis, though few modern linguists would argue that meaning should be the sole, main or indeed any criterion in the setting up of formal word-classes or other grammatical constituents, and in this sense they would categorically oppose a great many of the ideas of the Modistae. However, it must be emphasised that grammatical meaning was for the Modistae an active process while semantic meaning was as a result a passive one; this suggests, therefore, that meaning was implicitly widened to include formal relations and furthermore that the essential modes of signifying were an integral part of grammar and thus an active and not a passive process.

The consideration of the pre-grammatical modes had left us in effect with the dictio, the function of which is to designate the thing by means of the vox.

The dictio becomes a pars orationis by means of the modus significandi, and it is at this point that the grammarian states his understanding of the reality he has been considering in a form which is expressible in language, since, as Martin of Dacia says, whatever is connected with understanding is also connected with signifying.[142] To be quite true, it is not until we come to the modus significandi activus that the grammarian really begins to function. The Modistae used terms such as modus significandi really as generic terms – Thomas offers us no definition of modus significandi as such, nor does Siger in his *Summa* and even in his "Sophismata" he defines it only as an action of the mind in understanding the reality which it will express in speech.[143] For Martin of Dacia, however, the modus significandi is the property

---

[141] Bloomfield and his followers would dismiss it as mentalistic and impressionistic; nevertheless the modi significandi were a way of handling the same formal facts of Latin grammar that any modern linguist would have to deal with, and these prior modes were for the Modistae a very necessary piece of equipment in constructing and describing the modes of signifying.

[142] Martin of Dacia, #3: "quidquid enim contingit intelligere, contingit et significare".

[143] Siger de Courtrai, p. 130: "modus significandi existens in intellectu est illud mediante quo vox signat modum essendi circa rem".

of the thing signified by the vox,[144] and therefore just as the thing is distinguished by its properties, so the pars orationis is distinguished by its many modi significandi by means of which a grammatical statement may be made. The modus significandi is thus the raw material of the grammarian.

The modus significandi follows the modus intelligendi and is divided into active and passive; the passive mode is the modus essendi which has been signified, the active is the mode which leads to the various sub-modes which constitute the means whereby a language can begin to express its various concepts. These other aspects of the modus significandi are the absolute and respective modes, and the essential and accidental modes which will be discussed shortly. The structure of the metalanguage makes a parallel between the thing and its expression, thus:

res	= modus essendi
intellectus rei	= modus intelligendi
vox significans rem	= modus significandi.

The mode of signifying is sub-divided into the active and passive modes; the grammarian has, however, no concern with the passive mode, since by its very nature of being passive it cannot take part in the act of either signifying or consignifying. The grammarian's real interest will lie with the active mode of signifying and its operational dimensions, i.e. (i) the essential and (ii) accidental modes, (iii) the absolute and (iv) respective modes, and in the sub-modes of the essential mode, i.e. generalis and specificus (in the case of Siger) and generalissimus, subalternus and specialissimus (in the case of Thomas).

The essential mode is designed to express the essence of the pars in question, while the accidental mode is designed to treat those attributes of the pars which do not belong to its essence, though they occur by reason of its essence. The absolute mode refers to features of the pars which render it discrete from the other partes but without resorting to comparison with features of another pars. The respective mode deals with those features of the pars which permit it to operate in significant concord, both governmental concord and concord of gender, number,

---

[144]   Martin of Dacia, #11: "modus significandi est proprietas rei consignificata per vocem".

case, *etc.*,[145] with other partes orationis at a level higher than that of the word-class.[146]

There is a great measure of agreement between Siger and Thomas on the nature of the essential and accidental modes, but their *organisation* of the essential mode is substantially different. It would not serve any real purpose at this stage to discuss this organisational matter in detail, but it does have the effect of influencing the relationships between the dimensions already mentioned. In Siger's scheme, both the essential and accidental modes, by their natures, can be expressed in terms of absolute and respective in their inter-relationships: Thomas's organisation means that the essential mode has relationships with the other partes orationis[147] since it is partly specific, but its sub-divisions of subalternus and specialissimus, which are much more detailed lists of the various words which make up the pars orationis in question, are made always with reference to the specific essence of the pars in question, which is an absolute mode; the result is that only the accidental

(a) *Siger:*

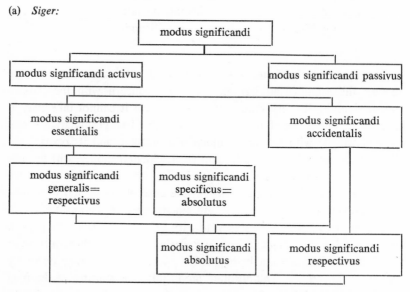

---

[145] Siger de Courtrai, p. 138: "est casus modus significandi accidentalis respectivus designans circa rem proprietatem per quam unum constructibile determinat dependentiam alterius".

[146] Thomas of Erfurt, #187: "intrinsecum sunt modi significandi respectivi, ratione quorum vel unum constructibile est ad alterum dependens, vel alterius dependentiam determinans".

[147] Thomas's modus generalissimus contains the features of Siger's modus generalis which is a respective mode and also of Siger's modus specificus which is an absolute mode.

(b) *Thomas:*

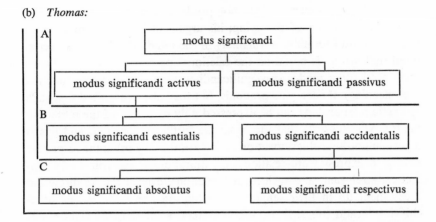

mode will be described in its absolute and respective relationships.[148] These dimensions can be represented by means of the diagrams above:[149]

A symbolises the bare outlines of the active and passive dimension; B the dimension of the essential and accidental modes: C is a combination of A and B, containing features of both, since the dimension of absolute and respective must contain features from the essential/accidental and active/passive oppositions.

The modus significandi deals with the linguistic unit at 'word' level; the modus significandi cannot create a sentence, since it is, to quote Siger, 'ens rationis simplex', whereas the sentence is something composite. The sentence is made up of partes orationis, which are established in terms of their modi significandi, but the modi significandi themselves play no active part in the syntax of the sentence; it must be stressed that they play no active part, but it remains a function of the respective modes of signifying, which are active modes of signifying, to realise the congruence of any sentence.[150]

There is then a necessary relationship between the modus significandi which is a concept or state of mind, and grammar which is the expression of this concept by means of 'sermo congruus'. But, as Siger con-

---

[148] Thomas of Erfurt, #22: "modus significandi accidentalis dividitur in modum significandi accidentalem absolutum et respectivum".
[149] It should be noted that Siger's general mode is always respectivus, and in the declinable partes at least, the specific mode is absolutus, since the specific mode is used to distinguish the pars in question from the other partes.
[150] Siger de Courtrai, p. 153: "omnis constructio congrua est per modos significandi proportionales".

cedes,[151] the grammarian does not produce this 'oratio congrua' by means of the modes of signifying; his argument is that the modus significandi is still formally (formaliter) in the mind. The Modistae recognised that syntax is based on the relationships between words – hence their need for a modus consignificandi to state the syntactic function (*i.e.* meaning) of each pars orationis, but they also recognised that such syntactic relationships can be expressed only by means of the respective modes. This suggests that the Modistae further recognised, and this is a very important achievement on their part, that, by using the respective modes to express word-relationships, morphology was sometimes syntactically relevant, and such formal relations, even if the Modistae did dress them up in their semantics, become in effect the means of achieving 'oratio congrua'. In Siger's system of analysis, all eight partes orationis differ in terms of their specific mode of signifying, but this specific mode has no syntactic function since it is absolute; the syntactic relations of each pars, which are its respective modes, are derived from one section of its essential mode, *i.e.* the modus significandi essentialis generalis, and the accidental modes of the pars in question.

However, these various sub-modes of signifying can now be considered as self-contained, since language is now operating by itself, having passed through the various stages of being, understanding, signifying; the pars orationis can be distinguished by operating by means of the modus significandi, and therefore the various submodes of signifying will of necessity be first considered inherently and then in relation to each other.

Modus significandi activus

It was stated in the last section that the modus significandi is the understanding of the thing as expressed in speech, but the active mode now becomes the final link whereby the word becomes grammatically functional, the dimensions of absolutus, essentialis, *etc.* being used to determine the actual grammatical status of the word. The vox qua vox, as we have seen, is not the subject matter of grammar, but the vox and the act of signification produce the dictio which is the word but without any grammatical attributes; the dictio, *i.e.* vox and significatio or expression and meaning, now acquires a mode of signifying and becomes a pars orationis, which is the smallest grammatical unit in the Modistic

---

[151] Siger de Courtrai, p. 129: "per modos significandi non reddit grammaticus orationem congruam".

system. The active mode of signifying is therefore the mode by means of which the vox signifies the modus essendi of the thing grammatically, or else some particular property of the thing, e.g. singular number which, though it may not be the thing itself, does refer to the property of the thing; the process of creating the pars orationis is with the active mode of signifying therefore complete. The modus significandi activus is derived eventually from the modus essendi, but there is not a direct line of development, since the mode of being must first become a mental concept (conceptus intellectus) and remain in the mind until it is expressed by the vox in the form of an active mode of signifying. It is therefore the systematic nature of the combination of the vox and the active mode of signifying which produces the pars orationis.[152]

It must be realised that, although these divisions of modus essendi, intelligendi, signandi and significandi are arbitrary and artificial, the actual modes themselves are fictional and inactive, i.e. the modus intelligendi does not function as such; it is the active mode which tells us that the intellect has perceived and comprehended the property of the thing. And so it is, right up the scale, until we reach the modus significandi activus which signifies what has been, in the case of Siger, designated by the (previous)[153] modus signandi passivus – in the case of Thomas, what has been understood by the intellect; thus the modus significandi activus takes over from the modus intelligendi passivus.[154]

[152] It is also possible to see why Thomas equates the ratio consignificandi to the modus significandi activus, and we see that they are not the same thing as would appear from a cursory examination of the text. The modus significandi activus possesses meaning merely by virtue of its being a mode of signifying, but this is not enough: clearly, notional meaning is not enough and if a grammatical system is to be set up in terms of meaning, it has to be done in terms of syntactic meaning, not root (or primary) meaning.

[153] The word 'previous' is used since Siger tends to give the impression of a temporal as well as a logical sequence in his description of the metalanguage, e.g. p. 94: "modum signandi sequitur modus significandi".

[154] Siger uses the modus signandi as the level where the dictio can be introduced into the logical sequence from the amorphous vox to the grammatically meaningful pars orationis. Thomas dispenses with the modus signandi, and instead gives the combination of vox and significatio a double role to play; he tells us that the intellect uses the vox to signify and to consignify, and in so doing ascribes a double system to it, i.e. (1) the ability to signify (ratio significandi), i.e. the significatio by means of which the signum is created which in combination with the vox formally becomes the dictio and (2) the ability to consignify (ratio consignificandi), creates the consignum and combined together they formally become a pars orationis. Siger has in the end a similar structure; at the end of his preamble, he tells us that a pars is a combination of vox and dictio, but a pars is really a pars only by virtue of the mode of consignification. What is implied here is that a dictio possesses meaning, what I call for this purpose 'potential' meaning; a dictio possesses vox too, but is is still pre-grammatical. It becomes grammatical by means

The importance to the Modistic system of the modus significandi activus acting with the ability to consignify or to differentiate this functional meaning will be appreciated from the fact that the thing can have several properties which are not mutually exclusive and which will require as many active modes of signifying to express them.[155]

The modus significandi activus must refer to some property of the thing: Thomas argues that the intellect is a passive power, indeterminate in itself and does not refer to any determinate act, unless this act has been determined in another manner. If then the intellect uses the vox to signify something by means of a determined modus significandi activus, this can only be by means of some determined property of the thing, which means that this property of the thing must correspond to some modus significandi activus.[156]

The modus significandi activus and passivus differ materially (materialiter) but are the same formally (formaliter); the passive mode refers to the property of the thing as it has been signified in terms of its functional or class-meaning,[157] whereas the active mode expresses the property of the thing in the form of its functional meaning.[158] They are alike 'formaliter' because it is the same class-meaning, *i.e.* ability to consignify, which is involved, the difference being caused 'materialiter' by virtue of the fact that the passive mode has no power of expression

---

of the active mode of meaning, which creates from the potential meaning a functional or distinctive meaning, which is the consignification. It is this consignification or functional meaning which distinguishes the pars orationis from the dictio and which permits the pars to operate grammatically. The commentators and critics have used 'dolor' and 'doleo' to illustrate; they both have the same vox and significatio, *i.e.* primary meaning but they possess different modi significandi, the former 'per modum permanentis' and the latter 'per modum fluxus' and it is this which represents the consignificatio; in other words, they possess one *Gesamtbedeutung*, but different *geformte Bedeutung* or modi significandi activi. It is then this *geformte Bedeutung* or consignificatio or the modus significandi activus which for the Modistae is the real matter of the grammarian.

[155] Thomas of Erfurt, #114: "in una et eadem re possunt reperiri diversae proprietates rei, non repugnantes, a quibus sumi possunt diversi modi significandi activi".

[156] Thomas of Erfurt, #6: "cum intellectus vocem ad significandum sub aliquo modo significandi activo imponit, ad ipsam rei proprietatem aspicit, a qua modum significandi activum originaliter trahit; quia intellectus cum sit virtus passiva, de se indeterminata, ad actum determinatum non vadit, nisi aliunde determinetur. Unde cum imponit vocem ad significandum sub determinato modo significandi activo, a determinata rei proprietate necessario movetur; ergo cuilibet modo significandi activo correspondet aliqua proprietas rei, seu modus essendi rei".

[157] Thomas of Erfurt, #12: "modus essendi est rei proprietas absolute".

[158] Thomas of Erfurt, #13: "modus intelligendi activus dicit proprietatem intellectus".

and therefore refers only to the property of the thing, whereas the active mode reveals the property of the 'vox significativa',[159] and this material difference might almost be described as the difference of content and expression.[160]

The modus significandi activus is divided into modus significandi essentialis and modus significandi accidentalis, modus significandi absolutes and modus significandi respectivus.

Modus significandi passivus

This is the mode which relates the modus essendi to the modus significandi activus; it is in fact the modus essendi as it has been signified by the vox. Its grammatical function is nullified by its very passivity: it is not a 'principium constructionis', nor is it, in Thomas's terms, a 'principium partis orationis' and as a result can play no grammatical role.[161] It is therefore not a matter for the grammarian; intrinsically, it does not interest the grammarian since it is not formally discrete from the active mode.

The passive mode is the same as the modus essendi and the modus intelligendi passivus 'materialiter' and 'realiter', *i.e.* substantially, but differs 'formaliter'. This is so because the same thing is referred to whether it be comprehended by the intellect or signified by the vox, but it will differ 'formaliter' since on the formal level the modus essendi refers to the property of the thing absolutely, the modus intelligendi passivus refers to the property of the thing but by means of the ratio intelligendi, and the modus significandi passivus refers to the same property of the thing but this time by means of the ratio consignificandi.

The modus significandi activus and passivus differ 'materialiter' but are the same 'formaliter'. They are the same 'formaliter' because the act of signification (ratio significandi) is the same; there will be no formal difference, since the active and passive modes are functionally different (*i.e.* materialiter), but significantly the same, *i.e.* at the same level (formaliter). They differ 'materialiter' because the modus significandi passivus belongs to the thing itself and constitutes the link between its properties and their signification, whereas the modus signifi-

---

[159] Thomas of Erfurt, #13: "modus significandi activus dicit proprietatem vocis, quae est ratio consignificandi".

[160] Thomas of Erfurt, #17: "modus significandi activus, cum sit proprietas vocis significativae, materialiter est in voce significativa, ut in subiecto".

[161] Thomas of Erfurt, #5: "modi significandi passivi, ad grammaticam non pertinent, nisi per accidens, quia non sunt principium partis orationis, nec formale, nec efficiens, cum sint rerum proprietates".

candi activus represents not the property of the thing but of the 'vox significativa' which expresses this property. The active mode is essentially dynamic, whereas the passive mode remains static.

Modus significandi absolutus et respectivus

It has been decided to treat this dimension as one, without making an organisational distinction between the two parts. In a sense (especially a Modistic sense) the division of absolute and respective modes of signifying is somewhat peripheral since it adds nothing *to* the description of either the essence or the accidents of the pars. It really is operational only at a stage when the modern grammarian would be deciding on the formal elements which permit a pars orationis to function: the function of the absolute/respective opposition is to separate those modes of signifying which can function syntactically from those which cannot.

The category of absolute is internal to the modus significandi, or more exactly the pars in question, and excludes all reference to the modi significandi of other partes orationis.[162] The modus significandi specificus, as opposed to the modus generalis (categories peculiar to Siger),[163] refers to an intrinsic feature of the pars in question, a feature which renders it discrete from the other partes orationis. This uniqueness of the modus specificus makes of it a modus significandi which will, in Siger's system, be absolute, since it is a modus significandi which refers to the modus essendi in question only. There are certain of the accidental modes, *e.g.* species and figura (in the nomen) which are intrinsic features of a particular pars, and as a result they are classed as absolute which also means that they cannot have any separate syntactic function; in Siger's system, one function of the modi significandi is to act as 'principium constructionis', *i.e.* as the member of a construction. This is not possible for any absolute mode: the congruity of any construction depends on the conformity of the various modi significandi, which means that these different modes must possess an inter-proportionality by virtue of which they can combine to produce an 'oratio congrua', but the absolute modes cannot enter in any such

---

[162] Thomas of Erfurt, #22: "modus significandi accidentalis absolutus dicitur ille per quem unum constructibile non habet respectum ad alterum, sed solum ad rei proprietatem".
[163] Siger de Courtrai, p. 96: "iste modus significandi (specificus) non est principium constructionis quia est absolutus".

relation, since by definition they take into consideration no other factors than their own intrinsic features.

Thomas has a slightly different organisation; in the first place, he has no modus significandi generalis, but his modus significandi essentialis generalissimus can be described as mid-way between Siger's general and specific modes, embracing features of both modes, which would suggest that the modus generalissimus would be respective by virtue of its similarity to Siger's modus generalis and absolute by virtue of its similarity to Siger's modus specificus.[164] In actual fact, Thomas arranges matters quite differently; in the first place, the dichotomy of absolute and respective is a matter for the accidental modes only, and in the second place, the modi significandi and partes orationis are divided into two levels – Etymologia and Diasynthetica. At the level of Etymologia, the partes orationis are considered purely and simply in terms of themselves without reference to other partes orationis, and thus they will be absolute; at the level of Diasynthetica, which is by definition the relationship of one pars orationis to another, these different modi significandi will become respective as a result of the fact that the partes orationis and their modi significandi are no longer considered by and for themselves but in their mutual relations to each other.[165]

Modus significandi essentialis

This mode, along with the accidental mode, constitutes the descriptive apparatus of the eight partes orationis in terms of themselves: Modistic syntactical doctrine makes use of these partes orationis as they have been described in the form of various modes and uses them as constructs in the modus construendi which will thus achieve the final end of grammar, the 'oratio constructa congrua'.

However, of all the co-dimensions of the modus significandi activus, this is probably the most important, since all the others derive their nature and function from the essence of the pars in question. Hitherto, we have found a large measure of agreement among the Modistae in dealing with the 'elements', and a similar agreement will be found in

[164]   Siger's modus generalis is a respective mode and his modus specificus is an absolute mode; thus Thomas's modus generalissimus of the nomen is the 'modus entis' which is equivalent to Siger's modus generalis, and 'determinatae apprehensionis' which is equivalent to Siger's modus specificus.

[165]   Thomas of Erfurt, #22: "primo prout sunt principium formale partis orationis absolute, secundum quem modum pertinent ad Etymologiam; deinde prout sunt principium intrinsecum constructionis unius partis cum alia, secundum quem pertinent ad Diasyntheticam".

dealing with the accidental modes. (This statement is made with obvious reservations, since the incompleteness of Siger's work becomes increasingly apparent). It should not however be imagined that it is suggested that in dealing with the essential modes, there is a large measure of disagreement between Siger and Thomas. There is disagreement between them, but it is not one of doctrine or substance, but one of presentation and descriptive apparatus, with Siger starting at a level 'earlier' than Thomas, who uses refinements of depth which are absent from Siger.

They both sub-divide the modus essentialis, but in the case of Siger the sub-divisions of generalis and specificus are equal and parallel, and both stem from the essential property of the modus significandi activus of the pars in question, whereas Thomas starts at a 'later' stage, *i.e.* mid-way between Siger's generalis and specificus and proceeds to subdivide, so to speak, in depth, adding refinements of 'subalternus' and 'specialissimus' to his sub-division of 'generalissimus'. This difference can be schematised thus:

(a) *Siger*:

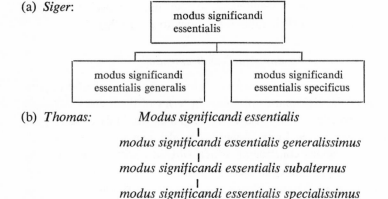

(b) *Thomas:*   *Modus significandi essentialis*
|
modus significandi essentialis generalissimus
|
modus significandi essentialis subalternus
|
modus significandi essentialis specialissimus

Michel de Marbais would appear to have followed a procedure somewhat like Siger's, whereas John of Dacia uses only the modus significandi essentialis generalis and the modus significandi accidentalis: Martin of Dacia, a contemporary and fellow-countryman of John's, uses a slightly different approach; he describes first of all the modus significandi essentialis generalis[166] of each pars orationis, and then he

---

[166] Martin's use of the general mode should not be confused with Siger's, since for Martin every pars orationis is distinct (and presumably discrete) by virtue of its general mode of signifying, which is thus much closer to Thomas's modus generalissimus.

analyses the modus significandi specialis and the modus significandi accidentalis of each. On the whole Martin's method is the same as Thomas's except for these minor variations: Roos suggests[167] that these might be pedagogical devices which supports the contention that it is procedure not subject matter which varies.

Siger tells us that the modus essentialis refers to the essence of the pars, and that it is divided into two parts, *i.e.* modus significandi essentialis generalis and essentialis specificus or specialis; for Thomas the modus essentialis is the mode by means of which the pars has its being, and is divided into the modus significandi essentialis generalissimus, subalternus and specialissimus.

For Siger, the modus essentialis therefore contains the essence of the pars, *e.g.* substance and quality in the nomen, but such a categorisation is not sufficient, for we shall see that certain partes orationis have certain essential features in common, *e.g.* substance (substantia) is common to both the nomen and pronomen, and yet they may vary through certain other essential features. He is aiming quite clearly at a procedure which would describe the partes orationis economically by first stating the essential features that some of them share, *i.e.* by means of the general mode, before giving a description of each pars orationis in terms which serve to distinguish it from the other partes orationis, *i.e.* by means of the specific mode. Siger thus produces a grammatical statement which is tantamount almost to a system of three word-classes[168] which can be defined by the general modes of *modus entis*, *modus esse*, and the *modus disponentis*, and these word-classes are then, by means of the specific mode, divided into the component partes orationis.

Siger is suggesting by implication that there are three essences involved, *i.e.* being, becoming, and disposition, and as a result he establishes three general essential modes, which is tantamount to saying that

---

[167] H. Roos, *Die Modi Significandi*, p. 141.
[168] Siger is, of course, working entirely with metaphysical and metalinguistic material; his theories, however, would be unacceptable to modern linguists because of their terms of reference, not perhaps so much because of their presentation. It might also be noted that arguments have been made in recent times in favour of certain universal features which are also suggested in Siger's description of the general modes of the partes orationis, *cf.* R. H. Robins, "Noun and Verb in Universal Grammar", *Language* 28 (1952), 289-298. Siger's procedure represents a radical departure from the pattern of his predecessors, and should be contrasted with Thomas's more orthodox presentation of the partes orationis by means of the partes orationis of Latin in the order that they had been presented by his classical models.

there are three 'archipartes',[169] but in order to achieve the eight partes orationis of traditional grammar, he subdivides these three archipartes into specific aspects of their essence; the difference between the general and the specific decides the nature of the individual partes orationis. It could be argued that in the first instance essence is considered as something common to all natures by which different entities are grouped into one main category; in the second instance, essence is considered as something primary by means of which the thing is distinguished from other things. Siger suggests as much when he defines 'generalis' as embodying an essence which can be found in other species of the pars and will be identical in all the other forms of this pars, but on the other hand 'specificus' is like the differentia specifica used in logical defini- tions – it separates one species from another, and in terms of Siger's system, it separates a pars from all the others so that it is entirely self- contained and separate from the others in terms of its essence and its function: this is why the modus specificus can have no syntactic func- tion.

Thomas starts his system a little 'later': he has no modus generalis which would embrace more than one pars. His modus generalissimus refers to the essence of a particular pars orationis and of any subordi- nate pars; this might appear at first sight to be a suggestion of some system of 'archipartes', but is in fact so arranged, so that certain partes which have certain features of their essence in common can be de- scribed without a separate unit having to be set up. Thomas's modus generalissimus is in many ways a more economic and at the same time a more detailed statement than Siger's, in that his modus generalissimus can be said to cover in effect the features of Siger's modus generalis and specificus; on the other hand, it might be argued that Siger is groping towards a more formal statement (even though it is stated in mentalist semantic terms), in that he is implying that, *e.g.* the noun and pronoun have formal characteristics in common.[170] Thomas, how- ever, having set up his modus generalissimus, is now in a position to add further refinements (which are in a large measure absent from Siger's description): he adds two sub-modes of the modus generalissimus, *i.e.* subalternus and specialissimus; the latter is the ultimate refinement. Just as the modus generalissimus is designed to describe the essential features which are shared by all the subordinate parts of the pars in

[169] The term 'archipars' has already been used, *cf.* p. 86; I have used the term in order to suggest that Siger's description, at least of the essential modes, is more modern and simple, *i.e.* in the Hjelmslevian sense, than Thomas's.
[170] By having the modus entis in common, they can become the suppositum.

question, the modus specialissimus describes the essence of some of the subordinate parts but in much more minute detail: the modus subalternus assumes a middle position between the modus generalissimus and specialissimus, and deals with the essence of the subordinate parts of the pars.[171]

The difference between Siger and Thomas is largely terminological; the apparent difference in their essential modes is resolved if we stagger the scale of relationship. There is no one-to-one relationship, because Thomas's modus generalissimus contains features which are found in Siger's modus generalis and other features which are found in Siger's modus specificus, but Siger has nothing which compares to the sub-divisions of Thomas's modus generalissimus, i.e. subalternus and specialissimus, and their analytical procedures can therefore be represented thus:

Siger   *Thomas*

generalis
                                          generalissimus
specificus   subalternus
                specialissimus

The result is a curious imbalance: Thomas presents us with a very detailed description of the modus essentialis, whereas Siger seems to imply that the essence of the pars is sufficient to speak for itself. Siger organises his material in such a way that his absolute and respective modes, which in Thomas's system are really sub-divisions of the modus accidentalis, are in some cases cross-dimensions rather than co-dimensions of the essential mode, and depend a great deal for their discreteness on features which differentiate the general from the specific mode. This discreteness would be much more apparent if Siger had described his general and specific modes with the same wealth of detail that Thomas gives us of his essential mode. The following diagram gives some idea of the cross-references beween the essential and accidental modes on the one hand and the absolute and respective modes on the other (see diagram on next page.)

The accidental modes have been added in order to make the picture more complete even at the danger of anticipating too much.

---

[171] Thomas of Erfurt, #21: "nec generalissime, nec specialissime, sed medio modo se habens".

			absolutus		*respectivus*
essentialis	Siger	*generalis* *specificus*	+		+
	Thomas	*generalissimus* *subalternus* *specialissimus*	+ + +		
accidentalis	Siger and Thomas	*casus* *coniugatio* *figura* *genus* *gradus* *modus* *numerus* *persona* *qualitas* *species* *tempus*	+ +		+ + + + + + + + +

Modus significandi accidentalis

The accidental modes play a significant role in the description of the partes in as striking a manner as Siger's (implied) 'archipars' did to the modus essentialis. Grammarians have always commented on the fundamental difference between declinable and indeclinable parts of speech:[172] the Modistae too had something to say on this topic.

They referred to the declinable partes as the 'partes magis principales' and to the indeclinable partes as the 'partes minus principales'; all the partes have essential modes, but as a result of what might be called the defective nature of their essence, the partes minus principales, *i.e.* the indeclinable partes have no accidental modes. Siger tells us in his Sophisma "O Magister", that certain things present themselves foremost to our minds, things such as 'ens' and 'esse' and their properties; modes of signifying which are derived from these properties are 'magis principales' and therefore the partes orationis which are derived from such modi significandi will be 'magis principales' too, and are in fact to be found in the nomen, pronomen, verbum and participium. These four partes have as their accidents number, person, case, mood, tempus and declension or conjugation. Siger continues that other partes are 'minus principales' for the simple reason that they are derived from properties which are 'minus principales', and are therefore

[172]   R. H. Robins, *A. and M.*, p. 85, *et al.*

"de bene esse orationis quam de esse".[173] Partes which have as their essence either 'esse' or 'ens' are 'magis principales', declinable, and therefore must possess a quota of accidental modes to express the variations which occur to their essence but originate from without their essence; accident can here be defined as "the quality which will *'happen' to a subject* in such a way that it does not constitute of the subject nor flow from its essence".[174] The partes orationis were devised to express the concepts of the mind by means of 'sermo congruus', but in fact some partes are equipped to do this, whereas others are not – this difference in function is attested by the presence or absence of the accidental modes: these accidental modes can be established only when the essence of the pars in question has been completely established and stated.

There is one difference between Siger and Thomas, but one which does not seem to be very important; it is however associated with their analysis of the modus essentialis. Thomas divides his accidental modes into absolute and respective; Siger does so obviously but not so categorically. The reason is that Siger's modus essentialis generalis includes more than one pars, so that these partes can be classified as respective at this particular level, at least as far as the partes magis principales are concerned, but since the modus specificus is so highly individual, it cannot permit a relationship such as must exist between respective modes. Thomas has no modus essentialis generalis, and his modus generalissimus which is roughly equivalent to Siger's modus specificus will not be a modus respectivus for the same reason that Siger's specificus is not respectivus. As for the accidental modes, in the case of both authors, some will be respective and others will be absolute, depending entirely on their intrinsic qualities,[175] *i.e.* whether they look back into themselves and are therefore absolute, or look out from themselves, finding their real functional values in terms of their higher relationship to other accidental modes, and are therefore respective.

---

[173] Siger de Courtrai, p. 144: What Siger is implying, of course, is that these properties do not derive from 'ens' or 'esse', which, as Siger's philosophical background suggests, are the only constituents of reality.

[174] R. McKeon, *Selections from Mediaeval Philosophers*, Pt. II, p. 424.

[175] Coniugatio is, for example, a respective mode because of its manifestation of other respective modes. As the Modistae say, coniugatio in the verb is somewhat as declinatio in the noun; in this instance we can say that it reflects the various properties of tense, number, mood, and person, and it will therefore be respective (though the Modistae do not actually discuss it as an absolute or respective mode). To be absolute a mode must refer to the property of the thing only, whereas coniugatio clearly refers to and derives from the properties of the other respective modes, *cf.* pp. 240-242.

IV

THE PARTES ORATIONIS

A. THE PARTES ORATIONIS IN GENERAL

The tradition of constructing a grammar on the partes orationis of a language was very old already by the Middle Ages,[1] but the conception of the nature and function of the partes changed by the 13th Century. Prior to the 11th century, grammarians seem to have been content to reproduce and comment on Donatus and Priscian, but without any logical or metaphysical undertones or implications. The Modistae continued to follow Donatus and Priscian in the organisation of their material, but their presentation of this material often differed very widely from that of their predecessors. Various factors had contributed to a lively and extensive renewal of grammatical study, but as a result of some of these factors, the study of grammar was much influenced by logic and philosophy, and the grammarians of the 13th Century could not have escaped from this legacy: "Men now sought, as the only sound method of research, to derive and justify rules of grammar from systems of logic and metaphysical theories about the nature of reality".[2] It was this concern with the metaphysics of reality along with similarly heavy emphasis on the theories of the grammarians of antiquity which created the concentration on the partes orationis rather than on syntax but at the same time coloured the whole approach of the Modistae to these same partes orationis, or as Roos has aptly put it "die philosophisch-spekulative Durchleutung der sprachlichen Kategorien (partes orationis)".[3] Factors such as the use of the methods of logic, the philosophical theories of the the day, which were obviously unknown to their models, *i.e.* Donatus and Priscian, produced a change not only in presentation but also in terminology and orientation of subject matter.

[1] H. Roos, *Op. cit.*, p. 144: "Nun hat zwar schon die antike und mittelalterliche Grammatik die Lehre von den 'partes orationis' gekannt."
[2] R. H. Robins, *A. and M.*, p. 75.
[3] H. Roos, *Die Modi Significandi*, p. 146.

Roos has called[4] the treatises on the 'modi significandi' "Lehre der Wortklassen", which is a revealing comment on the nature of these mediaeval grammars;[5] curiously enough, Roos has also stated[6] that 'diasynthetica', *i.e.* the section on syntax, was "das Hauptziel der mittel-alterlichen Grammatik". This is a statement which it is not easy to sustain – indeed Thurot, by implication, denies this,[7] and it would seem reasonable to argue that philosophical factors have the effect of laying stress on the theory of the partes orationis rather than on syntax.[8]

In the preceding chapter we saw the line and process of development from the vox to the dictio or word, and from the word to the pars orationis; the Modistae render a word grammatical, *i.e.*, make it a pars orationis by means of its aptitude or ability to signify such and such a mode of being, since all the partes orationis must signify some aspect or quality of things existing in the world of real things: the partes orationis were in fact considered correlatives of things in the world of external reality.

The ability to signify in combination with the verbal sign, *i.e.* the expression, constitutes the essence of a pars orationis. This is funda-mental to Modistic theory; and just as a general class is distinguished by different species, so the different partes orationis will constitute the various species of this particular general principle. Similarly, just as grammar is the expression of the general essence of reality with the

---

[4] H. Roos, "Sprachdenken im Mittelalter", *Classica et Mediaevalia* VIII (1946), p. 102.

[5] It shows also a direct line back to Thrax and the conception of grammar among the Alexandrian and post-stoic grammarians, *cf.* R. H. Robins, *A, and M.*, p. 39.

[6] H. Roos, *Die Modi Significandi*, p. 140.

[7] Ch. Thurot, *Op. cit.*, p. 237: "Il est singulier qu'aucun grammairien du moyen âge ne paraisse avoir cherché à établir systématiquement et a priori une division de la syntaxe, comme on aimait à le faire à cette époque". It is difficult to reconcile this statement with an earlier remark of Thurot's, in which he quotes a 13th-century grammarian, *i.e.* "Studium gramaticorum precipue circa constructionem versatur", and continues, "Un autre considère la syntaxe comme la fin de la gram-maire, et subordonne la doctrine des lettres et des parties du discours ... à celle de la construction". It suggests to me that he was not sufficiently aware of the wealth of material at present hidden in unpublished manuscripts, but more par-ticularly that he did not appreciate the aim of the Modistae in writing their sec-tions on syntax.

[8] A cursory examination of the materials available would seem to confirm this; Siger is incomplete and has no section at all on syntax, nor, as far as I can estab-lish, did Michel de Marbais. Thomas of Erfurt and Martin of Dacia have sections on syntax but they are much shorter in length, with much less detail, than their sections on 'etymologia'. Closer acquaintance with the manuscript tradition reveals a much greater interest in matters of syntax than one might suppose from the small amount of published material.

partes as its various species,[9] so each pars orationis must be a combination of its essence which it will share with another pars orationis[10] and its specific features which differentiate it from all other partes orationis.[11] In the hands of the Modistae, grammar becomes the expression of the species and fundamental kinds found in the world of reality; a species is made up of the general type (genus) and specific difference[12] – the type being represented by a general significative function which can be found in more than one pars,[13] and it is this which has to acquire a specific determination for a pars to be created.[14] There are certain metaphysical implications here; every material element demands matter and form which constitute its essence or nature, but it acquires accidental modalities, particularly of quality and quantity. Similarly, each pars consists of its essential constituents, *i.e.* its essential modes of signifying, and similarly its accidents, or more correctly, its accidental modes of signifying. The latter is a somewhat superfluous statement, since if we are to obtain a real definition and not merely a superficial description, the essence of a pars orationis can be defined only by the type to which it belongs and its

---

[9] Michel de Marbais: "ipsae partes distinguuntur per suos modos significandi quibus in specie partis reponuntur" (quoted by Wallerand, p. 48).

[10] The nomen and pronomen share the essence of 'modus entis', the verbum and participium the 'modes esse', and the indeclinables the 'modus disponibilis'.

[11] Siger de Courtrai, p. 95: "modus significandi specificus est modus significandi qui additus modo significandi generali constituit speciem". This is one matter of organisation on which Siger and Thomas differ: we shall see that Thomas's modus generalissimus contains the same subject matter as Siger's modus generalis and specificus, but Siger's division is done deliberately to set off the similarity of the pars with other partes and the individuality of the pars in question. The difference in their presentation is seen most clearly in the indeclinable partes, when Thomas's modus generalissimus is the equivalent of Siger's modus specificus only, and Siger's modus generalis, *i.e.* modus disponibilis which he states as the unifying factor between the indeclinables, is not mentioned at all by Thomas.

[12] Siger de Courtrai, p. 95: "sicut ad constitutionem speciei concurrunt genus et differentia specifica, sic ad constitutionem partis concurrunt modus significandi generalis et specificus".

[13] The same theories are presented by Thomas but are ordered and expressed differently; he uses the modus generalissimus to state the feature that the pars shares with other partes – (this will be the *general* type), and also the features by reason of which it is distinct from all the other partes orationis; *cf.* his definition of the essential mode, #20: "modus significandi essentialis est per quem pars orationis habet simpliciter esse, vel secundum genus, vel secundum speciem".

[14] I suggest that this makes the rationale of Martin of Dacia's ordering his material in the sequence of the modus essentialis of all the partes, then the modus specialis of all the partes, etc. more understandable.

specific difference, *i.e.* by its general and specific essential modes of signifying.[15]

There are two aspects above all which the grammarian must express, *i.e.* those of stability and becoming. The partes which express the element of stability or permanence are the nomen and the pronomen, while becoming is expressed by the verbum and the participium. (One of the weaknesses of the method of the Modistae can be seen in their treatment of the indeclinable partes, which, they say, do not belong to the essence of the language but merely serve to render language more adequate[16] – they are, however, not alone in this.[17]) The specific difference serves to distinguish the nomen from the pronomen, and the verbum from the participium.[18]

The Modistae followed Donatus in their classification of the partes orationis. Martin of Dacia described first of all the essential modes of all eight partes, then their special modes (and in the case of Martin 'specialis' must be considered the equivalent of Thomas's 'subalternus' and 'specialissimus'), and then the *six* accidental modes.[19] After this detailed review of the partes orationis, the grammarian would then examine them in terms of their syntax.[20] This would not seem to be absolutely true of all the Modistae; Thomas varies slightly from Martin, whereas Siger is in many ways quite different from both Thomas and Martin, *e.g.* he describes each pars orationis in terms of the equal subdivisions of its essential mode before proceeding to the accidental modes, which he certainly does not restrict to six.

The nomen and pronomen signify substance, *i.e.*, concreteness, *i.e.*, presence in the physical world and the permanence of things; this they have in common and this thus constitutes their general feature. Their specific difference represents a qualitative determination, because it is

[15] This is in contrast to the methods of antiquity where the different partes orationis were definable, *in part*, by the 'accidents' applicable to them; for this reason, it must be realised that accident and accidental mode are not by any means the same thing.

[16] Siger de Courtrai, p. 144: "non sunt de esse orationis sed de bene esse". *Cf.* also G. Wallerand, *Op. cit.*, pp. (49), (55).

[17] *Cf.* L. Tesnière, *Esquisse d'une grammaire structurale*, p. 7.

[18] Reference was made in the previous chapter to the idea of an 'archipars' implicit in Siger's modus generalis, and the modus specificus serves to differentiate members of the same 'archipars'.

[19] Martin uses six accidental modes of the nomen and verbum, in contrast to Thomas, who uses six for the nomen but eight for the verbum, and Siger uses nine for the nomen and eight for the verb.

[20] Thomas of Erfurt, #184: "principium efficiens constructionis et aliarum passionum sermonis".

quality or form which distinguishes one thing from another – in the case of the Nomen it is the ability to designate precisely and distinctively, whereas the Pronomen does not possess this, and does not represent any stable element, in the same way that prime matter is only the potential subject of any form. Siger has likened the function of the pronomen in grammar to that of prime matter in substance.[21]

The Nomen has as its meaning function the mode of the static, rest and determinate understanding which it expresses by means of the mode of being (modus entis) in contrast to the Verbum which signifies by means of the mode of becoming (modus esse).[22] The nomen, therefore, expresses a static state to the exclusion of all time connection which is a characteristic of the Verbum. The contrast between the Nomen and Pronomen is not one of time or becoming, but one of determinate understanding (modus apprehensionis determinatae).

The Pronomen signifies by means of the mode of state and inaction, as is the case with the Nomen, but also by means of indeterminate understanding which differentiates them. "Das Pronomen weist auf einem Gegenstand als Gegenstand hin . . . (dieser Gegenstand ist) nicht inhaltlich bestimmt . . . . als dieser und kein anderer. Die Bedeutungs-funktion des Pronomens kann daher mit Recht unbestimmt, besser nicht bestimmend genannt werden".[23]

The verb and participle express the features of becoming; Siger tells us[24] that the universal order of things requires, in any mass, the presence of an element from which all direction is derived and towards which everything converges. A similar state of affairs exists in grammar[25] in which several partes orationis seem to have to be governed by the verbum which, however, is not governed[26] by any other pars. This is a general

---

[21] Siger de Courtrai, p. 125: "pronomen substantiam solum non etiam qualitatem significat, ita quod consimili modo imaginandum in pronomine sicut in materia prima".
[22] Thomas of Erfurt, #25: "modus esse est modus fluxus, et successionis, rei inhaerens ex hoc quod habet fieri".
[23] M. Heidegger, *Die Kategorien und Bedeutungs-lehre des Duns Scotus* (1916), p. 199.
[24] Siger de Courtrai, p. 139: "in genere entium est devenire ad aliquod primum dignissimum et nobilissimum quod omnia entia regit . . . in omni multitudine aliquod unum regimen invenitur".
[25] Siger de Courtrai, pp. 139-140: "regimen in entibus grammaticalibus debet sumi ad similitudinem regiminis veri . . . ad similitudinem huius sumitur regimen inter partes orationis, ita quod est devenire ad aliquam partem orationis dignissi-mam respectu talis multitudinis, quia multitudinem et orationem complet, quae proprie regit omnes alias partes et a nulla alia regitur, videlicet verbum".
[26] 'Governed' is used here in the traditional sense of the term, *i.e.* the influence

feature common to the Verbum and Participium, *i.e.* the mode of signifying which embraces movement and becoming. Everything which is permanent derives from the substance, while everything which changes derives from an action or passion, from some movement. This becoming can be expressed in so far as it can be attributed to a subject – this is their special feature and serves to differentiate the Verbum and Participium, for the Verbum separates the action from the subject which produces it, while the Participium signifies the action in so far as it is joined to the subject,[27] what Siger called a mixture of action and potentiality.[28]

The Verbum thus signifies by means of the mode of becoming (modus esse et fieri),[29] and of separation from the substance (modus distantis a substantia). Whereas the Nomen represents an essentially static element, the mode of becoming is a dynamic element with time as the characteristic of the Verbum, *i.e.* Zeitwort! This mode of becoming is not sufficient, however, to differentiate the verbum from all the other partes orationis, since this feature, this general mode, is shared by the Participium; the feature which differentiates the verbum from all other grammatical word-classes is the mode of separation (modus distantis.)

The Participium signifies by means of the general mode of becoming which it shares with the verbum and also by means of the special mode of non-separation from the substance (modus indistantis a substantia). "Beim Partizipium ruht der Akzent seiner Bedeutung nicht so sehr auf der Zugehörigkeit des Sachverhaltes zum Gegenstand, als vielmehr auf dem Gegenstand vereinigt gedachten Sachverhalt."[30]

The accidental modes of these four declinable partes orationis follow and express variations of the essence of each pars orationis, some of which are derived from the form and others from the matter; this has an important influence on their syntactic function, inasmuch as some of these accidental modes will be absolute (and therefore non-syntactic) and some will be respective and therefore constructible with other partes orationis.[31]

---

of one word over another in determining the case of a noun or pronoun or the mood of a verb, in contrast to the much narrower use of the term current among some linguists today, *e.g.* C. F. Hockett, *A Course in Modern Linguistics*, p. 216.
27 G. Wallerand, *Op. cit.*, p. 52.
28 Siger de Courtrai, p. 123: "de actu permixto potentiae".
29 *Cf.* fn. 22.
30 M. Heidegger, *Op. cit.*, p. 219.
31 Siger de Courtrai, p. 131: "modi significandi absoluti dicuntur qui non conce-

In Siger's scheme, all the indeclinable partes have the same general mode in common, that of signifying the disposition of the 'ens' or the act (per modum disponentis), and are differentiated by the special mode (modus specialis), which is very similar in effect to Thomas's essential mode. The Adverbium marks a special determination which qualifies principally the act, and which therefore brings the Adverbium close to the Verbum. The Coniunctio derives its raison d'être from the fact that certain beings are unifiable; the Modistae distinguished between two types of coniunctio, *i.e.* coniunctio per vim and coniunctio per ordinem, the former acting as the link between two unifiable groups which do not require a particular link, and the latter serves to join up two groups which do require a particular link. The Praepositio is used to signify the relationships between certain properties, *i.e.* the cases, of the substantive element and the act, *i.e.* the verb to which they are linked; they may indicate an action in process or the limit of the action but this fact of linking substance to the action introduces higher correlative structures than those merely of stability or becoming. The Interiectio is used to signify various states of mind as apprehended by the intellect; it is close to the Verbum, since such emotional states will be caused by the feature of movement or as Heidegger says: [32] "Die Interjektion hat eine Beziehung zu den emotionalen Erlebnissen, sie determiniert nicht den Bedeutungsgehalt der Verba als solchen (wie die Adverbia); ihre determinierende Funktion geht auf die Beziehung der verbalen Bedeutungsakte zum Bewusstsein."

Wallerand argues[33] that the indeclinable partes cannot possess those properties which can be found in the declinable partes, and refers to Aristotle for authority, that a more noble and more perfect form implies more elevated and more numerous operations – the vegetable aspires

---

duntur dictioni in comparatione ad modum significandi alterius dictionis sed magis ut vox mediantibus illis designet talem modum essendi circa rem. Isti modi significandi non sunt principium constructionis quia non sunt principium unionis dictionis cum dictione". Thomas of Erfurt, #22: "modus significandi accidentalis absolutus dicitur ille, per quem unum constructibile non habet respectum ad alterum, sed solum ad rei proprietatem". Siger de Courtrai, p. 131: "modi significandi respectivi dicuntur qui conceduntur dictioni in comparatione ad modum significandi alterius dictionis eis proportionalem et tales sunt principium constructionis quia sunt principium unionis constructibilis cum constructibile". Thomas of Erfurt, #22: "modus significandi accidentalis respectivus est, per quem unum constructibile habet respectum non solum ad rei proprietatem, sed etiam per quem unum constructibile habet respectum ad alterum".

[32]   M. Heidegger, *Op. cit.*, p. 226.
[33]   G. Wallerand, *Op. cit.*, p. 55.

only to vegetative operations, the animal adds sensory acts, but man can reach up to higher intellectual operations. So it is with the partes orationis; the indeclinable partes can have only rudimentary modalities because the embrace of their meaning is inferior to that of the declinable partes. It is, of course, foolhardy to base any grammatical statement on such criteria, and would be totally unacceptable to modern thinking. However, granted all the limitations of a grammatical statement based on theories of meaning and despite the criticisms which can be made of his theory, it is reasonable to maintain that, of all the Modistae, Siger came closest to constructing a satisfactory grammatical statement by means of his modus entis, modus esse and modus disponentis;[34] at least this is based in part on syntactic criteria rather than on vague notions of higher and lower meaning.[35]

Wallerand also tells us[36] that the Modistae did not agree on the order or sequence of the partes orationis; for Siger, this order is essential,[37] since one pars either presupposes another or else is engendered from another pars, which explains, of course, the close links in his system between the Nomen and Pronomen, and the Verbum and Participium. Michel de Marbais, according to Wallerand,[38] maintained the rigorous independence of the partes orationis in the same way that one finds a similar independence between the various species of the world of reality. Thomas of Erfurt and Martin of Dacia follow a similar order, which, however, differs slightly from Siger's; this suggests that they too were not concerned about the inter-relationship of the partes, especially the declinable partes.

Thomas's division of 'Etymologia' and 'Diasynthetica' has been followed in presenting the theory of the partes orationis, *i.e.* a description of the partes orationis and then a description of syntactic theory,

---

[34] These are the characteristic features of the three 'archipartes'.
[35] *Cf.* Bloomfield's statement about the word-classes in Tagelog, L. Bloomfield, *Language*, p. 200.
[36] G. Wallerand, *Op. cit.*, p. 55.
[37] Siger de Courtrai, p. 108: "verbum sequitur immediate ipsum nomen, quia proprium sequitur immediate illud cuius est proprium, ut apparet in verbis. Nunc esse est proprius actus ipsius entis; cum nomen significat rem suam per modum substantiae seu entis, et verbum per modum significandi fieri, seu esse verbum immediate debet sequi ipsum nomen". Siger de Courtrai, p. 123: "participium sequitur immediate nomen et verbum quia solum ab eis partem capit". Siger's order of presentation is: nomen, verbum, participium, pronomen, adverbium, coniunctio, praeposito, interiectio; in contrast, Thomas's presentation follows this order: nomen, pronomen, verbum, adverbium, participium, coniunctio, praepositio, interiectio.
[38] G. Wallerand, *Op. cit.*, p. 55.

but Siger's division of the partes into declinable and indeclinable and also his sequence of the partes have been maintained in describing the individual partes.[39]

B. ETYMOLOGIA

Prior to the 13th Century and also in the early 13th Century, grammars were as a rule divided into four parts,[40] *i.e.* Orthographia, the science of letters and syllables, Etymologia, the science of the word and its meaning, Diasynthetica, the science of the sentence and its constructions, and Prosodia, the science of pronunciation.

By the 13th Century 'Etymologia' had come to mean everything that was relative to the declensions and conjugations of the different partes orationis and the formation of words. Thurot quotes[41] John of Genoa, *e.g.* "Sub ista (ethimologia) comprehenduntur octo partes orationis et earum accidentia"; Thurot added that the study of their meaning was not excluded.[42] In other words, the innovations brought by the Modistae to grammatical tradition refer principally to the definitions of the partes orationis and their accidents, and much less to the origin of their meanings.

[39]   Nomen, Verbum, Participium, Pronomen, Adverbium, Coniunctio, Praepositio, and Interiectio.

[40]   H. Roos, *Die Modi Significandi*, p. 138: "Die so definierte Wissenschaft der Grammatik teilte man im Mittelalter im Anschluss an die 'Institutiones' des Priscian in vier Teile ein". Roos quotes an extract from Peter Helias also quoted by Thurot, p. 132: "partes huius artis sunt quatuor: quarum nomina quoniam non habemus, dicatur prima pars scientia de litteris, secunda de sillabis, tertia de dictionibus, quarta de oratione".

Priscian and Donatus did not have this division: in Donatus, we find only 'vox, littera, syllaba' which really can be considered in this connection and these only in his larger *Ars Grammatica*. Priscian included 'vox, littera' in Book I and 'syllaba, dictio, oratio' in Book II.

Roos states that there seems to have been a tendency to reduce this to three parts, *i.e.* orthographia, prosodia and dyasynthetica and quotes an extract from the "Graecismus" also quoted by Thurot, p. 132: "Ortho. proso. dyasin. species tres grammatice sunt" – *i.e.* the sillaba, littera and dictio have all been included in the category of 'orthographia'. This tripartite division does not seem to have been general, and by the early 13th Century, the names of orthographia, ethimologia, dyasinthetica and prosodia were still in use. Thurot, pp. 146 and 212 explains the variant forms of ethimologia and dyasinthetica.

[41]   Ch. Thurot, *Op. cit.*, p. 147, fn. 1.

[42]   Ch. Thurot, *Op. cit.*, p. 147: "Au 13e siècle l'ethimologia comprend tout ce qui est relatif aux déclinaisons, aux conjugaisons et à la formation des mots ... mais n'exclut pas l'étude de leur signification".

The Modistae used two of the traditional divisions of grammar,[43] *i.e.* etymologia and diasynthetica.[44] They presented their material according to the following pattern: (i) the modus significandi essentialis of each pars orationis, (ii) the modus significandi specialis[45] and (iii) the modus significandi accidentalis of the various partes orationis. This general procedure of modus significandi essentialis, specialis, and accidentalis is in Martin and Thomas to a considerable extent the same, but Thomas, in contrast to Martin,[46] describes and analyses each pars orationis in turn, beginning with the modus essentialis and proceding via the modus subalternus and modus specialissimus to the modus accidentalis, whereas Siger and Michel de Marbais deal with each pars separately, and describe each pars in terms of the two equal subdivisions of the modus essentialis, i.e. generalis and specialis or specificus, before dealing with the modus accidentalis.

C. THE DECLINABLE PARTES ORATIONIS (47)

The Modistae stated quite categorically that the indeclinable partes had fewer modes of signifying (which is the Modistic way of saying that they

---

[43] H. Roos (*Die Modi Significandi*, pp. 139-140) argues that the Modistic division of 'etymologia' and 'diasynthetica' became the model for the division of morphology and syntax which has characterised grammatical description of the normative type down to the present.

[44] Siger does not use these terms at all and the incompleteness of his treatise makes it impossible to say with any certainty that he would have made use of such a division. At the end of his section on the nomen, there is a suggestion that he had in mind a separate section on syntax, but on the other hand his use of the theory of 'principium constructionis' suggests an even greater interpenetration of these two levels than would seem likely if he had followed the more traditional pattern of Thomas's or Martin's method, though there is a very great degree of interpenetration in Thomas's syntactic theory.

[45] The use of 'specialis' in Martin's descriptive scheme is not the same as Siger's use of 'specialis', since Siger's specialis is an equal member along with 'generalis' of the essential mode; Martin's modus specialis is much closer to Thomas's modus subalternus and specialissimus.

[46] Martin in fact describes the essential modes of an eight partes orationis and then their special and accidental modes. That part of his work dealing with the partes orationis can in a sense be divided into five sections of unequal length, *i.e.* (i) a short section on the nature of the essential mode as such, (ii) the essential modes of the partes orationis, (iii) a section on the special modes which Martin calls 'mediati' and 'immediati' which are derived from the essential modes, (iv) the special modes of the partes orationis, and (v) the accidental modes which he calls "posteriores" in contrast to the "priores" which are the essential modes. These technical terms are not without important implications in view of the progressions they represent.

[47] Appendix C sets out in diagram form the partes orationis, the essence they

had fewer formal features) than the declinable partes, since the meaning of such indeclinable partes rested on fewer properties or modes of being than the declinable partes.[48]

Siger made more of this than the other Modistae seem to have done, and divided the eight partes into two groups, which he called 'magis principales'[49] and ' minus principales'.[50] This further subdivision has been used in the description of the partes orationis, so that we find grouped together, (i) those partes magis principales, *i.e.* the declinable partes which in fact share the features of 'ens' and of 'esse' and (ii) those partes minus principales, *i.e.* the indeclinable partes, which do not possess 'ens' or 'esse' and which do not really 'belong' in any essential form but render the sentence more adequate as an expression of 'oratio congrua'.

D. THE INDECLINABLE PARTES ORATIONIS

Prior to the Modistae, mediaeval grammarians had little new to add to the definitions of the indeclinable partes orationis, and they, including Peter Helias, had been content to follow Priscian and Donatus. The Modistae too followed their predecessors, but did however make certain innovations in their general treatment of the indeclinable partes and their position in the grammatical hierarchy, and also in their definitions of some of the individual indeclinable partes.

One of the most serious flaws in the grammatical theories of Greece and Rome and also in the Middle Ages was the treatment of the indeclinable partes orationis; during this period in the history of grammar the indeclinables created a greater problem in grammatical description than their position in the hierarchy seemed to warrant, with the result that they were always considered as inferior members of the word-

---

share, and the quality of the essence by which they are distinguished; this Appendix also contains in more detailed diagrams the declinable and indeclinable partes, and also the modus entis and its sub-modes as they are used in the nomen and pronomen.

[48] Thomas of Erfurt, #183: "partes indeclinabiles, non tot modos significandi habent, quot partes declinabiles, quia significatum partium indeclinabilium paucis subsistit proprietatibus, sed significatio partium declinabilium multis: ideo pauciores sunt modi significandi partibus in declinabilibus, quam declinabilibus".

[49] Siger de Courtrai, p. 144: "partes quae significant per modum entis et esse sunt principales magis et declinabiles".

[50] Siger de Courtrai, p. 144: "aliae partes orationis sunt minus principalis quia modi significandi ipsarum sumuntur a proprietatibus minus principalibus, et sunt indeclinabiles quia carent illis accidentibus penes quae attenditur declinatio".

classes used in grammatical description. Such an attitude is, of course, inevitable in any system of grammatical description which relies entirely for its criteria on semantic or metaphysical factors, and one can almost imagine the dilemma that the Modistae must have found themselves in, *i.e.,* having defined the declinable partes in terms of 'ens' or 'esse' which are very closely related, how could they define the indeclinable partes in similar terms? What is the substance (substantia) or the becoming (fieri)[51] represented by these indeclinable partes? It becomes therefore inevitable that the Modistae, like their classical predecessors, should have to resort to other means in order to define the indeclinable partes; it will be remembered that Aristotle had dismissed them from the category of word,[52] and the Modistae, in particular Siger, dismissed them also as not belonging to language.[53]

Lest we should condemn our classical and mediaeval forbears too harshly, it must also be pointed out that a similar treatment of the indeclinables can be found among modern grammarians,[54] who have classified them by means of non-linguistic criteria, and have come to a similar conclusion, which is manifestly improper, since it is impossible to disregard a large proportion of the lexicon of a language simply because it does not fit into categories established according to a priori and nonlinguistic principles.[55]

The very existence of the indeclinable partes, requiring grammatical explanation, stresses the necessity for formal, intralinguistic explanation, since logical, metaphysical and philosophical means are manifestly incapable of explaining their presence and function in grammar.[56]

Why should they, in fact, present any problem at all? An explanation would seem to be connected with Aristotle's argument about the hierarchy of perfection which implies a commensurate hierarchy of oper-

[51] *Cf.* n. 22.
[52] R. H. Robins, *A. and M.,* p. 85: "One Modista ..., finding these uninflected parts of speech to fall outside the philosophical theory of language as it was then conceived, declared that such words 'did not belong to language as such', and were mere auxiliaries. This reminds us of Aristotle's similar rejection of 'syndesmoi' or 'grammatical words' as not words in the proper sense; and Aristotle was a thinker who ... approached grammar from philosophical or logical assumptions".
[53] Siger de Courtrai, p. 144: "sunt magis de bene esse orationis quam de esse".
[54] *Cf.* H. Sweet, L. Tesnière, *et al.*
[55] R. H. Robins, *A. and M.,* p. 86: "to say that such words are outside language is to ignore one of the most important parts of the structure of language, and to neglect just those words that are the prime concern of the grammarian".
[56] R. H. Robins, *A. and M.,* p. 86: "This should reinforce the principle that grammatical science must as far as possible be based on intra-linguistic or formal methods of analysis and statement".

ation, *i.e.* the greater the perfection, the higher the operation, and a similar hierarchy was thus imposed on the partes orationis;[57] the combination of Aristotelean theory and mediaeval metaphysics resulted in the creation of a hierarchy of properties for the partes orationis, and hence the indeclinable partes, by their very nature, cannot possess the same area of meaning or the same number of modes of meaning as the declinable partes because they derive from fewer properties than do the declinable partes.[58]

In order to appreciate the problem that the Modistae faced – (though it was entirely of their own creation by basing their grammatical classification on metaphysical criteria) – in setting up the indeclinable partes, we have to consider their whole conception of the 'word' in the form of partes orationis, which, in turn, are closely associated to the metaphysics of substance, matter, and form.

A mode of signifying is the means of expressing a mental concept, and a pars orationis had its status by means of the modes of signifying. The mental concept derives its importance from the importance of the object under consideration, *i.e.* from the properties of the thing itself, and as a consequence, the relative importance of the modes of signifying derives from the relative importance of the things they are used to express or signify. What suggests itself to one's mind first and foremost is 'ens' and its properties, and by extension 'esse' and its properties;[59] ens and esse must, however, be interpreted in the largest sense of the word as representative of the properties of the external world, *i.e.* as made up of things that are and which must be therefore they can act. This is closely connected with and derives from the moderate realism of the

---

[57] G. Wallerand, *Op. cit.*, p. 55: "D'après Aristote et son commentateur par excellence, une forme plus noble, d'une perfection plus grande, implique des opérations plus élévées et plus nombreuses ... Il en est de même dans les parties du discours. Les syncategoreumata ne peuvent avoir que des modalités rudimentaires parce que l'amplitude de leur signification est notablement inférieure à celle des parties déclinables".

[58] Thomas of Erfurt, #183: "Interiectiones et aliae partes indeclinabiles, non tot modos significandi habent, quot partes declinabiles, quia significatum partium indeclinabilium paucis subsistit proprietatibus, sed significatio partium declinabilium multis; ideo pauciores sunt modi significandi partibus indeclinabilibus quam declinabilibus".

[59] Siger de Courtrai, p. 144: "illud quod principaliter et primo occurrit intellectui nostro est ipsum ens et proprietates eius ... videlicet proprietates entis ut est ens et quiescens, magis extendendo ens ad esse genus entis sive in anima sive extra animam et proprietates ipsius esse et motus magis extendendo ipsum esse ad ipsum modum motus, sive proprie sive improprie dicti, propter quod modi significandi sumpti ab iis proprietatibus sunt magis principales et per consequens partes orationis constitutae per istos modos significandi sunt magis principales".

Modistae; moderate realism held that the universal has no existence apart from the individual things in which it is realised,[60] but the mind has the ability to abstract the universal from the individual in which it is realised, and it is thus possible to consider the universals apart from the individual sensible things in which they are realised; this means that the more 'real' a concept is, *i.e.* the more 'substantial' the object to which it refers is, the greater its importance and therefore the more important is the mode of signifying which is used to signify it. The result is that the modes of signifying that derive from them are more important and the partes orationis that exhibit them are similarly more important than the other partes which derive from modes of signifying which do not signify any essence which can be recognised as an 'ens' or its 'esse'; hence the pre-eminence that the declinable partes which do express 'ens' and 'esse' enjoy and as a result constitute the principal partes orationis, while the indeclinable partes, since they do not express ens or esse, derive from fewer and less important properties[61] and since they can hardly be said to derive from or to constitute any aspect of reality, they cannot possess those accidents which characterise the declinable partes and without which they cannot be declined.

It is to the great credit of the Modistae that they attempted to make much more of the indeclinables than their predecessors had done. They did this in at least two ways – by disagreeing with and restating, for instance, the definition of the preposition, but more particularly by the greater prominence they gave to the indeclinable partes as such. Thrax has been criticised for not making more of the binary opposition between the declinables and indeclinables;[62] it would not only be unjust but incorrect to accuse the Modistae, especially Siger, of similarly ignoring this distinction, because Siger particularly does make much of the contrast, and in his Sophisma "O Magister" in which he deals with the indeclinables, he discusses at some length the difference between them and the declinable partes. Thomas is perhaps less detailed in his discussion of this aspect of the declinable-indeclinable opposition, but he is much less concerned with the theory of the indeclinables[63] and dwells

---

[60] S. J. Curtis, *A Short History of Western Philosophy in the Middle Ages*, pp. 49-50.

[61] Siger de Courtrai, p. 144: "aliae partes orationis sunt minus principales quia modi significandi ipsarum sumuntur a proprietatibus minus principalibus". Martin of Dacia, #144: "plures et magis diversae sunt proprietates nominis et verbi et aliarum partium declinabilium quam adverbii et aliarum partium indeclinabilium".

[62] R. H. Robins, *Thrax*, p. 96 (n. 3).

[63] Thomas has much less to say about the indeclinable partes than Siger; indeed, all that Thomas has to say about the indeclinables as a group can be found at the

at greater length on the actual indeclinable partes of the Latin language and their various modes of signifying. Both of them, however, clearly suggest to us today, though obviously not using this terminology, a binary opposition between declinable and indeclinable partes orationis.

The Modistae then make a definite distinction between the declinables and indeclinables, and, as is to be expected, give the primacy to the declinables;[64] this is inevitable in terms of their analytical procedure. The declinables were kept discrete from the indeclinables on the grounds that the declinable partes derive from many more properties than the metaphysical factors which lie behind the establishment of the declinable partes, which Siger classified as 'magis principales'. There is no need to dwell at this stage on the metaphysical factors which lie behind the establishment of the declinable partes, except to say that they are derived by virtue of the fact that they signify ens or esse, and it is difficult to imagine what metaphysical essence could be expressed by the indeclinable partes. By a curious quirk, therefore, the Modistae were compelled to describe the indeclinable partes, rather than exclude them (which a metaphysician might well have done), in much more formal terms.[65] This problem of the indeclinables often left the Modistae in something of a cleft stick because, for instance, we find Siger at one stage saying something very reminiscent of Aristotle and tantamount to a denial of their grammatical status,[66] and then at another stage insisting that the indeclinable partes must be described in terms of a general and specific essential mode, just like the declinable partes, for the very reason that they are partes orationis,[67] albeit 'minus principales'. Little, however, will be achieved at this stage by dwelling on the inadequacies of the Modistae, and it becomes possible to say that

---

end of the section 'Etymologia', *i.e.* the section in which he describes the partes orationis. All that Thomas has to say about the indeclinables is that they have fewer modes of signifying than the declinable partes because their meanings subsist on fewer properties than the meanings of the declinable partes: *cf.* Thomas of Erfurt, #183: "significatum partium indeclinabilium paucis subsistit proprietatibus, sed significatio partium declinabilium multis: ideo pauciores sunt modi significandi partibus indeclinabilibus".

[64]   *Cf.* fn. 59.

[65]   Siger de Courtrai, p. 153: "partes indeclinabiles trahunt sua significata ab adiunctis, dicendum quod habent significata et modos significandi secundum se licet varientur secundum adiuncta, quod convenit, quia omnes per modum disponentis significant et dispositio variatur secundum variationem disponibilis".

[66]   Siger de Courtrai, p. 144: "sunt magis de bene esse orationis quam de esse".

[67]   Siger de Courtrai, p. 145: "omnes partes tam declinabiles quam indeclinabiles debent habere duos modos significandi essentiales, integrantes essentiam speciei illius partis".

by combining Siger and Thomas we can produce a fairly definitive idea of the Modistic conception of the indeclinables as a group and of the partes which make up this group.

The Modistae were agreed on the 'inferior' status of the indeclinable partes, but did not agree on the methods of describing them;[68] Michel explicitly and Thomas implicitly argue that these partes have only one essential mode of signifying[69] which constitutes in fact its specific difference, which Siger emphatically denies.[70]

A slight digression becomes necessary at this point in order to understand this: Michel de Marbais divides his essential mode into two, like Siger's dual modes of general and specific, and Thomas divided his modus generalissimus at least in the declinable partes, into a dual statement, which combines a definition of the pars in question and a statement about the essence it shares with another declinable pars.[71] The declinable partes share either 'ens' or 'esse' which is incorporated into Thomas's first statement, but since the indeclinable have no 'ens' or 'esse' to share, there becomes no need for a first statement, which will account for Michel's statement and Thomas's organisation. This, as has already been stated, is denied by Siger, and this represents one of his most important achievements; he has admitted that the indeclinables do not have the same grammatical status as the declinable partes, but they are partes orationis and therefore they must have the two essential modes just like the other partes.[72] He cannot introduce metaphysical criteria, and so he makes a general statement, which is in fact much more grammatical, *i.e.* much nearer to modern grammar than the statements made about the general essential modes of the declinable partes, *i.e.* that the indeclinable partes signify by means of the modus dis-

---

[68] Martin does not appear to have made a great deal of the relative status of the declinables and indeclinables except to state the declinables have more and varied properties than the indeclinables. Martin does, however, describe distinctive essential modes for all four indeclinable partes orationis and also sets up 'posterior' modes (modi posteriores) for these indeclinable partes orationis.

[69] Michel de Marbais: "cuilibet parti indeclinabili inest unus solus modus significandi essentialis, qui est sicut differentia specifica" (Thurot, p. 188).

[70] Siger de Courtrai, p. 143: "ad essentiam alicuius speciei consideratae a logico non sufficit natura generis, immo requiritur natura speciei, ergo similiter ad essentiam speciei grammaticalis non sufficit modus significandi generalis, immo requiritur specificus".

[71] *E.g.* Thomas's modus generalissimus of the nomen, *i.e.* per modum entis which it shares with the pronomen and determinatae apprehensionis which separates it from the pronomen.

[72] Siger de Courtrai, p. 145: "omnes partes indeclinabiles habent duos modos significandi essentiales quorum unus est generalis, alter specificus, sicut inducendo patebit secundum similitudinem quam in nomine reperimus".

ponentis, *i.e.* by means of their general syntactic relationship with other words; this is the general essential mode which all the indeclinable partes share. We have had reason to refer to the idea of 'archipars'[73] in his description of the indeclinable partes; it would seem then that the partes orationis can be classified, according to Siger's analysis, into a tertiary opposition consisting of two marked archipartes and one unmarked, *i.e.* we have two archipartes marked by 'ens' or 'esse' and the third unmarked in the sense that it possesses neither 'ens' nor 'esse'. Siger then describes the indeclinable partes, in terms of their specific modes which, as in the declinable partes, constitute their specific differences and render each one discrete from all the other partes; we shall see that in these specific modes Siger is very close to Thomas in his definition of the individual indeclinable partes.[74]

Siger's modus generalis is of great importance to him in that he recognises that certain features belonging to one species may well be found in another species, such as animal and man;[75] the general mode is used by Siger to express this overlap, and so far as the indeclinable partes are concerned, the overlap consists in the recognition that they have their raison d'être only by reason of their syntactical functions. Similarly, Siger sets up his specific mode, since he recognises that a species possesses a feature or features which distinguish it from all the others, *e.g.* rationality in man,[76] and so in the indeclinable partes, each pars is discrete from the others by reason of a syntactic function which is different from the others.

There is another possible explanation for Thomas's change in analytical procedure; in the declinable partes, his modus generalissimus was made up of two statements, which constituted the contrast of the matter and form, and which created the contrast between the declinable partes, *i.e.* the nomen and pronomen possess the same matter, but they differ in that the nomen possesses a discrete form while the pronomen is merely informable. Such a 'substantial' approach to the indeclinable

---

[73] *Cf.* p. 171-172.
[74] *E.g.* praepositio: Siger de Courtrai, p. 151: "modus specificus est modus significandi per modum retorquentis casuale ad actum". Thomas of Erfurt, #176: "modus significandi essentialis generalissimus praepositionis est modus significandi per modum adiacentis alteri casuali ipsum contrahens, et ad actum retorquens".
[75] Siger de Courtrai, p. 145: "sicut in diffinitione alicuius speciei consideratae a logico semper ponitur aliquid quod habet rationem generis in alia specie reperitur, sicut animal in diffinitione hominis".
[76] Siger de Courtrai, p. 145: "ideo ponitur aliquid quod habet rationem specificae differentiae quod speciem constituit et illam ab aliis distinguit, sicut rationale in diffinitione hominis".

partes is clearly impossible; it is as though Thomas recognised that this was impossible, and has therefore had recourse to the more traditional syntactic method of analysis.

We find therefore, that in this case, Thomas's modus generalissimus is to all intents and purposes identical to Siger's modus specificus, and Siger's modus generalis is used, since he did not make much use of the matter/form contrast, to make a general statement about the similar grammatical function of the indeclinable partes; this acts almost as a justification for their inclusion in his grammatical inventory. Such a justification may well have been forced upon him in view of the argument put forward by the Modistae that the meaning of the indeclinable partes, without the addition of the principal or declinable partes, is confused since they do not indicate any definite concept of the mind, but such confusion and indefiniteness disappears when in conjunction with the other declinable partes.[77]

It would be quite wrong, however, as Michel points out,[78] to imagine that the indeclinable partes signify nothing without the addition of the declinable partes, for, as Michel says,[79] some partes do not acquire their meaning from their adjuncts but possess their meaning before any construction is imposed upon them. This is a very important statement, for it is attributing to the indeclinable partes a much more vital position in linguistic hierarchy than had previously been given to them: what Michel is implying, is that if we interpret, as indeed we must, the modes of signifying to be mainly the semanticisation of the grammatical categories, we must accordingly treat the indeclinable partes and analyse them in a similar manner to the analysis of the declinable partes, since the indeclinables too will therefore have their modes of signifying, and that we cannot merely discard them as grammatical words. Regardless of any criticism which may be made of a system of grammatical analysis which uses meaning as its principal criterion, it must be appreciated that attaching a separate meaning to an indeclinable pars

---

[77] Michel de Marbais: "ipse per se sumpte significatum habent confusum sine partium aliarum adiunctione, ita quod non significant aliquem mentis conceptum certum sive finitum. Cum partibus declinabilibus aliquod significatum finitum significantibus adiunguntur, earum confusum significatum finitatur, ita quod ipsarum incertitudo vel confusio ab eis iam removetur" (quoted by Thurot, p. 188).
[78] Michel de Marbais: "plurimum peccant nostri gramatici dicentes quod ipse partes indeclinabiles per se sumpte nihil significant sine adiunctione declinabilium" (quoted by Thurot, p. 188).
[79] Michel de Marbais: "non enim alique partes suum significatum recipiunt ex adiunctis, sed ipsum habent ante omnem constructionem voluntate impositoris" (quoted by Thurot, p. 188).

considerably enhances its position among the partes orationis.

We find then that the loss of the matter/form contrast compelled the Modistae to resort to formal criteria in their description of the indeclinables, and since their morpho-semantics is equally impossible, the Modistae used formal syntactic criteria to establish their indeclinable partes. This was also necessary since the partes orationis were conceived for the expression of mental concepts by means of 'sermo congruus', and even if the indeclinable partes may not belong to language as such, they are nevertheless often required in order to make the expression of a concept possible;[80] the indeclinables are used, therefore, to render language more adequate,[81] and to do this they receive a vague signification, *i.e.* that of signifying by means of the modus disponentis, *i.e.* they are less easy to gloss in a dictionary.

---

[80] Siger de Courtrai, p. 145: "multi sunt conceptus qui nullo modo exprimerentur per sermonem congruum nisi essent partes indeclinabiles".

[81] G. Wallerand, *Op. Cit.*, p. 49: "Quant aux parties indéclinables, elles ne sont pas de l'essence du langage, elles ne servent qu'à rendre celui-ci plus adéquat: 'non sunt de esse orationis, sed de bene esse'; elles reçoivent une signification vague que les grammairiens appellent: 'per modum disponentis alterum'."

V

THE DECLINABLE PARTES ORATIONIS

A. NOMEN

Priscian and Donatus, in their definitions of the nomen, had insisted on the features of substance and quality along with case as the vital attributes of the nomen. The 12th Century had continued to accept Priscian's definition that the characteristic sign of the nomen was to signify substance and quality,[1] a definition which Peter Helias was content to repeat; 12th century grammarians, however, interpreted substantia as denoting an individual thing and qualitas as the universal nature in which it participates. The mediaeval grammarian interpreted "grammatical subject" as that which talk is about (id de quo sermo fit) which is par excellence an individual thing (or things), so that substantia and id de quo sermo fit will be the same, e.g. one anonymous 12th century commentator on Priscian identified the grammarian's use of substantia with the subject-matter of a discussion (id de quo sermo habetur); this is stated more precisely in another 12th century Priscian commentary which equates signifying "substance and quality" to signifying "that which underlies the verbal expression".

In the 13th Century, the grammarians felt the need to clarify and mark the opposition between the modes of signifying of the nomen and verbum, since there tended to be some confusion between the application of the terms 'substance' and 'existence' which had arisen as a result of Priscian's use of the term 'verbum substantivum'. As a result, the idea of permanence and repose was substituted for substance, and determined understanding (apprehensio determinata) for quality; similarly the idea of change and becoming (fieri) replaced action and passion as the characteristic feature of the verbum.

The Modistae came to accept, by and large, the 'permanent' con-

---

[1] Priscian (II.18): "Proprium est nominis substantiam et qualitatem significare." Cf. de Rijk, Op. cit. II, pp. 521-528. I am very much indebted to Professor de Rijk for drawing my attention to this important discussion of the nomen.

ception of the nomen in place of the traditional 'substantial' one as its definition; indeed they were almost compelled to do so, since, as Michel de Marbais points out, not every nomen will signify true substance as in the case of 'privatio', 'figmentum', and 'negatio', and he asks, what is the quality of 'Deus' or 'materia'? As it was, it required all their ingenuity to incorporate such terms into their nominal system.

It must not be imagined than the Modistae dismissed substance altogether from their definition of the nomen; it seems almost as if they were not satisfied with substance and quality as a definition and relegated them, so to speak, to be items in the description of the essential mode of the nomen. It also provides an interesting example of independent thinking within a general body of doctrine, since none of the Modistae agree in detail about the organisation and presentation of the nomen, though they do agree in general terms about their grammatical doctrine with reference to the nomen.

The Modistae, with the exception of Michel de Marbais, introduce the concept of 'ens' into their discussion of the nomen and similarly 'esse' into the verbum in order to contrast with 'ens'. Thomas tells us that the modus entis is the mode of permanency and repose inherent in the thing and this is how Martin of Dacia defined the nomen,[2] though he refers to the modus entis as an operative contrast to the modus esse of the verbum. Both Siger and Michel retain the idea of substance in their concept of the nomen, though in the case of Siger he gives it as a feature of the general mode of the nomen. Of the Modistae, Michel is closer than the others to the older (more classical) definitions of the nomen as the pars orationis which signifies the thing by means of the mode of determined substance.[3] Siger takes up a mid-way point, in that he retains the idea of substance, but introduces the idea of permanency and repose in his general mode and also introduces determined understanding in his specific mode as well as retaining qualitas as one of its features.[4] Thomas is the furthest from the traditional definition. He refers to this older definition of 'substantia cum qualitate' explaining that substance is the modus entis; this is derived from that property of the thing which is the mode of permanence and repose and which is

---

[2] Martin of Dacia, #16: "modus significandi per modum habitus et quietis et per modum determinatae apprehensionis".

[3] Michel de Marbais: "Nomen est pars orationis significans rem suam per modum substantie determinate" (quoted by Thurot, p. 164).

[4] Siger de Courtrai, pp. 95-96: "modus significandi essentialis generalis nominis est modus significandi substantiae, permanentis habitus seu entis ... modus significandi specialis est modus qualitatis seu distinctae apprehensionis a quolibet alio".

found *principally* in substance. He also explains that quality is the mode of determinate understanding derived from the property of form and quality. The nomen is thus, for Thomas, the pars orationis which signifies by means of the modus entis or the mode of determinate understanding.[5] One can almost sense in both Thomas and Siger a need to substitute the modus entis for the modus substantiae, in order to solve the problem of 'negatio', 'privatio', *etc.*; both of them answer the possible objection to 'negatio' *etc.* as belonging to the nomen, by reference to Aristotle.[6] It would seem difficult however to sustain the argument that 'figmentum' was a nomen by virtue of its possessing a mode of substance as its essential feature.

The Modistae did not agree entirely on the detailed analysis and description of the nomen, though there is a large measure of agreement on its essential general nature. Martin of Dacia and Thomas insist more on the contrast of its modus entis to the modus esse of the verbum; Siger and Michel de Marbais refer to the 'substantial' nature of the nomen, though Siger modifies his substantial statement by insisting also on the nature and function of 'ens'. None of them can accept this as a literal fact, since 'privationes' *etc.* obviously cannot refer to anything substantial.

Modus significandi essentialis

Siger and Thomas differed in their presentation of their material, although the subject matter and content of their material remained essentially the same; this becomes abundantly clear in their description of the essential mode of signifying of the nomen. The Modistae follow much more closely in the tradition of Plato and Aristotle than Priscian in that they lay great stress on the two principal parts of speech, *i.e.* nomen and verbum;[7] but whereas the Greeks appear to have established these parts on purely logical grounds, the Modistae based their distinction on the metaphysical criteria of reality. Thomas tells us that we can discover certain common properties or modi essendi, *e.g.* modus entis and modus esse, and this enables us to establish from which property of the thing a particular modus significandi is derived. The modus entis

---

5 Thomas of Erfurt, #25: "Nomen est pars orationis significans per modum entis, vel determinatae apprehensionis."
6 Thomas of Erfurt, #26: "licet privationes et negationes non sint entia positiva extra animam posita; sunt tamen entia positiva secundum animam, ut patet ex intentione Philosophi IV Met. text. 9, ubi dicit quod opiniones contrariae, hoc est, duo contradictoria extra animam sunt duo contraria secundum animam".
7 R. H. Robins, *A. and M.*, p. 18.

is the mode of permanence inherent in the thing from which it derives
being; the modus esse is the mode of flux and sequence inherent in the
thing from which it derives becoming.[8] The modus entis will be therefore
the modus generalissimus of the nomen and the modus esse will be the
modus generalissimus of the verbum.[9] Thomas refers to Aristotle for
authority[10] that there are principally two modi entium, *i.e.* modus entis
and modus esse, from which the two principal partes orationis, *i.e.*
nomen and verbum are derived. Thomas adds that the pronomen is here
implied by the nomen, and the participium by the verbum.

The Modistae were almost hoist with their own petard. Their metaphysics of reality and the traditional definition of the nomen had left
them with the problem of dealing with such things as fictions (figmenta),
negations (negationes), and absences (privationes), *e.g. nihil, caecitas,*
since they obviously cannot refer to anything possessing being,[11] nor
can they be called nomina by having recourse to the 'proprietas rei'.
Again the Modistae had recourse to Aristotle,[12] that these may not refer
to entia outside the mind, but they are entia according to the mind,
which can be justified in scholastic terms, *i.e.* that two terms containing
a contradiction outside the mind are antithetic according to the mind.
Since these negations and absences are entia in terms of the mind, or as
Siger says,[13] anything can be grasped by the mind, they possess the
property of permanence which is an attribute of the modus generalissimus of the nomen.

Siger is quite straightforward in his descriptive procedures; he describes the general mode and then proceeds to the specific mode, using
the general mode to state the essence of the pars in question which it
shares with other partes orationis, *e.g.* the nomen and pronomen share
the same modus generalis, *i.e.* modus entis, and the specific mode to

---

[8]   Thomas of Erfurt, #24: "modus entis est modus habitus et permanentis, rei
inhaerens, ex hoc quod habet esse. Modus esse est modus fluxus et successionis,
rei inhaerens, ex hoc quod habet fieri".

[9]   The modus generalissimus is used by Thomas to describe the essence of the
pars and the characteristic of the essence by means of which the pars is distinguished from all other partes.

[10]   Thomas of Erfurt, #24: "ad hanc intentionem Commentator IV Phys. cap. 14,
dicit quod duo sunt modi principaliter entium, scilicet modus entis, et modus esse,
a quibus sumpserunt Grammatici duas partes orationes principales, scilicet nomen
et verbum".

[11]   Negation is, however, only a way of stating a positive fact.

[12]   Siger de Courtrai, p. 95: "accipiendo ens secundum rationem eius maxime uni-
versalem, scilicet ad ens in anima et extra animam et ad omne id quod mente
potest capi: sive sit privatio, sive negatio, sive purum figmentum, aliquod est ens,
ut vult Aristoteles, IV Metaphysicae".

[13]   Siger de Courtrai, p. 95: "omne id quod mente potest capi".

state the particular essence of the pars by reason of which it can be distinguished from all the partes orationis.[14] His description of these essential modes is very succinct, and he prefers to dwell in much more detail on the accidental modes. Thomas begins with the modus generalissimus, proceeds to the modus subalternus (which he describes in great detail) and then to the modus specialissimus, which he also describes in very great detail. The very wealth of his description throws considerable light on his descriptive techniques. His modus subalternus derives from the modus generalissimus and details aspects of the essential nature of the pars in question, which he calls modi significandi essentiales subalterni generales, which he describes in turn as modi subalterni minus generales; these are then refined as modi specialissimi of the modi subalterni. Appendix C shows in detail the sequence from the modus generalissimus to the ultimate refinement of the modus specialissimus. The term 'sequence' is used quite deliberately with reference to Thomas, since Siger's technique suggests no such sequence.

Siger uses his general essential mode to describe that particular modus significandi which refers to the essence of more than one pars orationis, so that in the case of the nomen it is the mode of signifying substance, permanence, rest and the state of being,[15] which is very similar to Michel de Marbais's general mode.[16] It is the essential mode since it refers to the essence of the pars in question, and it is the general mode since it refers to the essence of more than one pars – in the case of the nomen it shares the attributes of substance, permanence and repose with the pronomen. The modus specificus is used by Siger to distinguish a particular pars from all the others; in the case of the nomen, the feature of this mode is that of quality (qualitas) or the mode of determinate understanding[17] which serves to distinguish the nomen from the pronomen which has as its modus specificus, that of nondeterminate understanding in opposition to the specific mode of the nomen. If we look at Thomas's modus generalissimus, we would see

---

[14] This binary opposition of generalis and specificus is clearly, though he himself does not say so unequivocally, exploiting the contrast of matter and form (to which reference has been and will be made frequently), which was a characteristic device in Modistic grammatical procedures.

[15] Siger de Courtrai, p. 95: "modus significandi essentialis generalis nominis est modus significandi substantiae, permanentis habitus seu entis".

[16] Michel de Marbais: "modus significandi substantie sive quietis vel habitus sive permanentis" (quoted by Thurot, p. 160).

[17] Siger de Courtrai, p. 96: "modus qualitatis seu distinctae apprehensionis a quolibet alio". Michel de Marbais: "modus significandi qualitatis sive determinati sive distincti" (quoted by Thurot, p. 160).

that this mode is one of being and distinct understanding;[18] there is no mention of substance but there is otherwise little difference between Thomas and Siger. Thomas adds that the modus entis possesses an attribute of matter which creates the bond between the nomen and pronomen, whereas the modus determinatae apprehensionis possesses the attribute of form which renders the nomen discrete from all the other partes orationis. Thomas's modus generalissimus fulfils the function of Siger's modus generalis and modus specificus.

Thomas avoids the use of the term 'substantia' in his definition of the nomen, though he does refer to the ancient grammarians (i.e. Priscian) who had said that the nomen signifies substance with quality, the implication being that the modus substantiae is equivalent to the modus entis, and qualitas can be equated to 'distincta apprehensio';[19] the latter, as Thomas tells us, is acquired from the property of the form, and quality is the property of determinateness, because the form determines and distinguishes the different meanings. It seems that Thomas deliberately avoided the use of the term 'substantia', since this term implies a combination of substantial form and matter, and in combination only substance can exist;[20] this would therefore exclude absences and negations from the category of nomen. Thomas insists on the dual nature of the modus generalissimus, i.e. the modus entis which is the attribute of matter and the modus determinatae apprehensionis which is the attribute of form; the nomen and pronomen possess the same modus entis but are distinguished by the form which would not have been possible if substance alone had been the feature of the nomen, since it would not then have been possible to distinguish the nomen from the pronomen.

We see then that Siger with his modus generalis and specificus achieves the same result as Thomas does with his modus generalissimus. Siger's modus generalis is a respective mode and his modus specificus an absolute mode – this is certainly true of the declinable partes; the modus generalis therefore is used to portray those partes orationis which have the same syntactic function separately from those which have not, and the modus specificus is used to distinguish the particular

[18] Thomas of Erfurt, #23: "modus significandi per modum entis, et determinatae apprehensionis".

[19] As Siger in fact does: p. 96: "modus significandi specialis est modus qualitatis seu distinctae apprehensionis a quolibet alio, quia qualitatis seu formae est distinguere".

[20] F. C. Copleston, Aquinas, p. 87: "every material thing or substance is composed of a substantial form and first matter. Neither principle is in itself a thing or substance; the two together are the component principles of a substance".

pars from all the others by means of mainly morpho-semantic criteria. At this stage, however, Thomas is not concerned at all with such a distinction.[21] The nomen and pronomen have the same modus generalis – which is the principium constructionis of the suppositum[22] and which we can call the 'subject' element – in contrast to the verbum and participium which have the same modus generalis and which is the principium constructionis of the appositum which we can call the 'predicate' element. The nomen and pronomen, in these terms, do not have separate syntactic function; it becomes therefore the function of the modus specificus in Siger's scheme to distinguish these two partes.[23] This device is of no concern to Thomas who accordingly combines that feature of the nomen which it possesses in common with the pronomen and that feature which distinguishes it from the pronomen into the one modus generalissimus.[24]

[21]   Thomas says quite clearly that the modi significandi will be considered first, purely and simply in terms of the partes orationis, and then in terms of their construction with other partes orationis. Siger has no separate section on syntax and therefore each mode of signifying is qualified, i.e. whether it is a 'principium constructionis' or not – the term 'principium constructionis' being taken to imply that the particular mode in question will have a grammatical function at a level higher than the word. Siger's interpretation of 'constructio' is very close to Priscian's, viz. 'si tollas nomen aut verbum imperfecta fit oratio', i.e. a two-term proposition of the nomen and verbum; Peter Helias had confirmed the use of suppositum and appositum as technical terms for the analysis of a particular type of construction and this must have suggested to Siger and Thomas a type of construction which Bloomfield has called the 'actor-action' type. This S P construction goes back to antiquity and constitutes one of the favourite sentence types of Latin. This type of construction plays a very great part in Modistic syntactic theory, and it is revealing to see to what extent the Modistae (and they are not alone in this) were unconsciously dominated, even in creating formalised logical statements and syllogisms, not to mention the fact that they constructed their syntactic theory round sentences of the N V and V N type, by the structure of the Latin sentence.
[22]   Martin uses the term 'principium constructionis' to indicate syntactic function, e.g. he does not for instance divide the modes of signifying into respective and absolute but, on the other hand, implies a syntactic function for the accidental modes, viz. #66: "ipsi dicuntur modi significandi accidentales, et hi sunt maxime principia constructionis sive construendi". Cf. also pp. 60-62, 289-290 for a discussion of the technical terms, 'suppositum', 'appositum', 'principium constructionis'.
[23]   This is Siger's method of presentation.
[24]   The modus generalissimus of the nomen is defined by means of the two terms 'modus entis' and 'determinata apprehensio' and the modus generalissimus of the pronomen by means of the two terms 'modus entis' and 'indeterminata apprehensio', so that we can see the nomen and pronomen have the 'modus entis' in common and are distinguished by the 'apprehensio' which is 'determinata' in the nomen but 'indeterminata' in the pronomen. This feature has already been discussed in some detail as an excellent instance of Thomas's use of the matter-form contrast to distinguish two partes orationis, i.e. the nomen and pronomen have the same matter, but do not have the same form.

Modus significandi essentialis subalternus

The modus subalternus and its various sub-modes are refinements of the nomen and represent a detailed inventory of the different kinds of word which can be included, in Modistic terms, under the general title of nomen. Consideration of the whole essential mode can be divided into two distinct parts; the first seeks to define the nature of the pars in question, the second to describe its morpho-semantic [25] content. The accidental mode consists of attributes of the pars which are derived from without its essence. The question is what does an accidental mode consist of, because on this point there is some disagreement between Siger and Thomas. This does not constitute a difference of doctrine but rather one of organisation and exposition, since in the end what Siger and Thomas have to say about, *e.g.* the substantivum, largely agrees, despite the fact that for the former it is an accidental mode and for the latter a modus subalternus. This fact is mentioned deliberately, since this divergence of exposition makes for a problem in the presentation of the material; for the sake of unity, *i.e.* in order to show that there is a unified grammatical doctrine, Siger's accidental mode of 'qualitas' (which Thomas does not consider to be a true accidental mode) [26] has been introduced at this stage alongside the modus subalternus of the nomen (which is a mode peculiar to Thomas).

There are two modes which must be considered under the modus subalternus, *i.e.* the modus communis and the modus appropriati. Thomas makes the very revealing remark that these are special modes with respect to the modus generalissimus but general modes with respect to the other modes; if we look at this through Siger's system, we find that all fits into place, *i.e.* the special modes describe features of the essence of a pars which serve to individualise it and differentiate it from all other partes, while the general modes must refer to its essence even if it transcends the one pars, *e.g.* we find that the modus per se stantis and the modus adiacentis, which belong to the modus

---

[25] The term 'morpho-semantic' used here is intended to express the idea of a morphology expressed in semantic terms; the term morpho-semantic should in this context *not* be understood in the the same sense as P. Guiraud (Les champs morpho-sémantiques, *BSLP* lii (1956), 265-288) and S. Ullmann (*The Principles of Semantics*, p. 313) have used it, *i.e.* to express sound-and-sense associations.

[26] Thomas of Erfurt, #28: "qualitas, quam assignat Donatus pro accidente nominis, dividens eam in qualitatem propriam et appellativam, nominat duos modos essentiales nominis subalternos, scilicet modum communis, et appropriati ... quae dicuntur accidere nomini, quia sunt praeter intellectum essentialem nominis simplicites et absolute sumpti".

communis, can also be found among the modi subalterni of the pronomen.

The modus communis is derived from that property of the thing which is the property of being divisible into or of being shared by several subordinates; [27] (the logician derives from the same property the 'intentio universalis'). This modus constitutes the nomen commune or appellativum,[28] what Donatus had called the qualitas appellativa.[29] The modus appropriati is derived from the property of not being divisible by several subordinates, (from which the logician derives the 'intentio individuationis'), and this mode constitutes the nomen proprium,[30] what Donatus had called 'propria qualitas'.[31]

From these modes which Thomas names modi significandi subalterni generales, we come to the modi significandi subalterni minus generales, which consist of refinements of the modus communis and modus appropriati or we might say of the nomen appellativum and the nomen proprium. The modus communis is divided into two sub-modes, i.e. the modus per se stantis and the modus adiacentis; the modus per se stantis derives from the property of finite essence,[32] and just as the modus generalissimus is derived from the property of absolute essence, so the modus per se stantis is derived from the property of definite essence and this constitutes the nomen substantivum. The modus adiacentis derives from the property of adhering to something according to its being[33] and constitutes the nomen adiectivum. Thomas then proceeds to describe the modus per se stantis in detail which he does in the form of five modi specialissimi which he enumerates, and then repeats the procedure for the modus adiacentis which he breaks down into twenty-four modi specialissimi. These merely describe the inventory of the nomen substantivum and adiectivum of the Latin lan-

---

[27] Thomas of Erfurt, #28: "modus significandi per modum communis sumitur a proprietate rei, quae est proprietas divisibilis in plura supposita, vel communicabilis pluribus suppositis".

[28] Thomas of Erfurt, #28: "nomen commune vel appellativum significat per modum communicabilis pluribus suppositis, ut urbs, flumen".

[29] Donatus (Ars Minor): "qualitas ... bipertita est: aut enim unius nomen est et proprium dicitur, aut multorum et appellativum".

[30] Thomas of Erfurt, #29: "modus significandi per modum appropriati sumitur a proprietate rei, quae est proprietas indivisibilis per plura supposita, a quo sumitur apud Logicum intentio individuationis; et hic modus facit nomen proprium".

[31] Donatus (Ars Minor): "qualitas nominum in quo est? Bipertita est: aut multorum et appellativum".

[32] Thomas of Erfurt, #31: "modus significandi per modum per se stantis sumitur a proprietate rei, quae est proprietas essentiae determinatae".

[33] Thomas of Erfurt, #32: "modus significandi per modum adiacentis sumitur a proprietate rei, quae est proprietas alteri adhaerentis secundum esse".

guage, and add nothing to the theory of Modistic descriptive technique; therefore, rather than render this exposition of the Modistic method very top-heavy with needless detail, the diagram[34] can be used to explain and illustrate in more detail the scheme of description from the modus essentialis generalissimus down to the various modi specialissimi. This applies too to the modi specialissimi of the modus appropriati, which is divided into four modi specialissimi which merely serve to describe in more detail the various types of the nomen proprium which Latin possesses, *e.g.* Marcus, *etc.* We see, then, that the development from modus essentialis generalissimus to modus essentialis specialissimus is exactly the same as for the nomen which goes, via the nomen appellativum and proprium, to the nomen substantivum and adiectivum which are sub-divisions of the nomen appellativum, and these are in turn divided into the various types of noun and adjective of the Latin language.

The modus subalternus is peculiar to Thomas, and we have to look to Siger's accidental mode of 'qualitas' before we can find any similar descriptive material of the nomen. Before considering Siger's qualitas which describes in a similar manner though perhaps in less detail the various forms of the nomen, it would be perhaps worthwhile to consider a possible explanation of this difference in descriptive method. Siger uses the terminology of Donatus, *i.e.* propria qualitas and qualitas appellativa; both, he tells us, are principia constructionis and must therefore be respective modes.[35] The specific or special mode (in which qualitas would have to be placed if it were to be considered under the rubric of essentialis) is for Siger an absolute mode, and Thomas's modus subalternus, which contains so much of this material, is, as he himself says,[36] a modus specialis with respect to the modus generalissimus; in Siger's system such a modus specialis could not possibly be a respective mode, and for this reason (if for no other) qualitas would have to be placed among the accidental modes. At the risk of anticipating things a little, it has to be pointed out that Thomas does discuss the nature of

---

[34]   *Cf.* Appendix B.
[35]   The principium constructionis as used by Siger (and Michel de Marbais) seems to have been a device to add to the definition of an accidental mode by stating whether or not the particular pars orationis to which this mode belonged was or was not potentially a member of a syntagm by reason of this mode; by definition a respective mode can be used only in a construction along with other accidental modes.
[36]   Thomas of Erfurt, #27: "(modi subalterni) sunt modi speciales respectu generalissimi, et sunt generales respectu aliorum modorum".

the accidental mode in contrast to the essential mode; Donatus had described qualitas and gradus in terms which in the Modistic system might well have become accidental modes – as indeed they do in Siger's system, though they are included in Thomas's system in the modi subalterni and specialissimi. Qualitas and gradus were considered accidents of the nomen by Donatus [37] according to Thomas, because they belonged outside the understanding of the nomen considered absolutely,[38] but then any modus significandi of the pars, if it is not the *modus essentialis generalissimus* of the pars, could be called an accident of the pars (in this case the nomen). This modus significandi under discussion may be an accidental mode, but if it constitutes a species, *i.e.* a particular type of sub-class of the pars in question, it will not be an accidental mode and will therefore be an essential mode, since by definition [39] an accidental mode may not constitute a different type of the pars in question. Therefore, 'qualitas appellativa', for instance, constitutes a particular type of nomen and becomes a subaltern essential mode even though it does not state the essence purely and simply of the nomen, whereas 'casus', which expresses a variation of the essence of the nomen, remains an accidental mode since it does not create any particular type of essence.

Siger divides his modus accidentalis of qualitas into propria and appellativa, which Thomas called modus communis and modus appropriati. The propria qualitas is the mode which designates the modus essendi of the thing which is not to be found in several subordinate forms.[40] Siger refers to Priscian that propria qualitas signifies the private substance or quality of something [41] and just as Thomas divides up his modus appropriati into the four modi specialissimi of praenomen, nomen, cognomen and agnomen, so does Siger divide up his propria qualitas. Similarly, Siger's qualitas appellativa designated the modus

---

[37] Donatus (II.1): "nomini accidunt sex, qualitas, conparatio, genus, numerus, figura, casus".
[38] Thomas of Erfurt, #66: "dicitur comparationem accidere nomini, quia hi tres modi sunt extra intellectum nominis absolute sumpti".
[39] Thomas of Erfurt, #20: "modus significandi accidentalis est, qui advenit parti post eius esse completum, non dans esse simpliciter parti, nec secundum genus, sed secundum speciem".
[40] Siger de Courtrai, p. 96: "qualitas propria est modus significandi accidentalis nominis designans circa rem modum essendi vel quod ei repugnat reperiri in pluribus".
[41] Priscian, II, 25: "proprium naturaliter unius cuiusque privatam et qualitatem significat et in rebus est individuis".

essendi of the thing which can be found in several subordinate forms;[42] this too he sub-divides into many different types, which he enumerates without the repetitive detail of Thomas. Both propria and appellativa qualitas are principia constructionis, the former with a vocative verb, the latter with signs expressing universality, *e.g.* omnis, nullus, and which cannot be properly constructed with propria nomina, and therefore it is incorrect to say, 'omnis Socrates'.

The adiectivum is an accidental mode of the nomen representing the property of "adjacency";[43] again Siger refers to Priscian[44] that adiectiva are so called because they are usually added to other nomina appellativa which signify substance or even nomina propria for the exhibition of praise or blame, *etc.* Siger reinforces his statement with a further reference to Peter Helias which considerably extends the province of the adiectivum,[45] *i.e.* to describe the accidental properties of the nomen. The substantivum is the accidental mode of the nomen which expresses the modus per se entis and the modus abstracti and will refer to 'entia' which are strictly speaking self-evident as in the case of substances, and 'entia' which are quite separate as in the case of abstract occurrences.[46] Both the modus per se entis and modus abstracti can be the principal constructible categories of sentence structure, *e.g.* principium constructionis; the substantivum will be the constructible member in the construction of the suppositum and appositum, *i.e.* subject and predicate, though the adiectivum cannot, because the verbum, which is the principal element of the appositum, signifies, as we shall see, by means of the modus dependentis and will, therefore, be proportionate to the modus significandi per se stantis and *not* to the modus significandi adiacentis.

In Thomas's scheme the modus significandi essentialis generalissimus

---

[42]   Siger de Courtrai, p. 97: "qualitas appellativa est modus significandi accidentalis nominis designans circa rem modum essendi prout rei non repugnat reperiri in pluribus".

[43]   Siger de Courtrai, p. 97: "adiectivum est modus significandi accidentalis nominis designans circa rem modum essendi adiacentis".

[44]   Priscian (II. 25): "adiectiva autem ideo vocantur, quod aliis appellativis, quae substantiam significant, veletiam propriis adici solent ad manifestandum eorum qualitatem vel quantitatem".

[45]   Siger de Courtrai, pp. 97-98: "cognitis substantialibus vel accidentalibus essentialibus, adinventa fuerunt adiectiva ut proprietates accidentales circa ea demonstrant".

[46]   Siger de Courtrai, p. 98: "substantivum est modus significandi accidentalis nominis, designans circa rem modum per se entis et abstracti sive sit proprie ens per se, sicut substantiae, sive sint entia per se distincta ab illo in quo sunt, et ut sic significata, ut in accidentibus abstractis".

nominis, which contains the modus entis, is divided into modi subalterni (which are modi speciales in relation to the modus generalissimus) and these modi speciales become modi specialissimi. Similarly the nomen is divided into the nomen commune or appellativum and the nomen proprium; the nomen commune is further divided into the substantivum and adiectivum, the former, *i.e.* the nomen substantivum becoming the nomen substantivum generale and the nomen speciale, which are the nomen patronymicum, collectivum and diminutivum. The adiectivum similarly is divided into twenty-four types,[47] and this might be very briefly described as a partly formal and partly semantic classification of morphological distinctions of the nomen in Latin. The nomen proprium is divided into proprie proprium, praenomen, cognomen and agnomen.[48]

The expositions of Thomas and Siger of the substantivum and the adiectivum suggest an interesting contrast in styles and also of attitude; Thomas presents us with a detailed description whereas Siger glosses over the inventorial analysis and attempts a discussion of the nature of the adiectivum and substantivum, which seems to be much closer to the Modistic and indeed mediaeval ideal of a descriptive grammar.

---

[47] These are: denominativum, generale, speciale, collectivum, possessivum, diminutivum, divisum, gentile, patrium, interrogativum, responsivum, infinitum, negativum, demonstrativum, relativum, positivum, comparativum, superlativum, ad aliquid, temporale, verbale, locale, numerale and ordinale.

[48] Thomas concludes his examination of the various types of nomina by including more for the sake of exhaustiveness rather than for any new feature of the nomen; these are certain nomina which do not differ so much in their meaning but rather in the expression (vox): *cf.* Thomas of Erfurt #65: "plura nomina usitata, quae differentiam specialem non habent secundum modos significandi, discrepantes magis secundum diversitatem vocis, quam significati". This means in effect that separate modes of signifying are not required, because if their root meanings do not differ, they can presumably be included among the modi specialissimi already described and will not require special modes of signifying to express them; their voces may be different, but this fact does not lead to the creation of special modes of signifying, since vox is merely the matter which is 'informed' into a pars orationis by means of the ratio significandi and vox is therefore never realised as vox but as a pars orationis which is expressed by means of modes of signifying but in the case of these particular nomina, the modes of signifying have already been listed and described. These nomina, to which Thomas is referring, are nomina such as "univocum, analogum, aequivocum, synonymum, absolutum, fictum", will be included either among the nomina substantiva or the nomina adiectiva which have already been described as modi specialissimi by the virtue of the essential modes of signifying they possess.

Modus significandi accidentalis

Thomas and Siger defined the essential mode of the nomen as the 'modus entis' which possesses a specific feature, that of designating with precision, *i.e.* by means of determinata apprehensio. Their presentation of this essential mode, though stating the same grammatical doctrine, had differed in that Siger had created the sub-modes of general and specific. Siger's definition of the essence of the nomen does not differ from Thomas's who states both parts as one mode, *i.e.* the modus generalissimus, and then describes the sub-modes of the essential mode, *i.e.* the modus subalternus and the modus specialissimus which he uses to list in greater detail those words which possess the same essence as the essence described in the modus generalissimus. Possessing this same 'basic' essence, they differ merely in that they represent some more individual property of this general essence, and as a result constitute a particular type of the pars. Different modi specialissimi are then used to specify in detail the types of words which express this general essence and its property by means of a more individualising feature, *e.g.* the interrogative adjective.[49]

Once their definition of the essential modes has been completed, Siger and Thomas discuss the accidental modes which represent variations of the general essence and its properties; Siger uses, for the nomen, *nine* accidental modes, while Thomas uses only six. These accidental modes are species, figura, genus, numerus, casus, gradus, qualitas, substantivum, adiectivum and persona; of these Siger does not include persona as an accidental mode of the nomen, while Thomas included qualitas, substantivum and adiectivum, as we have seen already, as his subaltern modes or in the case of 'gradus' as modi specialissimi derived from the subaltern mode, *i.e.* the nomen adiectivum.

Thomas's description of qualitas as a subaltern essential mode of the nomen in contrast to Siger's classification of it as an accidental mode merits comment in detail at this stage, since it reveals a great deal about their conception, use and organisation of the essential and accidental modes. In his introductory remarks to the accidental modes of the nomen, Thomas discusses Donatus's classification of qualitas and gradus as 'accidents' of the nomen (which Siger follows). Thomas states that this has been done since they describe something more than the

---

[49]   Thomas of Erfurt, #44: "modus adiacentis est modus significandi per modum denominantis alterum sub ratione interrogationis de ipso: et hic modus constituit nomen adiectivum interrogativum, ut quis, qualis".

pure and absolute essence of the nomen.[50] This is very important since it provides the key to Thomas's analysis in terms of the modus subalternus and modus specialissimus, and also to Siger's use of the general and specific essential modes. It will be seen throughout that Siger uses his essential mode merely to state the absolute essence of the pars in question and that qualification of the essence by means of which the pars is distinguished from all the other partes orationis; for this reason, he includes qualitas, *etc.* as accidental modes since they say nothing about the essence itself of the nomen, and this will be the procedure (in theory) in all the other partes orationis.

Thomas describes the features that Donatus classified as accidents, *i.e.* qualitas and gradus, along with his essential modes since any feature which does not belong to the pars by virtue of the modus generalissimus, *i.e.* its purest essence, can in fact be an accident.[51] Although the feature may be an accident, if we can restrict the essential mode to the expression of the essence in the narrowest sense and therefore exclude the feature from the modus generalissimus, it may still, however, be able to create a species of the pars and by definition this cannot be an accidental mode; it will thus become an essential sub-mode, *i.e.* subaltern, since it expresses a property of the essence and also constitutes a species of the pars. This is echoed by Siger in his Sophisma "O Magister", when he argues that 'whiteness' may be an accident of 'homo', but it is essential to 'homo albus'.[52] This is a characteristic of Thomas's analysis of the essential modes of the partes, and we shall find that any feature which expresses a property of the essence and also creates a species of the pars in question will be classed as a subaltern mode.[53] This is certainly so in the indeclinable partes, and any of Donatus's 'accidents' which yield a different species of the pars in question will, in Thomas's scheme, become a modus subalternus; conversely, however, qualitas in the verb, which Donatus classified as an accident, remains an accidental mode since it is not the expression of a property of the essence of the verb, nor does it create any species of

---

50 Thomas of Erfurt, #66: "dicuntur accidere nomini, quia sunt praeter intellectum essentialem nominis simpliciter et absolute sumpti".
51 Thomas of Erfurt, #66: "omnis modus significandi partis, qui non est modus essentialis generalissimus, potest dici accidens nominis absolute".
52 Siger de Courtrai, p. 147: "albedo sit accidens hominis et tamen est de essentia hominis albi".
53 Thomas of Erfurt, #128: "non est modus essentialis generalissimus, cum verbo non det esse simpliciter, sed sit praeter eius intellectum essentialem. Nec etiam est essentialis specialis (i.e. subaltern) cum non constituat aliquam speciem verbi".

verb. There are, of course, problems in such an analysis; Donatus was criticised for including qualitas, which he divided into demonstratio and relatio as a feature of the pronoun. Thomas is compelled to include demonstratio and relatio as subaltern modes of the pronoun; although they do not constitute different species of the pronoun, they represent mutually exclusive properties, *i.e.* presence and absence, of concreteness in the pronoun and become merely two complementary aspects of the pronomen substantivum.

Of the accidental modes, species and figura are absolute modes and the remainder are respective; species and figura represent derivational features of the nomen and are absolute modes since they themselves possess no syntactic function. Most of these respective modes are categories well known to most grammarians and require no further comment at this stage, genus being 'gender', numerus 'number', and casus 'case'. Qualitas, which Siger included as an accidental mode but which Thomas made into a subaltern mode, represents those features known traditionally as 'common' and 'proper' nouns; of these accidental modes, persona is the only one which requires any preliminary explanation. This mode was included by Thomas, and by Martin, but no mention is made of it by Siger; this use of persona as an accidental mode represents a very definite departure from tradition by Thomas and Martin, and this becomes especially worthy of mention, when it is realised that Thomas did not consider persona to be a genuine accidental mode of the verb (traditionally person is always ascribed to the verb) but admits it as an accidental mode of the verb only by virtue of its association with the suppositum. Person in the nomen is the mode of signifying by means of which it connotates the property of speaking[54] and this property is acquired by the verb by virtue of its association (by means of compositio) with its subject (suppositum).[55]

Donatus attributed six accidents to the nomen, *viz.* qualitas, comparatio, genus, numerus, figura, casus; Priscian attributed only five, *i.e.* species, genus, figura, numerus, casus.

In the 12th century, Abelard, for instance, had been content to follow his Latin predecessors, distinguishing the accidents of the nomen by means of their properties, or by means of their constructible potentialities, or by means of the nature of their expression, *i.e.* vox.[56] Peter

---

[54] Thomas of Erfurt, #94: "est persona modus significandi nominis, mediante quo nomen proprietatem loquendi consignificat".
[55] Thomas of Erfurt, #145: "numerus et persona insunt verbo, non ex proprietate suae rei per se loquendo, sed ex proprietate rei suppositi".
[56] Abelard: "sunt quedam nominum proprietates iuxta significationem pensande,

Helias did not use this classification, but preferred to relate many of the accidental modes to their function in a construction.[57] He admitted in the nomen only those accidents which had been enumerated by Priscian and he criticised Donatus in particular for having included qualitas and comparatio among the accidents of the nomen.

The Modistae are not alike in their classification and use of the accidental modes; Martin of Dacia and Thomas make use of only six accidental modes, *i.e.* those of Priscian and in addition 'persona', – these are what Thomas calls "de modis *pure* accidentalibus". Michel de Marbais however lists the six accidental modes which are those of Donatus. Siger is much more liberal and uses actually nine accidental modes, *i.e.* those of Donatus and also species, substantivum and adiectivum. Thurot states that by the 13th century there was a tendency to introduce accidents of the nomen which were not known to Donatus and Priscian; this is confirmed by Siger (a) by precept, and (b) by implication in his statement about the accidental modes.[58]

The following table shows the various accidental modes of the nomen described by the grammarians of antiquity and the Middle Ages:

	Donatus	Priscian	Martin	Siger	Michel	Thomas
qualitas	+			+	+	
species		+	+	+		+
gradus	+			+	+	
genus	+	+	+	+	+	+
numerus	+	+	+	+	+	+
figura	+	+	+	+	+	+
casus	+	+	+	+	+	+
persona			+			+
substantivum				+		
adiectivum				+		

quedam vero secundum positionem constructionis atendende, quaedam etiam secundum vocis compositionem accipiende" (Thurot, p. 164).

[57] Peter Helias: "accidentia nomini dicuntur convenientia ipsi, secundum que nomina inter se vel cum aliis dictionibus competenter habent construi" (quoted by Thurot, p. 165).

[58] Siger de Courtrai, p. 96: "modorum significandi accidentalium nominis quam plurimorum solum maiores et communiores enumerans, Donatus pro accidentibus posuit sex ... Priscianus autem quinque ..., sed de hoc non est vis". We shall see that this is also true of the verb, since Thomas introduces 'compositio' as an accidental mode of the verb, and by his account this is a category not used by his predecessors.

It has already been pointed out that Thomas did not include 'gradus' among his accidental modes, though he does list among the nomina adiectiva, the adiectivum positivum, comparativum and superlativum, but says in effect nothing more about them than to include them in his inventory. Since Siger, on the other hand, has much more to say about gradus as an accidental mode of the nomen, it has been included in this exposition of the accidental modes and not among the modi subalterni and specialissimi.

Species et Figura

The Modistae divided the accidental modes of a pars orationis into absolute and respective;[59] an absolute mode is a derivational[60] feature and in the Modistic scheme such a mode plays no part in either the inflectional paradigm or in the syntax of the pars in question, nor can it influence the congruence of a construction. A respective mode, on the other hand, in addition to the feature that it describes, represents it as a feature by means of which the pars orationis to which it belongs can fulfil a higher, i.e. syntactic function and therefore the sum total of the respective modes of a pars orationis will represent its potentiality as a member of a construction.

This is a very valuable distinction that the Modistae made, since it enabled them to define the derivational features of the pars without further reference to other accidental modes or to grammatical, i.e. syntactic, requirements. By making this division the respective modes can also be defined by means of their own criteria but by definition are related to the higher, i.e. syntactic function of the pars. This meant that the Modistae were able to avoid the severe distinction between morphology and syntax which so often occurs in the more normative type of grammar, and they were thus able to segregate those items, which cannot possess any further functional yield, from those items which show a degree of inter-penetration between the morpho-semantic and syntactic levels, which a great many traditional grammars ignore. Such accidental, i.e. respective, modes require, as a result, a definition and description which transcend the mere morpho-semantic and thereby produce a definition more in terms of the functional yield of the mode than of its particular morphology or semantics.

The Modistae used two accidental modes, i.e. species and figura, to

---

[59]   Martin of Dacia does not make any use of this contrast.
[60]   'Derivational' is used here in the synchronic sense, cf. Bloch and Trager, Outline of Linguistic Analysis, p. 55.

describe the derivational features of a pars orationis and these modes are absolute modes since they merely describe the pars in terms of the derivations which it manifests within the area of its meaning, *e.g.* 'albus' and 'albedo' are adjective and substantive, and are classed therefore as species of the nomen. 'Albedo', however, as a substantive contrasts with the verb 'dealbo' so that the distinction between them has gone beyond the semantic difference between one species of a pars and another species of the same pars. The difference between 'albedo' and 'dealbo' is now a functional, *i.e.* syntactic, distinction, and they are at this level distinguished by their different consignifications.

The two absolute modes in question are 'species' which can be described as 'type' and 'figura' which can best be interpreted by Thrax's term "skhema"; [61] these two absolute modes are considered together because of the fundamental difference between them and the other accidental modes. The Modistae used species and figura in every instance when derivation affected the intrinsic nature of the pars and these modes can therefore be applied to both declinable and indeclinable partes. In contrast to the absolute modes, all the other accidental modes must be considered, not only in terms of themselves, but in terms of their syntactic behaviour; this applies equally well to any accidental mode of an indeclinable pars which is not an absolute mode, and we shall see that, for instance, 'ordo' in the conjunction is used entirely with reference to its consignification, *i.e.* its syntactic meaning. The absolute modes represent, as we have said, the derivational features of the pars. Derivation is here used in a wider and different sense than the modern linguist would probably use it; derivation as conceived by the Modistae was not a formal, *i.e.* syntactic or morphological feature, but merely a meaning derived from another meaning. *Species*,[62] divided into primary and secondary, represents a root meaning, *i.e.* a species primitiva from which secondary meaning, *i.e.* species derivativa can be derived, *e.g.* mons > montanus, but these meanings must in the first place be semantically linked by means of a common essence. Figura [63] repre-

61   R. H. Robins, *Thrax*, p. 99.
62   Siger de Courtrai, p. 96: "species est modus significandi accidentalis nominis designans proprietatem determinandi ab aliquo vel a nullo". Thomas of Erfurt, #68: "species est modus significandi accidentalis nominis, mediante quo modum significandi primarium vel secundarium significat. Et dividitur in speciem primitivam et derivativam".
63   Siger de Courtrai, p. 102: "figura est modus significandi accidentalis nominis designans circa rem modum essendi indivisionis vel compositionis". Thomas of Erfurt, #82: "figura est modus significandi accidentalis nominis, mediante quo nomen proprietatem simplicis, compositi, vel decompositi significat".

sents a simple primary form which can be modified by means of a morphological change but it is nonetheless a change demanded in order to express a semantic change, *e.g.* 'dives' from which the compound form 'praedives' is derived; figura can be simple (simplex), compound (composita) and according to Thomas complex (decomposita), though Siger will not admit this as a discrete member of the accidental mode of figura.[64]

Species is not, however, described in formal terms, and thus 'mons' represents the primary species and 'montanus' the species derived from mons. Such a derivation, however, is not defined by means of any morphological criteria but by the semantic relationship of the two forms, *i.e.* 'montanus' must be derived from 'mons', since 'montanus' cannot signify 'mons' absolutely but only in relation to the inhabitant of the mountain. Such an explanation seems perfectly reasonable and could perhaps lend itself to a more formal statement, if similar derivations could be established systematically; but the Modistae, particularly Thomas, by insisting that the relation between the primary and derived species was entirely one of meaning and by excluding the different expression forms, *i.e.* vox – (this applies to Thomas only since Siger is prepared to admit[65] that vox along with the property of the thing or meaning can be a factor in producing a change of species), produced statements which, although they appear semantically logical, are in fact grammatically naïve. Thomas argues that vox must be excluded entirely from any consideration of species, since to include vox as a criterion would mean that the mode of signifying would be derived from the vox and not from the property of the thing and would produce what Thomas would undoubtedly consider an aberration, such as 'albedo' being derived from 'albus'.[66] Thomas, of course, argues the contrary, *i.e.* that whiteness must exist before white or white things can exist and bases his grammatical statement on such philosophical grounds.

Species is divided into primary (primitiva) and derived (derivativa –

[64] Siger de Courtrai, p. 103: "figura decomposita non designat circa rem aliquem modum essendi distinctum a praedictis (i.e. simplex and composita)".

[65] Siger de Courtrai, p. 103: "species determinativa est modus significandi accidentalis nominis designans modum essendi ut secundarium, seu rivulus, et ab alio descendens sive sit descenscus a parte vocis solum, sive ex parte proprietatis et passivae significationis".

[66] Thomas of Erfurt, #67: "species ... non attenditur ex parte vocis ... ita quod illud nomen sit primitivae speciei, cuius vox est primo ad significandum imposita: et illud derivativae speciei, cuius vox est secundario imposita, a voce primitiva descendens, ut albus descendit ab albedine; quia iam modus significandi activus a voce traheretur, et non a proprietate rei; quod est contra posita ... species sumitur a proprietate rei, quae est modus existendi primarie, vel secundarie".

Siger uses the term determinativa rather than derivativa[67]) and refers to the 'shape' of the word,[68] in this particular instance the nomen; species is therefore the accidental mode which designates the property of being determined from something or nothing. The Modistae argued that species primitiva, as an accidental mode of signifying, must refer to the modus essendi of the thing in its primary form – what might be called the root primary or root word, – and species primitiva thus expresses the primary or absolute essence as it is in its root form and incapable of any further sub-division.[69] (This statement is made to stress that the primary form cannot be reduced to any lesser meaning.) Derived species (species derivativa) refers to the creation of a new form by means of an internal change in the meaning of the pars and which must as a result find its formulation in a variation of the root meaning of the pars; the derived species is a free form but in contrast to the primary species, it is also a complex form. The term complex is used specifically in this instance to avoid confusion with composite since this term composite represents a sub-class of figura; it may well happen, and indeed it does happen, that in Siger's description the figura decomposita partakes of both a figura composita and a species derivativa – this does not however occur in Thomas's scheme.

Species thus represents the root meaning of a word, *i.e.* the primary form of the modus essendi or property of the thing to be signified, which is in fact its absolute essence since it cannot be derived from a lower, *i.e.* base-morphemic structure; such a primary form is capable of becoming a derived form by means of a change in meaning but which must, however, be derived from the primary meaning.[70] Species, and more particularly species primitiva, becomes the foundation of the structure of the whole pars since it represents that form of the pars which cannot be analysed into smaller segments, *i.e.* into lesser meaningful components. An additional factor is that any change of meaning between the primary and derived species cannot influence the syntactic function of the pars; once, however, as a result of a change in meaning,

[67] Clearly, 'determinata' has the meaning of 'derivativa' for Siger, if his use elsewhere of 'determinare' is any guide, *e.g.* " 'magnanimitas' a 'magnanimo' determinatur".
[68] Siger de Courtrai, p. 96: "species est positio vocabuli primaria aut secundaria".
[69] Siger de Courtrai, p. 96: "species primitiva est modus significandi accidentalis nominis designans modum essendi ut est primus et formalis et non ab alio descendens".
[70] Thomas of Erfurt, #68: "mons primitivae speciei est, quia significat rem sub essentia primaria, quae est essentia absoluta ... montanus derivativae speciei est, quia significat rem sub esse secundario, quae est essentia comparata".

a different pars orationis is created, we are then no longer dealing with the accidental mode of signifying but with the consignifications of two different partes orationis.

As a preamble to his analysis of species, Thomas had stated that species must not be considered in reference to the expression, *i.e.* the vox of the nomen; the vox merely gives expression to the derivation from the primary form which the mind has perceived and which it must express by means of another mode of signifying.[71] If vox were to play a vital part in the sequence, it would mean that the species derivativa would be structured on the vox of the species primitiva, so that 'albedo' would come from 'albus'; this would mean that the active mode of signifying is derived from the vox and not from the property of the thing – which is not the case.[72] Such a statement, *i.e.* that 'albedo' is derived from 'albus' as the result of the commutation of lexical items, would be quite acceptable to the modern linguist, but clearly the Modistae, as a result of the fundamental tenets of their theory, could never have accepted such a description. Arguing as they do, that the modes of signifying function in order to give meaning to the various properties of the thing under consideration, it is the root meaning that will be built upon and not the converse, and the very nature of their grammatical theory and descriptive technique must of necessity preclude any morphological criteria which would contradict the priority of their semantic criteria. As was pointed out in the chapter on the metalanguage of the Modistae, Thomas stated at a very early stage that the active mode of signifying must derive from some property of the thing.[73] Therefore species must be derived from the property of the thing which is either the mode of existing primarily in the case of the species primitiva or the mode of existing secondarily, *i.e.* derivatively in the case of the species derivativa, the former being the absolute mode of existing and the latter the comparative mode.[74]

If species is a means of creating a sub-class or a new form of the pars by means of a change of meaning which must be derived from the root meaning, figura is the means of creating a new form within the pars by means of a change in the shape of the word. Species can

[71]   Thomas of Erfurt, #6: "intellectus vocem ad significandum sub aliquo modo significandi activo imponit".
[72]   Thomas of Erfurt, #6: "cuilibet modo significandi activo correspondet aliqua proprietas rei, seu modus essendi rei".
[73]   Thomas of Erfurt, #6: "omnem modum significandi activum ab aliqua rei proprietate radicaliter oriri".
[74]   Thomas of Erfurt, #67: "voco modum significandi primarie, modum existendi absolute; et modum significandi secundarie, modum existendi comparate".

therefore be called semantic derivation within the word-class and figura the morpho-semantic change within the pars. Species and figura are complementary, in that species refers to the root meaning and forms which are created or derived as a result of meanings derived from the root meaning, while figura refers to the root or simple form and to the compound forms of the pars but is, however, attested by more formal criteria than in the case of species; with regard to figura, it is nevertheless change of meaning which produces a concomitant change in form, and it must not be imagined that it was a change of grammatical form which occasioned the change of meaning. Figura is, therefore, a derivational item, the method of indicating the difference in meaning between the different figurae of a pars being realised by means of the compounding of different forms with the root form to produce a compound word, 'composition' leading to two sub-classes of the compound form, i.e. compound (composita) and double compound or complex (decomposita).[75]

Donatus divided figura into two sub-categories which he called simple (simplex) e.g. decens, and composite (composita) e.g. indecens, and according to Donatus, these can be combined in four ways to create new words.[76] Priscian added a third sub-category, i.e. complex (decomposita) which can be derived from a compound word only. Figura in the nomen can therefore be defined as an accidental mode by means of which the nomen can signify the properties of indivisibility, composition and complexity.[77]

Of the Modistae, Michel and Siger preserved the dichotomy of Donatus, i.e. Michel describes figura as the mode of signifying used by the nomen to express the thing in the form of its simple or compound being (esse),[78] and Siger defines figura as the accidental mode which designates the modus essendi in its undivided or compound form; Siger,

---

[75] Martin seems to have been on the brink of a formal description and in fact makes a statement which is surprisingly 'modern', viz. #78: "hoc est quod dicitur quod figura est proprietas constandi ex litteris et sillabis vel veniendi a dictione composita. Unde dicitur quod illud est simplicis figura quod non potest dividi in duas partes intelligibiles eiusdem sensus capaces ut homo".

[76] Donatus (Ars Minor): "Figurae nominum quot sunt? Duae. Quae? Simplex, ut decens, potens, conposita, ut indecens ... Quibus modis nomina conponuntur? Quattuor: ex duobus integris, ut suburbanus; ex duobus corruptis, ut efficax ...; ex corrupto et integro, ut nugigerulus; aliquando ex conpluribus, ut inexpugnabilis".

[77] Thomas of Erfurt, #82: "figura est modus significandi accidentalia nominis, mediante quo nomen proprietatem simplicis, compositi, vel decompositi significat".

[78] Michel de Marbais: "figura est quidam modus significandi datus nomini ad designandum rem sub esse simplici vel compositi" (quoted by Thurot, p. 168).

it is true, talks about 'decompositio', but this is for him a variant (though not a free variant) of the composite form. Thomas of Erfurt follows Priscian[79] and introduces the third element of 'decompositio', as a result of which figura becomes the mode of signifying by means of which the nomen signifies the property of simple, compound and double compound or complex form, and by virtue of this triple property of the mode of signifying, the figura of the nomen varies in a three-fold manner, *i.e.* simple (simplex), compound (composita) and double compound or complex (decomposita). This triple division, Thomas tells us, results from the fact that these three properties of uncompounded, compounded and double compounded can be commonly found in the world of things, the third type representing a combination which derives from more than two components. It is as a result of this similarity between the structure of words and the structure of things that Thomas insists that figura, like species, does not refer to the expression, *i.e.* vox, since, as was pointed out in the section on species, the modes of signifying are derived from the property of the thing.[80] We have thus, in Thomas's scheme of things, a nomen of simple figura (form) – *e.g.* 'doctus' – a nomen of a compound figura – *e.g.* 'indoctus' – and a nomen of a double compound figura – *e.g.* 'inexpugnabilis'.

Figura simplex is defined as the mode of signifying the thing by means of the property of simple form, or as Siger would say, the property of indivisibility, *e.g.* 'dives';[81] Siger explains that indivisibility does not refer so much to the thing as to the understanding and therefore to the meaning of the thing, since it is possible to break off the /-x/ in 'senex' *etc.*, but to do so would be to destroy the meaning of the word since the separate parts mean nothing nor are they capable of having meaning.

Figura composita is defined as the mode of signifying the thing by means of the property of compound form, *e.g.* 'praedives'.[82] Siger described this feature as composition made up from the thing itself, the

[79]   Martin recognises the three elements of simple, compound, and double compound, but the latter in fact he considers a sub-mode of the compound, *viz.* #78: "illud autem decompositae est quod a composita venit dictione".

[80]   Thomas of Erfurt, #79: "figura, prout est modus significandi nominis, non accipitur vocis ... figura sumitur a proprietate rei".

[81]   Siger de Courtrai, p. 102: "figura simplex est figura designans circa rem modum essendi indivisionis intelligendo indivisionem non solum quantum ad rem sed quantum ad intellectum ut apparet in 'u' et 'x' et huius modi, cuius partes separatae nihil significant nec valent significare". Thomas of Erfurt, #83: "figura simplex est modus significandi rem sub proprietate simplicis, ut dives, pauper".

[82]   Thomas of Erfurt, #83: "figura composita est modus significandi sub proprietate compositi, ut praedives, praeclarus".

understanding and the expression (vox);[83] he continues that the parts of a nomen of compound figura, by the very fact that they are parts of such a nomen, do not always retain their own entirely separate parts.[84] However, these parts, when separated, have the ability to be considered separate meaningful parts in and of themselves although this meaning may not necessarily be entirely the same nor will the parts, of necessity, take the same shape as the whole; this must not be interpreted that the individual parts have no meaning but that as parts of a combination they have no separate meaning, *i.e.* separate from the composite form to which they now belong. Priscian[85] tells us, says Siger, that compound figura is made up from separate words with separately understood meaning, *i.e.* it is made up of free forms but not necessarily in their original shape, and which signify one thing when uttered with an accent which belongs to the whole form and not to either of the parts;[86] these parts are revealed in their entirety when considered separately and are seen to possess an independent meaning. We can compare, to illustrate this particular feature, the well known examples of 'green house' and 'green-house'.

Figura decomposita is defined as the mode of signifying the thing by means of the property of double composition and is made up from a composition of free forms and bound forms, *e.g.* 'inexpugnabilis'.[87] Siger denies that the figura decomposita designates any modus essendi distinct from either the simple or the compound figura, and for this reason Donatus used only the two categories, *i.e.* simplex and composita. Siger does however distinguish between the compound (composita) and the decomposite (decomposita), in that the decomposite must contain a bound form.[88] Siger explains that the Greeks used

[83] Siger de Courtrai, pp. 102-103: "figura composita est figura designans circa rem modum essendi compositionis, compositionis inquam rei, intellectus et vocis".
[84] Siger de Courtrai, p. 103: "licet partes nominis compositae figurae, ut partes, propinque, sunt et in actu talis nominis nihil significent separatae, quia sunt partes incompositae ... tamen partes nominis compositione figurae, remote, in potentia, partes secundum se consideratae, bene aliquid significant separatae et idem quod in composito vel non penitus idem".
[85] Priscian (V.56): "ipsa per se ex diversis componatur dictionibus separatim intelligendis sub uno accentu et unam rem suppositam [id est significandum] accipiat, ut est 'respublica' ".
[86] Siger de Courtrai, p. 103: "figura composita per se componitur ex divisis dictionibus separatim intelligendis, sub uno accentu unam rem significantibus ut est: 'respublica', quae per se prolata integra sunt et intellectum habent plenum".
[87] Thomas of Erfurt, #83: "decomposita est modus significandi sub proprietate decompositi, id est, sub proprietate collectionis".
[88] The ending /-bilis/ can never occur independently and with an independent meaning.

'parasyntheton', *i.e.* derived from the compound as a device to distinguish it from either the simple or compound; in this Priscian followed
the Greeks and separated the simple from the decomposita, arguing
that the latter cannot be a figura simplex because it is derived from a
figura composita in the way that 'magnanimitas' is derived from 'magnanimus'; it cannot be a figura simplex, nor can it be a compound figura
because it cannot be divided into intelligible parts.[89] Such then is
'magnanimitas' since 'animitas' cannot occur by itself, which means
that it cannot be a figura composita.

There is, in Siger's scheme, a very close link between the figura composita and the species determinativa in that a figura decomposita partakes of both of these;[90] there is, however, no such relationship in
Thomas's scheme between species and figura – for him a figura simplex
is a form which cannot be split into further component parts, while a
figura composita consists of two members and a figura decomposita of
more than two members. Siger considered figura simplex as a form
incapable of further division and the figura composita as made up of
two meaningful parts, though they may not have any further direct
association with the meaning of the compound form. The great difference between Siger and Thomas in their consideration of figura lies in
their different conceptions of the figura decomposita. As we have just
seen, for Thomas the decomposita is merely made of more than two
members.[91] Siger however argues that the decomposita does not designate any modus essendi distinct from either the simplex or composita;[92] following Priscian, who in turn had followed the Greeks, the
figura decomposita is a *derivation* from a compound figura but is not
a combination of free forms, *i.e.* of a simplex and compound and cannot therefore be broken down into its component parts. Siger says that
a word such as 'magnanimitas' is a double compound, *i.e.* complex form
and as such is derived from 'magnanimus' which is itself a compound
figure made up from 'magnus' and 'animus';[93] 'magnanimitas' itself

---

[89]   Siger de Courtrai, p. 103: "non potest esse simplicis figurae et a composita,
quia id non potest esse composite quod non potest dividi in partes intelligibiles".
[90]   'Magnus' can be considered the primary species which can become the derived
species of 'magnanimus' which as well as being a species derivativa will also be a
figura composita made up of 'magnus' and 'animus'.
[91]   Thomas of Erfurt, #83: "decomposita est modus significandi sub proprietate
decompositi, id est, sub proprietate collectionis, ut inexpugnabilis".
[92]   Siger de Courtrai, p. 103: "decompositam a simplici separat quia illud non
potest esse simplicis figurae quod a composita determinatur, ut 'magnanimitas' a
'magnamino' determinatur".
[93]   Siger de Courtrai, p. 103: "non potest esse simplicis figurae et a composita, quia

cannot be broken down into meaningful components. If it were a compound figura it would be possible to break it into 'magn-' and '-animitas', but 'animitas' as such does not exist and it cannot therefore be a compound figura. Siger excludes figura decomposita as a separate category, his argument being that some decompositae can be analysed into parts in such a way as to become a figura composita; he analyses 'impietas' as a combination of /in-/, the negative formant of adjectives, and /pietas/ to become a figura composita made up from two simple figurae, but it can also be analysed as compounded from 'impius, impi', in which the final /-i/ changes to /-e-/ and with the addition of /-tas/ becomes a figura decomposita. The first type of analysis is not always possible, though the second type can always be made; 'magnanimitas' cannot be described as a figura composita in the way that 'impietas' was shown to be made from the two meaningful segments of 'im-' and 'pietas'. 'Magnanimitas' cannot be analysed in this way, since there is no such segment as 'animitas', but it can be shown to be a *derivation* from a compound figura with the addition of the suffix /-tas/, *i.e.*

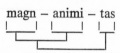

so that Siger can quote Peter Helias, that the only derived form possible from a composite figura is a figura possessing a figura decomposita.[94]

In these analyses of the figurae of the nomen we see the beginnings of a rudimentary IC analysis; this is seen quite clearly in Siger's concluding remarks that something can be at one and the same time a figura composita and a figura decomposita, as Siger himself shows by his two different analyses of 'impietas'. However in order to avoid giving the impression that the Modistae used a purely formal approach to their description of figura, we must consider Thomas's concluding remarks which summarise the features of the figura but in emphatically semantic terms. A dictio will be of a figura simplex which is imposed from a simple concept; similarly a figura composita will be imposed from a compound concept, and so it will be in the case of a figura decomposita, *i.e.* it will be established from more than two concepts. Such concepts are not imaginary, and therefore they must correspond

---

id non potest esse composite quod non potest dividi in partes intelligibiles; nunc 'magnanimitas' est huiusmodi quia 'animitas' per se non dicitur, ideo non potest esse compositae figurae".

[94] Siger de Courtrai, p. 103: "est ergo decompositae pro tanto quia a composito determinatur, ideo dicit commentator quod sola determinatio ex composito est figura decompositae figurae".

to the same properties in the thing, and those properties are the same as those which the nomen signifies by means of those concepts which have just been enumerated.

Gradus

We have already seen that Thomas included 'gradus' among the modi specialissimi of the nomen, since the three grades of positive, comparative and superlative represent three types of nomen adiectivum;[95] but he has nothing more to say about them and is content merely to include them in his inventory of the modi specialissimi which represent the different types of nomina adiectiva derived from the subaltern mode, *i.e.* modus adiacentis. Siger, on the other hand, includes gradus among the accidental modes of the nomen and discusses this feature in much greater detail.[96]

Michel de Marbais defined gradus as the mode of signifying by means of which the nomen can express the property of intensity of diminishing with regard to the thing either simply as it is or as it represents an extension beyond its limits.[97] Siger compared gradus in grammar to a flight of stairs, *i.e.* in actual life one climbs from the lowest to the top and vice versa by means of such a flight of stairs, and so it is in grammar;[98] therefore gradus is the accidental mode of the nomen which designates the modus essendi as it is in excess and is divided into positive, comparative and superlative.[99]

---

[95] Thomas includes comparatio in the adverb as an accidental mode; Thomas clearly saw the three grades of the adjective as three different adjectives, whereas in the adverb the comparison is derived from the accidental modes of species and figura and does not affect the fundamental role of the adverb.

[96] Donatus (Ars minor) stated that there were three degrees of comparison, that only nomina signifying qualitas or quantity can be compared, that the comparative degree can be used with the ablative without preposition, *e.g.* 'doctior illo', and that the superlative is used only with the genitive plural, *e.g.* 'doctissimus poetarum', *viz.* conparationis gradus quot sunt? "Tres. Qui? Positivus, ut doctus, conparativus, ut doctior, superlativus, ut doctissimus. Ouae nomina conparantur? Appellativa dumtaxat qualitatem aut quantitatem significantia. Conparativus gradus cui casui servit? Ablativo sine praepositione: dicimus enim 'doctior illo'. Superlativus cui? Genitivo tantum plurali: dicimus enim 'doctissimus poetarum' ".

[97] Michel de Marbais: "gradus est quidam modus significandi datus nomini ad designandum rem intensibilem vel remissibilem, ut est in subiecto simpliciter aut cum excessu" (*cf.* Thurot, p. 167).

[98] Siger de Courtrai, p. 98: "sicut per gradus proprie dictos fit acsensus de infimo ad summum et e converso descensus, ita in gradibus grammaticae considerationis fit ascensus in forma comparabili de infimo ad summum, et e converso".

[99] Siger de Courtrai, p. 98: "gradus est modus significandi accidentalis nominis

The positive is the degree of comparison which designates the modus essendi but without increase or excess; such a mode is not of itself the basis (principium) of a construction, although by reason of another mode of signifying which exists in this same positive form, *i.e.* that of being an adiectivum, the positive degree can be a principium constructionis; in other words the positive degree is the 'unmarked' term and does not require another nomen for support in a syntactic function, *e.g.* "he is clever" – whereas the comparative does require another nomen, *e.g.* "he is cleverer than X."

The comparative degree is the mode or the degree of comparison which expresses the modus essendi of the positive form along with its increase or excess. Siger tells us that Priscian [100] described the comparative as what is implied by the positive in conjunction with the adverb 'magis', *i.e.* indeterminate increase and indeed some adjectives have only this means of expressing such an increase. Siger continues that comparison cannot refer to 'one', and therefore the nomen proprium which possesses the property of one cannot be compared, and similarly the nomen appellativum cannot be compared, because 'magis' cannot be found in substance and therefore nomina signifying substance cannot be compared; [101] this leaves only the adiectiva which alone can be compared, and along with the gender and number which the adjective acquires from the nomen substantivum, these features of gradus, genus and numerus stress the separability of the adjective from the substantive and at the same time confirm the dependence of the adjective on the substantive that it qualifies. Siger adds a further refinement; 'magis' indicates a relative position between two contraries,[102] so that only adiectiva appellativa signifying quality or quantity can be compared. It may well have been this restriction which induced Thomas to list the comparative (as well as the positive and superlative) among the modi specialisimi of the adiectivum. We might therefore describe this definition of comparison as a 'logical justification' of a formal descrip-

---

designans circa rem modum essendi prout est in excessu vel cum excessu, et dividitur in positivum, comparativum et superlativum".

[100] Priscian (III.1): "comparativum est, quod cum positivi intellectu vel cum aliquo participe sensu positivi 'magis' adverbium significat: ut 'fortior', magis fortis".

[101] Siger de Courtrai, p. 99: "magis non determinatur inesse nisi per respectum ad substantiam, adiectiva solum comparantur et non substantiva seu abstracta".

[102] Siger de Courtrai, p. 99: "quia 'magis' attenditur penes accessum et recessum a contrario, quod solum in qualitate reperitur, vel penes extensionem in quanto, quod solum quantitati advenit, ideo nomina appellativa adiectiva significantia aut qualitatem aut quantitatem solum comparantur".

tion of Latin sentence structure, especially as we are given no grammatical expression of 'less' and 'least'.

The comparative is a principium constructionis with the ablative of either number because anything which signifies by means of the mode of excess can be properly constructed with anything which signifies the thing as that from which the excess is taken;[103] (we shall see that the ablative can be described in a quasi-formal manner as possessing the form 'ut a quo'). The comparative can also be constructed with the nominative, but in that instance, the adverb 'quam' which is the adverb of comparison or analogy must be used as in "Achilles est fortior quam Eneas"; Siger adds that in this case the comparison is achieved more by virtue of the adverb 'quam' than by the comparative itself. In conclusion, almost as an afterthought, Siger adds his belief that the nominative is governed by means of a verb understood rather than by the comparative,[104] i.e. in the form "quam Eneas [est]", and such a possible use of the verb 'est' produces a much more linguistically satisfactory explanation.

The superlative designates the modus essendi of the positive in so far as it is in excess which in this instance is the partitive;[105] the partitive is constructed with the genitive, the superlative is therefore constructed with the genitive, and since the partitive does not refer to one but to many, the superlative will be constructed with the genitive plural or with the genitive singular of a collective nomen, e.g. fortissimus gentis. Siger refers to Priscian's description of the superlative as whatever, compared to many of its kind, is placed above them all,[106] or else, it is whatever combines with 'valde', i.e. 'very' together with the positive form, i.e. optimus = valde bonus.

Genus

Priscian and more particularly the mediaeval grammarians had moved a long way from the formal definitions of Thrax and Donatus; it would

---

[103] Siger de Courtrai, p. 99: "omne id quod significat rem suam ut a quo exceditur, et quia ablativus utriusque numeri significat rem suam ut 'a quo', ideo comparativus cum ablativo utriusque numeri congrue construitur."

[104] Siger de Courtrai, p. 99: "credo tamen nominativum magis regi a verbo subintellecto quam a comparativo".

[105] Siger de Courtrai, p. 99: "superlativum est gradus comparationis designans circa rem positivi modum essendi prout est in vi excessus, et esse in vi excessus respectu aliorum illam formam participantium est quod partitivum".

[106] Siger de Courtrai, p. 99: "superlativum est vel quod ad plures sui generis comparatum omnibus superponitur, vel, per se prolatum, intellectum habet, cum 'valde' adverbio, positivi".

seem that Donatus had based,[107] to a large extent, his description of the Latin system of gender on Thrax's description of gender as "one of the concord categories of sentence structure",[108] and it would also seem reasonable to suggest that Donatus, in listing the genders of Latin as he did, *i.e.* masculine = hic magister, feminine = haec musa, neuter = hoc scamnum, common = hic et haec sacerdos, and hic et haec et hoc felix[109] and epicene = passer, aquila, had in mind that there is here a system analogous to the Greek system of using gender marking as one of the functions of the article.[110]

Priscian introduced the idea of generation in his description of gender,[111] which may well account for Thomas's statement that the ancients (antiqui) had defined gender as the difference of sex (discretio sexus), which means, according to Thomas and stated in his terminology that genus is the mode of signifying derived from the active or passive property which is more readily and definitely found in separate things.[112] As a preamble to this definition of genus, Thomas had stated that two general properties, *i.e.* the property of acting and that of suffering, are to be found in all things compounded of matter and form, but these properties belong more readily and distinctly to separate things; the first property is that of generating and the second of suffering.[113] In other things these properties are indifferently or indistinctly found. This duality of gender is entirely in keeping with the Modistic conception of things and material reality which contain the two proper-

---

[107] Donatus (Ars minor): "genera nominum quod sunt? Quattuor. Quae? Masculinum, ut hic magister, femininum, ut haec Musa, neutrum, ut hoc scamnum, commune, ut hic et haec sacerdos. Est praeterea trium generum, quod omne dicitur, ut hic et haec et hoc felix; est epicoenon, id est promiscuum, ut passer, aquila".

[108] R. H. Robins, *Thrax*, p. 99: who continues, that "gender is grammatically a category of concord and not the reflection of sex or inanimacy was noted by the scholiasts who pointed to gender marking as one of the functions of meaning of the article"; such a statement seems much truer of Donatus than of Priscian and their mediaeval commentators.

[109] Donatus actually refers to this as 'omne genus'.

[110] R. H. Robins, *T.P.S.* (1957), p. 99.

[111] Priscian, V, 141: "genera nominum principalia sunt duo quae sola novit ratio naturae, masculinum et femininum. Genera dicuntur a generando proprie quae generare possunt, quae sunt masculinum et femininum".

[112] Thomas of Erfurt, #69: "genus est modus significandi nominis, sumptus a proprietate activa, vel passiva, quae in rebus separatis magis prompte et determinate invenitur".

[113] Thomas of Erfurt, #69: "in rebus inveniuntur duae proprietates generales, scilicet proprietas agentis, et proprietas patientis, quae licet in omnibus rebus ex materia et forma compositis inveniantur, tamen in rebus separatis magis prompte et distincte videntur inesse; quorum unum est determinate generans, et alterum determinate patiens".

ties of acting and suffering which are to be found in all compound but equally all separate things. Gender therefore for Thomas is the active mode of signifying by means of which the nomen signifies either the property of acting or suffering or both of them.[114]

Siger took from Priscian the idea of 'engendering' in his description of genus;[115] Priscian had said,[116] according to Siger, that the natural scheme of things recognised two genders, *i.e.* masculine and feminine – these are the two principal genders and all the others are called 'genders' by virtue of their being predicated to the two principal genders.[117] Genus is therefore so called from the process of procreating, and in such a process we find the male (masculus) which possesses the active power of procreation and the female (femella) which possesses the passive power.[118] Once more we see a common doctrine in the Modistae; though Thomas and Michel do not go quite so far as Siger in ascribing the powers of procreation to the masculine and feminine, they both affirm the active and passive nature of the masculine and feminine. Gender can, therefore, be defined modistically as the accidental mode given to the nomen for signifying the active and passive force or for signifying that force which is indifferent to either of these other properties,[119] and thus in terms of these properties, gender is differentiated by means of the masculine, feminine, neuter, common, *etc.*; common, dubium and epicene may refer to different but not separate genders.

Of the various genders of the nomen, the masculine is the mode of signifying by means of the active property, *i.e.* the agency in the case of Thomas,[120] and in the case of Siger it designates the modus essendi

---

[114]   Thomas of Erfurt, #69: "genus est modus significandi activus, quo mediante nomen proprietatem agentis, vel patientis, vel utrumque significat".
[115]   Siger de Courtrai, p. 100: "dicitur genus a generando".
[116]   Priscian (V.1): "genera igitur nominum principalia sunt duo, quae sola novit ratio naturae, masculinum et femininum. Genera enim dicuntur a generando proprie quae generare possunt, quae sunt masculinum et femininum. Nam commune et neutrum vocis magis qualitate quam natura dinoscuntur, quae sunt sibi contraria".
[117]   Siger de Coutrai, p. 100: "alia dicuntur genera per attributionem ad ista".
[118]   Siger de Courtrai, p. 100: "masculinum genus, genus est nominis designans circa rem modum essendi masculi seu potentiae activae generationis ... femininum est genus nominis designans circa rem modum essendi femellae ratione passivae generationis".
[119]   Michel de Marbais: "genus est quidam modus significandi datus nomini ad designandum rem sub modo essendi virtutis active vel passive vel indifferentis ad utrumque" (Thurot, p. 167).
[120]   Thomas of Erfurt, #70: "genus masculinum est modus significandi rem sub proprietate agentis, ut vir".

of the male, *i.e.* the active power of procreating; similarly, the feminine gender is the mode of signifying the passive acceptance of an act,[121] *i.e.* in Siger's terms the passive participator in the act of procreation. The neuter is the mode of signifying that property which is indeterminate and does so without reference to either the masculine or the feminine; [122] Siger explains that its name 'nec utrum' is derived from the fact that it signifies the modus essendi of neither the masculine nor the feminine. Neuter gender must not be considered as representing the absence of the properties of the masculine and of the feminine, since to do this would imply that the neuter was not a mode of signifying but a fiction (figmentum); the neuter merely refers to a property which is neither masculine nor feminine, nor can it be considered as common gender since, in such an instance, it would refer to all three genders, *i.e.* masculine, feminine and neuter and would signify by means of the property 'omnis generis'.[123]

Thomas defined common gender as the mode of signifying by means of either property, active or passive,[124] *i.e.* it is the gender which differs neither from the masculine nor the feminine. Siger tells us that Priscian divided common gender into bi-partite, *e.g.* hic et haec sacerdos, and tri-partite, *e.g.* hic et haec et hoc felix, which Donatus called 'omne'; Thomas follows Donatus in this and has a small sub-section which he called an adiectivum 'omnis generis' because it can be assigned to a substantive of either masculine, feminine or neuter gender.[125] This becomes yet another criterion for the adjective [126] and furthermore, as we shall see in the section on syntax, the dependence of the adjective on the substantive in terms of gender and number is an integral feature of the constructio intransitiva personarum and the 'congruity' [127] (con-

[121] Thomas of Erfurt, #70: "genus femininum est modus significandi rem sub-proprietate patientis, ut mulier".
[122] Thomas of Erfurt, #70: "genus neutrum est modus significandi rem sub pro-prietate neutra, quae est indeterminata, et indifferenter ad utrumque".
[123] Thomas of Erfurt, #71: "quidam dicun, quod neutram genus sit modus sig-nificandi rem sub privatione utriusque proprietatis. Quo posito, vel genus neutram non erit modus significandi, sed figmentum; vel a privatione accipietur, quae nul-lius est causa; quae ambo sunt inconvenientia".
[124] Thomas of Erfurt, #70: "genus commune est modus significandi rem sub utraque proprietate determinate, ut homo".
[125] Thomas of Erfurt, #72: "adiectivum ... omnis generis potest attribui sub-stantivo masculini generis, feminini, vel neutrius, ut felix".
[126] Thomas of Erfurt, #71: "hoc tantum convenit adiectivis, quae genus non habent ex proprietate suae rei subiectae, sed ex proprietate rei substantivi no-minis".
[127] *Cf.* also pp. 303-307, 319-321.

gruitas) of such a construction. Siger describes the bi-partite type of common gender as the gender which embraces the modus essendi of the masculine and feminine while actively designating the modus essendi of the thing under consideration; it is used in constructions of either the masculine or the feminine and yet is distinct from them just as the whole is distinct from the pars.[128] The tri-partite form of common gender designates the modus essendi actively and at the same time embraces the modus essendi of the masculine, feminine and neuter and is used in constructions of all three genders.[129] It is interesting to note that both Siger and Thomas provide us, unconsciously, with a purely formal definition of this common gender by means of their description of the paradigm of the adjective in two or three genders.

Epicene gender is defined by Thomas as possessing the masculine and feminine but designated by means of the one expression, e.g. hic passer, haec aquila.[130] Siger defines it, etymologically, as 'supra commune' in that it will signify by means of one member and will do so mixedly as in the case of 'piscis'; what this means is that since it may convey the modus essendi of either the masculine or feminine, it does so with reference to a masculine gender and yet at the same time implies the feminine as in 'piscis', or the converse may be the case as in 'aquila'.[131]

The final subdivision of gender is the dubium genus, which can designate separately a modus essendi of either the masculine gender or the feminine, which means that it can occur sometimes in a masculine construction and at other times in a feminine construction, e.g. hic et haec dies, hic et haec finis, and this too might be briefly described as a formal description of this particular gender.

Genus is a principium constructionis and as such demands concord of gender, i.e. masculine with masculine; the reason for this is two-fold:

---

[128] Siger de Courtrai, p. 101: "omne duorum est genus nominis designans circa rem modum essendi actualiter et simul et includentem modum essendi masculini et feminini et amborum servat constructionem et distinguitur ab eisdem sicut totum a partibus".

[129] Siger and Thomas say nothing about anomalous, irrational or inanimate genders.

[130] Thomas of Erfurt, #73: "(genus epicoenum) habet masculinum et femininum genus sub uno articulo designatum".

[131] Siger de Courtrai, pp. 100-101: "epicoenum dicitur promiscuum, quia mixtim seu promiscue modum essendi masculini et feminini importat; ideo aliquando significatur sub modo essendi masculini, ut ... piscis, nihilominus tamen, modum significandi feminini mixtim seu promiscue importat, et aliquando significatur sub modo essendi feminini, tamen mixtim seu promiscue modum masculini importat, ut ... aquila".

(a) the male and female cannot exist together in a thing in mutual symmetry but the male requires the male and the female requires the female, and (b) whatever depends on something else for its essence, acquires its essence from it and as a consequence its generation will be thus ordained.[132] Adjectives derive their essence from their substantives and therefore they must be of the same essence as their substantives. Siger concludes that a thing can possess several modi essendi or properties because such properties belong to things and there can be several accidents particular to the one thing; therefore one and the same thing, designated by reference to different modi essendi, can be of more than one gender.

Numerus

This is, of course, a well known category which refers to the inflection of the nomen in terms of quantity. The Modistae are in entire agreement on the nature of numerus, though their terms inevitably show minor variations, i.e. Siger defines number as the accidental mode which designates the property of one or of many,[133] while Thomas states that it expresses the property of indivisibility or divisibility.[134]

Siger continues that one or many are aspects of quantity and refers therefore to Priscian that numerus is the form of the word which can express differences of quantity.[135] He also refers to Peter Helias who suggested that because the mode of signifying presupposes the vox, numerus therefore can be expressed in two ways, (a) according to the thing so that singularity or plurality will be signified, or (b) according to the realisation (vox) which is the form of the word from which it can be established whether the expression refers to one or to more than one.[136] This can be construed as a formal statement of number.

Thomas bases his definition of number on Boethius who had stated, according to Thomas, that the 'numerus' existing in things outside the mind represents a multitude of many unities collected together,[137] which

---

132   Siger de Courtrai, p. 101: "illa quae dependent in esse ab aliquibus, ab illis habent esse et per consequens generationem ordinatam ad esse".
133   Siger de Courtrai, p. 101: "numerus est modus significandi accidentalis nominis designans circa rem modum essendi unius aut multi".
134   Thomas of Erfurt, #77: "in utroque numero duae proprietates inveniuntur, scilicet: proprietas indivisibilitatis ... et proprietas divisibilitatis".
135   Priscian, V, 172: "numerus est dictionis forma quae discretionem quantitatis facere potest".
136   Siger de Courtrai, p. 101: "numerus ... dicitur ... secundum vocem prout est forma dictionis ex qua discerniur utrum ad unum vel ad plura pertineat locutio".
137   Thomas of Erfurt, #79: "numerus in rebus extra animam, secundum Boethium, est multitudo ex unitatibus aggregata, et profusa".

is close to Michel de Marbais's definition of numerus as the accidental mode given to the nomen to designate the thing in the form of the property of actual unity or actual multiplicity.[138] However, Thomas points out that unitas can be considered as having a two-fold representation, the first of which refers to the singleness, the indivisible oneness of the thing, and thereby reveals the 'multitudo' as one out of a very great number[139] – this is the numerus essentiarum, and by means of this the multiplicity of the different species of things is reckoned. The second representation of unitas refers to the unbroken continuity of the thing – this is the 'numerus materialis', and by means of this the individual differences within the species are reckoned.[140] In this context, therefore, the 'numerus essentiarum' refers to the different types of nomen, while the 'numerus materialis' refers to the different nomina within each type of nomen.

Thomas continues that in both numbers two properties are found, *i.e.* the property of indivisibility which is found in the thing by virtue of its unity (quae est in re ratione unitatis), and the property of divisibility which is found in the thing by virtue of the multitudo which is revealed by the repetition of the unity (quae est in re ratione multitudinis, quae ab unitatis replicatione profunditur); from these properties in the nomen numerus is derived. Numerus is therefore the accidental mode of the nomen which signifies the property of divisibility which is the property of the plural (multitudo).[141]

Singular number is the mode of signifying by means of the property of indivisibility, *i.e.* the property of one;[142] this is all that Thomas tells us, which Siger also confirms, but the latter dwells at greater length on the nature of the singular number. Number, this way, is similar to the number of various forms but not to the number, which is a species of a definite quantity; such a number is really more the basis of a number rather than a number itself because strictly speaking a

[138] Michel de Marbais: "numerus est quidam modus significandi datus nomini ad designandum rem sub modo essendi actualis unitatis vel actualis multitudinis" (Thurot, p. 168).
[139] Thomas of Erfurt, #75: "ab ista unitate multoties iterata profunditur multitudo, quae est unum de transcendentibus, ut ens, et unum".
[140] Thomas of Erfurt, #76: "ab ista unitate multoties reiterata profunditur multitudo, quae numerus materialis vocatur, id est individuorum secundum differentiam materialem differentium".
[141] Thomas of Erfurt, #77: "numerus est modus significandi accidentalis nominis, mediante quo nomen proprietatem indivisibilitatis, quae est proprietas unius, vel proprietatem divisibilitatis, quae est proprietas multitudinis, significat".
[142] Thomas of Erfurt, #78: "numerus singularis est modus significandi rem sub proprietal indivisi, quae est proprietas unius, ut homo".

number cannot be found in *one*.[143] Singular number should not properly be called a number, unless it were argued that it is called number, (a) because any material increase of it creates a number, and (b) because all numbers are constructed from it or resolved into it. Plural number is the mode of signifying by means of the property of divisibility which is the property of 'multitudo'.[144] Because the concept of many or number increases infinitely by means of the addition of unities, then plural number, as Siger quotes from Priscian, is infinite,[145] and as a result numeral nomina were devised to determine this infinity.

Siger concludes that number is the basis (principium) of a construction of the adiectivum and the substantivum and of the appositum with the suppositum, because those elements, which are dependent on something else for their being (esse), will be equally so as far as number is concerned; adiectiva depend on their substantiva just as accidents depend on their substance, and equally then, the adiectiva depend on the substantiva in so far as numerus is concerned. In other words, elements which use number as an accidental mode evolve syntactic relations with verbs and other partes orationis, but also demonstrate a mutual dependency within the word-class to which they and this accidental feature belong.

Casus

This is, of all the accidental modes of the nomen described by the Modistae, the most difficult to analyse and assess; the reason is that whereas the other accidental modes of the nomen were described in terms which were fairly solidly and consistently semantic with a formal suggestion added occasionally, one might say fortuitously,[146] there seems to be real confusion in the criteria for case, which renders any exposition problematical. An additional complication is that, for once, there

---

[143] Siger de Courtrai, pp. 101-102: "numerus ... habet similitudinem cum numero formarum, extendendo formam ut prius extensum est unum, et non cum numero qui est species quantitatis distinctae, et quia ipsum unum est magis principium talis numeri quam numerus eo quod in uno proprie numerus non reperitur".

[144] Thomas of Erfurt, #78: "numerus pluralis est modus significandi rem sub proprietate divisi, quae est proprietas multitudines, ut homines",

[145] Siger de Courtrai, p. 102: "multum seu numerus crescit in infinitum per additionem unitatis ... ideo numerus pluralis est infinitus".

[146] In the sections on 'genus' and 'numerus' I have referred to formal statements, but these are *my* interpretations of *their* statements; the Modistae did not seek to make what the modern linguist would call a 'formal' statement, since this would have entailed a conscious departure on their part from their normal descriptive procedures.

seems to be no one single Modistic case theory which can perhaps be explained by the fact that in this particular instance they seem to have fallen between the two extremes, *i.e.* of reproducing in their own semantic terms the ideas of their predecessors or of trying to produce something entirely new. What has happened is that Siger describes a case theory which can be described as an account vaguely reminiscent of his models, but it is an account which is completely unsystematic and does not reproduce by any means all the criteria which had been represented in the grammars which had been his models; the result is an exposition of the cases of Latin in terms which are partly functional, partly semantic, with a half-hearted attempt to add formal justification to his categories by making use of the quasi formal criteria of 'ut quod', *etc.* Thomas seems to have tried to open new territory; he too makes use of this quasi formal criterion 'ut quod', *etc.*, but he too fails because he has been content with vague semantic criteria to justify his distinctions of the cases on the more formal criteria of word order as a functional, *i.e.* syntactic feature, and furthermore he has ignored morphological criteria which would of course have justified his more functional approach to case theory.

Thrax had listed the cases of the Greek noun on a semantic basis, though his case system is morphologically based.[147] Priscian too retained a morphological definition of case, which he described as the declension of the nomen or other words possessing a case feature.[148] The Modistae, as we have said, ignored morphology altogether as a feature of case, and indeed it should be noted that they abandoned altogether the use of case of a positive feature in their definitions of the nomen or as a negative feature in their definitions of the verb, though the Greeks and Priscian had included case as a criterion for the nomen and absence of case as a criterion of the verb.[149] Michel de Marbais did retain however a purely functional approach to case by insisting on the concord of the cases in any construction.[150]

There is then little similarity between the case theories of Thomas and Siger. Siger follows the line adopted by the Greek grammarians and Priscian, that the nominative is the starting-point and that all the other

---

[147]   R. H. Robins, *Thrax*, p. 100

[148]   Priscian (V. 183): "casus est declinatio nominis vel aliarum casualium dictionum, quae fit maxime in fine".

[149]   R. H. Robins, *A. and M.*, pp. 40, 65.

[150]   Michel de Marbais: "casus est principium alicuius constructionis cum in unione constructibilium requiratur proportio vel convenientia casum invicem" (Thurot, p. 224).

cases are in fact derived from the nominative and are therefore in opposition to the nominative. Siger has nothing to say about a possible morphological analysis of case but does make a little use of the quasi formal criteria of the analogy of the different forms of 'quod', but this is far from satisfactory data since this 'ut quod' criterion merely represents a definition of the different cases based on the translation equivalent of 'quod, cuius', *etc.* Siger does provide certain definitions of the different cases according to their uses, but this is unsystematically presented and not exhaustively described; furthermore there is no attempt to set up a case theory based on the oppositions created between the various cases, and which had been achieved by the Greek grammarians, *e.g.* Apollonius. Hjelmslev refers to the systems of oppositions described by Greek and Byzantine grammarians[151] which constitute the essential of their theories, but nothing of such a systematic nature is found in Siger – nor for that matter in Thomas.

According to Thomas, every case of the nomen is defined by means of two criteria, (a) whether it is the mode of signifying of the first or final constituent of the construction, *i.e.* proprietas principii et proprietas termini, and (b) according to the morpho-semantic criterion of its analogy to the inflections of 'quod'. Therefore, the nominative signifies as the first member and is as 'quod' is; the vocative signifies as the final or terminant[152] member only and has no special formal distinguishing features to equate with the scatter of 'quod'.[153] The genitive signifies as either member with the formal mark of 'cuius', and similarly, the dative possesses the formal mark of 'cui', the accusative the formal mark of 'quem' and the ablative the formal mark of 'a quo'. The formal features of the cases of the nomen will be paralleled by a similar concord in the government between the verb and the case-form. Thomas does attempt to make word-order a functional criterion for each case, so that each case is defined by its syntagmatic function which will vary according to whether it is the first or final element in a construction; *e.g.* "Socratis interest" shows the genitive as the first element in the syntagm and "misereor Socratis" shows it as the final element in the syntagm. These are the only general criteria that Thomas uses, and he makes no attempt to define the cases of the nomen in any further detail or in terms of their mutual dependence or independence.[154]

---

[151] L. Hjelmslev, *La Catégorie des cas*, pp. 1-13.
[152] *Cf.* pp. 310-312 for the use of this term.
[153] *Cf.* also pp. 176-177.
[154] Hjelmslev looks upon the dependence and independence of cases as one of

Case for Thomas is the accidental mode of signifying which consignifies, *i.e.* connotates the two common properties of principium and
terminus,[155] which, as we have argued, suggests that principium and
terminus are syntactic values attached to relative word-order. For
Siger, case is not quite so complicated; he defines it in semantic terms
as the accidental mode which designates the ending of the nomen and
also the way that the mode of being of the thing subject to declension
is expressed and understood.[156] The Modistae continued to divide case,
as Donatus and Priscian, *etc.* had done, into six component cases
of nominativus, genitivus, dativus, accusativus, vocativus, and ablativus.

The nominative case is so called, according to Siger, for two reasons:
(a) because it leads from its own ending to other endings, and (b)
because it can create other cases, and hence it possesses the quality of
leading[157] and by so doing creates all the other cases.[158] This case is
called the nominative because naming is done by means of it.

The nominative case, however, according to Thomas, is the mode
of signifying which belongs to the first constituent of a construction, its
morphological shape belonging to the pattern of 'ut quod'. Thomas
makes no reference to the nominative with the copula or to its use in
instances such as "Socrates vocatur philosophus". In his discussion of
the constructions, he refers to the type of construction *e.g.* 'sum albus'
and 'vocor Adrianus' as intransitive personarum constructions,[159] in
which the verbum substantivum, *i.e.* 'sum', and the verbum vocativum,

---

the major contributions of the Byzantines to case theory, *cf. La Catégorie des cas*,
pp. 11-12.
[155]   Thomas of Erfurt, #85: "casus est modus significandi accidentalis nominis,
mediante quo, nomen proprietatem principii, vel termini consignificat".
[156]   Siger de Courtrai, p. 104: "casus est modus significandi accidentalis designans
circa rem modum essendi cadentis, inquam rei, intellectus et vocis, seu eiusdem
nominis".
[157]   This definition of the nominative case goes back to the Stoics, *cf.* R. H. Robins,
A. and M., p. 32: "The Stoics fixed the use of term 'case' as we have it today: the
nominative was 'the upright case' . . ., and the rest were 'oblique'.
[158]   Siger de Courtrai, p. 104: "nominativus dicitur casus, tum quia cadit a sua
terminatione in alias, tum quia facit alios casus, tum naturam habet ut cadere
possit et cadendo facit omnes casus, quippe cum casus non dicitur solum illud in
quo cadit aliquid sed etiam ipsa res quae cadit". It will have become clear that the
accidents of the nomen have been listed and described by the Modistae in terms
of the properties of the res, vox, and intellectus with no clear and real distinction
made between inflectional and derivational categories, a tendency apparently
general in antiquity, *cf.* R. H. Robins, *Thrax*, p. 98; the modes of absolute and
respective however do suggest a definite step in the direction of making a distinction between derivational and inflectional categories.
[159]   This type of construction is described in greater detail in Chapter VII, section G.

i.e. 'vocor' are determined by a declinable pars orationis; the implication is that the dependence between the two constructibles is a 'backwards' relationship but he has nothing specific to say about the use of the nominative in such constructions. Thomas tells us, furthermore, that in the construction "Socrates amat", the nominative 'Socrates' becomes the first member of the construction with the verb 'amare' by virtue of the property 'ut quod est alterum', which implies that the nomen 'Socrates' in isolation [160] is different – hence the 'alterum'. In the construction "Socrates amatur", 'Socrates' remains in the same relationship, *i.e.* ut quod est alterum, to the dependent verb with the same morphological shape, and the passive nature of the verb does not alter the one-to-one relationship between the verb and nominative case. Thomas refers to Peter Helias to support his definition of the nominative case based on morphological scatter; Peter Helias argues that the cases are derived according to the pattern of the inflections of 'quod, cuius, cui', *etc.*, and although Thomas had to add a semantic reflex to his statement, *i.e.* that this mode of signifying is called the nominative because in this mode names (nomina) are given to things, it must be conceded that Thomas's main criterion for the nominative and for its discreteness from all the other cases was the property of 'ut quod est alterum'.

The nominative is the principium constructionis *i.e.* of an intransitive [161] construction with a finite personal verb, because such a verb signifies by means of the mode 'ut illud' [162] which has important implications for the congruence of the nomen and verb or the suppositum with the appositum, since a verb in the mode of signifying 'ut illud' will be predicated to a nomen which designates the mode or property 'ut quod'.[163] Throughout his discussion of case, Thomas has fragmentary suggestions about case concord and rection between the verb and case, *i.e.* in the nominative, the concord will be 'ut ipsum est alterum' on the pattern of 'ut quod' as a morphological feature of the nominative, since the concord of this verb whether active or passive, is governed by the

---

[160]   M. Heidegger, *Op. cit.*, p. 196: "(In) 'Socrates amat', Sokrates ist Principium der Bestimmung 'lieben', er ist zugleich in seiner Identität als Sokrates ein Anderes, ihm zufallendes, er liebt, ist liebender Sokrates".

[161]   This is the Modistic use, not the traditional use, of the term 'intransitive'.

[162]   Siger de Courtrai, p. 104: "iste modus significandi est principium constructionis intransitivae cum verbo personali finiti modi, quia tale verbum significat rem suam per modum significandi 'ut illud' qui circumloquitur per personam et modum finitum".

[163]   Siger de Courtrai, p. 104: "modus significandi 'ut illud' apponitur modo nominativi designantis modum 'ut quod' ".

nominative.[164] This is an important statement, since it implies that the form, *i.e.* the nominative, is demanded by the rection of nominative and verb.

According to Siger the genitive case is so called because it possesses a natural bond (naturale vinculum); based on the morphological criteria of being, it can be deduced from the nominative [165] because all names (to the Greeks) used to come from it,[166] and by analogy and response to the form 'cuius'. The genitive, according to Thomas, is the mode of signifying of both the first and final constituent in a construction and possesses the form of 'cuius' from the property 'ut cuius est alterum'.[167] In the construction 'Socratis interest', the genitive form 'Socratis' signifies as the first member, *i.e.* as the logical subject with reference to the verb 'interest', and in the construction 'misereor Socratis' it functions as the second member, *i.e.* as the logical object and grammatical oblique nominal form with reference to the verb 'misereor'. In his definition Thomas stated that the genitive signifies differently according to the property of principium or terminus; in the first instance, it seems to be the subject, at least the logical subject of 'interest' and in the second, it functions as the oblique of 'misereor'; *i.e.* the former is an intransitive construction, the second a transitive construction.

Siger describes at some length the genitive as a principium constructionis, *e.g.* of a construction suggesting possession, *e.g.* 'capa Socratis', or the partitive, *e.g.* 'fortissimus Graecorum', *etc.* These constructions are established on purely semantic criteria with the quasi formal criterion of 'ut cuius' introduced in each case as confirmation, so to speak, of the genitival element in the construction.

Since these constructions refer to Latin only, and seem to add nothing to the definition of the genitive case, it seems pointless to overload this exposition of the theories of the Modistae. (This is also true of Siger's description of the dative and ablative cases). Siger certainly never makes use even of Thomas's distinction of principium and terminus; in his definition of the genitive, Siger is much more orthodox than Thomas and is content to reproduce some of the ideas of his predecessors.

---

[164]   Thomas of Erfurt, #87: "huic modo proportionatur in verbo modus, ut ipsum est alterum, scilicet: principiatum, et causatum a re nominativi active, vel passive".
[165]   Siger de Courtrai, p. 104: "genitivus casus dicitur genitivus tum quia naturale vinculum possidet, tum quia nascitur a nominativo et generat alios obliquos".
[166]   Siger de Courtrai, p. 104: "apud Graecos omnes deconominationes ab eo solent fieri".
[167]   Thomas of Erfurt, #88: "genitivus est modus significandi rem in ratione principii, vel termini differenter, proprietate, ut cuius est alterum, superaddita".

Siger has nothing to say about a definition of the dative except to give the formal 'ut cui' as its pattern, and leaves any discussion of the dative until he describes it as a principium constructionis; this use by Siger of 'principium' must not be confused with Thomas's use of 'principium'. They are quite distinct, for one thing, by reason of their entirely different collocations. Siger's use of principium in principium constructionis was a device he used to define a feature by its syntactic potentialities while still analysing the feature in question as a mode of signifying of a pars orationis; in this respect the use of principium constructionis is no different from any other of Siger's uses of the term, *i.e.* to describe an additional feature of some mode of signifying. Thomas defines the dative as the mode of signifying of the first or final member according to the pattern 'ut cui est alterum',[168] but this time it would seem that the proprietas principii or the proprietas termini does not have any distinctive semantic value, though they do have a different grammatical potentiality. In the construction 'Socrati accidit', the dative signifies as the principium and in 'faveo Socrati', it signifies as the terminus, and although we are dealing with two different types of construction, according to Thomas, the meaning of the dative case as such is the same.

Siger lists four different types of construction and it is interesting to see the various criteria applied to the definition of the dative in addition to the general criterion of 'ut cui'; it proves to be a curious mixture of semantic and syntactic criteria, *i.e.* it signifies possession, *e.g.* 'Evandro filius fuit Pallas', or it signifies by means of the mode of favour or the contrary, *e.g.* 'fortis patriae', or it is used with adverbial forms ending in /-lis/ and /-dus/, *e.g.* 'amabilis mihi', or it signifies relationship (ad aliquid), though the latter may also be constructed with the genitive.

Siger dismisses the accusative in only a few words, since it is not, for him, the basis of any construction. He does, however, give us a formal definition of the accusative, that it designates the property of the thing in the form 'ut quem'.[169] According to Thomas it is the mode of signifying as the final member of a construction in the form 'ut quem', *e.g.* 'amo Deum';[170] in this instance the accusative signifies by virtue of its ending

[168] Thomas of Erfurt, #89: "dativus casus est modus significandi rem in ratione principii, vel termini *indifferenter*, proprietate ut cui alterum acquiritur superaddita".

[169] Siger de Courtrai, p. 107: "accusativus ... est casus nominis designans circa rem modum essendi 'ut quem' ".

[170] Thomas of Erfurt, #90: "Accusativus casus est modus significandi rem in ratione termini, proprietate ut quem, superaddita".

the act and at the same time it signifies dependency on the verb.[171] There are occasions when the accusative can signify and be at the same time the first member; in such cases it involves an infinitive or impersonal verb, *e.g.* 'me legere', 'me oportet', and the special property of 'ut quem' will not be introduced as an additional criterion.[172] Once more we are dealing with two different types of construction, *i.e.* 'amo Deum' is a transitive construction, and 'me legere' is an intransitive construction, in which the accusative is complementary[173] to the verb without any special quality attached to it, which would be the case if it were functioning as the end member (*i.e.* terminus) of a construction.[174] Thomas adds that sometimes the accusative acts quite simply as the end member without any linking device as in 'lego librum'; sometimes it is linked in its position as second constructible to the first constructible by means of the preposition subject to the accusative, *e.g.* 'curro ad campum'.

The vocative is based, both for Siger and Thomas, on criteria which cannot in any way be described as formal. It is, for the Modistae, the case which designates the property of excitement or vehemence;[175] it is an absolute case and is not the basis of any construction with other nomina. Thomas tells us that it is the final constituent of a construction but it must be a dependent constituent on the adverb 'o'. Such a dependence arises, not from a syntactic relation, but from the feelings implicit in the adverb; therefore it can express no relation which will account for the absence of distinguishing morphological marks[176] as part of its criteria.[177]

Meaning, for the Modistae, became the criterion for the *inclusion* of the vocative in the case system of the nomen; morphological criteria were excluded, though it was in the first place morphology that had

---

[171]   Thomas of Erfurt, #90: "iste accusativus, Deum, significat sub proprietate terminandi actum, et dependentiam huius verbi, amo".

[172]   Thomas of Erfurt, #90: "accusativus est modus significandi rem, sub ratione principii simpliciter, id est, proprietate speciali non superaddita".

[173]   The use of the term 'complementary' with reference to the Modistic term of 'proportio' is discussed in Chapter II.

[174]   Thomas of Erfurt, #90: "hic significat accusativus rem, sub ratione principii a nulla proprietate speciali contracta, nec contrahibili, cui proportionatur modus verbi simpliciter".

[175]   Siger de Courtrai, p. 107: "vocativus ... est casus nominis designans circa rem modum essendi excitati".

[176]   L. Hjelmslev, *La Catégorie des cas*, p. 4.

[177]   Thomas of Erfurt, #91: "vocativus casus est modus significandi rem sub ratione termini dependentis, actus exerciti, vel exercitati, nulla differentia dictarum proprietatum superaddita".

caused Thrax to include the vocative in the scatter of cases.[178] Thomas does not moreover include his quasi formal criterion of 'ut quod', *etc.* in order to justify his inclusion of the vocative, and syntactic criteria (although they may well be included in a negative way, *i.e.* in that the vocative case can never be the first constituent of a construction, but fits into the position of terminus of a construction and in reality acts semi-independently with the adverb 'o'), – are used only to stress the absence of any rection between the verb and the case form as in 'lege, o puer'.

The quasi formal criterion for the ablative agreed upon by the Modistae is, as Siger defines it, the modus essendi 'ut a quo'; Siger again defines the case by its meaning and illustrates from Latin usage, *i.e.* the ablative is used to demonstrate something possessed, *e.g.* 'vir magna virtute', *i.e.* 'a man possessing great virtue'.[179] Thomas defines the ablative as the mode of signifying of either the first or final constituent of a construction and possesses the formal characteristics of 'a quo', *e.g.* 'utor pane'; the ablative in such a construction is the 'terminus', although its position does not seem to have any influence on the meaning, *i.e.* whether it is the first or final constituent, and so, according to Thomas, it signifies in the same way in either position.[180] Thomas concludes that the ablative can be used with or without preposition, *e.g.* 'in domo', 'acutus oculis'.

Siger has nothing to say about 'declinatio', but tells us that declinatio, which Donatus actually included in his consideration of case, is derived from the property of the cases and is the mode of signifying by means of which the nomen is inflected, and varies by means of the different properties of the cases;[181] it becomes in fact the realisation (vox) of these different properties. The treatment of case by Thomas and Siger is disappointingly jejune, the more so in view of the importance of the category and the possibilities that Latin case theory present to any grammarian, regardless of the criteria on which he may base his descriptive technique. It would show the Modistae in an even poorer light if we were to dwell on their inadequacies and to compare their descriptions

---

[178]   R. H. Robins, *Thrax*, p. 100.
[179]   Siger de Courtrai, p. 107: " 'a quo' est quando aliquid habere demonstratur, ideo ablativus, ut sic, est principium constructionis cum omni illo quod significat rem suam per modum ut habens illud, ut: vir magna virtute, id est, magnam virtutem habens".
[180]   Thomas of Erfurt, #92: "ablativus casus est modus significandi rem, in ratione principii, vel termini *indifferenter*, proprietate, ut quo, superaddita".
[181]   Thomas of Erfurt, #95: "declinatio est modus significandi rem nominis, per quem inflectitur. Et variatur per diversas casuum proprietates".

of case to those of their predecessors. Hjelmslev points [182] in particular to the achievement of the Byzantine grammarians in particular to Maximus Planudes who described the cases of Greek by means of localist theory which bases its definition of case and the different cases of Greek on the abstract notion of direction; unfortunately, this theory which anticipates much of the work on case theory of the 19th and 20th centuries, had, as Hjelmslev points out, no influence on the general development of case theory, and Roman (and therefore mediaeval grammarians) followed the theories of the Stoics and Apollonius. This is lamentably clear as far as the Modistae are concerned.[183] It is to be regretted that Michel de Marbais's work so far remains unpublished; from the extracts published in Thurot it would seem that he shows something of a localist theory of case in relation to the use of the preposition with the accusative and the ablative, but it would be wrong to make more of this than the mere sketching of a theory which is different from Thomas or Siger.[184] The Modistae are even more guilty, and this is a criticism which applies particularly to Thomas, of making such little use of the theories of Apollonius and Thrax; Siger has, like the Greeks, a general conception of case as consisting of the opposition between the nominative and all the other cases, a theory which dates back to the Stoics, but the Modistae, unlike the Greeks, do not seem to have made any use at all of the relationship between case and the voice of the verb.

It seems in fact possible to argue that there are at least two distinct Modistic case theories; Siger's is more orthodox and shows a certain kinship with the theories of the Stoics, Apollonius and Priscian, but on the other hand, Thomas's case theory appears quite new but palpably thin, and it is indeed difficult to associate Thomas's theories with any theory of the past, except perhaps Stoic theory.

It would, however, be unfair to dismiss Modistic case theory entirely because of a certain jejuneness in their exposition. Modistic case theory

---

[182] L. Hjelmslev, *La Catégorie des cas*, pp. 9-13.

[183] Martin of Dacia does not have an extensive section on case, but his description is quite formal, being a mixture of syntax and morphological analogy. Even so, his treatment is thin and contributes nothing to case theory in general; he is perhaps more straightforward than Thomas in that he prefers to talk about function rather than consignification, *viz.* Martin of Dacia #83: "modus significandi qui facit casum est modus significandi secundum quem aliquid se habet in ratione principii vel in ratione termini".

[184] Michel de Marbais: "non solum isti casus pro accidente assignantur prepositioni tanquam servitium eius vel officium consequens eius modum significandi essentialem, sed potius tanquam aliquis modus significandi accidentalis, qui dicitur modus significandi retorquentis casuale ad actum in ratione termini terminantis vel in ratione principii initiantis" (Thurot, p. 197).

is not in fact devoid of interest but, paradoxically, it is not their theory of case qua case which is of interest but it is their exposition of their case theory in its relation to their wider syntactic theory; in this sense Thomas seems to have made an important innovation, if not in case theory then in general grammatical theory. Hjelmslev has pointed out[185] that the introduction of 'regere, regimen' brought with them a theory of rection which is a much broader one than their predecessors had envisaged; the Modistae, in particular Thomas, did not make any extensive use of the term 'regere',[186] but they saw the government of the verb on the nominative as well as the cases of the oblique nominal form. Thomas built most of his case theory on the rection of the verb with the pre-posed nominative or any other case-form which, in a particular construction, acts as the subject, and on the rection of the verb with the post-posed oblique nominal regardless of the case, though even Thomas has to admit that the vocative cannot function in such a system. If it is feasible to argue that Thomas produced his case theory in order to demonstrate the necessary rection of all the case forms (except the vocative), it does not justify the paucity of his case theory as a description of the Latin case system; it does suggest the recognition of a very important fact, *i.e.* that an inflectional system such as a case system is both syntagmatic and paradigmatic.[187]

Persona

This mode represents a radical departure, one might almost say a cleavage, between the Modistae; Thomas and Martin of Dacia describe persona as the last of the accidental modes of the nomen, whereas Siger and Michel de Marbais make no mention of it whatsoever as an accidental mode of the nomen.

Thomas tells us that in rational things a certain property of the category of case can be found, *i.e.* the property of speaking from which the feature of person is derived and as such is an accident of the nomen. Persona is therefore the mode of signifying of the nomen by means of which the nomen consignifies, *i.e.* connotates the property of speaking;[188] as a result of the difference of the speech whether it is 'de se',

---

[185] L. Hjelmslev, *Principes de grammaire générale*, pp. 158-159.
[186] Modistic use of this term is discussed in more detail in Chapter II.
[187] L. Hjelmslev, *La Catégorie des cas*, p. 22.
[188] Thomas of Erfurt, #94: "persona modus significandi nominis, mediante quo nomen proprietatem loquendi consignificat. Et secundum diversitatem loquendi,

i.e. 'of oneself', 'ad alium', *i.e.* 'to another', or 'de alio,' *i.e.* 'of another', the person will vary in a similar threefold manner, the first person being the mode of signifying by means of the property of speaking of oneself, the second person being the mode of speaking to another person, and the third person the mode of speaking of another person.

Thomas concludes his very short discussion of persona with a strange piece of etymology, no doubt to explain what is, at least, the equally strange fact of including persona as an accidental mode of the nomen. He states that because the mode of speaking of oneself is not without a mode of signifying 'de se', then this mode is called persona, named from 'per se sonando'.[189]

B. PRONOMEN

The Greek grammarians, *e.g.* Thrax and Apollonius had defined the pronoun as a 'part of speech used in place of the noun and indicative of specific personal references'.[190] Priscian followed the Greeks in his definition of the pronomen in that it is used instead of a nomen and signifies certain persons.[191] There is one significant difference between Priscian and his predecessors, *i.e.* he abandons their formal definition to the extent of admitting as pronouns only those words[192] which designate substance, independently of its qualities.[193] It would not do to make too much of this, because Priscian did not develop his theory of substance as a feature of the pronoun, and it must also be remembered that matters such as the relation of matter and form to substance are subjects quite foreign to Priscian, who, as a 'literary' grammarian, was not interested in philosophy and made use of logic only in so far as it contributed to the definition of a grammatical feature.

---

de se, ad alium, vel de alio, variatur persona per triplicem differentiam, scilicet: primam, secundam et tertiam".

[189] Thomas of Erfurt, #94: "quia modus loquendi de se non est sine modo significandi de se, ideo ipse modus dicitur persona, a per se sonando nominata".

[190] R. H. Robins, *A. and M.*, p. 40.

[191] Priscian (XII.1): "pronomen est pars orationis, quae pro nomine proprio uniuscuiusque accipitur personasque finitas recepit".

[192] Priscian (XVII, 37): "pronomina et finita volunt esse et loco propriorum accipiuntur et substantiam solum sine qualitate significant, quantum in ipsa voce est eorum, cum supra dicta generalia nomina penitus sunt infinita confusione omnium sub se specierum".

[193] This question of substance is, however, of some importance in discussing the pronomen since it indicates a definite difference between Priscian and Donatus, and has important implications for the development of the theory of the pronoun in the Middle Ages.

Priscian's grammatical categories have been referred to as 'semi-formal' – 'semi' being used to indicate that he also used other, *i.e.* semantic criteria in his definitions. One of the criteria he had introduced into his definition of the nomen had been substance, but a substance with a specific or common quality.[194] In contrast to the nomen, the pronoun, although it too suggested substance, did so without referring to any quality, so that this substance became the principal criterion for the *semantic* content of the pronoun. Priscian and the Modistae made no deliberate use of the idea of linguistic compensation – naturally enough, – but Priscian introduced a concept which in fact compensated to some extent for the loss of quality as a criterion for the pronoun. This concept was the use of 'demonstratio' and 'relatio' – (we shall see very shortly that the Modistae, especially Thomas, made great use of this); demonstratio and relatio were used to express the idea of the presence (demonstratio) or absence (relatio) of substance in the pronoun. (This was associated with person,[195] and can be thought of, as far as some pronouns are concerned, in equivalent terms to subjectivity and objectivity). It must be stated quite emphatically at this stage that the Priscianic and Modistic use of demonstratio and relatio bears no resemblance to the conventional use of demonstrative and relative as features of the pronouns of the standard Indo-European languages. This concept of the pronoun led Priscian to consider only fifteen words as pronouns, *e.g.* ego, tu, ille, ipse, iste, hic, is, sui, meus, tuus, suus, noster, vester, nostras, vestras, all of which express to a greater or lesser extent the presence or absence of substance, and all other words which are traditionally referred to as pronouns, *e.g.* demonstrative, relative, interrogative pronouns, were rigorously excluded. Thomas followed Priscian in his description of the pronoun, in that although he does not list all the words he considers to be pronouns, it is quite clear that he accepted as pronouns the fifteen pronouns that Priscian described.

This stresses a very important difference betwen Priscian and Donatus and which was to have a very great influence on their successors in the Middle Ages; Priscian used demonstratio and relatio, not as accidents of the pronoun, but as features of the substance which he introduced as a characteristic of the pronoun.

[194] Priscian (II, 18): "proprium est nominis substantiam et qualitatem significare". Priscian (II, 22): "nomen est pars orationis, quae unicuique subiectorum corporum seu rerum communem vel propriam qualitatem distribuit".
[195] Priscian (XII, 14): "in prima quidem et secunda persona pronomen ponitur, in tertia vero non, nisi demonstratione egeat vel relatione". Priscian (XVII, 65): "prima et secunda persona, in quibus sola est demonstratio".

Donatus, on the other hand, included qualitas which he divided into specific (finita) and non-specific (infinita), (Thomas informs us[196] that *qualitas finita* is *demonstratio* and *qualitas infinita* is *relatio*), as an accident of the pronoun,[197] but this is in complete contrast to Priscian who had excluded qualitas altogether as a feature of the pronoun. Donatus had used qualitas finita to describe those pronouns which are restricted in concord to a particular person of the verb, *e.g.* ego, tu, ille, and qualitas infinita to describe those pronouns which are not so restricted, qui, quae, quod, etc. Priscian disagrees with this and argues that words such as 'quis, qui', *etc.* are in fact unspecified nomina which signify substance and an infinite quality, which is in opposition to his own definition of the pronoun as signifying substance *but without quality*.[198]

This has important implications since it was quite clearly Priscian and not Donatus whom Peter Helias and the Modistae followed; Thomas refers to Donatus explicitly only in order to demonstrate how he, Thomas, differs from Donatus. The difference between Thomas and Donatus is in this instance largely one of organisation and terminology, whereas their grammatical doctrine is very much the same, *e.g.* Donatus assigns qualitas, which he divides into qualitas finita and qualitas infinita, to be an accident of the pronoun, but, as we shall see, demonstratio which he (Thomas) derives from Donatus's qualitas finita and relatio which he derives from qualita infinita become in Thomas's scheme subaltern modes of the pronoun. Thomas and Donatus differ terminologically in that Thomas restates the more formal definitions of Donatus in his own characteristically semantic terms. Thomas makes demonstratio and relatio into subaltern modes[199] stating that these are

[196] Thomas of Erfurt, #106: "notandum, quod qualitatem, quam Donatus assignat pro accidente pronominis, dividit in qualitatem finitam et infinitam; et vocat illos duos modos significandi essentiales speciales pronominis, scilicet demonstrationem, et relationem".

[197] Donatus (Ars minor): "qualitas pronominum in quo est? Bipertita est: aut enim finita sunt pronomina aut infinita. Quae sunt finita? Quae recipiunt personas, ut ego, tu, ille. Quae sunt infinita? Quae non recipiunt personas, ut quis, quae, quod".

[198] Priscian (XIII, 31): " 'quis' quoque quamvis substantiam sine aliqua certa qualitate demonstret, hoc tamen interest inter substantiam illam, quam pronomina significant, quod illa pro speciali et propria uniuscuiusque accipiuntur substantia, quae demonstratione praesentium vel relatione absentium personarum intelligitur, hoc autem generalem et infinitam substantiam, quae pertinet ad universarum rerum generare et species et partes, demonstrat. Quomodo igitur numeros et quantitates inter species qualitatis nominum accipimus, sic etiam infinitam et generalem substantiam, quae ex eo componuntur, in hoc esse dicimus qualitatem. Habet igitur etiam qualitatem, quam desiderat nomen".

[199] Thomas of Erfurt, #100: "modus significandi, qui vocatur demonstratio,

the same as Donatus's qualitas divided into qualitas finita and qualitas infinita. Thomas does this, not because the pronomen demonstrativum and the pronomen relativum constitute a sub-class of pronoun but because demonstratio and relatio are used to represent aspects of the essence of the pronomen, *i.e.* presence (praesentia) or absence (absentia) of the essence of the pronoun, *i.e.* presence or absence as features of substance, which is itself the essential feature of the pronoun.[200] The difference between Modistic and modern or even traditional use of demonstratio and relatio cannot be sufficiently stressed.[201] Priscian, it will be remembered, excluded words such as 'quis, qui, cuius', *etc.* from the category of pronoun on the grounds that they *signified substance with quality*. Demonstratio and relatio represent the presence or absence of certain properties and because they derive from the property of matter, they are potentially present in every pronoun.[202]

---

sumitur a proprietate rei, quae est proprietas certitudinis, et praesentiae ... hunc modum Donatum vocat qualitatem finitam; et hic modus constituit pronomen demonstrativum".

Thomas of Erfurt, #101: "modus significandi, qui vocatur relatio, sumitur a proprietate rei, quae est proprietas absentiae, et incertitudinis ... unde Donatus appellat istum modum qualitatem pronominis infinitam; et hic modus constituit pronomen relativum".

[200] Thomas of Erfurt, #100: "sic contingit dare diversos modos certitudinis, et praesentiae; et secundum hoc erunt diversi modi demonstrationum; et ex consequenti diversa pronomina demonstrativa. Contingit enim rem esse praesentem et certam, et maxime vertam vel praesentem, et sic demonstratur per hoc pronomen 'ego'; vel non maxime esse certam et praesentem, et sic demonstratur per hoc pronomen 'tu', et alia similia".

[201] It is possible to argue that Thomas arrived at his conception of demonstratio and relatio by means of a form of reconciliation of Donatus and Priscian; Donatus used qualitas to differentiate between the pronouns that could possess person and those that cannot, while Priscian associated person with demonstratio and relatio. Thomas used Donatus's division of qualitas finita and qualitas infinita to suggest Priscian's division of demonstratio and relation, *i.e.* the degree of the presence or absence of substance in the pronoun. These features can never be present together at the same time in the same pronoun, though certain pronouns may be capable of suggesting both features but, of course, in different contexts. In certain pronouns, *e.g.* the substantive pronouns, demonstratio and relatio can be associated with the idea of subjectivity or objectivity; the first person pronoun is entirely subjective, the second person pronoun is less subjective that the first person pronoun but more so than the third person pronoun which is in fact entirely objective. The first person pronoun could be described modistically as demonstrative, the second person pronoun as less demonstrative and to some degree relative, and the third person pronoun may well be relative but will be demonstrative to a much lesser degree than either the first or the second person pronouns.

[202] F. C. Copleston, *Op. cit.*, p. 86: "If we think away all forms and all determinate characteristics we arrive at the notion of a purely indeterminate constitutive principle which is capable of existing successively in union with an indefinite multiplicity of forms."

It is not entirely fortuitous that in the whole of his discussion of the pronoun, Thomas refers only to pronouns such as *e.g. ego, tu, sui, hic, ille, meus, tuus, suus, nostras, vestras,* which were those defined by Priscian as pronouns, and makes no mention whatsoever of 'quis, qui', *etc.,* which had been included by Donatus as pronouns.[203] Thurot tells us[204] that Michel de Marbais sought to reconcile the definitions of Donatus and Priscian, but had to admit defeat, though Michel does, furthermore, suggest that even among his, *i.e.* Michel's, contemporaries there was disagreement about the nature of 'quis, qui', etc.;[205] (this could well be a reference to Siger's probable inclusion of qualitas as an accidental mode and hence possible inclusion of 'quis, qui' among the pronouns).

The Modistae were obviously also influenced by Peter Helias whom they tended to accept often as their immediate model;[206] he followed Priscian in his theory of the pronoun, but moves forward in the sense that he developed the idea of pronouns designating substance further than Priscian had done. Peter could call on contemporary philosophical theories of substance, matter and form to support his theory; Peter distinguished three senses of the word 'substantia' according to which it signifies matter, form or a composition of matter and form.[207] This last meaning agrees with the definition of the nomen as signifying substance and quality and the first agrees with definition of the pronoun as signifying substance but without quality. This is a dualism which we find throughout Modistic grammatical analysis, especially in their description of the partes orationis, and represents a major advance on their

[203]   A major divergence between Thomas and Siger in the nomen had been their assignment of qualitas – Thomas as a modus subalternus and Siger as a modus accidentalis; it would have been interesting to compare them on their assignment of qualitas in the pronoun – it seems probable that Siger would have included it as an accidental mode, following Donatus in this, which would, of course, have been entirely consistent, but Siger is unfortunately incomplete and this section is lacking from his work.

[204]   Ch. Thurot, *Op. cit.,* p. 173.

[205]   Michel de Marbais: "quis et qui non sunt pronomina, sed potius nomina ... Et hoc etiam est de intentione Prisciani. Unde Donatus et Priscianus de hoc fuerunt contrarie opinionis, et adhuc moderni grammatici contrariuntur super hoc plurimum" (Thurot, p. 173).

[206]   It is interesting and revealing to compare the relationship between Peter Helias and his successors who might be said to constitute his school, and between the creators and members of many modern schools of linguistic doctrine, and how the founder left to his followers the task of refining the original inspiration.

[207]   H. Roos, *Die Modi Significandi,* p. 147: Roos argues that Peter, though he used the contrast of materia/forma, did not apply the theory to his description of the partes orationis.

part from Peter Helias;[208] it is particularly fundamental to their separation of the pronomen from the nomen, and the participium from the verbum. All four declinable partes possess materia – *i.e.* modus entis in the nomen and pronomen, and modus esse in the verbum and participium – but only the nomen, verbum and participium possess forma, *i.e.* determinata apprehensio in the nomen, distantia in the verbum, and indistantia in the participium.

As far as the nomen and pronomen are concerned, we can say that the nomen possesses form and that the pronomen does not. Roos argues [209] that the modus entis represents the form of the pronomen, and the indeterminata apprehensio the matter of the pronomen; this seems difficult to reconcile, and it seems more accurate to say that the pronomen, as Thomas implies, does not possess form but is capable of being determined by form[210] – it would be mistaken to say that this represents an absence (privatio) of form but rather that form is neither included nor excluded but present as a *potential* element to determine the first matter *i.e.* something 'uninformed' but 'informable',[211] what Copleston described as 'a purely indeterminate potential element which has no definite form of its own and no definite characteristics'.[212]

[208] H. Roos, *Op. cit.*, p. 148: "Martinus de Dacia hat als einer der ersten das Begriffspaar: forma/materia systematisch in die Behandlung der 'partes orationis' aufgenommen."

[209] H. Roos, *Die Modi Significandi*, p. 147: Roos is, of course, referring to Martin, and here we find one major divergence between Martin and the later Modistae. Martin describes the mode of permanence and repose (modus habitus et quietis) as the material part of the nomen but as the formal part of the pronomen. This derives in part it would seem, from the fact that he dismisses undetermined understanding (indeterminata apprehensio) altogether as a feature of the pronomen and he similarly dismisses quality as the form of the pronomen. It seems difficult, however, to account for Roos' assertion that 'indeterminata apprehensio' is the material part of the pronomen, since Martin specifically excludes it, viz. "modus significandi pronominis est modus habitus et quietis sive modus substantiae merae, id est, *nudae vel non cum qualitate vel indeterminatae apprehensionis* [my emphasis]".

[210] Thomas of Erfurt, #96: "ab ista proprietate materiae primae, quae est proprietas de se indeterminata, determinabilis tamen per formam, sumitur modus significandi essentialis generalissimus pronominis".

[211] Thomas of Erfurt, #97: "illud, quod sic est indeterminatum, quod non excludit, nec includit formam, nec formae determinationem, non est privativum; et sic se habet modus significandi pronominis, qui est modus indeterminati de se, determinabilis tamen". F. C. Copleston, *Op. cit.*, p. 93: "First matter, considered in abstraction, is pure potentiality for successive actualisation by substantial forms, each of which stands to its matter as act to potentiality, actualising the matter's potentiality."

[212] F. C. Copleston, *Op. cit.*, p. 86. Siger de Courtrai, p. 125: "finitatio est formae et quia materia prima non determinat sibi aliquam formam, sed est in potentia ad omnem formam".

This was a fundamental distinction for the Modistae and had a profound effect on their organisation and analysis of the four declinable partes orationis. We have already seen in the nomen, that Thomas, for whom determinata apprehensio was the equivalent of qualitas, *i.e.* derived from the property of form, used this factor of form and its varieties, to distinguish in his subaltern modes *different types of nomen*. In the pronomen, however, the feature of indeterminata apprehensio, which implies that form and quality are immanent[213] rather than absent, is not capable of distinguishing different types of pronoun, and demonstratio and relatio in the subaltern modes do not create different types of pronoun but different values of the same pronoun. Thomas includes 'qualitas' as a feature of the pronoun, but it cannot be a criterion of the modus generalissimus since the pronoun does not possess form; qualitas in the nomen he derived from Donatus and defined as the subaltern modes which produced the 'nomen proprium' and 'nomen appellativum'. In the pronoun, qualitas is also included as a criterion for the subaltern modes but does not create different types of pronoun (as qualitas had done in the nomen) – instead qualitas produces 'demonstratio' and 'relatio' which can be described briefly as two qualities, never present together, of the pronoun.

There was a large measure of agreement between the Modistae in their definition of the pronoun; they were agreed on its 'substantial' nature, on the close relationship between the nomen and the pronomen, and on the absence of qualitas as a feature of the pronomen. Michel de Marbais describes the pronoun as a pars orationis signifying substance which is specifiable by means of another element,[214] which is very much the same as Thomas of Erfurt[215] for whom the pronoun signifies by means of the modus entis, a term he chose in preference to substantia (which however the nomen and pronomen both express), and by means of indeterminata apprehensio which distinguishes the pronomen from the nomen. As we have seen, this indeterminata apprehensio is derived from the property of first matter but is determinable by means of form, a statement very similar in intent to Michel's. Siger represents a combination of the ancient and contemporary tradition; he too describes the

---

[213]   Thomas of Erfurt, #96: "materia prima, extra indeterminata est, respectu cuiuslibet forma naturalis, *quae in est de se*, ita quod nec includit nec excludit formam [my emphasis]".

[214]   Michel de Marbais: "pronomen est pars orationis significans per modum substantie specificabilis per alterum unumquodque" (Thurot, pp. 171-172).

[215]   Thomas of Erfurt, #98: "pronomen est pars orationis significans per modum entis, et indeterminatae apprehensionis".

pronoun as signifying by means of the modus entis,[216] which he equates, as he did with the nomen, to the mode of substance, state or permanence, and which is identical to his definition of this aspect of the nomen. Siger, however, prefers Priscian's terms that the pronomen signifies without qualitas, and makes no use of the idea of indeterminata apprehensio; determinata apprehensio was a term used by Thomas to refer to qualitas, and is derived from the property of form,[217] — this suggests that indeterminata apprehensio indicates the absence or non-presence rather than the deprivation of form.

Modus significandi essentialis

A great deal has perforce been said on the use of the metaphysical device of matter and form by the Modistae to distinguish and compare the four declinable partes orationis. This particular feature is mentioned at this stage of the discussion of the essential mode of the pronomen, since it has a very striking effect not only on the theory of the pronomen but also on the presentation of Modistic theories of the pronomen.

As in the nomen and verb, the Modistae remain consistent in their presentation of the essential mode of the pronoun and divide the essential mode into two parts by means of the contrast of matter and form. The nomen and the pronomen are alike materially but differ formally – but this is not the whole picture, because the pronoun differs in fact from the nomen by virtue of the fact that the pronoun does not have form but is merely informable.[218] This absence of form does not in any way prevent Thomas from describing the pronoun by means of the subaltern modes, etc., and then by the accidental modes; but it does have the effect that the subaltern modes are no longer the stage at which the pronouns are categorised but described in more detail.

One of the most distinctive features of Thomas's method of presenting his grammatical theory was his use of Donatus's *organisation* of grammatical data, as well as the data itself; in this he differs a great deal from Siger, the reason for this being probably Thomas's use of

---

[216] Siger de Courtrai, p. 124: "modus significandi per quem pronomen est pronomen est modus significandi substantiae, habitus permanentis, seu entis".
[217] Thomas of Erfurt, #25: "per qualitatem modum qualitatis, qui est modus determinatae apprehensionis, sumptus a proprietate formae et qualitatis, qui est modus determinationis".
[218] Thomas of Erfurt, #96: "ab ista proprietate materiae primae, quae est de se indeterminata, determinabilis tamen per formam, sumitur modus significandi essentialis generalissimus pronominis".

the modi subalterni and specialissimi to catalogue those words which possess the same essence and 'secondary' or distinctive feature of this essence, *e.g.* the nomen possesses modus entis as its essence and 'determinata apprehensio' as its secondary or distinctive feature. Siger, as we have already seen, merely stated the essence and the distinctive feature of the pars in question with the result that Siger assigns certain categories which he has derived from Donatus's accidents, *e.g.* qualitas in the nomen, to be an accidental mode, whereas Thomas described the same material as a subaltern mode.

Thomas's use of the subaltern mode must not be interpreted as making it a *sub-mode;* he assigns what Donatus called 'qualitas' to the subaltern mode since the subaltern mode is used to represent different aspects of the 'pure' essence of the pars and may thereby create certain sub-classes of the pars in question, *i.e.* the subaltern modes of the nomen are used to express two properties of the essence, *e.g.* modus per se stantis and modus adiacentis which constitute the substantive and adjective sub-classes of the nomen. It does not follow that the subaltern mode will always be used to set up the various sub-classes in the pars in question, nor does it follow that an accident taken from Donatus will be in every instance included as a subaltern mode nor will it always create different sub-classes of the pars. Thomas described qualitas in the verb as an accidental mode, since it neither created a sub-class of verb nor represented any feature of the essence. Qualitas, which Donatus made into an accident of the pronoun becomes a subaltern mode in Thomas's scheme – but it does not create any sub-class of the pronoun; it does, however, express different features of the essence of the pronoun, and for this reason demonstratio and relatio (Thomas's qualitas) can be used to represent two aspects of the same pronomen. Because the nomen and pronomen possess the same essence, it follows that they will possess the same accidental modes which will be expressions of the *same properties,* and for this reason Thomas did not describe the accidental modes of the pronomen in any detail but refers to the nomen for an equivalent description of them.

Siger, in the nomen, divided his essential mode in terms of the matter and form contrast but the lack of the formal element in the pronoun has an unexpected effect on his presentation in that the pronoun has only one mode of signifying,[219] *i.e.* the general, or we might even call it the material, but it cannot have a specific mode since it has no form and the

---

[219]   Siger de Courtrai, p. 124: "pronomen non habet nisi unum modum significandi qui dictus est" [*i.e.* the general essential mode].

specific mode is thus replaced by an indeterminate, unordered mode of signifying substance without quality.[220] Thus we find that Siger's general mode of the pronoun is the same as the general mode of the nomen, but the pronomen has however no specific mode; Thomas does not entirely agree, and he seems to have been concerned about the symmetry existing between the declinable partes.[221] His modus generalissimus of the pronoun states that the pronoun signifies by means of the modus entis and indeterminata apprehensio;[222] the first part of his definition, the material, agrees with the nomen and compares with Siger's statement, but it might be argued that the term indeterminata apprehensio was introduced in order to balance the determinata apprehensio of the nomen, although it cannot be the formal element of the pronoun in the way that determinata apprehensio is the formal element of the nomen.

Thomas explains that indeterminata apprehensio is derived from the property of first matter[223] although it is the unmarked member of the contrast between the determinata apprehensio,[224] *i.e.* the formal element of the nomen and the indeterminata apprehensio, *i.e.* the potentially informable element of the pronoun. Martin of Dacia is quite different on this point, in that he makes the material component of the nomen the formal component of the pronomen and the formal component of the nomen the material component of the pronomen.[225] Thomas insists that the use of indeterminata apprehensio as the distinctive feature of the essence of the pronoun must not be interpreted as absence of form (privatio formae) since this would imply a privative mode, and any mode of signifying must be positive;[226] what Thomas is in fact saying is that this facet of the pronoun, by deriving from first matter which is innate and immanent,[227] merely implies that the pronoun possesses the

---

[220] Siger de Courtrai, p. 125: "modus significandi indeterminati, confusi, substantiae mere seu sine qualitate, accidit pronomini, unde pronomen est".

[221] *Cf.* Diagrams, pp. 354-374 in Appendix B and also in Appendix C.

[222] Thomas of Erfurt, #96: "modus significandi essentialis generalissimus pronominis est modus significandi per modum entis et indeterminatae apprehensionis".

[223] Thomas of Erfurt, #96: "modus indeterminate apprehensionis oritur a proprietate, seu modo essendi materiae primae".

[224] The term 'unmarked' is used to suggest that the nomen is 'marked' because it possesses a 'form', but the pronoun is 'unmarked' because it is only 'potentially informable'.

[225] Martin of Dacia, #19: "quod materiale est in modo significandi nominis, hoc est formale et completivum pronominis".

[226] Thomas of Erfurt, #97: "illud quod est ita indeterminatum, quod excludat formam, et formae determinationem, est privativum".

[227] Thomas of Erfurt, #96: "materia prima in se, extra indeterminata est, respectu cuiuslibet formae naturalis, quae inest de se, ita quod nec includit nec excludit formam, nec determinationem formae".

same essence as the nomen which constitutes a common mode of signifying[228] that the first matter of the pronoun is informable, *i.e.* capable
of acquiring form, and that it will be informed by means of the nomen.
The pronoun thus signifies substance without quality,[229] *i.e.* it consists
of matter and potential form.

Modus significandi subalternus

In the nomen, the second feature of its essential mode, *i.e.* determinata
apprehensio, is derived from the property of qualitas and represents the
formal element in contrast to the material element of the nomen,[230] *i.e.*
the modus entis; this distinguishes the nomen from the pronomen, but
its counterpart is not the formal element of the pronoun nor does it
represent qualitas, since by definition the pronoun does not possess
qualitas as a feature of its essence as a result of not possessing form.
In the nomen, Thomas had interpreted Donatus's qualitas divided into
appellativa and propria as aspects of the subaltern mode of the nomen,
i.e. nomen commune and nomen proprium. In the pronoun, Thomas
interpreted Donatus's qualitas divided into finita and infinita as demonstratio and relatio and described them as subaltern modes. However,
the pronoun, as we have just said, does not have by definition qualitas
or form (though it is informable) so that, whereas in the nomen the
determinata apprehensio which is derived from form and quality is
responsible for the creation of the basic division of nomen commune
and nomen proprium, the indeterminata apprehensio, which is the
second feature of the essential mode of the pronoun, cannot create a
basic division in the *type* of pronoun and instead represents different
aspects of the pronoun potentially present in every pronoun, just as
first matter is potential in every form.[231] Thus indeterminata apprehensio,
which Thomas tells us, is derived from the property of first matter, is
potentially present in every pronoun, and we shall see that this is so as a
result of demonstratio and relatio.

---

[228]   Thomas of Erfurt, #97: "per modum istum privativum grammatici circum-
loquuntur modum significandi positivum, qui est modus significandi communis
simpliciter".
[229]   Thomas of Erfurt, #96: "pronomen significare substantiam meram, vel substantiam sine qualitate".
[230]   Thomas of Erfurt, #25: "per qualitatem, modum qualitatis, qui est modus
determinatae apprehensionis, sumptus a proprietate formae et qualitatis, qui est
modus determinationis".
[231]   Siger de Courtrai, p. 125: "materia prima non determinat sibi aliquam formam, sed est in potentia ad omnem formam".

Thomas divides the subaltern modes into three groups, *i.e.* demonstratio and relatio, primitive and derivative, substantivum and adiectivum, but it does not seem that all these subaltern modes should be treated as equal; this is not very astonishing since in the nomen we saw that certain subaltern modes took 'precedence' over the others,[232] *i.e.* we found the division of modus communis and modus appropriati in a position of priority, and the modus communis was divided into modus per se stantis and modus adiacentis, which were then divided into their modi specialissimi. This pattern can be applied to the subaltern mode of the pronoun; the contrast of proprium and commune is not possible since the pronoun does not possess qualitas, but in its place we have the contrast of demonstratio/relatio which, although they are potential in every pronomen, do not however create different types of pronoun. The fundamental division in the subaltern mode seems to be substantivum – adiectivum and demonstratio and relatio are always potential in these pronouns; every pronomen adiectivum can also be a primitive or have a derivative and these too can constitute different types of pronoun.[233] The following diagram attempts to set out the relationships established within the subaltern mode:

Pronomen

Substantivum		Adiectivum		
D	R	D	R	
		p	d	p	d

D = Demonstratio
R = Relatio
p = primitivum
d = derivativum

The modus per se stantis and the modus adiacentis in the pronoun derive from the same properties as in nomen.[234] There are three substantive pronouns – ego, tu, sui – which, possessing demonstratio or relatio, are used without the help of any other substantive,[235] what would be stated in modern terms as 'independent substitutes, requiring no

[232] Thomas of Erfurt, #27: "sunt duo modi significandi, qui immediate sub hoc modo continetur, scilicet modus communis, et modus appropriati; qui sunt modis speciales respectu generalissimi, et sunt generales respectu aliorum modorum".
[233] Thomas of Erfurt, #102: "primitio et derivatio constituunt diversas species in pronomine, scilicet pronomen primitivum, et derivativum".
[234] Thomas of Erfurt, #103: "modus adiacentis et per se stantis ab eisdem proprietatibus sumitur, a quibus sumebatur in nomine, scilicet modus per se stantis a proprietate essentiae distinctae et modus adiacentis a proprietate inhaerentis alteri secundum esse".
[235] Thomas of Erfurt, #103: "a grammaticis ponuntur tria pronomina substantiva, scilicet, ego, tu, sui, quia huiusmodi usi sunt poetae virtute demonstrationis et relationis in sermone perfecto, sine adiunctione alterius substantivi".

antecedent utterance of the replaced form'.[236] All other pronouns are adiectiva, since they can be used adjectivally, *i.e.* by means of the modus adiacentis,[237] and all are potentially demonstrative or relative.

The primitive and derivative modes of signifying which constitute the pronomen primitivum and the pronomen derivativum, are derived from the same properties as species primitiva and species derivativa, the accidental mode of the nomen.[238] Thomas does not specify his reason for making this rather radical change in organisation, nor does he illustrate. The reason seems to be however that in the nomen, primitiva and derivativa represented *modifications* only of the species of the nomen, whereas in the pronoun they represent different types of pronoun.[239] The pronoun 'ego' is described as a pronomen substantivum but its derived form 'meus' would be a pronomen adiectivum derivativum, and a change, such as this, between the modus subalternus and the modus specialissimus of the pronomen serves to create a different kind of pronoun; by means of 'species' therefore it becomes possible to create sub-classes of the pronoun. This distinction is especially necessary, since otherwise there would be no means, in view of the absence of qualitas, of creating different types of pronoun, except by means of the substantivum-adiectivum contrast.

As we have already stated, demonstratio expresses the property of certainty and presence, while relatio expresses the property of uncertainty and absence;[240] demonstratio, which Donatus called qualitas finita, constitutes the pronomen demonstrativum, and relatio, which Donatus called qualitas infinita, constitutes the pronomen relativum.[241]

---

[236]   L. Bloomfield, *Language*, p. 255.

[237]   Thomas of Erfurt, #103: "aliis usi sunt adiective; ideo grammatici omnia alia pronomina adiectiva posuerunt".

[238]   Thomas of Erfurt, #102: "modus significandi, qui est primitivus, et derivativus, sumitur ab eadem proprietate in pronomine, a quo sumitur species primitiva et derivativa in nomine . . . in nomine, species primitiva et derivativa modi significandi accidentales nominis nominantur".

[239]   Thomas of Erfurt, #102: "primitio in pronomine idem est quod species primitiva in nomine, et derivatio in pronomine idem est quod species derivativa in nomine. Sed habent se differenter, quia primitio et derivatio constituunt diversas species in pronomine, scilicet pronomen primitivum, et derivativum".

[240]   Thomas of Erfurt, #106: "per qualitatem finitam dat intelligere demonstrationem quae rem finitam et certam significat et repraesentat, scilicet sub accidentibus realibus, quae oculis conspici possunt. Per qualitatem infinitam dat intelligere relationem, quae rem incertam et infinitam repraesentat, scilicet sub notitia secunda per recordationem, quae est incerta respectu notitiae primae".

[241]   Thomas of Erfurt, #100-101: "pronomen demonstrativum significat rem sub ratione vel proprietate praesentiae seu notitiae primae . . . pronomen relativum significat rem sub proprietate absentiae, et incertitudinis, seu notitiae secundae".

It must be repeated that these are *not* the equivalent of the modern demonstrative and relative pronoun – indeed the Modistae, like Priscian before them, excluded what would have been called today the relative pronoun altogether from their inventory of the pronoun. There are, of course, different degrees of demonstratio and relatio, *e.g.* the pronoun 'ego' represents the property of demonstratio to the greatest possible degree, the pronoun 'tu' to a lesser degree, and so forth;[242] this is pure semanticisation of the degree of subjectivity and objectivity in the pronoun.[243]

Of the subaltern modes of the pronoun, only the pronomen adiectivum derivativum divides further into modi specialissimi, of which it has two; the first one signifies possession, and thus becomes a possessive pronoun, a type which traditional grammars describe as pronominal adjectives. It signifies the mode of connection by means of the mode of possession, *e.g.* meus, tuus, suus.[244] The other modus specialissimus is the pronomen derivativum gentile, and it signifies the mode of connection but by means of the mode of gentility or heredity, *e.g.* nostras, vestras.[245] Once more we have a formal description of certain Latin pronouns restated in semantic terms.

The structure of the essential mode of signifying of the pronoun can be expressed by means of these sequences (see diagram on next page).

Modus significandi accidentalis

We have to rely entirely on Thomas for our knowledge of Modistic theory of the accidental modes of the pronoun; Siger's treatment of the pronoun breaks off abruptly when he completes his examination of the essential modes of the pronoun.[246]

---

[242] Thomas of Erfurt, #100: "contingit rem esse praesentem et certam, et maxime certam vel praesentem, et sic demonstratur per hoc pronomen ego; vel non maxime esse certam et praesentem, et sic demonstratur per hoc pronomen tu, et alia similia".

[243] This can be compared to the very rich types of demonstration found, for example, in certain Amerindian languages, which often express the presence or absence of the object under discussion by means of a demonstrative device.

[244] Thomas of Erfurt, #104: "pronomen derivativum possessivum est, quod significat per modum adiacentis alteri per modum possidentis ipsum, ut meus, tuus, suus".

[245] Thomas of Erfurt, #104: "pronomen derivativum gentile, est, quod significat per modum adiacentis alteri, sub ratione gentis, vel patriae, ut nostras, vestras".

[246] Siger does say something of the indeclinable partes in his Sophisma "O Magister", but this cannot be said to complete his treatise.

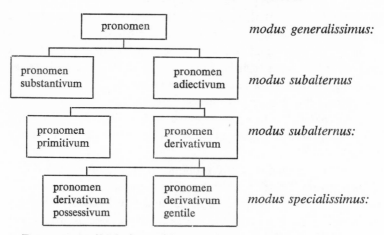

Donatus ascribed six accidents to the pronoun, *i.e.* qualitas, genus, numerus, figura, persona and casus.[247] In the pronoun, qualitas cannot, except negatively, be a feature of the essential mode, and therefore Thomas does not follow Donatus in this.[248] The other accidental modes which belong to the pronoun are genus, numerus, persona, figura and casus, and whatever was said of these categories in the nomen applies to them as accidental modes of the pronoun.[249] This reaffirms the intimacy between the nomen and the pronomen, which has been observed already in their essential modes.

Donatus had included qualitas as one of the accidents of the pronoun, but Priscian did not include demonstratio and relatio among the accidents of the pronoun – indeed Priscian excludes qualitas altogether from his definition of the pronoun but does include demonstratio and relatio in his description as aspects of the substance (substantia),[250] a characteristic attribute of the pronoun. Peter Helias and other grammarians of the 13th century had discussed this and had concluded that demonstratio and relatio are substantial features, *i.e.* properties of the

---

[247] Once more it must be pointed out that the terms 'accidentia' as used by the classical grammarians and 'accidental mode' as used by the Modistae are by no means always the same, although they do often coincide. We had cause to refer to this when discussing qualitas in the nomen and verbum, when it was shown that, for internal considerations, qualitas became a feature of the essence of the nomen, but an accidental mode of the verbum.

[248] In the nomen, qualitas and its divisions create different types of nomen, and are therefore included as subaltern modes, but in the pronoun, qualitas, *i.e.* demonstratio and relatio, create different aspects of the pronoun.

[249] Thomas of Erfurt, #106: "de genere, et numero, persona, figura, et casu in pronomine idem intelligatur, quod de ipsis dictim est de nomine".

[250] Priscian (XVII, 73): "pronomen unum pro omnibus accipitur nominibus, id est quod demonstrationem vel relationem habet alicuius certae substantiae".

pronoun and cannot be an accident since they refer to part of the definition of the pronoun – though Peter states it differently, *i.e.* that accidents refer to the inflections of the declinable partes.[251]

Much of this problem is a question of organisation and rests on the difference between accidents and the accidental mode of the Modistae; an accident was a consequential attribute derived from the morphological characteristics of the pars in question in contrast to a property peculiar to the pars in question and which forms part of its definition.[252] An accidental mode in the Modistic scheme contrasts to an essential mode and must be considered, therefore, as external, *i.e.* a feature which the pars acquires to express the variations which occur to its essence but originate from without its essence.[253] An accident was, therefore, for the classical grammarian, a *formal* term of reference, whereas the accidental mode is for the Modistae something which is, according to their professed belief, semantic and contains formal criteria only incidentally, but is however based on morphological criteria.

It becomes clear that demonstratio and relatio, since they represent aspects of the substance (substantia), an essential feature of the pronoun, cannot be included as an accidental mode, but since they do not represent the essence of the pars in question, they cannot be the modus generalissimus; they become a subaltern mode, not because they represent different types of pronoun, but because they represent different aspects of the essence of the pronoun and are yet capable of further refinement to the modus specialissimus.

This analysis of qualitas and its inclusion by Donatus as an *accident* of the pronoun and its exclusion by the Modistae from the *accidental modes* of the pronoun show more clearly the closeness of the relationship between the nomen and the pronomen in terms of the essence they share and the accidental modes which they also share and which are variations of this same essence.

---

[251] Peter Helias: "demonstratio, relatio, discretio pronomini sunt quasi sub-stantialia quoniam propter demonstrationem vel relationem nec non etiam discretionem reperta sunt. Licet tamen auctor dicat hec omnia pronomini accidere, ideo quod principaliter significat substantiam, secundario illa. Vel fortasse illa sola dicuntur declinabilium accidentia que ad aliquam eorum pertinet inflexionem" (Thurot, p. 173).

[252] R. H. Robins, *Thrax*, p. 105.

[253] Thomas of Erfurt, #20: "modus significandi accidentalis est, qui advenit parti post eius esse completum, non dans esse simpliciter parti, nec secundum genus, nec secundum speciem".

C. VERBUM

In the classical period and the early Middle Ages, there tended to be a divergence between the grammarians and logicians in their definitions of the nomen and verbum. In the 12th century, with Peter Helias, we can discern a marked change in the definition of the verbum, and Peter represents an attempt to combine the definitions of Aristotle and Priscian, the leading exponents in the western world of the logical and grammatical traditions, into one definition of the verbum. After Peter, and during the 13th century and with the Modistae, we find a further refinement in the definition of the verbum in which certain criteria were no longer considered the principal features of the verbum; we also find contemporary metaphysical considerations introduced as criteria to replace the more traditional features of the definition. We reach thus an interesting point at which the definitions of the Modistae have replaced the traditional grammatical elements with their own metaphysical ideas and at the same time, the traditional logical elements are either omitted or modified by new grammatical considerations; the features of being, becoming, succession and flux (esse, fieri, successio and fluxus) replace the features of action or being acted upon (actio and passio) used by the ancient grammarians, and the feature of 'tempus' which was the logician's principal criterion is relegated to the accidental modes of signifying. Affirmation is ignored except by Michel de Marbais though this had been a feature of Aristotle's definition, and the feature of separation from the substantial element, *i.e.* the nominal element (in contrast to the participium which can adhere to the nominal) is introduced. In other words the traditional logical SP relationship now becomes a *grammatical* feature, *i.e.* it is not so much that the nomen and verbum are to be segregated in order to express the predication of an action or condition,[254] but rather to express, in quasi formal terms, the separation of the verbal member from the nominal member which exemplifies syntactic dependence [255] of the verbal element on the subject nominal element.[256]

---

[254] R. H. Robins, *A. and M.*, p. 18.

[255] This term is discussed in Chapter II in relation to the verb as well as its general use in Modistic syntactic theory. There is, in addition, an important philosophical concept involved which induced the Modistae to consider dependence as a grammatical matter in the noun-verb relationship, especially the S P favourite sentence type; the concept in question derives from 'ens' and 'esse', the features which constitute the essence of the nomen and verb; 'ens' must precede 'esse' since some thing has to 'be' before it can 'become' *i.e.* be talked about.

[256] Siger de Courtrai, p. 108: "omne verbum requirit aliquid in ratione suppositi quod dependentiam eius sustentat".

Why there should have been such a divergence between the logician and the grammarian cannot be a matter for discussion at this point, but it must be pointed out that the logician needed only the nomen and the verbum to express his essential S and P relationships, whereas the grammarian, especially in the early Middle Ages, is heir to a system of grammatical description which possesses many more partes orationis than does the logician, and which were set up for a different purpose. Thrax and Apollonius had established their word-classes on formal criteria, especially Thrax,[257] and they had in addition ensured the analysis of the word-classes into the now traditional eight, *i.e.* noun, pronoun, verb, participle, adverb, conjunction, preposition, and article (in the case of Greek) or interjection (in the case of Latin). Priscian followed Apollonius in his definitions of the partes orationis, and apart from a slight divergence on the part of Apollonius himself,[258] this analysis in formal terms survived until the Middle Ages, *i.e.* the time of Peter Helias, and from the time of the Stoics and the scholars of the schools of Alexandria, grammar was until the latter Middle Ages considered a separate branch of knowledge.[259]

This dual development is seen quite clearly from the definitions of the logicians and grammarians; Plato defined the verb in terms of its predicability on the nomen, but Aristotle first[260] introduced the concept of 'time' into his definition of the verb, and it was this definition of the verb which was followed thereafter by the logician.[261] Beginning with Thrax and continued by Apollonius, an entirely different definition of the verb was used by the grammarian, *i.e.* the verb is a part of speech without case-inflection, admitting inflections of tense, person and number, signifying an activity or a being acted on;[262] although tense was not by any means excluded, the definition relies on the morphological distinction of the case-inflection of the noun and the absence of the case-inflection in the verb along with the definition of

---

[257] R. H. Robins, *Thrax*, p. 96.
[258] R. H. Robins, *A. and M.*, p. 43.
[259] R. H. Robins, *A. and M.*, p. 25.
[260] R. H. Robins, *A. and M.*, p. 23.
[261] Boethius: "Verbum est, quod consignificat tempus, cuius pars nihil extra significat, et est semper eorum quae de altero praedicantur, nota ... Verbum distat a nomine in hoc solo quod nomen sine tempore est ... verbum vim temporis in significationibus trahit" (*In librum Aristotelis de interpretatione, Commentaria minora*). Peter Abaelard: "Verbum est illud quod consignificat tempus ... id est significat nomen inhaerens personae cum temporali adverbio, sibi adiect(iv)o in constructione, ut 'currit' significat 'cursum' cum temporali adverbio".
[262] R. H. Robins, *A. and M.*, p. 40.

the verb signifying an action or being acted on. This is the definition used by Priscian and Donatus, the only difference between them being that Priscian includes the features of tense and mood[263] and Donatus the features of tense and person,[264] whereas Thrax had referred particularly to the features of tense, person and number. The grammarians of the Middle Ages, until Peter Helias, followed Priscian or Donatus, as can be seen quite clearly in the definitions of Aelfric, Bede, Cassiodorus, Isidorus, etc.;[265] it is interesting to note that Alcuin, although he refers in the first place to the Aristotelian definition, teaches (and defines) the verb[266] according to the model established by Priscian.

With this link back to the Greek grammarians, who themselves were conscious of Greek as a literary language, and the close association, for Priscian and the grammarians of the early Middle Ages, between grammar and literature and the complete divorce of grammar and logic during this period, it becomes quite futile to look for logical terms in their grammars. A great deal has already been said of the change and the causes for the change in the relationship during the 11th and 12th centuries between grammar and the other disciplines of the Trivium and the change in the attitude to grammar on the part of contemporary scholars; apart from anything else, it led to the exploitation of logical terminology in grammatical description as well as the introduction of metaphysical and philosophical considerations into the description of grammatical features.

The whole question and debate on the nature of the *verbum substantivum* provides us with yet another excellent example of the extent of the interplay between the logicians and grammarians of the period. The problem can in a sense be traced back to Priscian who had translated 'hyparxis' as 'substantia' and 'hyparktikon rhema' as 'verbum substantivum'; this was based on a confusion between existence and substance which, according to Thurot,[267] seems to have led the logicians and gram-

---

[263]   Priscian (VIII, 1): "verbum est pars orationis cum temporibus et modis, sine casu, agendi vel patiendi significativum".

[264]   Donatus (II, 11): "verbum est pars orationis cum tempore et persona sine casu aut agere aliquid aut pati aut neutrum significans".

[265]   Aelfric: "verbum est pars orationis cum tempore et persona sine casu aut agere aliquid aut pati aut neutrum significans. Cassiodorus: verbum est pars orationis cum tempore et persona sine casu ... verbum aut agentis aut patientis habet significationem" (*Commentarium de Oratione et de Octo Partibus Orationis*, Chapter II).

[266]   Alcuin: "verbum est vox significativa, secundum placitum, cum tempore, definitum aliquid significans et accidens ... verbum est pars orationis cum temporibus et modis, sine casu, agendi vel patiendi significativum".

[267]   Ch. Thurot. *Op. cit.*, p. 178.

marians to understand 'verbum substantivum' *not* as a verb signifying existence but as a verb meaning substance. (Such a confusion seems to have been carried on into the 13th century, when definitions, *e.g.* that the verb 'est' does not signify an action or being acted on but substance, can still be found).[268]

In the 11th century a variety of views were expressed by the grammarians who had, as de Rijk points out,[269] resorted to non-grammatical grounds in order to clarify the functions of the verbum substantivum. It was with Abelard that the important change took place and this was to exert a powerful influence on William of Conches and Peter Helias; though at first Abelard had regarded the copula as signifying a relation of inherence, he abandoned this view in favour of the identity theory, *i.e.* that the copula is a sign of identity.[270] Thus we find Peter Helias, for example, in his discussion of the signification of the verb, dealing with the verbum substantivum in terms of the identity theory[271] and this approach to the problem can be attributed to the impact of specific developments in 12th century logic.

The effect of these changes on Modistic theory is worth noting. It has been shown in the section on the nomen that permanence and repose were substituted for substance as the criteria for the nomen and similarly change and becoming instead of action and passion became the criteria for the verb, the terms used by the Modistae being 'ens' in the nomen and 'esse' on the verb; to this change can be related the metaphysical implications of the dependence of 'esse' or 'ens' to which reference will be frequently made in this section, *i.e.* an 'ens' has to be before it can become (esse) anything. It is reasonable to argue that two

[268] "Hoc verbum 'est' actionem et passionem non significat sed substantiam." An anonymous MS of the 13th century which I shall refer to as Digby 55; I must acknowledge the very kind loan by Dr R. W. Hunt, Keeper of Western MS in the Bodleian Library, Oxford, of his transcript of this MS.

[269] L. M. de Rijk, *Op. cit.* II, pp. 101-108.

[270] W. and M. Kneale, *The Development of Logic*, pp. 206-210.

[271] Peter Helias: "Dicimus itaque quod ens significat illud idem quod et substantia, sed aliter, quoniam substantia significat discernendo, ens vero diffuse, sicut dictum est. Unde quamvis ens nichil aliud significet quam substantia, tamen quia ei datum est secundum hoc quod accidentia recipit in se, inde est quod hoc nomen ens transumitur ad accidentia significandum, id est ad nominandum accidentia, licet solam substantiam significet, veluti cum dicitur 'Albedo est ens'. Si enim vere inspicias, sola substantia proprie est, accidens vero inest. Dicimus ergo quod, 'sum, es' significat substantiam, scilicet ut de altero, scilicet cum tempore, et in verbali terminatione. Et quoniam substantia est unitiva omnium aliarum rerum – accidentia namque sibi unit et copulat –, inde est quod 'sum, es' copulativum est, eo quod substantiam que sibi cetera unit et copulat significet". (*cf.* R. W. Hunt, "Studies on Priscian", p. 231).

considerations at least led to the change in the criteria of the nomen and verb, (a) to avoid the confusion between 'substance' and 'existence' which had arisen out of Priscian's use of 'verbum substantivum', and (b) the metaphysical implications of the dependence of 'esse' on 'ens'.

Such a change began, it would appear, with William of Conches and the other immediate predecessors of Peter Helias who sought to combine the logical tradition of Aristotle and the grammatical tradition of Priscian by arguing that the verb makes a statement about the other element [272] (*i.e.* the suppositum) of the perfect construction, and at the same time it expresses an action, *etc.* with the idea of duration by means of the tense placed on a secondary level.[273] By the 13th century, the idea of change and becoming came to replace the idea of action and passion as the principal features of the verbum; this must not be taken to mean that the ideas of action and passion were dismissed from the verb, but they merely came to be looked upon as aspects of movement and becoming which now took their place as the principal criteria of the verb.[274]

Thus with the Modistae, we find a definition of the verbum which is quite different from both Priscian's and Aristotle's. The verb signifies becoming, change, flux and shares this feature with the participium as a general essential mode; by means of its specific mode, it signifies as a member of a proposition but one which is separate from its subject, and in this it is distinguished from the participle, which can 'adhere' to the subject as a result of the adjectival nature of some of its features. This is a logical restatement of a grammatical tradition which distinguished the verbum and the participium in Latin as separate word-classes. It is interesting to compare this logical description of the two partes orationis with Jespersen's theory of junction and nexus.[275]

Just as the Modistae came to accept the 'permanent' nature of the nomen in place of the traditional 'substantial' definition, so the Modistae replaced the traditional definition of the verb as action and being acted

[272]   Aristotle had described 'affirmation' as one of the principal features of the verb.

[273]   Peter Helias: "reperta sunt verba ad designandum quid de altero dicitur et primo propter actionem et passionem ... omne verbum formam actionis vel passionis significat, id est agere vel pati ... verbum consignificat tempus quantitative – 'cucurri' actum quidem 'currendi' ... principaliter designat, sed quando significat secundario" (Thurot, pp. 179, 180, 182).

[274]   Digby 55: "verbum significat motum vel fieri quia significat conceptum aliquem sub proprietate motus vel fieri et sicut motui vel fieri accidit actio vel passio, et sicut modo significandi per modum motus vel fieri accidit modus significandi actionis vel passionis, ita significato verbi accidit agere vel pati".

[275]   O. Jespersen, *The Philosophy of Grammar*, p. 108 *et seq.*

on by the counterpart to the permanent and static nature of the nomen, *i.e.* the verb represented for them flux, succession and becoming; in other words, the two principal partes, for such were still the nomen and the verbum to the Modistae, represent the opposition of 'ens' and 'esse'. The Modistae did not abandon substance as a feature of the nomen, nor did they deny that a verbum could signify action or passion, but they no longer included them as items in the description of the essence of the verbum. They were not, however, the originators of this, because already in the 13th century, grammarians had begun to dispute action and passion as the characteristic of the verbum; 'Digby 55' shows this quite clearly. What is interesting is to see the transition already at work, by which 'motus' and 'fieri' are in the process of replacing 'actio' and 'passio' which are in fact made to belong to 'motus' and 'fieri'. By the time of the Modistae, the change had been completed and 'motus' and 'fieri' (or 'fluxus' and 'successio') in the verbum were accepted as the counterparts of 'habitus' and 'permanens' in the nomen.

There is acceptance among the Modistae of the broad outlines, but there are a few minor variations, though not nearly so many as in the nomen, and once again we find a division between them which has been encountered on more than one occasion. Thomas and Martin seem to be in complete agreement in their definition of the verbum as the pars orationis which signifies by means of the mode of being separated from the substance,[276] while Siger and Michel, although they too refer to becoming (fieri) *etc.* as the characteristic feature of the verbum, rejecting 'actio' and 'passio', retain aspects of older definitions.[277] They both suggest that the verb must say something about the nomen; this has already been referred to because 'ens' (*i.e.* the nomen) must precede 'esse' *(i.e.* the verb) since there must be something (ens) before there can be any 'becoming' (esse). The verb will thus become, as we shall see in the section on syntax, along with the nomen the constructible elements in constructions which will constitute the favourite sentence type of suppositum and appositum, since the nomen and verb combination in the S P construction represents the minimal constructible pair. Hence Michel defines the verb as the pars orationis which signifies by means of the mode of becoming and which is potentially able to

---

[276] Thomas of Erfurt, #117: "verbum est pars orationis significans per modum esse distantis a substantia".
[277] Siger uses 'modus fluxus, fieri seu motus, seu esse' in that order to describe the essence of the verb, but Thomas uses only 'modus esse'.

express something about the other constructible.[278] This is very reminiscent of the Platonic definition of the noun and verb;[279] moreover there is in Siger a suggestion of the Aristotelian and contemporary logical definition of the verbum, *i.e.* as consignifying tense[280] which is totally absent from Thomas.

There is another fact which reveals an interesting difference between Thomas and Siger, and which suggests that in some ways Siger is more conservative than Thomas. Roos says, rightly so,[281] that the whole history of the definitions of the nomen and verbum, back to Aristotle and Priscian, means that the analysis of these two partes will be much richer in content than that of the other six partes orationis. What is revealing is the hold that tradition seemed to have had on Siger, who described first the nomen and then the verbum, and quite deliberately; in contrast to this, Thomas describes the nomen and then the pronomen, presumably because they have many essential features in common, before embarking on an analysis of the verbum. Siger explains that 'esse' refers to an action peculiar to 'ens',[282] and since the nomen signifies by means of the modus entis and the verbum by means of the modus esse, then the verbum must follow the nomen. In view of Siger's analysis of the four declinable partes in the form of two 'archipartes', one of which is characterised by 'ens' and the other by 'esse', it would seem much more reasonable and logical to describe together the two declinable partes which were members of the same archipars; that Siger did not do this and preferred to describe the two principal partes, *i.e.* the nomen and the verbum, in that order before coming to the other partes, suggests that he was more bound by tradition than he was prepared to follow up the implications of his theory of the 'archipars'. Thomas, on the other hand, came after Siger and one

[278] Michel de Marbais: "verbum est pars orationis significans per modum fieri de altero dicibilis" (Thurot, p. 181).

[279] Roos refers to the Aristotelian and logical tradition as defining the nomen as the modus esse and the verbum as the modus fieri; Roos implies here (though he makes no actual statement to this effect) that there was once more a wide divergence between the grammarian and the logician, because Thomas and Siger state quite explicitly that the modus esse is, along with the modus fieri, an essential feature of the verbum. The answer may well lie in the fact that 'esse' for Aristotle and the Schoolmen did not mean quite the same thing, but that is outside the scope of this work.

[280] Siger de Courtrai, p. 108: "verbum est quod consignificat tempus et est semper nota eorum quae de altero dicuntur".

[281] H. Roos, *Die Modi Significandi*, p. 146.

[282] Siger de Courtrai, p. 108: "esse est proprius actus ipsius entis; cum nomen significat rem suam per modum substantiae seu entis, et verbum per modum significandi fieri seu esse, verbum immediate debet sequi ipsum nomen".

cannot help feeling that he had succeeded to a great extent, both in his descriptions and in the plan of his work, in throwing off the incubus of tradition, though this should not be interpreted as implying that Siger is at all inferior to Thomas as a grammarian.

We can say, then, that there was a large measure of agreement among the Modistae on the nature of the verbum; in contrast to the nomen, which signifies by means of the mode of permanence and repose, the verbum signifies by means of the mode of change and becoming which in turn implies action or passion.[283] This opposition between the nomen and verbum might be described as one of different essences; there remains a further opposition which concerns the verb, *i.e.* the opposition between the verbum and the participium since they too have essential features in common, and which must be expressed in their definitions. The difference between the nomen and verb remains one of essence despite the fact that there may be a relationship between 'ens' and 'esse' which may on occasion create problems, but this does not alter the fact that their essences are different, and for this reason their consignifications will be different. The verb and the participle share the same matter, *i.e.* the modus esse, but differ by reason of the form which means that the participle can have some of the same consignification, *i.e.* syntactic meaning, but cannot ever be the appositum in an S P construction – this difference is however created by the form which cannot affect the matter,[284] *i.e.* the essence of the two partes. The verbum signifies by means of the mode of separation from the substantial element, *i.e.* the nominal suppositum, in contrast to the participium which, because the participium can also possess features like those of an adjective, will signify by means of the mode of adhering to the nominal suppositum.

---

[283] Michel de Marbais: "propter quod intelligendum est verbum significare actionem vel passionem pro tanto quod ipsum significat quicquid significat sub modo essendi vel proprietate fluxus vel fieri, qui quidem est modus actionis vel passionis, eo quod omnis actio vel passio est in quodam fluxu vel fieri sive in quadam transmutatione. Unde sicut quicquid permanet per naturam substantie permanet, sic etiam quicquid fluit vel in fieri est per naturam actionis vel passionis sive motus fluit vel in fieri est" (Thurot, p. 181).

[284] The terms materia and forma should, in this context, *not* be confused with substance; a pars orationis consists of its essence and its distinctive feature, *e.g.* in the nomen, the modus entis is the essence and the 'determinata apprehensio' is the distinctive feature. The terms materia and forma are used as members of a binary opposition, which the Modistae used descriptively to distinguish the essence and the distinctive feature, so that materia is the term used to symbolise the essence and forma to symbolise the distinctive feature – in this instance the 'determinata apprehensio'.

Siger adds one further fact about the verbum which is full of interesting and important implications which have, however, not been ful-
filled since his work is incomplete. He states that the verbum signifies
by means of the modus fieri, which is quite in keeping with the other
Modistae; he adds, however, and this is the interesting implication since
it suggests a great deal about his syntactic theories, that the mode of
becoming is dependent and that every verbum signifies by means of a
mode of signifying which is dependent (modus significandi dependentis).
This dependence of the verb refers to the philosophical problem of
dependence, since a verb requires something that it can talk about,
something that the verb can be capable of asserting, which is one of
Michel de Marbais's requirements for the verb. This means that no
verbum will be the subject of a verbum and that every verbum will
therefore require something in the nature of a subject (suppositum) in
order to support such a dependence.[285] This suggests a form of syntax
which might well have been very similar to Thomas's, because, as we
shall see, in every construction there is a dependent constructible; in
an intransitive construction, it is the second constructible as in "Socrates
currit" which is the dependent and in a transitive construction, it is the
first constructible as in "video Socratem" which is the dependent. In
both cases, however, the verb has been the dependent element and this
is very similar to Siger's statement. Siger makes, as we have said, the
verbum always a dependent of the suppositum; this suggests that his
syntax might well have been to a very large extent the S P (suppositum-
appositum) of traditional logic, but it also suggests that Siger was less
interested in the minutiae of syntax, especially of Latin syntax, than
Thomas was.

Modus significandi essentialis

It will be apparent already that there is between the Modistae a great
measure of agreement on their grammatical doctrine and that such
divergences as do exist are really matters of presentation. Furthermore,
it is quite clear, that once their premises have been established, there
is considerable consistency in their analytical procedure. The weakness
of their system is revealed sharply by the need the Modistae felt to
rationalise apparent exceptions in their system, e.g. privatio and fig-

---

[285] Siger de Courtrai, p. 108: "omne verbum significat rem suam per modum
fieri, et ipsum fieri est dependens, ideo omne verbum significat rem suam per
modum significandi dependentis et par consequens nullum verbum, in quantum
tale, poterit supponere verbo, immo omne verbum requirit aliquid in ratione suppositi quod dependentiam eius sustentat".

menta as members of the nomen-class and the position of the verbum substantivum in the verbal system. It is this type of rationalisation which reveals perhaps their greatest failing, *i.e.* their grammatical procedure claimed universality and yet needed to indulge in such tortuous arguments in order to justify certain exceptions to their statements.

The structure of their presentation of the verbum reveals that consistency to which reference has just been made. It will be remembered that in the essential mode of the nomen, Siger states his criteria for the essential mode, divided into general and specific, in a very succinct manner, and then allows himself much more space in which to expatiate on the accidental modes; in contrast to this, Thomas presents his modus generalissimus which is, in effect, an equivalent statement to Siger's general and specific modes, before beginning his more detailed description of the pars in question by means of the modus subalternus which he continues to refine by means of the modus specialissimus. Thomas's approach to the whole problem of defining the essential mode might be said to represent a contrast of theory and practice; in the modus generalissimus he states his theoretical criteria for establishing this particular pars and in the modus subalternus and specialissimus he merely seems to describe in detailed grammatical terms the application of this philosophical theorising to the pars in question, *i.e.* we find a contrast between philosophical theorising and grammatical description. Once this has been done, he is then free to deal with the accidental modes.

The procedure in the verbum, then, is exactly the same as in the nomen, and it will facilitate this exposition of Modistic doctrine, if the same plan is followed in this section on the essential mode of the verbum. The diagram in Appendix C shows the different presentations of Siger and Thomas of the essential mode of the verbum and at the same time permits us to see that the final result is the same. As in the nomen, we see then that Siger's modus generalis and specificus are the equivalent of Thomas's modus generalissimus and that Thomas's modus subalternus and specialissimus consist of refinements which Siger does not discuss at all. In order to present a unified statement on the essential mode of the nomen, it became necessary to displace some of Siger's accidental modes and consider them along with Thomas's modus subalternus; in this exposition of the verbum, no such change in order of presentation has been necessary in order to achieve unity of subject matter.

As in the nomen, Siger uses his general essential mode to describe a feature which is possessed by more than one pars orationis, in this instance the verbum and the participium, and Siger defines this mode as the mode of flux, becoming or movement, or being;[286] it is the essential mode since it refers to the essence of more than one pars. It is very similar to Michel's general essential mode which he describes as the mode of flux and becoming[287] and it is also very similar to a description of the general essential mode of the verbum to be found in the Digby MS (to which reference has already been made).[288] The modus specificus is used by Siger to distinguish a particular pars from all the others; therefore Siger gives as the specific mode of the verbum the feature of separation or discreteness from the substance, *i.e.* the nominal element,[289] and this also serves to segregate the verbum from the participium which, of all the other partes orationis, is closest to the verbum by virtue of a common general essence.[290]

[286] Siger de Courtrai, p. 108: "modus significandi generalis essentialis verbi est modus significandi per modum fluxus, fieri seu motus, seu esse, quod idem est extendendo ista sicut prius modus significandi entis extendebatur".

[287] Michel de Marbais: "modus significandi fluxus vel fieri.

[288] Digby 55: "significatum verbi est significare conceptum aliquem sub modo fieri vel motus, ex qua proprietate motus vel fieri accipitur modus fieri inclinabilis ad substantiam ... non est modus specificus sed essentialis generalis ... in hoc communicant verbum et participium".

[289] Siger de Courtrai, p. 108: "modus specificus verbi est modus significandi essentialis de aliquo seu significare per modum distantis vel facientis alterum extremum orationis".

[290] This is one of the many instances of the use of the matter-form contrast to produce a grammatical opposition. Siger does not make very much use of the terms 'materia' and 'forma' but this does not mean that he avoids the actual opposition; in actual fact, his use of the modus generalis and the modus specificus as sub-modes of the essential mode, and this is shown quite clearly if we compare his statements to those of Thomas who does use the terms 'materia' and 'forma', can be considered the equivalent of the matter-form contrast. In this respect, *i.e.* the definitions of the essential modes, Siger goes much further than Thomas, in that he, Siger, quite clearly uses this contrast (though he never says so specifically) to distinguish the general and specific modes of the indeclinable partes and, by implication, to distinguish the indeclinable partes themselves – this Thomas does not do. The Modistae had recourse to this dichotomy of matter and form in order to clarify the difference between the verbum and the participium. Siger is perhaps less overt in his use of this division but he did refer to the *formal* aspect of the specific mode of the nomen, *viz.* "qualitatis seu formae est distinguere, in quo modo significandi nomen differt a pronomine". Thomas confirms that matter refers to the general mode and that form refers to the specific. Thomas points out that the modus esse represents the material which brings the verbum and participium together but that separation (distantia) represents the formal and thus segregates the verbum from all the other partes orationis, *viz.* "comparando verbum ad participium, modus esse habet rationem materiae, respectu verbi, quia facit verbum cuius participio convenire; sed facere convenire est proprietas materiae; modus distantis habet rationem formae, quia facit verbum ab omnibus aliis distare et differre".

It is interesting to note that Michel's special mode is not quite the same as Siger's, whereas the Digby MS is;[291] Michel reverts, as has already been suggested to the older logical tradition of the verb being capable of asserting something,[292] his argument being that what is in a state of flux or becoming can be predicated to the subject.[293] Michel admits that separation (distantia) is a feature of the verbum, otherwise it would not be capable of making any assertion,[294] but he denies that it is an essential mode of the verbum, his argument being that such distantia does not refer to any discreteness by the actual designation of whatever process the verb refers to, *i.e.* this discreteness is not in the mind, but rather to the actual physical separation of the verbum from the nomen.[295] The participle is near to the verb in meaning and some syntax, but is distinct from the verb with regard to the minimum SP sentence structure of Latin; in other words, the participle and the verb can stand in a one-to-one relationship but the participle cannot constitute the appositum in the favourite SP sentence type of Latin.[296] Thomas's modus generalissimus combines these two modes of the other Modistae, and defines the essential mode of the verbum, as we might expect from the definitions given by the others, as the mode of signifying by means of the modus esse and the mode of separation from the substance – a definition which is identical to Martin of Dacia's.[297] In the nomen, the characteristic had been the modus entis and it was pointed out that this mode operates in contrast to the modus esse, which represents the mode of flux and succession and which is

---

[291] Digby 55: "specificus est modus inclinabilis ad substantiam in ratione distantis et alterius extremi".

[292] Michel de Marbais: "modus significandi dicibilis de alio" (Thurot, p. 181).

[293] Michel de Marbais: "illud quod est in fluxu vel fieri est aptum natum dici de subiecto vel enunciari. Unde habet proprietatem vel modum essendi de alio dicibilis" (Thurot, p. 181).

[294] Michel de Marbais: "verbum significat sub ratione distantis, eo quod omne illud quod enunciatur de altero in oratione distat ab eo" (Thurot, p. 181).

[295] Michel de Marbais: "remotio situs verbi a situ nominis" (Thurot, p. 181).

[296] Reference has already been made to Siger's theory of the 'archipars'; it is not possible to state with absolute certainty, from the few extracts available in Thurot, whether Michel suggests any similar theory, though there seems every likelihood that he did, but it does seem true from the two extracts just quoted that the author of the Digby MS sought to organise his material in such a way as to suggest an embryonic theory of the 'archipars' very similar to Siger's. It would be inappropriate to say more since this MS is clearly pre-Modistic, and the material is not ordered in the same systematic manner of the Modistae.

[297] Thomas of Erfurt, #110: "modus significandi generalissimus essentialis verbi est modus significandi rem per modum esse, et distantis a substantia".

the other common property found, as Thomas tells us, in things,[298] the first being the modus entis, and is in opposition to the property of repose and permanence; it must be remembered that this dichotomy of ens and esse is fundamental to Modistic grammatical theory.

It is revealing to note that neither Siger nor Thomas could entirely exclude syntactic material from their descriptions of the essential modes of the verbum; this is not to suggest that this should be construed as a flaw in their grammatical method, far from it, but it does represent a weakening in the rigour of their whole approach, especially Thomas's.[299] Siger, in describing the specific mode of the verbum, in which distantia is the important and distinguishing factor, reinforces his argument by stating that the verbum will become the other member of the construction (alterum extremum orationis) in contrast to the participium which can join with the suppositum. Distantia thus becomes their way of expressing this syntactic feature and is an especially valuable distinction since the participle can be endocentric with either the suppositum or the appositum. Thomas employs syntactic criteria as a justification for his modus generalissimus, so that the modus esse of the verbum will be proportionate, i.e. complementary to the modus entis, i.e. the mode of repose and permanence which will be found in both the suppositum and in the oblique, i.e. terminant, constructible.[300]

We saw in the section on the nomen that the Modistae showed great skill in applying their metaphysics to their grammatical theories, but that this also left them with the serious problem of reconciling metaphysics and grammar, which they did by resorting to metaphysics, the final result being that the inadequacy of their non-formal grammar is brought out into very sharp relief. A similar problem arose in the verbum, and Thomas was faced with the problem of reconciling the statements that if 'esse' implies flux and succession, what then is the succession in the use of the verb in "Deus est": Thomas finds a solution

---

[298]   Thomas of Erfurt, #24: "in rebus invenimus quasdam proprietates communissimas sive modos essendi communissimos, scilicet modum entis, et modum esse".
[299]   This is rather like certain modern linguists who rigorously eschew meaning as a criterion in linguistic analysis and then appeal to meaning to produce the final and decisive argument.
[300]   Michel de Marbais was the only one of the Modistae to exclude 'ens' from his description of the nomen, and so too in the verbum he is the only one to exclude 'esse' from his definition; again, just as in the nomen he stood closer to the older classical definition, so too in the verbum he is much closer to the older logical statement of the assertability of the verbum. Siger and Thomas both consider 'esse' to be one of the principal criteria – indeed for Thomas it is, apart from distantia, the only one, whereas Siger refers to action and passion as features of the verbum, though not as features of the essence of the verbum.

by resorting to tortuous arguments about the non-temporal but eternal nature of the succession implied in the statement "Deus est", *i.e.* that the eternal has to be imagined in terms of the temporal.[301] This is a long way from descriptive linguistics and it is mentioned in detail to show some of the problems which a grammatical theory, relying almost entirely on non-linguistic and metaphysical criteria, can create for itself. The copula, also, appears to have presented an awkward problem for the Modistae which their morpho-semantic descriptive technique was quite clearly incapable of answering except by resorting to non-linguistic arguments, or else by using formal criteria to explain something which semantics could not do.[302]

Modus significandi subalternus

If it is reasonable to argue that the general essential mode of the verb is described along lines similar to the description of the equivalent mode of the nomen, it is equally reasonable to suggest that the modus subalternus of the verbum will be identical in pattern to the modus subalternus of the nomen. It will soon be realised that this is what we actually do find.

As in the nomen, the modus subalternus of the verbum is peculiar to Thomas but this time it has not been necessary to include certain material, *i.e.* some of Siger's accidental modes for the sake of a unified description of their grammatical doctrine.[303] The modus generalissimus

---

[301] Thomas of Erfurt, #112: "licet esse Dei ... non sit successivum successione temporis, est tamen successivum successione aeternitatis; et licet aeternitas sit tota simul et perfecta possessio ... tamen, quia intelligimus ex istis inferioribus, ideo imaginamur ibi successionem et durationem aeternitatis per diversa spatia temporis".

[302] The whole problem arises from the argument that 'distantia' cannot be used as a general criterion for the verb, since 'esse' does not signify anything essentially distinct from any 'ens', because anything distinct from 'ens' would be 'non ens': Thomas of Erfurt, #115: "dicendo: 'ens est', esse non significat aliquid essentialiter distinctum ab omni ente, quia quod est essentialiter distinctum ab ente non ens". In Chapter II as part of the discussion of the materia-forma contrast, the use of the technical term 'ratio' as an indication of potential word-order was discussed since the Modistae seem to have considered word-order to be grammatically relevant. The difference between 'ens' and 'est' in the construction 'ens est' is much more satisfactorily explained by means of the formal criterion of potential word-order than by resorting to semantics.

[303] It will be remembered that Thomas had described the substantivum and adiectivum, which Siger had classified as accidental modes, as modi subalterni and specialissimi of the nomen; in order to make a unified statement on Modistic theory, it was decided to include the consideration of Siger's accidental modes of substantivum and adiectivum along with our description of Thomas's subaltern

is divided into three modi subalterni, only one of which will be sub-divided into modi specialissimi; the first subalternus refers to verbs such as 'sum' which is otherwise referred to as a verbum substantivum. The verbum substantivum is capable of specifying some special being while signifying by means of the modus esse;[304] unlike the verbum neutrum it is also capable of being contracted to some case-form. It is as a result of its contractability with its post-posed case-form that it becomes a verbum substantivum, not because of the feature of 'per se stantis' which characterises the nomen substantivum, but because it signifies some being and is also capable of further specification by means of a post-posed nominal form;[305] 'vocor' becomes a verbum vocativum with the post-posed nominative form which in this instance acts also as the 'further specification' of the verbum substantivum as well as being the specification of the verbum vocativum. The second modus subalternus contains verbs such as 'vocor' and this subaltern mode constitutes the verbum vocativum. The verbum vocativum signi-fies the general property of naming which will be specifiable by means of the special property of naming which will be brought to it by means of the dependent constructible,[306] e.g. 'vocor' represents the general quality of naming but it becomes specific with the addition of the dependent as in "vocor Adrianus". The third modus subalternus would seem to refer to all other verbs, differentiated by their modi specialissimi, since all verbs in this category which constitutes the verbum adiectivum possess the ability to signify action or passion, which as we have seen, was long considered the principal feature of all verbs.

The verbum adiectivum is divided into four modi specialissimi, i.e. modus actionis, modus passionis, modus neutri, and modus utriusque and constitute the verbum activum, passivum, neutrum and commune. The whole process from the modus generalissimus to the modi special-issimi can be presented diagrammatically (see diagram on next page).

These modi specialissimi constitute, in modern terms, verbs which are active transitive, passive transitive, intransitive, and active and passive,

---

modes and modi specialissimi. In Thomas's system the modi subalterni and spe-cialissimi are used to catalogue the various types of word which constitute the particular pars orationis in question.

[304]   Thomas of Erfurt, #118: "verbum substantivum est, quod significat per modum esse generaliter, specificabile per quodlibet esse speciale".

[305]   Thomas of Erfurt, #118: "dicitur substantivum, non ex modo per se stantis, sed quia significat esse generale specificabile; ideo potest stare specificativum cuiuscumque specificantis ipsum".

[306]   Thomas of Erfurt, #119: "verbum vocativum significat nominationem in generali, specificabilem per quamcumque nominationem propriam in speciali".

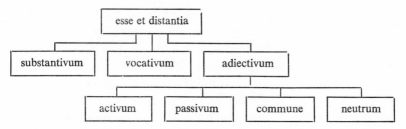

but it must be stressed that the inherent criteria for these verb-classes
are purely semantic, *i.e.* the verbum adiectivum activum signifies 'action'
only,[307] *e.g.* 'amo', while the verbum adiectivum passivum signifies
'being acted on' only,[308] *e.g.* 'amor'. We shall discuss very shortly the
difference between these modi specialissimi which, by virtue of their
inherent semantic criteria, constitute verbs which signify 'action' or
'being acted on' and the accidental mode of genus, which, by virtue of
imposed quasi formal criteria, refers to the nature of the relationship
between the verb and any post-posed nominal oblique form. It is
interesting to note, and yet Thomas is quite consistent in this, that he
excludes the verbum deponens as a modus specialissimus of the verbum,
since there are no criteria at all, in terms of its essence, (not even
morphologic, though Thomas seems, on this small point, to have moved
outside his frame of reference in order to reinforce his argument[309]),
for setting up the verbum deponens as a separate verb-class.[310] The
verbum commune signifies both action and being acted on, *e.g.* 'criminor
te' and 'criminor a te'. The verbum neutrum, or in modern terms, the
intransitive verb, signifies neither action nor being acted on,[311] *e.g.*
'vivo', *i.e.* it signifies by means of the absence (privatio) of action or

---

[307]   Thomas of Erfurt, #121: "verbum adiectivum activum est, quod significat
tantum actionem ut amo, doceo".
[308]   Thomas of Erfurt, #122: "verbum adiectivum passivum est, quod significat
passionem tantum, ut amor, doceor".
[309]   Thomas of Erfurt, #125: "verbum deponens non potest esse distincta species
ab activo et passivo, nisi per terminationem vocum, quod non est specie differre,
cum plures partes orationis possint in una voce et terminatione convenire".
[310]   Martin of Dacia divides the verb into substantivum, vocativum, and adiectivum, and the latter he subdivides into activum, passivum, neutrum, commune,
and deponens. By virtue of his organisation, he is able to set up the verbum
deponens as a separate sub-class; he also uses formal criteria to justify this, since
Modistic semantic criteria are insufficient for this distinction, *viz.* #120: "verbum
deponens non differt ab activo et passivo *nisi penes terminationes vocales hinc
et inde* [my emphasis]. Martin's organisation can be seen from the following
diagram:
[311]   Thomas of Erfurt, #123: "verbum neutrum est, quod nec actionem, nec passionem significat, ut vivo".

passion rather than by means of some positive attribute expressed by means of some mode of signifying. More important still is that the verbum neutrum is contractable with itself, *i.e.* it is self-contained but will not be used with any postposed oblique form.[312]

The modus specialissimus represents the full semantic quotient which combines to make up the essence of each of these verbs; if we take the verb 'amo', we see that it contains as its essence, (i) esse, (ii) distantia as the modus generalissimus (or the modus generalis and specificus to use Siger's terminology), (iii) it is a verbum adiectivum by means of its modus subalternus, and (iv) it signifies action by virtue of its modus specialissimus -- this can be interpreted as a positive feature even for a verbum neutrum, which by virtue of its modus specialissimus may not

	modus generaliss- imus		modus subalter- nus	modus specialissi- mus		
	esse	distan- tia	adiec- tivum	actio	passio	privatio actio/ passio
amo	+	+	+	+		
amor	+	+	+		+	
vivo	+	+	+			+
criminor	+	+	+	+	+	

[312]   Thomas of Erfurt, #124: "verbum neutrale significat esse contractum de se, non contrahibile, ut vivo significat esse absolute secundum esse vitae".

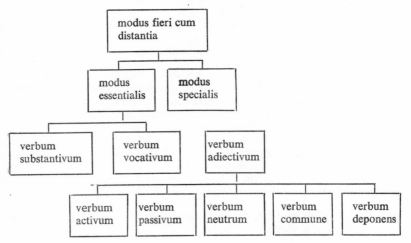

signify action or being acted on. This process of development from the modus generalissimus to the modus specialissimus can be described in diagram form for all the four kinds of verbum adiectivum (see p. 212).

Reference was made, in discussing the nomen, to a procedure in Thomas's analysis of the modus subalternus, which suggested that the modus subalternus will be a special mode with respect to the modus generalissimus, *i.e.* it will describe features of the essence of the pars which serve to individualise it, but that the modus subalternus will be at the same time a general mode with respect to the other modes, *i.e.* the modi specialissimi, since a general mode will refer to its essence even if it transcends one pars orationis in doing so. This is confirmed by the fact that the modus subalternus of the participium, as we shall see, can be divided into participium substantivum, vocativum and adiectivum. Even more important perhaps, is that this underlines the fact that the establishment of the modus subalternus and its sub-divisions is made on semantic criteria alone, and that morphologic and syntactic criteria are excluded. These modi speciallissimi represent different types of verb, the distinction being treated as a purely semantic one. It should be mentioned that in 'genus' two formal criteria are involved, (a) morphological, since the difference between the active and passive genus is that the active ends in /-o/ but can be changed to /-r/ and the passive ends in /-r/ but can be changed to /-o/- (meaning is introduced but only as a secondary criterion), and (b) syntactic since these verbs can have the following possible relationships:

(a) active — post-posed oblique nominal
(b) passive — post-posed nominal oblique governed by a preposition
(c) neutrum — no possible relationship
(d) commune — either (a) or (b).

But these relationships are expressed by the accidental modes of significatio and genus. The absence of morphological and also syntactic criteria in establishing the modus specialissimus is thus in striking contrast to the accidental mode of genus in the verbum and these sub-divisions of the verbum adiectivum serve to illustrate the fact that all the essential modes represent the semantification of mainly formal distinctions which the Modistae inherited from Priscian; for this reason semantic criteria will take pride of place although syntax is admitted occasionally, but only as a last resort.

We can summarise the essential mode of the verbum thus: the modus generalissimus is sub-divided into three modi subalterni, which are in effect the verbum substantivum, the verbum vocativum and the verbum adiectivum. The verbum adiectivum is further subdivided into four modi specialissimi which constitute the verbum activum, the verbum passivum, the verbum neutrum, and the verbum commune. Just as the modus generalissimus leads to the modus subalternus, which in turn is divided into the modi specialissimi, so the verbum considered simply as such can be divided into the verbum substantivum, vocativum and adiectivum, the last named sub-dividing into verbum activum, passivum, neutrum and commune. This last sub-division of the modi specialissimi should not be confused with 'genus' in the verbum[313] since genus, *i.e.* voice, is the accidental mode by means of which the quality of the relationship between the verb and the post-posed oblique is made. Modi specialissimi merely represent different types of verb, *i.e.* they are the further refinement of the modus subalternus; the VN relationship is entirely another matter.

Modus significandi accidentalis

There are potentially many more accidents[314] to a pars orationis than are described in any Modistic grammar, just as the Modistae tended to add one or more additional accidental features,[315] having either taken over or omitted some of the accidental features found already in the grammars of their classical predecessors. Siger in the nomen followed Donatus closely except that he added 'species' to the list of accidents, but Siger differed from Priscian who did not include either 'qualitas' or 'gradus' among his accidents of the nomen; on the other hand, Thomas followed Priscian closely, though Thomas too went one stage ahead of Priscian and added 'persona' to the accidents of the nomen.

As for the verbum, Siger tells us that Donatus ascribed *seven* accidents to the verbum, *i.e.* modus, coniugatio, genus, numerus, figura, tempus and persona, while Priscian ascribed *eight, i.e.* all those of Donatus with 'species' in addition. Thrax, in his definition of the verb,

---

[313] Thomas of Erfurt, #126: "non sit idem dicere, verbum activum, et activi generis; passivum, et passivi generis".

[314] R. H. Robins, *Thrax*, p. 105, which is the definition of 'accident' in this instance: it should not be equated with modus accidentalis or with 'accidentia', a metaphysical term associated with 'substantia'.

[315] In many respects the Modistae present a much more unified body of doctrine for the verbum than they did for the accidental modes of the nomen.

had listed eight categories which were applicable to the verb, *i.e.* mood, voice, type, form, number, tense, person and conjugation, which can be stated in Modistic terms as modus, genus, species, figura, numerus, tempus, persona, coniugatio; so we see that Priscian followed Thrax closely as far as the accidents of the verbum are concerned. The Modistae followed Priscian closely, *i.e.* Siger has the same features as Priscian for his accidental modes of the verbum, but Thomas introduces the category of 'qualitas', which the others mentioned do not use. He divides this into the sub-modes of 'modus' and 'forma'; he equates the latter to 'species' in the nomen and this is in fact the same as Siger's category of 'species' in the verbum. Furthermore, he uses an additional accidental mode, and it would seem that this accidental mode of 'compositio' is, to him, the most important. He himself classifies it as a modus significandi accidentalis communissimus verbi, and he states quite categorically that the ancient [316] grammarians made no use of this category, although this is a feature present in all verbs; [317] for this he refers to Aristotle to support his argument. [318] Michel too seems to have included, according to Thurot, an accidental mode of the verbum which he called the modus specificabilis and which would appear to be like Thomas's accidental mode of 'compositio', but unfortunately Thurot gives us no further information about it. Compositio is quite clearly a most important feature of the verbum; quite apart from its intrinsic importance as the first of the accidental modes of the verbum, it plays an important role in syntax by providing the link between the suppositum and the appositum.

After dealing with compositio, Thomas proceeds to analyse the other accidental modes in more or less the same way that the others do, attributing the same importance to them all. Donatus, Priscian and Siger equate 'genus' to 'significatio' and do not create a separate accident of the verbum for 'significatio', but Thomas follows Peter Helias (who had described 'significatio' as 'significatio accidentalis') and makes

---

[316] 'Antiqui' does not necessarily mean the ancient Greeks and Romans; it was also sometimes used in the Middle Ages to refer to their immediate predecessors, and in this instance could refer to Peter Helias just as well as to Priscian and Donatus, since Peter did not describe 'compositio' as a separate feature of the verb.

[317] Martin attaches great importance to 'compositio' and places it before all the other accidental modes; as in so many other instances, however, he does not provide us with the extent of detail that Thomas does.

[318] Thomas of Erfurt, #128: "hoc verbum 'est' significat quandam compositionem, quam sine extremis non est intelligere; et tamen hoc verbum 'est' in omni verbo includitur, tamquam radix omnium ideo compositio omni verbo inhaeret, per quam verbum distans a supposito ad suppositum ... inclinatur".

of 'significatio' another separate accidental mode. So far as this exposition of Modistic theory is concerned 'significatio' has been treated as a preamble to an examination of the feature of 'genus/significatio', an accidental mode of the verbum common to all the Modistae.

The Modistae present the accidental modes in slightly differing order, e.g. Thomas begins with compositio and then discusses qualitas (which he subdivides into modus and forma), coniugatio, significatio, genus, persona, numerus, figura and tempus. Siger follows a different order of presentation; [319] he begins with genus which he, like Donatus and Priscian, equates to significatio and which Thomas treats separately. Siger then describes tempus, modus, species, figura, numerus, coniugatio, and persona in that order.

To facilitate the presentation of this material and to show the similarities and differences in doctrine, some changes have been necessary in the order of presentation, which should be understood as though divided into three main groups: (i) Compositio followed by modus, since, as Thomas tells us, [320] modus is the quality of the compositio, and then significatio followed by genus since this is the quality of the significatio; [321] the correlation of compositio and significatio deals with the verb in its transitive and intransitive functions, compositio dealing with the verb in its relations with the suppositum, and the significatio with the verb and its relations with the post-posed oblique nominal form; (ii) species or forma and figura which are absolute modes as in the nomen and although they may represent features which may be described as 'synchronic derivation' their primary criteria are, as always, semantic; [322] (iii) tempus, numerus, persona, which are respective ac-

---

[319]   Siger has no accidental mode of 'compositio', and his 'genus' and 'significatio' are equivalent terms but are not expressly designed to state the relationship between the verb and the post-posed oblique nominal form. Thomas's compositio and significatio coupled with modus and genus, are perhaps his most significant contributions to the theory of the verb, and have their ramifications well beyond the verb; they serve to throw a great deal of light on his syntactic theories and especially his system of transitive and intransitive constructions. We find here a major divergence between Siger and Thomas as far as their treatment of these accidental modes of the verb concerned; as we have just stated, Siger makes no use of either compositio or significatio, nor does he describe these features by any other means.

[320]   Thomas of Erfurt, #131: "modus, ut est accidens verbi, est qualitas compositionis".

[321]   Thomas of Erfurt, #137: "genus non est formaliter significatio, sed qualitas significationis ipsam contrahens et disponens".

[322]   The primary or principal criteria in the description of all categories are, in the Modistic grammatical scheme, always semantic; secondary is used to refer to other criteria, e.g. syntactic, to support the primary criteria. What it really amounts to is that Modistic procedure was to take the formal categories of Priscian and

cidental modes, and which, along with mood (modus), combine to be
present in any coniugatio of the verbum, though they do not, strictly
speaking, belong to the verb, but are acquired either from the suppositum or from the sentence as a whole.[323]

Compositio

Thomas introduces two accidental modes into his description of the
verb, *i.e.* compositio and significatio, which are not to be found in
either Siger or Michel de Marbais (though Siger does use the term
significatio in the same way as Priscian, *i.e.* as an equivalent term for
voice (genus)); Thomas maintains in fact that his predecessors did not

---

restate them in semantic terms; when this failed or could not very well be applied,
as in the indeclinable partes, the Modistae resorted to more formal criteria for their
statements.

[323] The following diagram shows the various accidental modes of the verbum
described by the grammarians of antiquity and the Middle Ages; Martin has seven
accidental modes, Michel, Siger and Thomas each have eight. Asterisks have been
used to indicate, in the case of Michel, that his modus specificabilis has been included under the rubric of 'compositio', and in the case of Thomas, that 'modus'
and 'species' which he actually calls 'forma', are in fact sub-modes of 'qualitas'. It
should also be noted that Michel does not appear to have included 'species' as an
accidental mode, and that 'coniugatio' cannot genuinely be listed among Martin's
accidental modes of the verbum since he subordinates it as a feature of 'tempus'
just as 'declinatio' was a feature of # 'casus', *i.e.* Martin of Dacia, #136:
"per coniungationem non intelligo aliud quam modum intelligendi rem sive fieri
secundum quod cadit sub diversis inflexionibus temporum, sicut declinatio in
nomine est modus intelligendi rem ut cadit sub diversis inflexionibus casuum".

	Thrax	Dona-tus	Pris-cian	Mar-tin	Mi-chel	Siger	Thomas
compositio					*		+
modus	+	+	+	+	+	+	(+)*
significatio							+
genus	+	+	+	+	+	+	+
species/forma	+		+	+		+	(+)*
figura	+	+	+	+	+	+	+
tempus	+	+	+	+	+	+	+
numerus	+	+	+	+	+	+	+
persona	+	+	+	+	+	+	+
coniugatio	+	+	+			+	+
qualitas							(+)

make use of 'compositio' at all,[324] which seems to be true as far as compositio can be considered an accident of the verb, but Priscian does refer to compositio as a feature of the syntax of the noun and verb.

Thomas took the unusual step of declaring this accidental feature of compositio to be a modus communissimus, and there is considerable justification for placing it at the head of all the accidental modes. Aristotle had argued[325] that a verb does not itself indicate anything but implies a copulation, and Thomas argues from this that the copula element is to be found in every verb; as a result compositio is inherent in every verb, and serves to link the verb to its suppositum. This is a very important concept, since the essential mode of the verb declares discreteness of the verb from the suppositum – Michel de Marbais had indeed argued against discreteness being considered an essential mode of the verb since it would produce precisely that situation which compositio had to remedy – to be one of its most important characteristics. For this reason, Thomas cannot make of compositio an essential mode since it is in diametric contrast to the essential mode of separation, and it is equally not a feature of the modus esse of the verb nor does it constitute a specific type of verb;[326] it is therefore an accidental mode of the verb, which states the fundamental syntactic relationship, *i.e.* of S and P, between the nomen-suppositum and the verbum-appositum.

It is true that other accidental modes, *i.e.* number and person, play a part in the relationship between the suppositum and the verb, but such a relationship cannot be compared to the relationship between the suppositum and the verb exemplified by compositio. Compositio is inherent in the verb, whereas number and person are in fact derived from the suppositum and not in and of themselves as features of the verb, and they occur only as a result (and this can be said of all the other accidental modes with the exception of significatio) of the relation between the suppositum and verb which has *previously, i.e.* logically, been established by the accidental mode of compositio.

We find then governmental concord[327] between the compositio,

---

[324]   This statement requires a minor qualification. Thomas in this context says 'grammatici antiqui'. Siger and Michel do not include 'compositio' among the accidental moods. But Martin does and like Thomas gives it pride of place.

[325]   Aristotle, *De Interpretatione*, Chap. III.

[326]   Thomas of Erfurt, #128: "non est modus essentialis generalissimus, cum verbo non det esse simpliciter, sed sit praeter eius intellectum essentialem. Nec etiam est essentialis specialis, cum non constituat aliquam speciem verbi".

[327]   This term has been borrowed from Hockett, *A Course in Modern Linguistics*, pp. 215-216, but I have used it differently to account for the particular relationship realised by *compositio*.

which is the property of linking the verb to the suppositum,[328] and the substantival element in the suppositum,[329] and once this relationship has been stated, the other accidental modes will follow. This is (at least to the present writer) one of Thomas's most significant contributions to the theory of the verb, *i.e.* that the accidental modes can be established only when the fundamental relationship of nomen-verbum has been made, – in other words the formal relationship of noun and verb must dominate all other morphologic features which are, in many senses, useless until this primary formal factor has been established. The same is, as we shall see, true also of significatio, though this is restricted somewhat by the fact that this accidental mode will feature in certain types of construction only. The result is something which can be very satisfying aesthetically; we begin with a fundamental relationship of noun and verb, and from this stems the operation of the other accidental modes in a beautifully staggered scheme – (we can except species and figura, since they as absolute modes play no part whatsoever in the syntactic relationships of a construction). Thus we find, in Thomas's scheme, compositio leading to mood which expresses the quality of the compositio and these dominate the whole atmosphere of the sentence; significatio and genus express further relationships of the more complex construction, for genus is primarily a *relational* feature and concerned with the relationship between the verb and the postposed nominal oblique (obliquum). When once these fundamental relationships, implicit in compositio-mood and significatio-voice, exemplified in SV, SVO and (S)VO[330] have been established, it is then possible to move on to the purely inflectional features of tense, person, number and conjugation which can become grammatical (as opposed to paradigmatic) only as a result of the interpenetration of compositio and these inflectional accidental modes.

Compositio is therefore the accidental mode of the verb by means of which the verb consignifies the property of connection in terms of 'esse', and by means of which the verb, discrete from the suppositum (as a result of its essential mode), is linked to the suppositum.[331]

---

[328] Thomas of Erfurt, #128: "cum verbum sit alterum extremum in oratione, distans a supposito, et inclinetur ad suppositum, huius inclinationis principale et communissimum principium, inter ceteros modos accidentales verbi, est compositio".

[329] Thomas of Erfurt, #128: "huic modo verbi, qui est compositio, proportionatur ex parte suppositi modus per se stantis".

[330] S = suppositum, O = obliquum.

[331] Thomas of Erfurt, #128: "compositio est modus significandi accidentalis

Modus

Siger and Thomas show a very large measure of agreement in their theory of mood as an accidental mode of the verb, and their definition of the feature is almost identical. Their analytical procedures, as we shall also see in the section on voice (genus), differ quite appreciably, since Thomas is much more interested in the feature as such and devotes little space to the various moods; Siger has little to say about the phenomenon of mood, but dwells at great length on the moods of the Latin verb, and furthermore considers under the rubric of mood, the gerund and the supine, since they have the value of an infinitive mood.[332]

Thomas introduces the accidental mode of qualitas which he divides into mood and form or species; more will be said of this when species is considered, but it must be stated at this point, that Thomas is here following Donatus by his use of qualitas and its subdivisions of modus and forma. We had cause, while considering the nomen, to take into account Siger's accidental mode of qualitas subdivided into appellativa and propria, which Thomas, however, included as subaltern modes of the essential mode, but on this occasion Thomas makes of qualitas an accidental mode of the verbum, and its sub-categories of modus and forma will be considered as accidental modes along with Siger's accidental modes of modus and species. The association of mood with qualitas seems, in Thomas's scheme, to have important implications, since mood is, by definition, the quality of the compositio which creates the link between the suppositum and the verb[333] and thereby repairs the 'damage' created by the discreteness (distantia) required as an essential feature of the verb.

Mood is derived from the property of the verb, *i.e.* the property of the qualification, arrangement and relationship of the verb to the subject element of the verb,[334] which signifies the quality of indication, command, wish, doubt or non-specification. Mood is therefore the accidental mode of the verb which designates the property of various

---

verbi, mediante quo verbum consignificat proprietatem inhaerentis secundum esse, et quo mediante verbum distans a supposito, primo et principaliter ad suppositum inclinatur".

[332] Siger de Courtrai, p. 115: "gerundia, participialia seu supposita vim infinitivorum habent et funguntur voce eorum".

[333] Thomas of Erfurt, #131: "modus, ut est accidens verbi, est qualitas compositionis, qua verbum inclinatur ad suppositum".

[334] Thomas of Erfurt, #131: "modus sumitur a proprietate rei verbi, quae est proprietas qualificationis, dispositionis, et inclinationis rei verbi ad suppositionem".

states of the mind and consignifies, by means of the various qualities, *i.e.* indication, command, *etc.* which are derived from these states of mind expressed by mood, the dependence of the verb on the suppositum.[335]

Peter Helias had defined mood as the different inclinations of the mind revealed in the different effects it achieves, but Thomas however is very insistent, and this is most important for an understanding of Thomas's whole procedure, that mood is *not* this inclination of the mind but its *quality*,[336] and therefore mood becomes the quality of the compositio which provides the link between the verb and the suppositum. This is, in Thomas's eyes, clearly a fundamental relationship, which, as we shall see, will be paralleled by a similar fundamental relationship between the verb and the post-posed oblique form exemplified by significatio, the quality of which will be expressed by means of the voice (genus). These fundamental relationships can be stated by means of the following diagram, and it will be seen that they state the governing associations in any construction, either transitive or intransitive, which contains a verb. The other factors which are to be found in any such construction, *i.e.* the accidental modes of tense, number, person and conjugation, can be introduced when once these primary relationships have been set up; we have thus, as these primary relationships:

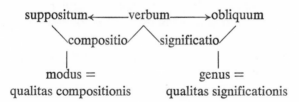

Compositio is therefore going to be a vital factor in any constructio intransitiva actuum which consists of NV or suppositum-appositum, one of the favourite sentence types of Latin in which compositio will express the relationship between the S and the dependent P; similarly significatio will play an analogous function in the constructio transitiva

---

[335] Thomas of Erfurt, #131: "modus verbi nihil aliud est quam modus significandi accidentalis verbi, mediante quo proprietatem verbi per modum indicii, imperii, voti, dubii, vel infiniti circa verbi dependentiam ad suppositum consignificat". Siger de Courtrai, p. 112: "modus in verbo est modus significandi accidentalis verbi designans circa rem modum essendi variae inclinationis animi, varios eius affectus demonstrans et dicitur in indicativum, imperativum, optativum, coniunctivum, infinitivum".

[336] Thomas of Erfurt, #131: "sed non quod modus sit ipsa inclinatio sed qualitas inclinationis, non ea, qua anima inclinatur ad enuntiandum actus de substantia".

actuum which also represents a favourite sentence of Latin, *i.e.* VN or
verb and post-posed nominal oblique, in which significatio will express
the relationship between the dependent V and the post-posed N. It will
also be seen that the relationship between the suppositum and the verb
is basically one of modus entis and modus esse; the modus esse assures
that the verb will remain discrete from the suppositum and thereby
function as the constructible separate from the nominal constructible
in the construction – which will also occur in any construction consisting
of verb and oblique nominal. Compositio serves therefore to assert the
fundamental relationship between the verb and suppositum but also
refines it so that mood, which is the quality of the compositio, can
associate with the substantival (modus per se stantis) element in the
pre-posed suppositum.[337] The basic relationship between the verb and
the suppositum in any SP construction consists of the thing and what
is said about it, and the attitude of mind which is involved in expressing
this.[338] Compositio functions by creating the link between the N and
the V so that we can know the thing and what is said about it, while
mood is used to express the attitude of mind which 'governs' the creation and purpose of the relationship. Mood is therefore the expression
of certain attitudes of mind and is diversified, in terms of the different
qualities of the relationships thus made between the verb and suppositum, into indicative, imperative, optative, conjunctive and infinitive.

The indicative is that mood of the verb which designates the property
of indication,[339] and possesses the full complement of person and tense;
the imperative mood expresses the property of command[340] but lacks
the first person of the singular and the preterite tense; the optative is
the mood designating the property of choice[341] and possesses the full

---

[337]   Thomas of Erfurt, #133: "sicut verbum per modum esse exigit in supposito
modum entis per se stantis; sic per modum, qui est qualitas compositionis, exigit
in supposito modum per se stantis, in ratione principii se habentis".
[338]   This can be linked to the moderate realism of the Modistae, which argues that
words are not vocal noises but correlates of reality, though subjected to the
moderating influence of the mind which perceives, understands, and seeks to
express this reality. This metaphysical theory acts as a substrate to their grammatical theories and from time to time appears to exert a more direct influence
on a particular aspect of their theory; the relationships of NV expressed by compositio and mood are one example of such 'interference'.
[339]   Siger de Courtrai, p. 112: "indicativus est modus verbi designans circa rem
verbi modum essendi indicantis".
[340]   Siger de Courtrai, p. 113: "imperativus est modus designans circa rem verbo
modum essendi imperantis".
[341]   Siger de Courtrai, p. 113: "optativus est modus designans circa rem modum
essendi optantis".

complement of person and tense; the conjunctive or subjunctive is the mood expressing doubt, confirmation or possibility [342] and has the same tenses and persons as the indicative. (It should be noted that all these definitions given by Siger are done for and by means of Latin.) It would be needless to dwell at any further length on these moods, since they are, at least in Siger's descriptions, merely expansions of any descriptions of the moods of a Latin verb, and add really nothing more to the earlier definition of mood as the designation and signification of certain states of mind.[343]

The infinitive was included in mood, at least by Thomas, by virtue of the fact that all moods can be resolved into the infinitive,[344] which is therefore a common factor in all moods of the verb, so that 'lego' can be resolved into "indico me legere" and 'lege' into "impero te legere". The infinitive for Siger becomes the mood which designates the property of non-specification without reference to the properties of the other moods, rather like neuter gender in the nomen which expresses its property without reference to the masculine or the feminine.[345] The infinitive lacks voice, number and person, but despite such imperfec-

[342] Siger de Courtrai, p. 114: "coniunctivus, subiunctivus, seu dubitativus ... aliquando significat dubitationem aliquando confirmationem seu comprobationem, aliquando possibilitatem".

[343] The Modistae, by basing their criteria for mood on purely semantic terms, were able to insist on the distinction between the subjunctive and the optative; it is not possible to make such a distinction in any formal system of Latin grammar. Priscian, whose own quasi formal categories are based on those of Thrax, had presumably noted the distinction in Greek though he was not able to make for Latin a similar distinction. Cf. Priscian (XVIII, 125-126): "Latini quoque omnibus temporibus subiunctivi modi etiam in optativo utuntur, ostendit tam usus quam antiquiores Donato artium scriptores". Virgilius in VI: "Hac Troiana tenus fuerit Fortuna secuta", ecce hic (fuerit) optative posuit in precatione Aeneae hoc verbum, quod tam praeteriti perfecti quam futuri potest esse: quod Donatus et quidam alii subiunctivi tantummodo putant esse, cum aliae omnes voces optativi communes sint etiam subiunctivo. Ergo non immerito in supra dicta Attica constructione, qua illi optativis utuntur, hoc quoque tempore indifferenter nostri sunt usi".

The Modistae, who deliberately set out to establish a new grammatical theory by semanticising Priscian's more formal divisions, were thus able to produce criteria for distinctions between the optative and subjunctive. This is however a hollow achievement, since a distinction such as this, which is not supported by formal criteria, will not be a productive feature in a system of grammatical description and detracts from the general economy of their procedure.

[344] Thomas of Erfurt, #132: "dicitur infinitivus, quia omnibus communis est, cum omnes modi in ipsum resolvantur".

[345] Siger de Courtrai, p. 114: "infinitivus est modus designans circa rem verbi modum essendi infiniti seu indefiniti et indifferenter se habentes ad modum essendi aliorum modorum, sicut neutrum in nomine designat circa rem modum essendi indifferenter se habentem ad modum essendi masculini et feminini".

tions it can combine with verbs of other moods, expressing a particular state of mind, to produce complete constructions, rather like imperfect matter which will combine with other matter to produce a complete entity.[346]

It has already been stated that Siger includes the gerund as a mood of the verb – (Thomas excludes the gerund entirely from his grammar) – because it has the value of an infinitive; it does not seem that Siger was able to extract, from his consideration of the gerund, anything which contributes to the discussion of mood.

Mood is therefore the expression of a state of mind involved in the operation of compositio, and herein lies the importance of mood as an accidental mode of the verb; compositio is the means by which the verb is able to offset the feature of discreteness (distantia) which is a feature of its essence and linked up to the suppositum, and mood expresses the state of mind necessarily entailed in such a relationship. We have seen that compositio requires mood as a concomitant since compositio cannot suggest the state of mind involved; the NV relationship is an expression of assertion, and mood therefore signifies the state of mind involved in such an expression. Indeed it can be stated more positively, that the verb, by virtue of its essential mode, can stand discrete from the nominal suppositum, and by virtue of its accidental mode of compositio these two entities can be linked together to form a construction; and the mood which is the material expression of this compositio, enhances the nature of the relationship between the suppositum and the verb, not by altering the relationship but by stating its quality in terms of the different attitudes of mind it can express.

Significatio

This is a category which is found in Thomas and Martin; Donatus, Priscian, and Siger[347] use the term but include it in their analysis of the voice (genus) of the verb, whereas Thomas[348] keeps it separate and

---

[346] Siger de Courtrai, p. 115: "materia imperfecta exigens debitam unionem quae dat ei esse perfectum, sic infinitivus affectum animi imperfectum importans congruam constructionem habet cum verbis aliorum modorum certum affectum animi importantium".

[347] Siger de Courtrai, p. 109: "genus seu significatio".

[348] Martin is quite critical of Peter Helias's definition of 'significatio' and substitutes a definition which is much closer to Thomas's. Martin does not perhaps deliberately use 'significatio' to balance 'compositio', but he associates it as a feature of the verb in terms of its relationships with the post-posed oblique nominal – unlike Thomas, however, Martin restricts it to the accusative, viz.

makes of it a very significant section by using it to balance compositio, which, as we have seen, he had used to discuss the relationship between the verb and its suppositum; it stands in a very close relationship to the mood of the verb. Significatio balances the pattern by referring to the verb and its relationship with the post-posed oblique nominal and is thus very closely associated to the voice (genus) of the verb. It is the expansibility of the verb and in instances such as the verbum neutrum, the significatio will be zero since there cannot be a post-posed oblique, *i.e.* the dependent verb will have as its terminal a zero oblique. It is an accidental mode for the same reasons that compositio is an accidental mode, *i.e.* it does not refer to the modus esse of the verb, nor is it a special mode, since it cannot in itself constitute a different species of verb.[349] The relationships can be represented diagrammatically thus:

$$\text{compositio} \qquad \text{significatio}$$
$$\text{suppositum} \longleftarrow \text{verbum} \longrightarrow \text{obliquum}$$

This accidental mode must be seen in conjunction with the other accidental mode of compositio; they both govern the relationship between the verb and the post-posed oblique nominal or the pre-posed nominal suppositum. Significatio is derived from that property of the verb which is its property of being dependent on some post-posed oblique,[350] and we shall see that this is in effect equivalent to Thomas's definition of the transitive construction; Thomas points out that Peter Helias too had, by using the term 'significatio accidentalis', intended modus transeuntis.[351]

Significatio (and compositio) represent an interesting innovation on the part of Thomas; the other accidental modes are expressions, regardless of the fact that they are described in purely semantic terms, of morphologic features which will be either inflectional or derivational. Significatio and compositio have recourse to syntactic criteria, which are governmental concord (proportio) between the substantival element represented by the modus per se stantis in the oblique form (and the

---

Martin of Dacia #125: "significatio accidentalis est modus transeundi in aliud et hoc solum in accusativum".

[349] Thomas of Erfurt, #128: "non est modus essentialis generalissimus cum verbo non det esse simpliciter, sed sit praeter eius intellectum essentialem. Nec etiam est essentialis specialis cum non constituat aliquam speciem verbi".

[350] Thomas of Erfurt, #136: "significatio sumitur a proprietate rei verbi, quae est proprietas dependentiae ad quemlibet obliquum post se, habentum se in ratione per se standi".

[351] Thomas of Erfurt, #136: "per significationem accidentalem vult intelligere modum transeuntis, id est, modum dependentis ad quem libet obliquum post se".

mode of dependence in the verb or the substantival element in the suppositum); we have already seen that compositio is achieved by means of a similar concord between the substantival element and the mode of dependence.

Genus

Consideration of this accidental mode affords an excellent study in contrast between the methods of Siger and Thomas. Siger gives no definition whatsoever of genus, which is clearly for him a synonym of significatio, and divides it into the five categories of active, passive, neuter, deponent and common, which he proceeds to describe at some length with particular reference to the Latin verb. On the other hand, Thomas discusses at length the feature of voice, but dismisses very summarily the five sub-divisions just mentioned. This means that our exposition of the Modistic analysis of voice (genus) will depend largely on Thomas for the theory of the feature and largely on Siger for illustration and discussion of the different sub-modes.

Voice (genus) is derived from that property of the verb, the property of dependence on the post-posed oblique nominal form which will be the final element in the construction but which, as far as the voice of the verb is concerned, needs only to be potential;[352] in other words, a transitive verb may have an object but does not necessarily have to have one. Voice is, therefore, that accidental mode of the verb by means of which it signifies its dependence on the post-posed oblique nominal form.[353] This is quite in keeping with Peter Helias's definition of voice as 'significatio accidentalis' with the ending of /-o/ or /-r/, which is, therefore, the modus transeuntis with the ending /-o/ or /-r/ and which serves to differentiate the different species of voice. Peter's definition of genus is in effect a combination of significatio and genus, i.e. a combination of the relational and its different expressions, and Siger is more or less in accord with this. Thomas differs sharply from Peter in that significatio for Thomas is the relation between the verb and the post-posed substantival element contained in the obliquum by means of the modus per se stantis; genus thus becomes the quality of this

---

[352] Thomas of Erfurt, #137: "genus in verbo sumitur a proprietate rei verbi, quae est proprietas dependentiae rei verbi, post se ad obliquum, sub ratione termini non contracti sed contrahibile".

[353] Thomas of Erfurt, #137: "genus in verbo est modus significandi accidentalis verbi, mediante quo proprietatem dependentiae rei verbi post se ad obliquum, sub ratione termini, significat".

relationship,[354] just as mood became the quality of the compositio. This is an important step forward on Thomas's part, and the distinction between significatio and genus must be clearly understood. In Thomas's terminology, this definition is a material not a formal one [355] – and this applies also to mood with regard to compositio. If it were formal, this would imply a different relationship with the post-posed oblique according to the different voice, but since it is material, this means that the relationship will be the same in every instance but its quality will vary; it will thus be the function of voice, *i.e.* to express this different quality, so that we can have active voice and oblique, or passive voice and oblique in which the relationship is always one of the verb dependent on the oblique (even if the dependence is only potential). This also suggests that if the different voices do not result from different relationships, then they will derive from internal factors – Thomas interprets it by means of what may appear to be false etymology, though there is certainly another explanation possible,[356] that the expression of one voice is 'bred' from the expression of another voice, as the passive is generated from the active.[357] As far as 'genus' is concerned, genus as an accidental mode of the verb functions in association with significatio in the same way that mood did with compositio; it would seem, therefore, that genus is the expression of a state of mind created by the relationship involved between the verb and the postposed nominal oblique, while significatio is responsible for the actual relationship.

An understanding of this association between genus and significatio is most essential for an understanding of the difference between the different voices of the verb and the different modi specialissimi of the

[354] Thomas of Erfurt, #137: "sicut se habet modus verbi ad compositionem, sic se habet genus ad significationem ... genus non est formaliter significatio, sed qualitas significationis ipsam contrahens et disponens".
[355] Thomas of Erfurt, #137: "haec definitio generis non est formalis, sed materialis. Genus non est formaliter significatio, qui unus modus non est alius, sed genus est quasi qualitas significationis determinans sive specificans significationem".
[356] The Modistae did not often resort to etymology to explain a feature; it is as well that they used this method as infrequently as they did, since etymology was clearly one of their weakest points. Mention has already been made of Thomas's curious use of etymology to explain the origin of 'persona' as an accidental mode of the nomen. It may be that Thomas has shown considerable sophistication in making what can just as well be interpreted as a formal statement which would be quite acceptable to the modern linguist.
[357] Thomas of Erfurt, #137: "vocatur iste modus significandi genus, a generando dictum, quia vox unius generis generatur a voce alterius generis, ut vox passiva generata a voce activa".

verb. The modi specialissimi represent different types of verb and in this context 'amo' is considered different from 'amor' because 'amo' signifies an action and 'amor' being acted on; similarly, a verbum adiectivum commune is defined as signifying either an action or being acted on. Such a definition is made purely and simply in intrinsic terms, *i.e.* in terms of the essence of the verb. Voice, on the other hand, is established as a result of the quality of the relationship between the verb and the post-posed oblique; in the two constructions 'doceo litteras' and 'doceor litteras', the relationship between the verb and the noun oblique is the same but the quality of the relationship is different in either case, and it is this which decides the voice which is expressed by means of the ending /-o/ or /-r/. Thus we see that in terms of the modus specialissimus 'doceo' and 'doceor' are different types of verbs since 'doceo' expresses an action and 'doceor' expresses being acted on, but in terms of voice, they are different because they express a different quality of relationship; the difference between action and passion becomes in this instance a secondary matter, a matter of consignification.[358]

We can say then that the difference in voice (genus) is to a large extent a matter of the expression, which is supported by reference to Donatus who said that the active voice of a verb is that which ends in /-o/ and can acquire /-r/ added to the /-o-/ and thus become the passive voice.[359] Quite clearly, such a formal definition could not possibly be sufficient for the Modistae, since for them the ending of /-o/ or /-r/ alone cannot establish whether a verb will be of active or passive voice.[360] Significatio sets up the relationship of VN so that we know the result of the action or passion of the verb, and genus therefore signifies the dependence of the verb on the post-posed oblique form of a transitive construction.[361] But genus tells us more of this relationship

---

[358]   Thomas tells us that, *e.g.* 'timeo', although it possesses in its form the active voice, in reality signifies not an action but being acted on; it would be interesting to know whether Thomas would have classified this, when dealing with the modi specialissimi of the verb, as a verbum adiectivum passivum, which, it will be remembered, he defined as signifying a passion only; *viz.* Thomas of Erfurt, #139: "ista verba, timeo, liceo, metuo, quae sub voce activa modum passionis significant".

[359]   Donatus (Ars Minor): "activa quae sunt? Quae in 'o' desinunt et accepta 'r' littera faciunt ex se passiva, ut lego, legor".

[360]   Thomas of Erfurt, #138: "verbum per vocis terminationem non magis determinat sibi actionem quam passionem, ideo dubium est quare verbum sub terminatione vocis in 'o' magis debet esse activi generis, quam passivi, et sic de caeteris".

[361]   Thomas of Erfurt, #138: "genus verbi sit ratio significandi dependentiam rei verbi post se ad obliquum sub ratione termini".

and does this by means of different formal criteria, *e.g.* the morphological criterion of the conjugation, *i.e.* /-o/ or /-or/, the syntactic criterion of the post-posed case, *i.e.* "lego librum" in contrast to "legitur a Socrate", or the syntactic criterion of the zero post-posed oblique which indicates a neuter voice (genus neutrum) *etc.* This will be done in Modistic terms by means of a combination of the expression (vox) and the semantic element of action, passion, *etc.*, to signify, however, a similar fundamental relationship of verb and a potential post-posed oblique. It is interesting to note that Thomas does nevertheless give expression pride of place over content in establishing the voice of the verb.[362]

Siger describes the active voice as the accidental mode of signifying of the verb which can end in /-o/ and can acquire /-r/ and thus make it the passive,[363] which is entirely in keeping with Donatus's definition; similarly Siger defines the passive voice as ending in /-r/, and if this is lost then it becomes the active voice.[364] He defines the other voices, *i.e.* neuter, deponent and common in somewhat similar quasi formal terms. Thomas describes the various sub-modes of genus in similar quasi formal terms but adds, as part of the definition, that, *e.g.* the active voice usually (frequentius) signifies an action, though there are verbs which have an active voice and yet have a passive signification, and similarly for the other sub-modes. Siger stays closer to the more formal definition than does Thomas, and despite the fact that Siger also states that the active voice is used to designate the property of acting, and that it may also signify by means of the modus transeuntis (which, it is true, is common to the active, passive, and indeed in some cases to the deponent and neuter voices),[365] he seems to be able to account more easily for the apparent exceptions than Thomas apparently can with his very bald statement that the active voice usually signifies an action

---

[362] Thomas of Erfurt, #138: "oportet praeter hoc ad vocis terminationem attendere, si velimus genera verborum servare".

[363] Siger de Courtrai, p. 109: "activum est modus significandi accidentalis verbi signatus per vocem quae desinit in 'o' et potest recipere 'r' et facere ex se passivum, designans circa rem modum essendi agentis".

[364] Siger de Courtrai, pp. 109-110: "passivum genus est genus verbi signatum per vocem quae desinit in 'r', et, ea dempta, redit in activum, designans circa rem modum essendi patientis".

[365] Siger de Courtrai, p. 109: "et quia significant per modum transeuntis qui est communis activis, passivis, etc., et quibusdam deponentibus et neutris, ideo dicuntur transitiva". This suggests that Siger is using 'transitive' here in the traditional sense rather than in the Modistic sense as Thomas uses it.

but can also signify being acted on;[366] Siger, for example, explains[367] the fact that 'timeo' has an active voice but implies a being acted on by stating that 'timeo' really means 'timorem patior'.[368] The passive voice is indicated by the ending in /-r/ and can, by the loss of /-r/, become an active voice;[369] the neuter voice ends in /-o/ as in the active voice but may not acquire the /-r/ of the passive;[370] the deponent and the common voices[371] end in /-r/ but may not lose the /-r/ and thus become an active voice.[372] Siger's theory of 'principium constructionis' (which he uses to indicate a constructible member) reveals interesting extensions of the possible relationships between the verb and the postposed oblique forms in Latin. We find that the active voice can create a relationship by means of the accusative case in the oblique, *e.g.* oro te, but also with the genitive, or dative, or ablative, *e.g.* intelligo a te; the passive voice uses the ablative, *e.g.* doceor a te, the dative or the accusative, and similarly for the other voices. However, these relationships are expressed in terms of the syntax of Latin and they too add little to the theory of relationship and voice.

The relationship of suppositum and verb is one of modus entis and modus esse, and compositio becomes the means of stating more accurately the relationship between them as the substantival, *i.e.* modus per se stantis, in the suppositum and the verb; by stating the quality of the

[366]   Thomas of Erfurt, #139: "illud verbum est activum, seu activi generis, quod sub terminatione vocis in o, potest mutari in r, et frequentius actionem significat, ut amo. Et dicitur frequentius, propter ista verba, timeo, liceo metuo, quae sub voce activa modum passionis significant".

[367]   A mistake, common to the Modistae and the modern normative grammarian, is their failure to recognise that any definition or 'rule' which produces so many exceptions, no matter how plausible the explanations may be, is quite clearly based on faulty criteria.

[368]   Siger de Courtrai, p. 109: "voce actionem significant: nihil enim aliud est 'timeo' quam 'timorem patior' et 'timeor' quam 'timorem facio' ".

[369]   Thomas of Erfurt, #140: "verbum passivi generis est, quod sub terminatione vocis in r, potest mutari in o, et frequentius passionem significat, ut amor. Et dico frequentius, propter liceor, quae sub voce passiva actionem significant".

[370]   Thomas of Erfurt, #141: "verbum neutri generis est, quod sub terminatione vocis in o, non potest mutari in r, et sub indifferentia, vel indeterminatione actionem vel passionem significat, ut curro".

[371]   Little would be achieved by describing in detail Siger's analysis of the different voices, which is in effect a description of the Latin verb and would add little to any discussion of the theory of voice as a feature of the verb.

[372]   Thomas of Erfurt, #142-143: "verbum deponentis generis est, quod sub terminatione vocis in r non potest mutari in o, et consignificat actionem, deposita passione, ut loquor . . . Verbum communis generis est, quod sub terminatione vocis in r non potest mutari in o, et consignificat actionem et passionem simul, ut criminor".

compositio, we state the moods of the construction, whereupon the dependent modes of tense, person, number and conjugation can be established. Similarly, the relationship of verb and oblique is one of modus esse and modus entis, and by means of the significatio we can state the relationship more accurately as verb and the substantival element;[373] thus, by means of the quality of the significatio, *i.e.* by means of the voice, the whole valence of the relationship between the verb and the post-posed oblique form will be influenced.

Species/forma

Thomas tells us in fact that forma in the verb is the same as species in the nomen and is derived from the same properties as in the nomen, *i.e.* from the primary or secondary modus essendi;[374] both Siger and Thomas describe this feature as divided, as it was in the nomen, into primitive and derivative. Their analysis of species shows considerable light on their method of description in terms of meaning; species is a morphological, *i.e.* derivational[375] category and might well be expected to consist of a primary root-word, *i.e.* the primitiva, from which some other form is derived by a morphological or analogous formal procedure. The species primitiva does, it is true, represent the minimal form for the Modistae, but not in the modern formal sense; Siger tells us that Donatus used the term 'forma perfecta' (which may well have inspired Thomas to use this term) to describe the primitive type[376] which can be taken to represent the minimal member of the verb-class. The other species of verb are derived[377] from this primary form, which

---

[373] Thomas of Erfurt, #144: "sicut verbum per modum esse requirit modum entis in supposito, sic per eumdem modum esse exigit modum entis in obliquo. Et sicut verbum per compositionem exigit per se stantis in supposito, sic per significationem accidentalem exigit modum per se stantis in obliquo ... sicut verbum per modum distantis exigit modum per stantis pro supposito, ito per eumdem modum esse exigit modum entis in obliquo. Et sicut verbum per modum compositionis exigit modum entis per se stantis in ratione principii in supposito, sic per modum generis exigit modum entis per se stantis in ratione termini in obliquo".

[374] Thomas of Erfurt, #134: "forma, quae est accidens verbi, idem est, quod species in nomine, et ab eadem proprietate sumpta, scilicet a modo essendi primarie vel secundarie. Forma est modus significandi accidentalis verbi, mediante quo verbum modum existendi primarium vel secundarium significat".

[375] Derivation is used in the sense of synchronic derivation.

[376] Siger de Courtrai, p. 117: "est primitiva quae primam positionem ab ipsa natura accepit, ut: lego, quam Donatus appellat formam verborum perfectam".

[377] There is a slight divergence in terminology between Siger and Thomas; in the nomen Siger talks about species primitiva and *determinativa* while Thomas talks about the primitiva and *derivativa*: in the verb both Siger and Thomas talk

signifies the thing absolutely,[378] *not* however by virtue of any morphologic change but by virtue of the fact that they add something, *i.e.* some additional meaning or meaningful feature, to the primary form of the verb which in the first place was devised to indicate some feature of reality. There are, for both Siger and Thomas, many different types of derived species, six for Siger and five for Thomas;[379] Siger goes on to list in some detail the various categories of derived verb to be found in Latin.[380]

One example will suffice to show that the derived form is made by the addition of some further refinement of the primary meaning by means of the addition of an 'ending' which changes the meaning; Thomas has nothing more to add and makes no attempt to introduce formal criteria.[381] Siger does, however, introduce formal criteria to support his semantic criteria and describes each derived 'species' in terms of the additional or derived meaning; he supports this by the use of morphological changes to demonstrate the change in structure, *e.g.* the inchoative verb signifies the beginning of an action or passion – it ends in /-sco/ and all are to be found in the third conjugation, *e.g.* 'calleo' – 'callesco'. Siger does not, however, describe the morphological process as the addition of an infix, *i.e.* /calle - o/ to become /calle - /sc / - o/. What Siger is in fact saying is that the process is one of stating the formal structure in semantic terms, *i.e.* the basic meaning which is the species primitiva (which may have no reference to the morphemic root) to which is added the feature of inchoateness, repetitiveness, *etc*. It matters less that his formal criteria should be incorrect, *e.g.* he describes the formation of 'callesco' as constructed from the second person singular of the indicative of the primitive 'species' with the addition of /-co/, *i.e.* 'calleo' - 'les' -'callesco', than that he should have used formal criteria at all, especially when describing a derivational (*i.e.* absolu-

---

about the primitiva and derivativa. It was seen, when discussing species in the nomen, that 'derivativa' is distinct from 'determinativa', but in the verb, both use 'derivativa' identically.

[378]   Thomas of Erfurt, #134: "per formam perfectam debet intelligi species primitiva, quia guae sunt perfectae formae sunt primitivae speciei, quia significant rem verbi absolute".

[379]   Siger de Courtrai: "inchoativa, meditativa, frequentativa, desiderativa, diminutiva, imitativa. Thomas of Erfurt: meditativa, frequentativa, inchoativa, diminutiva, desiderativa".

[380]   This seems to be typical of Siger, who goes to some length, in most of the accidental modes, to illustrate in detail his descriptive statement of Latin grammar.

[381]   Thomas of Erfurt, #134: "sed quae sunt inchoativae formae, et sic de caeteris, sunt derivativae speciei, quae non significant rem verbi absolute, sed cum quadam additione, scilicet, sub inchoatione, frequentatione, etc.".

te) mode. Furthermore, he is prepared to face the fact that there will be verbs with the same formal characteristics as inchoative verbs but which are not themselves inchoative verbs, *e.g.* 'quiesco', 'pasco';[382] unfortunately he does not dwell on this, and characteristically implies, by his silence, that semantic distinctions are in such instances the vital, conclusive factor.

In the verb, Donatus had included mood (modus) and form (forma) as subdivisions of qualitas and as accidents of the verb; Thomas follows Donatus closely in this and considers them accidental modes, presumably because mood and form do not indicate different types of verbs and therefore could not be re-classified as subaltern modes of the essential mode of the verb. It is interesting to see the influence that Donatus and Priscian held over the Modistae, despite their temporary eclipse in the 13th century schools by 'inferior' grammarians such as Alexander of Villedieu. This alone can surely explain Thomas's curious retention of mood and form together, especially as they are clearly different in his scheme in that mood must be a respective mode and form an absolute mode; although they are both morphologic categories, mood is quite clearly inflectional and form derivational, despite the fact that Thomas did not describe either of them in such terms. In the nomen, the link between species and figura was quite clear, and they were classed together as the absolute derivational modes; in the verb, the link between them is similarly obvious, though it was ignored by Siger (as is also true of the nomen) and implicitly denied by Thomas. It might have been more appropriate to group mood and voice together[383] in view of their definitions as subdivisions or submodes of qualitas. We have seen the close relationship between compositio and mood, and significatio and voice, and we should bear in mind that Thomas stated that mood is the quality of the compositio[384] and voice is the quality of significatio.[385] Thomas, however, grouped forma and modus together as subdivisions of qualitas.[386]

---

[382] Siger de Courtrai, p. 115: "inveniuntur tamen quaedam primitiva inchoativorum, formam habentia, non tamen sunt inchoativa, ut: quiesco, posco, pasco, etc.".
[383] Thomas of Erfurt, #137: "sicut se habet modus verbi ad compositionem, sic se habet genus ad significationem".
[384] Thomas of Erfurt, #131: "modus ... est qualitas compositionis".
[385] Thomas of Erfurt, #137: "genus ... est ... qualitas significationis".
[386] It will be remembered that in discussing the nomen, a certain amount of reorganisation of material became necessary in order to make a united statement on the nature of the nomen and that this was done because Siger included in his description of qualitas certain material which Thomas had described in his subaltern modes of his essential mode of the nomen. Thomas, in the verbum, includes

This affords an excellent example of Thomas's procedure. In every case of his using qualitas, *i.e.* in the nomen, pronomen and verbum, he has followed Donatus (almost 'au pied de la lettre'), but has of course restated Donatus, retaining at the same time the principal facts which Donatus had stated; thus we find that 'appellativa' and 'propria' which for Donatus are accidents of the nomen, become for Thomas different types of nomen, *i.e.* different aspects of the essence of the nomen and are therefore included as subaltern modes of the essential mode, which is entirely in keeping with his definition of the subaltern mode.[387] Similarly in the pronomen, demonstratio and relatio, which were for Donatus accidents, become for Thomas different aspects of the pronomen, which he includes therefore in the subaltern mode of the essential mode. Like figura, and like species in the nomen, species/forma in the verb is an absolute mode; it is thus not syntactic and represents a morpho-semantic statement of the quasi formal classification of the primary and derived types of verb as Priscian and Donatus had previously described them.

Figura

Neither Siger nor Thomas add anything to their previous description of figura as an accidental mode of the nomen in their discussion of figura as an accidental mode of the verbum.[388] It follows then that figura will be an accidental mode of signifying of the verb and can be divided into simple and compound, and in the case of Thomas, into the third subdivision of decomposita. As in the nomen, it will be an absolute mode, and together with species it forms the two derivational sub-classes of the verb; as in the nomen, we might consider figura as the 'morphemic base structure'.[389]

---

qualitas as an accidental mode which he subdivides into mood (modus) and forma; he does this in conformity with Donatus who had also subdivided qualitas in the nomen into 'appellativa' and 'propria' as indeed Siger has subdivided his accidental mode of qualitas, but which Thomas, however, made into an essential mode. Furthermore we have seen in the pronomen that Thomas included qualitas once more as an essential mode, this time subdivided into demonstratio and relatio.

[387]　Thomas of Erfurt, #21: "modus significandi essentialis subaltermus est, qui est de essentia suppositorum illius partis, nec generalissime, nec specialissime, sed medio modo se habens".

[388]　Siger de Courtrai, p. 119: "figura et numerus sunt modi significandi accidentales communes nomini et verbo et aliis partibus orationis, ideo dicta de eis in nomine ad praesens sufficiant".

[389]　R. H. Robins, *Thrax*, p. 99.

Tempus

The inclusion by the Modistae of tempus as an accidental mode of the verb represents almost the final step away from the logical definition of the verb and its relation to the time factor, which had characterised the definition of the verb since Aristotle, who had said[390] that a verb carries with it the notion of time. For the Modistae, time is no longer an essential feature of the verb (though it is argued by Thomas that time is a factor in the becoming (fieri) or succession (successio), which are characteristics of the essence of the verb,[391] and has been 'relegated' to be an accidental mode of the verb, *i.e.* a feature which is not derived from the essence of the pars orationis in question.[392]

Peter Helias sought to reconcile the logical and grammatical definitions of the verb and in so doing came to consider tempus as an accidental mode of the verb, though the time element remained as a feature of his definition of the verb. The significant fact of Peter's treatment of tense is that he excluded from his definition of tense all idea of duration which, according to Thurot, had been the theory in the earlier Middle Ages; time became for him a reference not duration, and time became therefore subordinate to the act itself, *i.e.* the location of the act in time.[393]

This new attitude to time characterises the Modistic use of tense as an accidental feature of the verb. Michel de Marbais described two kinds of time – the first represents an uninterrupted quantity and as such is the measure of movement and rest,[394] but this is a matter for the natural philosopher and not for the grammarian; the feature of time, which is a matter for the grammarian, is the accidental mode of the verb which designates the action as it occurs at some point in time, present, past or future.[395]

[390] Aristotle, *De Interpretatione*, Chap. III.
[391] Thomas of Erfurt, #147: "modus temporis secundum esse rationis consequitur modum esse, qui est modus fluxus et successionis".
[392] Thomas of Erfurt, #20: "modus significandi accidentalis est, qui advenit parti post eius esse completum, non dans esse simpliciter parti, nec secundum genus, nec secundum speciem".
[393] Peter Helias: "nec illud dico quod verbum consignificet tempus quantitative, quod antiqui dicebant, sed potius quod consignificat tempus ut ad predicamentum 'quando' pertinet. Qui dicit 'cucurri' actum quidem currendi . . . principaliter designat, sed quando significat secundario" (Thurot, p. 182).
[394] Michel de Marbais: "tempus . . . est continua quantitas, et tale tempus est mensura motus et quietis" (Thurot, p. 184).
[395] Michel de Marbais: "tempus . . . est quidam modus significandi datus alicui voci ad designandum diversas partes temporis reales, utpote presentationem, preteritionem vel futuritionem" (Thurot, p. 184).

Tense is derived, as we have seen, from the flux and succession of the essence of the verb by means of which the verb consignifies time,[396] which is divided into present, past and future.[397] Unlike the other accidental modes, except species and figura, tempus is not a respective accidental mode with reference to the verb itself, since tense depends neither on the pre-posed suppositum nor on the post-posed obliquum,[398] but is respective with reference to temporal adverbs, since it is obviously incongruous to utter such sentences as "Plato disputat heri". It becomes a respective mode by virtue of the sequence of tenses in composite sentences, i.e. tempus is a respective mode not by virtue of any intrinsic feature of the verb, but as a result of inter-clausal relation and the concomitant colligation of the tenses. Tense thus represents, in addition to compositio and significatio, a further relational attribute of the verb, and clearly the Modistae, especially Thomas, were at pains to discuss this as fully as they did the conventional semantic (and morphological) categories of the verb.

Thomas and Siger are largely in agreement on their description of tense,[399] though Siger does provide more detail, and in so doing discusses one aspect of the present tense which Peter Helias had quite clearly abandoned as fruitless, i.e. whether the present tense refers to that point of time when the verb is uttered – Peter had been content with the idea that the present tense refers to something which takes place at some point in the present time rather than be the consignification of present time.[400] Siger may, of course, have been led astray by his false etymology of 'instans' as being 'non stans', a term which he used as the equivalent of 'praesens'. However, he comes to the conclusion that we cannot categorically state what the present is, and therefore every form of the present is expressed in the same way,[401]

---

[396] This is an excellent example of consignification used in the sense of connotation, i.e. the second use of 'consignificatio'.

[397] Michel de Marbais: "tempus presupponit modum significandi fluxus vel fieri" (Thurot, p. 183). Thomas of Erfurt, #147: "tempus est modus significandi accidentalis verbi, quo mediante verbum, citra rem, modum temporis consignificat".

[398] Thomas of Erfurt, #149: "tempus non est accidens respectivum verbi, cum secundum ipsum non dependent ante se ad suppositum nec post se ad obliquum".

[399] Siger de Courtrai, p. 112: "tempus est modus significandi accidentalis verbi designans circa rem modum essendi praesentialitatis vel praeteritionis vel futuritionis et dicitur in praesens, praeteritum et futurum".

[400] Peter Helias: "verbum non consignificat presens tempus, sed significat aliquid in presenti tempore" (Thurot, p. 183).

[401] Siger de Courtrai, p. 112: "plerumque nobis incertum est et cognitio eius nobis angustissima et dubia, propter quod intellectus noster non potens certe distinguere inter praesentia, una voce contentus est".

which seems a somewhat clumsy way of saying that Latin has no inflectional aspect of the present tense, *i.e.* the present tense is the least marked of all the tenses of Latin. Siger divides the preterite into imperfect, perfect and pluperfect, and of the future he states, again in semantic terms, that it has no inflectional aspect.[402]

Numerus

As in figura, the Modistae had very little to add to their description of this category beyond what they had said in their description of number as an accidental mode of the nomen. Siger had nothing to add except to say that it was, like figura, a category common to the nomen, verbum and other partes orationis (presumably declinable partes) and that whatever he had said of numerus in the nomen would apply to numerus as a category of the verbum.[403]

Thomas has little more to add, but what he does have to say is significant for its implications for his syntactic theories. He states that number, like person, is derived from the same properties as in the nomen, *i.e.* the properties of divisibility and indivisibility,[404] but in the case of the verb these are not properties which are innate in the verb but which it acquires by association with the suppositum.[405] This anticipates an important aspect of his syntactic theory, *i.e.* his theory of concord; he argues that the relationships between the members of a construction can be either those of government and rection, *i.e.* proportio, or of concord, *i.e.* similitudo;[406] when the dependent constructible possesses certain modes of signifying which it acquires however from the properties of the terminant constructible,[407] these

[402] Siger de Courtrai, p. 112: "futurum tempus . . . quia plerumque incertum, est intellectus noster in una voce in ipso contentus".
[403] Siger de Courtrai, p. 119: "figura et numerus sunt modi significandi accidentales communes nomini et verbo et aliis partibus orationis, ideo dicta de eis in nomine ad praesens sufficiant".
[404] Thomas of Erfurt, #77: "in utroque numero duae proprietates inveniuntur, scilicet: proprietates indivisibilitatis . . . et proprietas divisibilitatis".
[405] Thomas of Erfurt, #145: "numerus et persona insunt verbo, non ex proprietate suae rei per se loquendo, sed ex proprietate rei suppositi".
[406] Thomas of Erfurt, #220: "quandoque constructibile dependens habet aliquos modos significandi, non ex proprietatibus suae rei per se, sed ex proprietatibus rei constructibilis terminantis; et tunc inter illos modos significandi exigitur similitudo et non proportio".
[407] Thomas of Erfurt, #220: "constructibile terminans debet habere modos significandi constructibilis dependentis, ut patet de constructione adiectivi cum substantivo, et in constructione suppositi nominativi casus cum verbo personali".

properties will refer to relationships of concord, not of rection,[408] and the verb thus will acquire number and person from the properties found in the suppositum.[409]

Persona

Thomas and Martin of Dacia had set up person as an accidental mode of the nomen, and we have seen that person in the pronomen is defined as the same as in the nomen. This has important implications for Thomas's theory of person in the verb, since he has stated already, *i.e.* when dealing with number, that person and number belong as features of the verb not by virtue of properties inherent in the verb but by virtue of certain properties of the suppositum.[410] This means that person in the verb, at least for Thomas, is the accidental mode of signifying by means of which the verb consignifies the property of speaking; this property is however not itself inherent in the verb, but represents a potential connection with the suppositum which already possesses those properties of speaking. It is more marked formally in the verb but represents nonetheless the link with the person of the nominal suppositum which still remains the head of the NV construction; hence person belongs to the verb by virtue of its ability to be linked to the suppositum according to the different predicates the suppositum may have.[411] The person of the verb depends, therefore, on the person of the suppositum with which it is connected, *i.e.* it will be the first person if its suppositum possesses the property of speaking of itself.[412]

This means that person, like the other respective accidental modes, is only respective by reason of its association with another feature in the construction, and apart from species and figura which are in any

---

[408]   Thomas of Erfurt, #220: "verbum personale habet numerum, et personam, ex proprietatibus rei suppositae; ideo hos modos requirit in supposito, non proportionabiles, sed similes".

[409]   This description of number provides an interesting example of the Modistic procedure of taking the semi-formal descriptions of their predecessors and restating them in their own semantic terms.

[410]   This is a typical Modistic way of stating semantically a concord category.

[411]   Thomas of Erfurt, #145: "persona est modus significandi, quo mediante verbum proprietatem loquendi consignificat non inhaerentem de se, sed ut res verbi applicabilis est rei suppositi subsistentis per se secundum proprietates loquendi. Unde persona inest verbo ex aptitudine attribuendi supposito secundum variam attributionem".

[412]   Thomas of Erfurt, #146: "illud verbum dicimus esse primae personae attributum, quod est applicabile supposito, prouti stat sub proprietate loquendi de se, et sic de aliis".

case absolute modes, compositio and significatio are the only true respective modes.[413] Every other respective mode must be stated in terms of its possible relationship, and person must be included in this general statement, either with the suppositum or the obliquum, or else, as in the case of tempus, with the construction as a whole; compositio thus represents the sum total of mood, person, number and conjugation, just as significatio is the totality of every voice and its relations to the obliquum.

Siger's attitude to the question of person is somewhat different; in the first place, he did not include person as an accidental mode of the nomen, nor did he conceive of the accidental modes of the verb in any form of hierarchy with compositio as a kind of super-mode and with other modes, *i.e.* mood, person, number and conjugation as its sub-modes. His definition of person is, moreover, almost identical to Thomas's definition of person in the nomen as the property of consignifying the property of speaking and the person speaking,[414] so that it will be divided into three persons. Here again, Siger's definition of the three persons is almost identical to Thomas's, these persons are 'de se', *i.e.* 'of oneself', 'ad alium', *i.e.* 'to another', and 'de alio', *i.e.* 'of another'.[415] Person was, for Siger, a respective mode, and though he does not follow Thomas in asserting a necessary dependence of the property of the person of the verb on the person of the suppositum, Siger does mark out as an important feature of person as a constructible element its necessary concord with the suppositum.[416]

Siger also introduces the impersonal verb into his section on person and discusses it at great length. He states in effect that an impersonal verb is to all intents and purposes the same as any other verb except that it lacks person and number.[417] This is itself an interesting and

---

[413] It will be remembered that tempus was described as a mode which was not respective with regard to the verb but was respective with regard to adverbs of time.

[414] Siger de Courtrai, p. 120: "persona est modus significandi accidentalis verbi designans circa rem modum essendi prout convenit alicui sub aliquo modo loquendi".

[415] Siger de Courtrai, pp. 120-121: "prima persona verbi est persona designans circa rem verbi modum loquendi prout convenit alicui sub modo loquendi de se ... Secunda persona verbi est persona designans circa rem verbi modum essendi prout convenit alicui sub modo loquendi ad alium ... Tertia est persona verbi designans circa rem verbi modum essendi prouti convenit alicui sub modo loquendi de alio".

[416] Siger de Courtrai, p. 121: "prima est principium constructionis ex parte ante cum supposito sub modo proportionali loquendi".

[417] Siger de Courtrai, p. 121: "verbum impersonale ... actum significat semper

revealing statement in view of Thomas's argument that the verb possesses person and number only by virtue of its association with the suppositum and derives its person and number from the properties of the suppositum, so that an impersonal verb in reality cannot have a nominal suppositum. The Modistae and in particular Thomas would not, of course, look upon a construction such as 'percutit Socratum' as an impersonal construction; this is a transitive construction of the VN type similar to 'lego librum' with the suppositum subsumed, since, as Thomas tells us,[418] it is possible to have a 'congruent' construction in which one member is understood.[419] In a construction such as 'me oportet' however, the 'me' though the accusative, would be in the first position (in ratione principii), but it would not possess the special property of 'ut quem' which it would otherwise have if it were acting as the terminant constructible in a transitive construction such as 'lego librum'. There would be proportionality of mood with the accusative but no concord[420] of number or person, and 'oportet' is thus a true impersonal verb. Otherwise the impersonal verb, apart from its lack of person and number, possesses like any other verb the same moods, voices, tenses, and conjugations.

Coniugatio

This has been placed last among the accidental modes since it results, as Thomas says, from the various properties of tense, number, mood and person.[421]

It is interesting to see how different the Modistae could be in dealing with the same accidental mode. Michel does not even consider conjugation to be a mode of signifying at all but merely a variation of the

---

finitum et perfectum, et omnes modos sub modis significandi dependentis et fieri distantis et omnibus modis significandi verbi a quo nascitur, persona et numero tamen solummodo deficiens".

[418] Thomas of Erfurt, #222: "congruitas secundum intellectum est, quando ambo constructibilia secundum vocem non sunt expressa, sed alterum ipsorum est ab intellectu apprehensum".

[419] Thomas does, in fact, imply that this is a feature with verbs of the first or second person but it seems reasonable to maintain that this would also be true for the third person with the suppositum understood.

[420] Concord is used here as the equivalent term of 'similitudo'.

[421] Thomas of Erfurt, #135: "est coniugatio modus significandi rem verbi prout inflectitur per diversas proprietates temporum, numerorum, modorum et personarum".

expression (variatio vocis).[422] Siger, typically enough, does not dwell on the feature as such, and as in the other accidental modes, he is more concerned with a description of the conjugations of the Latin verb. He follows Priscian closely in defining conjugation as the declension of verbs,[423] and a conjugation becomes the result of the similar declension of a large number of verbs;[424] Siger then describes the four declensions of the Latin verb in similar formal terms.

Thomas likens conjugation in the verb to declension in the nomen, and it will be remembered that he did make a separate statement for declinatio though not as a separate mode of signifying; whereas, however, declinatio is derived from the inflection of one accident only, *i.e.* case, and for that reason, like Donatus, declension is included under case, conjugation is the result of the inflections of several accidents, *i.e.* tense, number, mood and person, and for that reason cannot be placed under any other particular accidental mode. Since it must be included as an accident of the verb, it will therefore be described as a separate accidental mode.[425] Like Siger, Thomas describes the various conjugations of the verb in formal terms (even if he does not define the feature as such in formal terms),[426] since each conjugation is recognised by means of its expression; such a statement allows Thomas to admit that verbs such as 'sum' and 'volo' have their own conjugation.

The interesting thing is that Thomas's definition of conjugation draws attention to the fact that any definition of conjugation by means of a mode of signifying implies a difference of meaning along with a difference of form. It is however difficult to apply the criterion of meaning to this particular accidental mode, since one may well ask what the semanticisation of coniugatio might be. The difference of form that the Modistae refer to, is not a purely formal matter, and will of course demand commutation on both sides, *i.e.* the change of form

---

[422] Martin likens it to declension in the nomen but associates it with tense only; like Michel, he associates it with the expression, *viz.* a parte vocis hoc attenditur, and as such is not really a mode of signifying.

[423] Siger de Courtrai, p. 119: "coniugatio est consequens verborum declinatio".

[424] Siger de Courtrai, p. 120: "nominatur coniugatio quasi una eademque ratione declinationis plurima verba coniunguntur".

[425] Thomas of Erfurt, #135: "coniugatio autem attenditur penes inflexionem plurium accidentium; ideo sub nullo proprie et determinate potest comprehendi; et ideo inter alia accidentia Verbi numeratur".

[426] Thomas of Erfurt, #135: "coniugatio sit prima, secunda, tertia, vel quarta, consequens, vel inconsequens, hoc totum a parte vocis attenditur. Et ex hoc patet, quod sum et volo habet coniugationem, licet non primam, secundam, tertiam, vel quartam".

which occurs with any change of conjugation commutes with some equivalent change in the meaning as a result of some concomitant change of meaning in the tense, mood, person and number.

D. PARTICIPIUM

The actual status of the participium has exercised grammarians since the days of Ancient Greece; modern grammarians classify the participle as a part of the verb, but throughout the period of Greek and Latin antiquity and during the Middle Ages it was considered a separate word-class and treated as such, since it shared features treated as essential to the noun and verb, which prevented its being assigned to either of these word-classes.

Looking back into antiquity from the period of the Modistae, we find a remarkable consistency in the definition of the participle, and it is not until we reach the Modistae that we find any serious departure from the traditional definition, although the Modistae too recognise and state emphatically that the participle shares features belonging to the noun and verb. Thrax defined it as a part of speech sharing the formal and functional characteristics of verb and noun.[427] This is the definition which Donatus[428] and Priscian followed, though their definitions do not accentuate the formal and functional to the extent that Thrax and Apollonius did; indeed Priscian does not give any specific definition of the participle and seems to have been content to draw attention to the similarities between the participle and the nomen and verb. This method provides its own form of definition by contrast, since the features in the participle and the nomen that are alike are quite distinct from those features that the participle and the verb share.[429] They seem to have been content merely therefore with stating the similarities between the participle and the verb and the participle and the noun in the form of the accidental features they share, *i.e.* gender, number and case from the noun

---

[427] R. H. Robins, *A. and M.*, p. 40.

[428] Donatus (*Ars Minor*): "participium quid est? Pars orationis partem capiens nominis, partem verbi; nominis genera et casus, verbi tempora et significationes, utriusque numerum et figuram".

[429] Priscian (XI.18): "participium in se separatur a verbo. quod et casus habet, quibus caret verbum, et genera ad similitudinem nominum, nec modos habet, quos continet verbum". Priscian (XI.8): "participium est igitur pars orationis, quae pro verbo accipitur, ex quo et derivatur naturaliter, genus et casum habens ad similitudinem nominis et accidentia verbo absque discretione personarum et modorum".

and tempus from the verb, though Donatus is perhaps more explicit in that the participle acquires genus and casus from the nomen, tempus and significatio from the verbum, and numerus and figura from both the nomen and verbum.

R. H. Robins, in his discussion of Thrax,[430] draws attention to the uneconomical method of separating the participle from the verb, and points out that 'the class membership of the two classes, participle and verb, stand in a fixed numerical relation to each other', adding that the scholiasts noted that participles were always derived from and pre-supposed a verb. This too was noted by Priscian,[431] and in a double manner by the Modistae, in that they (the Modistae) bring the verb into close association with the participle by means of the mode of becoming, flux and succession, which they shared as their essential mode of signifying,[432] i.e. they have the same matter (materia), modus esse, but are differentiated by means of their form. The Modistae also recognised the derived nature of the participle by making no mention whatsoever of the accidental mode of species, which suggests that they recognised the derived nature of the participle without feeling the need to express this explicitly. We have already seen that the verb and nomen possess two 'species', i.e. primitiva and derivativa, and by this means different verbs and nouns with the same root meaning are derived; the participium is, to begin with, a derived form from another pars orationis, so that in the case of 'fervescens' which is a derivation from 'fervesco', there is the same one-to-one relationship as 'fervens' and 'ferveo', but 'fervescens' and 'fervens' are both members of the participle word-class. The difference between the participle and the verb is one of consignification and therefore syntactic, so that the use of 'species' to account for this distinction must be ruled out, since such distinctions are syntactic.[433] If, however, the participle were con-sidered, as it is today, as part of the verb, the difference would be inflectional and would be described by some other accidental mode.

---

[430] R. H. Robins, *Thrax*, pp. 97-98.
[431] Priscian (VIII, 90): "participia sine verbis esse non possint". Priscian (XI, 2): "participium separatim non tradebant partem orationis quod nulla alia pars ora-tionis semper in derivatione est nullam propriam positionem habens, nisi parti-cipium".
[432] Siger de Courtrai, p. 123: "est modus significandi generalis participii, modus significandi fieri, motus, fluxus seu esse, qui est principium constructionis, ut dictum est in verbo". Michel de Marbais: "participium est pars orationis significans per modum fieri informantis" (Thurot, p. 187).
[433] *Cf.* pp. 43, 53-56, and 58-59 for discussion of 'consignification' and *species*.

Siger places the participle immediately after the nomen and verb because it portrays features common to these two major declinable partes, *i.e.* substantia in the nomen and hence the accidental features which stem from substantia, *i.e.* genus and casus, and action (actus) and hence the accidental features of tempus and significatio from the verb. The participle is therefore midway between the nomen and verb.[434]

Thomas agrees that the participle derives from the nomen and verb, hence the origin of the term 'participium', a statement which Siger echoes;[435] the participle is therefore for Thomas a pars orationis which signifies by means of the modus esse[436] and belongs to the same binary division of the sentence as the nominal element (substantia).[437] Thomas does not, however, share Siger's idea that the participle acquires substance from the nomen and action from the verb; he agrees that the participle derives from the nomen and verb but *not* in terms of the essential part or mode of either, since this would mean that the participle would signify by means of the modus entis *and* the modus esse – therefore it derives from the nomen and verb because they have certain accidental modes in common.[438] It is interesting to compare the Modistae and the modern critic of Thrax on this particular question and to note their similarity.[439]

The difference between Siger and Thomas on the matter of the relation of the participle to the nomen and verb can perhaps be accounted for in terms of the accidental modes of the verb, which are differently organised by Siger and Thomas, the difference being accentuated by their different treatment of the feature of compositio, and also in terms of the materia/forma contrast which refers particularly to this problem.

---

[434]   Siger de Courtrai, p. 123: "est participium medium inter nomen et verbum".
[435]   Thomas of Erfurt, #163: "divitur participium, quasi partem nominis, et partem verbi capiens". Siger de Courtrai, p. 123: "participium sequitur immediate nomen et verbum quia solum ab eis partem capit; a nomine, scilicet, substantiam et per consequens accidentia eius, scilicet, genus et casum; a verbo actum et per consequens tempus et significationem; ab utroque numerum et figuram".
[436]   Thomas of Erfurt, #163: "modus significandi essentialis generalissimus participii est modus significandi per modum esse indistantis a substantia".
[437]   It is as a result of the difference of its formal element, *i.e.* indistantia that the participle can function in the same segment of the sentence as the nominal element.
[438]   Thomas of Erfurt, #163: "dicitur participium capere partem nominis et verbi, quia habet quosdam modos significandi accidentales modis accidentalibus nominis et verbi consimiles".
[439]   R. H. Robins, *Thrax*, pp. 97-98. Siger de Courtrai, p. 123: "rationabiliter hoc nomen est ei a grammaticis inductum per conformationem duarum partium orationis principalium; nec est participium ab aliqua propria vi sed ab affinitate nominis et verbi nominatum".

The verb and the participle possess the same matter, *i.e.* the mode of becoming (fieri) but differ by reason of their form, which is expressed in the verb by means of the feature of separation or discreteness (distantia) but in the participle by means of non-separation (indistantia). The difference of distantia and indistantia does not affect the subaltern modes of the verb and participle;[440] distantia might almost be described as the most verb-like features of the verb and serves to distinguish it from all the other partes orationis. It also represents the definition of the verb by means of syntactic criteria, since the verb, by means of *distantia*, becomes the appositum, and with the suppositum creates the basic favourite sentence type of SP, which was, as we shall see, the only type of construction that the Modistae considered a complete sentence (constructio perfecta). The verb, therefore, can in effect be distinguished from the participle by means of syntactic criteria since the participle by virtue of its essential criterion of 'indistantia', cannot be constructed with a suppositum; there may be intransitive constructions of the NP or PN type, *e.g.* 'homo legens' or 'legens librum', but the first will not be an exocentric construction, since the participle can be constructed only endocentrically but with either a pre-posed or post-posed nominal form. Therefore a construction of the type NP cannot be a constructio perfecta such as Thomas described, nor can a construction of the PN type be considered a similar type of construction to the NV type, since the VN type possesses in this relationship the accidental mode of significatio, an accidental mode of the verb. The type PN possesses only the accidental mode of 'significatio' which corresponds to 'genus' in the verb.[441] The loss of the 'significatio' in the PN type, like the loss of compositio in the NP type, prevents them from becoming complete 'congruent' constructions.

Indistantia is derived from the same property as the modus adiacentis in the nomen and compositio in the verb, *i.e.* the property of inherence in terms of esse;[442] it is this similarity of the form of the participle to the adjective and that feature of the verb, *i.e.* compositio, which estab-

---

[440]   It will be seen that the organisation of the subaltern modes of the verb and participle and the categories which are derived from such modes are identical.

[441]   Thomas of Erfurt, #167: "significatio in participio, secundum grammaticos, idem est, quod genus in verbo, et ab eadem proprietate sumitur. Genus autem in verbo ... est modus significandi per modum dependentiae verbi ad obliquum post se, in ratione termini; et hoc idem est significatio in participio".

[442]   Thomas of Erfurt, #163: "modus indistantis a substantia, seu modus uniti substantiae, sumitur ab eadem rei proprietate in participio, a qua sumitur modus adiacentis in nomine, et compositio in verbo; et haec est proprietas inhaerentis alteri secundum esse".

lishes the *concord* between the participle and the pre-posed nominal form (though in the case of the verb it is concord of the verb with the suppositum). It is moreover this relationship of form which permits the participle to function like an adjective and acquire certain features of the adjective, for the participle derives certain of its accidental modes as a result of its form, *i.e.* genus, numerus; casus and persona are acquired from its association or connection with the pre-posed nominal and significatio and tempus are the only accidental modes which it derives from the verb and which have no connection with its form. The following catalogue of the accidental modes of the participle has been made in terms of the material-formal divisions and shows quite clearly how these features are shared between the nomen and verb as a result of this contrast:

It may well have been the confusion created by this formal problem which induced the Modistae to retain the participle as a separate pars orationis, when in reality the participle is clearly, even in Modistic terms, a part of the verb, *i.e.* by virtue of the essence they have in common.

Modus significandi essentialis

At this stage of our exposition, it is almost possible to predict the nature of the participle, especially as the Modistae were, despite all the criticisms one may make of their theory and especially the criteria used, very consistent in their analytical procedures. We have seen that the nomen and the pronomen constitute a group which combine in terms of their essence and which are differentiated by means of the matter/form contrast; similarly we can say that the verb and participle make up a group by virtue of the fact that they both possess the features of flux and succession as their essence, and they too are separated by means of the matter/form contrast.[443] We have already seen the organisation

---

[443]   *Cf.* pp. 187-190 and 203.

of the verb and the effect of form on the organisation of the verb and participle; it is also possible to see in Appendix B by means of the diagram the different modes of the participle and compare them to the nomen and verb to which the participle is closely connected. The following diagram attempts to show in more detail the interrelationships between the nomen, verb and participle:[444]

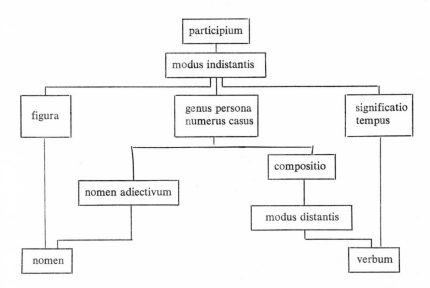

The presentation by the Modistae of the participle follows along the lines already discussed in the nomen and verb. Siger describes the essential mode as general and specific, the general linking the pars in question with the associated pars, and the specific separating it from all the other partes; Thomas starts with his modus generalissimus which is divided into modi subalterni and specialissimi which as a rule consist of different types of the pars in question, and which are divided further into sub-categories.

[444] The lines on this diagram are intended to show how these accidental modes result from the similarity of the participle to the nomen and the verb. The dotted line linking 'compositio' with the four accidental modes of genus, numerus, persona, and casus is used to indicate that these four accidental modes do not derive from the same property as 'compositio' but from the pre-posed nomen-suppositum, a relationship which is first established by compositio which is used by the verb to counteract the 'distantia' of the verb; the participle, by virtue of its link *i.e.* non-separation (indistantia) from the nomen, which it derives from its essence, acquires these modes as the nomen adiectivum does, *i.e.* from the pre-posed substantival form.

As in the other partes, there are minor divergencies between the Modistae, but these do not amount to a different doctrine, and are more often matters of presentation or terminology. Siger describes the general essential mode of the participle as the mode of signifying becoming, movement, flux or esse, and the specific mode as the mode of signifying non-separation from the nominal element.[445] Michel de Marbais defines the essential mode of the participle similarly by means of two modes, the first being the mode of becoming and flux, and the second the mode of signifying the active or passive union with the nominal element[446] – which suggests that Michel was seeking to stress, more than the other Modistae, the verbal quality of the participle in so far as the specific mode is concerned; Michel describes this second mode as the modus informantis, i.e. the mode of conferring form on the pars.

Thomas describes the modus generalissimus of the participle as the modus esse which is not separated from the nominal element;[447] in discussing the verb, he had shown how the modus esse represents in fact the total of becoming, movement, flux and succession (fieri, motus, fluxus, successio), so that Thomas does not differ from either Siger or Michel in the essential mode of the participle – Michel does, however, differ in one way, i.e. as in the verb, when he denied distantia as an *essential* feature, so he denies indistantia as an *essential* feature of the participle, though he would admit them as features of these two partes. His argument follows very much the pattern he made with reference to distantia in the verb, though of course in contrast, i.e. that the non-separation of the participle from the suppositum refers to its membership of the nominal piece and what is predicated of the participle belongs to the nominal element – the participle is near to the verb in meaning and some syntax, but is distinct from the verb with regard to the minimum SP sentence structure of Latin.

[445] Siger de Courtrai, p. 123: "modus significandi specificus participii est modus significandi indistantis seu uniti substantiae; ita quod participium non significat actum ut alterum a substantia sed unitum substantiae. This is yet another example of the matter-form contrast being used to differentiate the essential modes of a pars orationis and stresses the fact that the formal element, i.e. distantia in the verb and indistantia in the participle serve to 'inform' differently the matter, i.e. modus esse, of the verb and participle, with consequent syntactic differences.

[446] Michel de Marbais: "duo ... sunt modi essentiales ipsius participii, scilicet modus significandi fluxus vel fieri et modus significandi uniti vel concreti cum substantia agente vel patiente, qui ab aliquibus dicitur modus significandi informantis" (Thurot, p. 187).

[447] Thomas of Erfurt, #163: "modus significandi essentialis generalissimus participii est modus significandi per modum esse indistantia a substantia".

Modus significandi subalternus

As in the other declinable partes, this division is peculiar to Thomas, and in fact follows exactly the same pattern of analysis as the equivalent section in his description of the verb, and as in the verb as in the other declinable partes the modus generalissimus is used to *define* the participle and the modus subalternus and specialissimus to describe and catalogue its morphologic stock, but in semantic terms.

There is a little need to dwell at any length on Thomas's exposition of the subaltern mode and the modus generalissimus since it follows on the pattern of the verb, with the same divisions and sub-divisions. The modus generalissimus of the participle is divided into three subaltern modes: the first constitutes the participium substantivum and is the mode of signifying some special being by means of the modus esse, *e.g.* 'ens, existens';[448] the second constitutes the participium vocativum and signifies the property of naming by means of the modus esse, *e.g.* 'vocans, nominans';[449] the third is the mode of signifying action or passion,[450] and would seem to contain all the participles except those mentioned in the first two subaltern modes – this constitutes the participium adiectivum and is the only subaltern mode to be subdivided into modi specialissimi.

There are four modi specialissimi of the participium adiectivum – again as in the verb; the first is the mode of signifying action only, *e.g.* 'amans', the second is the mode of signifying passion only, *e.g.* 'amatus', the third is the mode of signifying neither action nor passion, *e.g.* 'currens', and the fourth is the mode of signifying both action and passion, *e.g.* 'criminans, criminatus'.[451] The modus specialissimus thus represents the full semantic statement of the essence of the participle; we start with the modus generalissimus which is the general description of its essence, *i.e.* esse and indistantia, the modus subalternus defines

[448] Thomas of Erfurt, #164: "primus modus est modus significandi per modum esse generaliter respectu cuiuslibet esse specialis. Et hic modus constituit participium substantivum, ut ens, existens".
[449] Thomas of Erfurt, #164: "secundus est modus significandi per modum esse generalis, respectu nominationis propriae tantum. Et hic modus constituit participium vocativum, ut nominans, vocans".
[450] Thomas of Erfurt, #164: "tertius est modus significandi per modum esse specialis actionis, vel passionis. Et his modus constituit participium adiectivum".
[451] Thomas of Erfurt, #165: "primus est modus significandi per modum actionis tantum ... ut legens, amans. Secundus modus est modus significandi per modum passionis tantum ... ut amatus, legens. Tertius est modus significandi per modum neutrius ... ut currens. Quartus est modus significandi per modum utriusque simul ... ut criminans, criminatus".

it as substantive, vocative, or adjective, and if adjective, the modus specialissimus types it as active or passive or neither, *etc.*

Modus significandi accidentalis

The Modistae do not have a great deal to say about the accidental modes of the participium, but the little they do say reinforces earlier statements about the intimacy which is very necessary between the essential and accidental modes of the pars in question, and about the doubtful status of the participle, at least in modern practice.

Both Siger and Thomas retain, as the accidental modes of the participle, the six accidents which Donatus and Priscian had ascribed to the participle, *i.e.* significatio, genus, tempus, numerus, figura and casus; to these Thomas added persona, which he includes as an accidental mode of the participle for the same reason that he included it as an accidental mode of the verb, *i.e.* that it is in effect derived from the suppositum, *i.e.* the nomen. These, significatio and tempus, are derived from the verb, and genus, numerus, figura, casus and persona are derived from the nomen; significatio is derived from the same property as genus in the verb.[452] This is very reminiscent of Donatus and Priscian and also very close to Siger, since it will be remembered that Thomas had made of significatio in the verb an accidental mode which was related to but separate from the accidental mode of genus, whereas Donatus, Priscian and Siger had used significatio as a synonym of genus. The other accidental modes derive from the same properties as in the nomen or verbum.

Significatio is an accidental mode of the participle and is derived from the same property as genus in the verb.[453] It seems indeed to

---

[452]   One of the most important features of Thomas's exposition of the accidental modes of the verb was the use of compositio and significatio to express the relations between the verb and the suppositum and the verb and the post-posed oblique; the quality of these relationships was expressed by further accidental modes, *i.e.* mood (modus) expressed the quality of the compositio, and voice (genus) expressed the quality of the significatio.

[453]   Thomas of Erfurt, #167: "significatio in participio, secundum grammaticos, idem est, quod genus in verbo, et ab eadem proprietate sumitur". Just as compositio is not needed in the participle in view of its indistantia from the nominal element which will be the suppositum, since compositio in the verb serves to restore the relationship between the subject and the predicate, so significatio, which serves as a balance to compositio, will not be required in the participle and becomes in fact the same as genus, which, as we saw in the verb, states the quality of the relationship between the verb and the post-posed nominal-oblique.

represent a combination of significatio and genus which, as has been stated, were closely related as accidental modes of the verb. Significatio in the participle thus represents the dependence of the participle on a post-posed oblique nominal;[454] this relationship is potential rather than actual in that, like the verb, it can have a transitive object but does not necessarily have to have one.[455] The actual quality of the relationship may be, as in the verb, active or passive and this opposition is exponentialised by the expression, *i.e.* vox,[456] which is in fact a formal statement and thus a morphological one.

Thomas has nothing to say of tempus as an accidental mode of the participle except to say that it derives from the same property as in the verb; in such a case, tempus as we have seen does not result from relations with either the suppositum or the oblique. Siger has a little more to say but adds little if anything to the theory of tempus as a feature of the participle; his account is, as is so often the case in Siger's discussions of the other accidental modes, a discussion of tempus as a feature of the *Latin* participle, and in particular its various shortcomings as a Latin participle.

Thomas has nothing at all to say about figura in addition to what he said of it in the nomen. Siger, however, does say of figura, that a participium such as '*indocens' can be described either as a figura composita, and as such will be analysed as /in-/ and /-docens/, or else as a figura decomposita and as such will presumably[457] be analysable as from '*indocens' and may be /*indoc-/ and /ens/. Therefore, as in the nomen, a participle can be of either figura simplex or figura composita, or figura simplex or figura decomposita, but there is no real difference between composita and decomposita, since they have the same class membership[458] and therefore they do not constitute, as in

---

[454] Thomas of Erfurt, #167: "genus in verbo ... est modus significandi per modum dependentiae verbi ad obliquum post se, in ratione termini; et hoc idem est significatio in participio".

[455] Thomas of Erfurt, #167: "hic modus est modus significandi in ratione termini absolute, et non contracti, tamen contrahitur".

[456] Thomas of Erfurt, #167: "aliquod participium sit significationis activae, vel passivae, et sic de aliis, hoc totum de parte vocis attenditur".

[457] 'Presumably', because Siger does not in fact offer any analysis of any decomposita.

[458] Siger de Courtrai, p. 124: "participium ut: indocens ... diversiter possunt considerari. Uno modo, prout a verbo compositione figurae determinantur, et sic, omne participium aut est simplicis figurae aut decompositae. Alio mode, prout componitur ab 'in' et 'docens' et sic est compositae figurae, ita quod unum et idem diversis respectibus potest esse compositae figurae vel decompositae".

the nomen, separate sub-modes of figura.[459] Siger in the participle sets up thus two hierarchical oppositions of simplex-composita and simplex-decomposita, but the opposition of composita-decomposita is absent. The reason for this can probably be related to the absence of 'species' as the companion absolute mode, since the participles were always considered to be derived (therefore it can only be a species derivativa) from a verb and presupposed a verb;[460] the participle, itself a derived form, will always be structured on a verb of either simple or derived species. The participle with a figura composita will be derived from a combination of figura simplex with a figura simplex already derived from a verb, but the participle with a figura decomposita must be derived from a verb with a figura composita. A figura decomposita must always presuppose a figura composita; a figura composita will always presuppose a figura simplex, but a figura decomposita may never presuppose a figura simplex. A participle with a figura composita must therefore consist of a combination of a figura simplex and a figura simplex, *i.e.* '*indocens' will be a figura composita consisting of 'in' and 'docens' which is itself however derived from 'doceo'[461] or it can be made up of parts which as parts have no separate individual meaning, *but whatever its composition, the meaning will remain the same.*

There are two interesting gaps in the inventory of accidental modes of the participle, *i.e.* species and compositio with mood (modus). Much has already been said about the similarities and dissimilarities between the nomen and pronomen, and the verb and participle; the verb and participle have the same essential features which in both partes are derived from the property of flux and succession, but they are rendered distinct by the fact that the verb must also be discrete (distans) from the suppositum while the participle will not be discrete (indistans) from the suppositum. It will be remembered that compositio and its concomittant of mood (modus) were required to 'repair the damage' caused by discreteness as an *essential* feature of the verb; if, however, the whole concept of discreteness is abandoned, there is clearly no need to retain compositio and mood, which accounts for their absence as accidental modes of the participle.

---

[459]   Thomas, in the nomen, required three types of figura, *i.e.* simplex, composita, and decomposita. Siger had postulated two, *i.e.* simplex and composita with decomposita really as a sub-class of composita.

[460]   R. H. Robins, *Thrax*, p. 97, fn. 3.

[461]   There is however no such verb as '*indoceo', so that '*indocens' cannot be a derivative of it.

It must not be imagined, however, that compositio is ignored altogether as a feature of the participle; Thomas tells us that the mode of non-separation from the substance is derived from the same property from which modus adiacentis in the nomen and compositio in the verbum are derived. This has important implications for the creation of the accidental modes of the participle in that the adjectival nature of the participle and the accidental modes which ensue from this are created as a result of this ability to associate with and be dependent on the suppositum; Thomas has already stated that the verb acquires the accidental modes of person and number not from its own properties but from the properties of the suppositum. Similarly, he tells us that the participle acquires the accidental mode of gender,[462] number, and case, as the nomen adiectivum does, as a result of a property in common,[463] and the participle thus acquires the features of person and number, as the verb does, from this same property, *i.e.* proprietas inhaerentis. This serves to underline those features that the nomen, verb and participle have in common and which they derive in fact from the nomen,[464] but it also illustrated that between the verb and the participle it is the necessary presence of compositio in the verb and its necessary absence in the participle which render these accidental modes possible.

Species is not included among the accidental modes of either the pronoun or the participle;[465] in fact, the absence of species as an accidental mode of the participle is very revealing. It will be remembered that species in the verb was divided into primitive and derivative, and that the derivative changed the morphemic shape of the verb by the process of adding a meaning to a meaning, – in others words the verb is built on a semantic root which does not change. This is, of course, not possible in the participle and serves to underline the precariousness of the independence of the participle as a separate pars orationis. The rea-

---

[462]   Siger argues that genus in the participle derives from the same property in the nomen, which is the property of active or passive creation, *e.g.* generans is masculine and nubens is feminine; Siger de Courtrai, p. 124: "natura participii ita communis est trium generum quod sine vituperationis causa sive figurae participia apta maribus".

[463]   Thomas of Erfurt, #163: "proprietas inhaerentis alteri secundum esse".

[464]   Thomas of Erfurt, #168: "nomina adiectiva, et pronomina, quae tot sunt adiectiva, et participia adiectiva, habent casus, numerum, genus, et personas, non ex parte suae rei, per se loquendo, sed ex parte rei subiectae".

[465]   Thomas tells us that what was species in the nomen, an absolute accidental mode, becomes in the pronomen a subaltern mode and is used to create different types of pronoun.

son for the absence of species is that any participle is a derived form in the first place, so that 'docens' will be derived from 'doceo' though not in the same sense that 'montanus' was derived from 'mons' and in instances such as 'fervescens' we have a derived form from a verb that is already a 'species derivativa'. This reinforces the argument that morphology was not considered by the Modistae as ever really pertinent to grammatical analysis; the Modistae for the most part described the inflectional and derivational systems according to their adaptation of the 'word and paradigm' method,[466] i.e. by stating each of these according to their meaning and not according to their form. The participle shares its general essential features with the verb and yet is discrete from the verb by virtue of a feature of its essence, i.e. indistantia, which brings it close in effect to the nomen; its accidental modes are derived from both the nomen[467] and the verb.[468]

It has been pointed out[469] that Greek (and also Latin) has two major syntactical relations, and this was also suggested by the Modistae almost to the exclusion of any other type of construction; the first is the concord of gender, number, case and (in the case of Thomas) person with the pre-posed nominal suppositum, and the second is that of government between the verb and the post-posed oblique which is expressed by means of significatio. It should be noted that the participle derives all the accidental modes which express the first relationship *from the nomen*, as indeed the verb, as we have already seen, derives its number and person from the pre-posed suppositum; the participle derives the accidental modes, which express the second relationship, from the verb, so that the participle can 'contract both these sorts of relations, and can exhibit them both in the same sentence'.[470] It is implied here that the Greek grammarians kept the participle as a separate word-class as a result of the duality of its syntactic relations; the Modistae were not overtly prompted by such formal considerations, but quite clearly were

---

[466]   C. F. Hockett, "Two Models of Grammatical Description", *Word* 10 (1954), p. 210. R. H. Robins, *Thrax*, p. 92.

[467]   Nomen is used throughout in preference to noun, since nomen includes both substantive and adjective, and in order to distinguish them (nomen) substantivum and (nomen) adiectivum would be used; verbum does not present any such division and the term 'verb' can be used without any danger of confusion.

[468]   Thomas refers more than once to the adjectival nature of some of the functions of the participle; it is this duality which has produced, in traditional grammars, expressions such as 'verbal-adjective'.

[469]   R. H. Robins, *Thrax*, pp. 97-98.

[470]   R. H. Robins, *Thrax*, p. 98.

impelled to do so as a result of the 'mixed' nature of the participle,[471] and it may have been metaphysical criteria just as much as grammatical considerations which induced them to do this.[472]

[471] Siger de Courtrai, p. 123: "eodum modo imaginandum est de participio sicut de actu permixto potentiae".
[472] This is of course a reference to one of the major influences on their work, *i.e.* contemporary metaphysics: in this instance the retention of the participle as a separate word-class also coincides with the scheme of the classical grammarians, another great influence on the theories of the Modistae who were thus able to order their semanticised word-classes which are restatements of the more formal divisions of their classical predecessors to fit both the requirements of contemporary metaphysics and the organisation of their classical predecessors.

VI

THE INDECLINABLE PARTES ORATIONIS

A. ADVERBIUM

The Greek[1] and Roman[2] grammarians had defined the adverb very narrowly as being associated grammatically with the verb and said nothing about its possible associations with other partes orationis, *i.e.* adjective or another adverb.[3] One important advance of the Latin grammarians had been the separation of the interjection from the adverb which had been included as a sub-class of the adverb by the Greeks. The Modistae, as is to be expected, followed their classical predecessors very closely; it must be remembered that Modistic grammar is largely a re-statement in semantic terms of Priscian's and Donatus's grammar and therefore we must expect that they will follow Priscian and Donatus closely in subject matter, if not in grammatical doctrine.

The treatment by the Modistae of the adverb and the other indeclinable partes provides an interesting study in contrasting styles and theoretical attitudes. As far as subject matter is concerned, the Modistae are to all intents agreed on the nature of the adverb, but it is the organisation of their material which is the most interesting aspect of their work. Thomas and Michel take largely the attitude that there are four separate partes orationis which put them on a par with the four declinable partes; Siger on the other hand groups them together by means of their general essential mode making of them a group very reminiscent of the 'particles' of the modern grammarian,[4] so that we

---

[1] R. H. Robins, *A. and M.*, p. 40: "the adverb is a part of speech without case inflection, further specifying the verb".
[2] Priscian (XV.1): "adverbium est pars orationis indeclinabilis, cuius significatio verbis adicitur".
[3] R. H. Robins, *Thrax*, p. 101.
[4] O. Jespersen, *The Philosophy of Grammar*, p. 87. C. F. Hockett, *A Course in Modern Linguistics*, p. 222.

have nominals (made up of substantives, adjectives and pronouns), verbals (made up of verbs and participles) and syntactic relatables[5] (made up of adverbs, conjunctions, prepositions and interjections).

Thomas devotes more time and space to a description, which is almost exhaustive, of the adverb than of any other pars with the exception of the nomen; this fact, moreover, plus the fact that Thomas includes the adverb, which he defines in syntactic terms[6] immediately after the verb and prior to the participle, suggests a morphological link between the nominals but a syntactic association with the verb, which would in fact make a very formal statement of the adverb, except that the Modistae do not deliberately use formal criteria. It is possible to see in this a direct link with the Greek grammarians who considered the adverb as morphologically associated with the nominals but syntactically with the verbs. It does, however, show up a certain inconsistency in Thomas which is not found in Siger, certainly as far as the essential modes are concerned; whereas Siger seems content to state the theory of the essential mode without any particular language in mind, Thomas tends to reinforce his statement by means of a more exhaustive description of the pars in question[7] as exemplified in Latin. Siger, by his use of the general essential modes to demonstrate certain fundamental grammatical functions which distinguish in effect three types of groups of partes orationis, is much more 'modern' than the other Modistae who are, as their treatment of the indeclinable partes shows, much more traditional in their grammatical theory.

The adverb, for the Modistae, is an indeclinable pars which signifies by means of the mode of specification[8] or attachment to something which signifies by means of the mode of becoming;[9] as was pointed out in the introductory section on the indeclinable partes Thomas's modus generalissimus expresses the same doctrine as Siger's specific mode, his general mode having been used to describe its status as a member of its

---

[5] Siger de Courtrai, p. 146: "modus significandi generalis adverbii est significare per modum disponentis et dicitur generalis quia reperitur in aliis speciebus orationis, videlicet in praepositione et quibusdam aliis".
[6] Thomas of Erfurt, #150: "adverbium est pars orationis, significans per modum adiacentis alteri, quod per modum esse significat ipsum esse absolute determinans".
[7] By means of his analysis of the modus subalternus and the modus specialissimus. This is shown in more detail on pp. 261-266, when Thomas discusses the modus subalternus and specialissimus of the adverb.
[8] Thomas of Erfurt, #150: "Sumitur iste modus determinantis a proprietate terminantis in re."
[9] Michel de Marbais: "adverbium est pars orationis significans per modum fluxus vel fieri in alio" (Thurot, p. 189).

'archipars'. The adverb is thus an indeclinable pars which specifies a verb or participle, since they signify by means of the modus fieri a narrow definition which quite clearly is derived from Priscian.

How is it that there should be such a close connection between the adverb and the verb? This goes back, in reality, to Priscian[10] and the Greeks who talked about the adjectivality of the adverb with regard to the verb. The Modistae developed this by arguing, as Michel de Marbais does,[11] that the mode of substance is divided into the mode of substance in itself, by means of which the nomen substantivum signifies and the mode of substance in something else, by means of which the nomen adiectivum signifies, and it will be remembered that the nomen adiectivum derives its essence from the nomen substantivum;[12] similarly the mode of becoming is divided into something which becomes by itself and something which becomes in something else.[13] The adverb and the adjective have this in common that they derive their being by their power to associate with the pars which gives them their being.

Thrax has been criticised for saying nothing about the possible associations of the adverb with other partes orationis;[14] the Modistae touch very tentatively on this subject and come to the conclusion that certain adverbs can construct endocentrically with other partes besides the verb or participle. However, the tentative nature of this new development must be stressed; Siger says very little about it at all, and while Michel insists that the adverb cannot determine the nomen or pronomen which signify by means of the mode of substance,[15] he is, however, prepared to admit that an adverb can properly determine another adverb, as in the sentence 'lego multum bene'. Thomas is more positive than the others, though it would be misleading to exaggerate this; he states that

---

[10] Priscian (XVII.21): "adverbium vero quod verbi est vi adiectivum . . .".
[11] Michel de Marbais: "modus significandi substantie vel permanentis dividitur in modum permanentis in se, per quem significat id quod significat nomen substantivum, et in modum permanentis in alio, per quem significat id quod significat nomen adiectivum" (Thurot, p. 188).
[12] Siger de Courtrai, p. 101: "adiectiva dependent in esse a suis substantivis".
[13] Michel de Marbais: "modus significandi fluxus vel fieri dividi potest in modum significandi fluxus vel fieri per se et in modum fluxus vel fieri in alio" (Thurot, p. 188).
[14] R. H. Robins, Thrax, p. 101.
[15] Michel de Marbais: "ipsum adverbium non potest specificare sive determinare, nisi aliquid habens modum significandi fluxus vel fieri. Unde nomen vel pronomen determinare non potest, cum utrumque per modum substantie significet" (Thurot, p. 189).

the adverb, by reason of its modus generalissimus, can determine only the verb or participle, which signify by means of the modus esse – however the adverb may determine other partes by means of some other mode, *i.e.* specialis[16] or accidentalis, as in the case of the exclusive adverbs, *e.g.* 'tantummodo', 'solummodo', which can determine anything which is capable of being excluded.[17] The little that Siger did have to say does throw some light on the use of the accidental mode in this context. He argues that in a sentence such as 'tantum Socrates currit', the adverb 'tantum', by virtue of the mode of exclusibility, seeks to exclude this particular act from all other possible authors of this action.[18] This seems to be the Modistic way of saying that by means of the modus generalissimus, the adverb modifies the verb only, but it can have syntactic relations with other partes orationis by means of various other modes of signifying. This is not confined to verbs or participles, and a nomen and other partes are capable of being excluded and can therefore be determined by an adverb as in 'homo tantummodo legit'. Michel was clearly not happy about this and argues that in a sentence such as 'tantum ens rerum opponitur falso', the adverb 'tantum' does not determine the nomen but the verbum substantivum or the participial element, so that we can have as an alternate the sentence 'tantum quod est rerum opponitur falso'.[19] Unfortunately, Michel did not offer any interpretation of the sentence 'homo tantummodo legit', so that we cannot say whether Michel would have described this as determination of the nomen or verbum.

[16] Thomas uses modus specialis as an alternative term for the modus subalternus: at a later stage in his discussion of the adverb, he tells us that the subaltern modes derive from Donatus's significatio (which Donatus called an accident), and then defines 'significatio' as a modus essentialis specialis, *cf.* Thomas of Erfurt, #153: "significatio non est modus accidentalis, quia est extra rationem adverbii absolute". Furthermore, when discussing the conjunction he uses 'specialis' as an intermediate stage between the modus generalissimus and specialissimus, *cf.* Thomas of Erfurt, #174: "modus significandi essentialis generalissimus dividitur in duos modos speciales, ad specialissimus descendendo".
[17] Thomas of Erfurt, #150: "adverbium, de suo modo significandi essentiali generalissimo, tantum determinat ea, quae per modum esse significat; licet de aliquo modo essentiali, speciali, et accidentali, possit alia determinare ut patet de adverbiis exclusivis ... quae, propter modum significandi per modum excludentis, possunt determinare omne illud, quod habet se per modum exclusibilis".
[18] Siger de Courtrai, p. 147: "dicendo: tantum Socrates currit, hoc adverbium 'tantum' in quantum adverbium est, disponit actum per comparationem ad Socratem, in quantum tamen exclusivum excludit actum illum ab omnibus aliis".
[19] Michel de Marbais: "Hoc adverbium 'tantum' non determinat nomen, sed determinat verbum substantivum vel eius participium subintellectum de bonitate tamen intelligentis, ut 'tantum ens verum opponitur falso' vel 'tantum quod est verum opponitur falso' " (Thurot, p. 190).

Modus significandi essentialis

The Modistae describe the essential mode of the adverb[20] and of the other indeclinable partes according to the same methods that we have encountered in their descriptions of the declinable partes,[21] *i.e.* Siger divides his essential mode into two equal parts, the general and specific, while Thomas begins with his modus generalissimus which, as has been pointed out, is in the case of the indeclinables the equivalent to Siger's specific mode. Thomas uses his modus generalissimus to define the pars in question, and subdivides it into the modus subalternus and further into modus specialissimus, which, as we have seen in the other partes orationis, is the means he adopts for describing more exhaustively the types and classes of word which go to make up this particular pars orationis.

Siger's general mode is the mode of syntactic relatability[22] (modus disponentis), *i.e.* the syntactic relationships which the adverb has with other words, and this is clarified and narrowed down – since it cannot have similar and equal syntactic relationships with all other words, – by means of the specific mode which states that the adverb signifies by means of the mode of determining the act or anything else which signifies by means of becoming,[23] *i.e.* the verb or participle.

It is at this stage that Thomas starts; his modus generalissimus defines the adverb as a pars orationis signifying by means of the mode of adjacency to another which signifies by means of the modus esse which is the essential mark of the verb and participle, and by doing so determines it, *i.e.* the verb or participle.[24] This modus generalissimus, as defined by Thomas, stresses that feature, *i.e.* the mode of adjacency, which brings it close, in syntactic function, to the adjective. Thomas points out the 'adjectivality' of the adverb and suggests that there are some adverbs which do not determine the participle, since some adverbs may determine the verb by reason of the verb's accidental modes of compositio and mood which the participle does not possess – Thomas

---

[20] *Cf.* Appendix B, pp. 375-377: the diagram shows, in particular, Thomas's organisation of the adverb.

[21] *Cf.* the diagram on p. 111 which shows the relationship between Siger's general and specific modes, and Thomas's modus generalissimus.

[22] *Cf.* pp. 129-130, 257.

[23] Siger de Courtrai, p. 146: "significare per modum determinantis actum vel aliquid quod rem suam significat per modum esse, fieri, motus vel actus".

[24] Thomas of Erfurt, #150: "modus significandi essentialis generalissimus adverbii est modus significandi per modum adiacentis alteri, per modum esse, significans ipsum simpliciter et absolute determinans".

goes so far as to suggest that this may have been at the back of Priscian's mind when he called the adverb the 'adiectivum verbi'.[25]

The definition of the essential mode of the adverb, and indeed of all the indeclinable partes, stresses that Siger is in fact a very real grammarian; he seems to have realised, as others did, that semanticisation was not going to be as successful as in the declinable partes, and although he was able to define the specific mode in syntacto-semantic terms, he stated the general mode, common to all the indeclinable partes, in formal syntactical terms. By stating a common function to the indeclinables by means of the general mode which is at the same time a respective mode,[26] Siger has tried not so much to place the indeclinable partes on equal footing with the declinable partes, but to give a very formal account of their occurrence in grammar, and Siger thus lays much less stress on their dissimilarities and much more on their similarities.[27]

Modus subalternus

As in the other partes, Thomas alone uses this sub-division of the essential mode along with its own sub-division of modus specialissimus as a means of describing in more detail the various kinds of adverbs; the modus specialissimus becomes, in fact, a fairly exhaustive inventory of the adverb in the Latin language, and little need be said of this section, since it adds nothing to Thomas's theory of the adverb.

The first division of the modus generalissimus is the subaltern mode and there are in the adverb two subaltern modes, the first being the mode of signifying by means of the mode of determining the verb or participle by reason of the meaning of the adverb, e.g. 'unde', 'multum',

---

[25]   Thomas of Erfurt, #150: "licet adverbium dicatur adiectivum verbi, hoc est ideo, quia adverbium, secundum omnes species eius, determinat verbum, sed non participium; quia adverbia determinantia verba genera compositionis, et genera sui modi, qui est qualitas compositionis, participia determinare non possunt, cum participium compositionem et modum verbi non habeat. Et sumitur iste modus determinantis a proprietate terminantis in re".

[26]   Siger de Courtrai, p. 131: "modi significandi respectivi dicuntur qui conceduntur dictioni in comparatione ad modum significandi alterius dictionis eis proportionalem et tales sunt principium constructionis quia sunt principium unionis constructibilis cum constructibili". This suggests a double reason for the formal syntactic nature of the general mode, i.e. the respective mode is by definition a syntactic mode and the general mode of the adverb is similarly by definition a syntactic mode.

[27]   O. Jespersen, The Philosophy of Grammar, p. 87.

'qualiter', 'prudenter',[28] and the second by means of the mode of determining the verb or participle by reason of the mode of signifying of the verb or participle, *e.g.* 'cur', 'forsan', 'etiam', 'non', 'utinam', 'quando', 'nunc',[29] *i.e.* the first subaltern mode contains those adverbs which remain discrete from the verb by reason of their own denotative meaning and the second subaltern mode contains those adverbs which must operate with the verb by reason of certain accidental modes of the verb. These accidental modes are compositio, modus and tempus; such adverbs have a much more restricted use – *i.e.* they are collocationally restricted adverbs, – than those adverbs deriving from the first subaltern mode, and require further comment. Clarification is to be found in the appreciation of the particular natures of the three accidental modes of the verb to which the adverbs of the second subaltern mode refer; compositio and modus refer to the relationships between suppositum and appositum of the favourite SP type of sentence, and tempus is an accidental mode of the verb only by virtue of the temporal adverb which therefore signifies more about the action of the verb caused by the suppositum. Adverbs of the first subaltern mode are therefore to determine the verb by virtue of their own denotative value, while adverbs of the second subaltern mode are very restricted in their function, the adverbs of compositio and mood being restricted to a determination of the verb by virtue of its dependence on the suppositum, and the adverbs of time are also considerably restricted, not by the NV relationship but by the very necessary colligation of tenses of the verb, since it is obviously incongruous to colligate a future tense with an adverb of 'past time'.[30]

Donatus posited three accidents for the adverb, *i.e.* significatio, degree (conparatio) and figura; the Modistae did not describe in any detail the accidental modes of the adverb, (in fact Siger makes no mention of them at all) and Thomas dismisses them very summarily, *e.g.* Thomas of Erfurt, #162: "de comparatione, specie et figura dicendum est hic sicut in nomine", which is all he has to say about the accidental modes

---

[28] Thomas of Erfurt, #151: "primus est modus significandi per modum determinantis verbum, vel participium ratione significati".
[29] Thomas of Erfurt, #151: "secundus modus est modus significandi per modum determinantis verbum vel participium ratione modi significandi".
[30] We shall see in the section on syntax that the adverb can determine either member of an intransitive constructio which represents the favourite SP or NV type: if the adverb determines the V element, it can in theory be any type of adverb, but if it determines the suppositum it will be an adverb of the second subaltern mode only.

of the adverb,[31] but what became of the accidents described by Donatus? Thomas tells us quite baldly at the end of his description of the essential modes that comparatio, species and figura in the adverb are the same as in the nomen;[32] significatio, Thomas tells us,[33] is contained in two subaltern modes just described. Significatio in the adverb, like qualitas in the nomen, was clearly a device used by Donatus[34] to establish certain basic types of the pars in question, i.e. qualitas was used in the nomen to establish the fundamental types of nomen, i.e. nomen proprium and nomen appellativum,[35] and similarly Thomas uses significatio to create the two subaltern modes which constitute the two fundamental types of adverb. This relationship to qualitas in the nomen and the verb further enhances the position of the adverb, as morphologically associated with the nominal, since qualitas establishes two fundamental morphological types of nomen (though they are semantically dressed), and as syntactically linked with the verb, since qualitas in the verb creates the accidental mode of mood (modus) which represents the quality of compositio which is one of the most important accidental modes of the verb;[36] together they control the syntax of the verb and its subject. It should be noted that one of the subaltern moods of the adverb, the mode which determines the verb by reason of its mode of signifying, divides into the modi specialissimi of compositio, modus and tempus which are syntactical and not inflectional accidental modes of the verb. Significatio is thus the mode of signifying by means of which the adverb determines the verb or participle either by means of the denoted meaning of the adverb, e.g. 'ubi', 'qualiter', or by association

---

[31]   Martin of Dacia has more to say on the subject of the accidental modes of the adverb but this would appear to be more a matter of organisation rather than doctrine.

[32]   Apart from anything else, this serves to confirm that accidentia and declinatio were not the same for the Modistae; in the nomen, comparatio was included as one of the modi specialissimi, while species and figura were absolute modes, so that it is quite clear that the Modistae were prepared to set up accidental modes to explain the derivational items, but obviously there could be no inflectional accidental modes for the indeclinable partes.

[33]   Thomas of Erfurt, #151: "hos duos modos Donatus appellat significationem adverbii ... per significationem in adverbio, dat intelligere duos modos essentiales subalternos mediatos".

[34]   The Modistae did not make quite the same use as Donatus did of qualitas in the pronomen; they did however, make a comparable use of significatio in the adverbium.

[35]   Donatus (Ars Minor): "qualitas nominum in quo est? Bipertita est: aut enim unius nomen est et proprium dicitur, aut multorum et appellativum".

[36]   Thomas goes so far as to call it a "modus significandi accidentalis communissimus".

with a particular mode of signifying of the verb,[37] *e.g.* 'cur', 'forsan'.

An interesting feature of the treatment of the indeclinable partes was a tendency on the part of the Modistae, especially Thomas, to describe certain features of the indeclinable partes quite exhaustively; this is certainly true of Thomas's subaltern modes of the adverb and their subdivisions of modi specialissimi, which he describes in some considerable detail. This does, of course, suggest a slight inconsistency on Thomas's part; it has already been pointed out[38] that the Modistae had a pedagogy always, to some extent, in mind, but we have also argued that it is not so much Latin grammar as grammar that the Modistae had in mind, and yet some of the Modistae show, from time to time, curious departures from an otherwise considerable consistency, *i.e.* Thomas by his relatively exhaustive description of certain aspects of the nomen like the nomen adiectivum and adverb, and Siger by his tendency to describe the accidental modes of the nomen and verb in terms of Latin syntax. It would be pointless to consider this an animadversion of the Modistae, since they obviously viewed Latin in the light of the intellectual spirit of their day as the universal language from which alone grammar should be illustrated. It does not seem possible to offer any valid explanation for Thomas's excursion into exhaustiveness as far as the adverb is concerned, except to say that both instances of exhaustiveness, in the nomen and adverb, are connected with the 'adjectivality' of the nomen and adverb. This, along with the definition of the adverb as a determinant of a verbal or participial member, serves to accentuate the near syntactic parallelism and morphological non-parallelism which the Modistae had wrongly assumed to exist in Latin, between the nomen substantivum, nomen adiectivum and adverbium, which places the adverb in an almost mid-way position between the great word-classes.[39]

The subaltern modes are each divided into various modi specialissimi; the diagram in Appendix B shows the whole structure of Thomas's organisation of the different essential modes of the adverb. It seems therefore that little more would be achieved by a detailed analysis of these modi specialissimi since they merely represent an inventory of the adverbs of Latin dressed up in Modistic terminology.

---

[37]   Thomas of Erfurt, #153: "significatio in adverbio est modus significandi, quo mediante adverbium repraesentat specialem modum determinandi verbum, vel participium, aut ratione significati, aut ratione modi significandi".
[38]   H. Roos, *Die Modi Significandi*, p. 141.
[39]   R. H. Robins, *Thrax*, p. 102.

The first subaltern mode of the adverb[40] is divided into four modi specialissimi, which constitute four species of adverbs, *i.e.* the adverbs of place, quality, quantity and appellation (vocandi.) The adverb of place is divided into two, by means of the modes of enquiring about or referring to place,[41] which are further divided until we reach a detailed list of the adverbs of place of Latin. Similarly the adverbs of quantity and quality are each divided into two,[42] which produces a detailed if not exhaustive list of such adverbs; the fourth modus specialissimus constitutes the adverb of appellation[43] which is in effect the adverb 'o' used with the vocative of the substantive as in "O Henrice, lege".[44]

The second subaltern mode[45] is divided also into three modi specialissimi, which clearly derive by virtue of certain of the accidental modes of the verb they determine, *i.e.* by means of (i) compositio, (ii) modus, and (iii) tempus. The first is made up of 14 modi specialissimi which serve to determine the inherence of the verb[46] and it will be remembered that compositio, as an accidental mode of the verb, serves to establish the relationship between the suppositum and the verb, *e.g.* the interrogative adverb, which constitutes one of these modi specialissimi, determines the inherent quality of the verb in the shape of asking

---

[40] Thomas of Erfurt, #154: "modus significandi per modum determinantis verbum vel participium ratione rei significatae, dividitur in quatuor species essentiales quatuor species adverbiorum constituentes".

[41] Thomas of Erfurt, #155: "adverbium loci ... determinat rem verbi ratione loci ... vel per modum requirentis locum, vel respondentis ad locum".

[42] Thomas of Erfurt, #156-157: "adverbium quantitatis significat per modum determinantis rem verbi vel participii ratione mensurae continuae vel discretae ... et hoc vel per modum requirentis mensuram, ut quantum; vel per modum respondentis mensuram, ut semel, bis, ter ... adverbium qualitatis significat per modum determinantis rem verbi vel participii ratione qualitatis ... vel per modum requirentis rem verbi, ut qualiter; vel per modum respondentis ad qualitatem, ut docte, prudenter".

[43] Thomas of Erfurt, #158: "adverbium vocandi est quod verbum ratione actus exercitandi determinat, prout ad ipsum resolvitur substantia vocativi vocata, ut, o Henrice, lege".

[44] Siger de Courtrai, p. 154: " 'O' est adverbium et est tale adverbium, scilicet vocandi. Ratione qua adverbium est, semper construitur cum verbo, vel expresso vel subintellecto, sicut videmus in aliis adverbiis quae aliquando construuntur cum verbis subintellectis."

[45] Thomas of Erfurt, #159: "modus significandi per modum determinantis rem verbi vel participii ratione modorum significandi dividitur in tres modos, scilicet: in modum significandi per modum determinantis verbum vel participium ratione compositione; et ... ratione temporis; et ... ratione qualitatis sive modi; qui dicuntur indicativum, optativum, imperativum, etc.".

[46] Thomas of Erfurt, #160: "modus significandi per modum determinantis verbum ratione compositionis est modus significandi per modum determinantis inhaerentiam verbi".

the cause, *e.g.* 'cur'.[47] The second modus subalternus is made up of two modi specialissimi which constitute two types of adverb, *i.e.* the interrogative adverb of time, *e.g.* 'quando', which might also be included as one of the modi specialissimi which, as just mentioned, are derived by means of 'compositio', and the answering adverb of time, *e.g.* 'nunc, hodie', the first one signifying by means of the mode of determining the verb by means of the mode of asking the time, and the second signifying by means of the mode of answering.[48] The third, *i.e.* the mode of signifying by means of mood, is divided into two modi specialissimi which constitute the adverbs of wish and exhortation,[49] and are closely connected with the mood of the verb they determine, *i.e.* the adverb of wish, *e.g.* 'utinam', is closely connected with the optative mood.[50]

The subaltern modes and their modi specialissimi demonstrate a definite division among the adverbs: the first subaltern mode and its modi specialissimi which constitute the adverbs of place, quantity, quality and appellation, represent adverbs which have their own denotative meaning, and the second subaltern mode and its modi specialissimi of compositio, mood (modus) and tempus represent adverbs which must operate with the verb and by reason of these same accidental modes of the verb.

Thus the adverb can be derived, by means of its modi subalterni and specialissimi, into adverbs of place, quantity, quality and appellation which determine the verbs by virtue of their mode of signifying and consist of (i) adverbs which determine the adverb by virtue of the accidental mode of compositio,[51] (ii) adverbs which determine the verb by virtue of its mood, and (iii) adverbs which determine the verb by virtue of its accidental mode of tempus.

---

[47] Thomas of Erfurt, #160: "adverbia interrogandi determinant inhaerentiam verbi sub ratione requirentis causam, ut cur".

[48] Thomas of Erfurt, #161: "modus significandi per modum determinantis verbum ratione modi, qui est qualitas inclinationis, subdividitur in duos modos specialissimos, duas species adverbiorum constituentes, quae sunt adverbia optandi, ut utinam, et hortandi, ut eia, age".

[49] Thomas of Erfurt, #161: "modus significandi per modum determinantis verbum sub ratione temporis subdividitur in duos modos speciales, duas species adverbiorum constituentes, scilicet; adverbium temporis interrogativum, ut quando, et responsivum, ut nunc, hodie".

[50] It must be remembered that Siger described this mood as a 'principium constructionis' in conjunction with this adverb.

[51] Thomas of Erfurt, #162: "adverbium determinans verbum ratione compositionis subdividitur in adverbium interrogandi, dubitandi, affirmandi, negandi, modificandi, ordinis, similitudinis, eventus, prohibendi, eligendi, congregandi, demonstrandi, residendi, excludendi".

B. CONIUNCTIO

Thrax defined the conjunction as 'a part of speech connecting the train of thought and filling in gaps in its interpretation',[52] a definition which Priscian tightened considerably by expounding it in much more formal terms as the part of speech which connected other words,[53] though he too resorted to semantic criteria to explain the conjunction further, in that it provided this link according to the meaning it gave the words it linked or else it served to demonstrate the relationship between these words; Donatus's definition[54] is to all intents the same as Priscian's, and this too is therefore a more formal definition than Thrax's definition. It was this definition that the mediaeval grammarians accepted and so we find the Modistae defining the conjunction as the pars orationis which signifies – we must not attach too much value to the strained sense of 'signify' in this context[55] – by means of the mode of joining two elements of a construction, and essentially this definition is to be found in Michel de Marbais, Thomas of Erfurt and Martin of Dacia;[56] Siger, as we know, is incomplete and we have to rely on the account given in his grammatical sophismata, but his specific essential mode is usually his vehicle for the definition of the pars in question, and so we find that he varies only a very little from the other Modistae by defining the conjunction or perhaps more exactly, the specific mode of the conjunction, as signifying by means of the mode of uniting.[57]

The Modistae distinguished two types of conjunction in keeping with Priscian's definition; these conjunctions are not divided in a way which could be compared to the normative grammar of today – the Modistae

[52] R. H. Robins, *A. and M.*, p. 40.
[53] Priscian (XVI.1): "coniunctio est pars orationis indeclinabilis, coniunctiva aliarum partium orationis, quibus consignificat, vim vel ordinationem demonstrans".
[54] Donatus (*Ars Minor*): "coniunctio quid est? Pars orationis adnectens ordinansque sententiam".
[55] The Modistae are, however, quite consistent in using 'signify' here as a grammatical criterion since this is a general criterion throughout their treatises. It must be pointed out that in their indeclinable partes, 'signify' comes to mean 'function syntactically', which has a modern touch to it, since the late Professor Firth would argue that grammatical meaning of a word is the way it is used, *cf*. J. R. Firth, "The Technique of Semantics", *Papers in Linguistics*, pp. 7-33.
[56] Michel de Marbais: "coniunctio ... est pars orationis significans per modum coniungentis" (Thurot, p. 191). Thomas of Erfurt, #170: "coniunctio est pars orationis, per modum coniungentis duo extrema significans". Martin of Dacia: "coniunctio significat per modum coniungentis vel connectentis".
[57] Siger de Courtrai, p. 148: "modus specialis coniunctionis est significare per modum unitatis extendendo unionem".

ignored the subordinating conjunction[58] – this may, of course, be the result of their syntactical theories, since, if we are to take Thomas's theories on syntax[59] as typical, a construction is made up of two members, one of which is the dependent and the other the terminant, and the conjunction is always used with reference to one member of the construction or between two constructions, and will be the determinant, and as such will be the link between two equal parts.

The conjunction, in Modistic language, was divided into two and as such constituted two types of conjunction: the first one joins by means of meaning (per vim), e.g. 'et, vel', and the second by means of the relationship existing between the two parts (per ordinem) e.g. 'ergo'; in the first instance no particular link is required by either of the two members, but in the second instance one member may require a particular link with reference to the other member – this second type of conjunction can be considered logically subordinating, but it is the subject-matter of either member and not the structure of the parts or the whole which calls for this second type of conjunction. This means in effect, as Wallerand suggests,[60] that there is an equal relationship between each member; in the first place, the two parts will be linked together either with regard to a third member, e.g. 'Socrates et Plato currunt' and 'Socrates vel Plato', but in the second instance, the relationship is either one of cause and effect or antecedent and consequence, e.g. 'Socrates currit, ergo movetur', and 'terra interponitur inter solem et lunam, ergo luna eclipsatur'.[61]

Donatus had by means of the accident of 'potestas', established five species of conjunction, i.e. copulative, disjunctive, expletive, causal and rational: Thomas divides his subaltern modes in terms of Donatus' potestas, i.e. the copulative and disjunctive are sub-members of the first modus subalternus which contains the first type of adverb mentioned previously, i.e. which joins by means of its meaning,[62] and the causal and rational conjunctions are sub-members of the second subaltern mode which contains the second type of conjunction, i.e. which

---

[58] Thomas does, in fact, introduce the question of the subordinating conjunction *once* in his consideration of perfectio.
[59] Martin of Dacia sets up similar requirements.
[60] G. Wallerand, *Op. cit.*, p. (55).
[61] Thomas of Erfurt, #173: "modus significandi per modum coniungentis duo extrema secundum ordinem ex parte ante se tenentia . . . per modum coniungentis duo extrema secundum ordinem ex parte consequentis se habentia".
[62] Thomas of Erfurt, #172: "modus significandi per modum coniungentis duo extrema per vim est modus significandi, uniendi duo extrema, quae inter se dependentiam non habent".

joins by reason of the mutual relationship between the two parts.[63] Thomas included the fifth species set up by Donatus, *i.e.* the expletive conjunction, but really only as an after-thought after describing the modi subalterni and specialissimi. His argument for doing this is quite simple: such conjunctions are not truly conjunctions since they do not join but merely decorate the parts to be joined, and therefore are not very necessary in a sentence.[64] If they are to be included in a general statement about the conjunctions, it is sufficient to say that the conjunction either joins or decorates, but it is the conjunction which does actually join which must be described in detail, since it is the only true conjunction.

There was one problem which, in the light of the definition of the conjunction as the pars orationis signifying by means of the mode of joining, must have caused the Modistae some little trouble, since both Siger and Michel refer to it and discuss it at some length. It is, once more, a problem of their own creation and as a result of their semanticisation of a formal definition: curiously enough, it is a problem which Thomas, as a result of the organisation of his procedure, was able to avoid. It was a question of how to reconcile the definition of their specific mode as the mode of joining with the species of conjunction described by Donatus as a disjunctive conjunction; in other words, how do we reconcile the apparent contradiction of a specific mode which signifies by means of the mode of joining and an accidental mode which signifies by means of the mode of separation.[65] Both Siger and Michel[66] answer this query in an almost identical manner, and mention of it is made only to show once more the tortuous argument they had to make

---

[63]   Thomas of Erfurt, #173: "modus significandi per modum coniungentis duo extrema secundum ordinem est modus significandi unientis duo extrema per ordinem inclinata".

[64]   Thomas of Erfurt, #174: "quaedam coniunctiones dicuntur expletivae, quae secundum veritatem non sunt coniunctiones, quia non coniungunt, sed tantum coniuncta ornant, et in sermone non sumuntur propter necessitatem, sed propter ornatum".

[65]   Siger de Courtrai, p. 149: "modus significandi accidentalis non debet repugnare modo specifico, nunc potestas est accidens coniunctionis secundum Donatum et potestas disiunctiva repugnat modo specifico coniunctionis quia significare per modum unientis et significare per modum distinguentis repugnant, quia distinguere et unire repugnant; dico quod aliquid unum et idem bene distinguit et unit respectu diversorum ... et ideo haec coniunctio 'vel' dicendo: 'Socrates vel Plato currit', unit Socratem respectu Platonis, tamen distinguit alterum respectu cursus".

[66]   Michel de Marbais: "coniunctio disiunctiva habet rationem coniungentis et disiungentis, non tamen respectu unius, sed respectu diversorum. Habet enim rationem coniungentis respectu vocum, ... et rationem disiungentis respectu significatorum" (quoted by Thurot, p. 192).

in order to answer a problem which a formal definition would have answered so easily. Both Siger and Michel agree that a conjunction can both join and separate, but with regard to different things, *i.e.* in 'Socrates vel Plato currit', the disjunctive conjunction 'vel' joins Socrates with regard to Plato and vice versa, but it separates 'Socrates' and 'Plato' as far as the running (cursus) is concerned;[67] the disjunctive conjunction, in that it is a conjunction, joins the two parts grammatically,[68] but in that it is disjunctive, it separates them semantically with regard to the meaning of the verb.[69] Such an analysis is quite close in effect to a modern Immediate Constituent analysis, but is, however, clothed in very different language; 'Socrates' and 'Plato' are capable of being linked together, in this instance by 'vel',[70] and they are also capable of being separated, again in this instance by 'vel', with regard to the verb 'currit'.[71] We can represent the analysis thus:

> Socrates vel Plato /currit
> Socrates / vel Plato / currit.

Michel is less wordy in his explanation that such a conjunction, though as a conjunction it signifies by means of the mode of joining, joins two members but separates them with regard to a third;[72] this explanation is very close to Thomas's definition of a disjunctive conjunction, but Thomas saved himself the trouble of such a lengthy and dubious explanation by making of it a sub-mode, *i.e.* modus specialissimus[73] of the first subaltern mode of the conjunction.

---

[67]   Siger de Courtrai, p. 149: "haec coniunctio 'vel' dicendo: 'Socrates vel Plato currit', unit Socratem respectu Platonis, tamen distinguit alterum respectu cursus".

[68]   Siger de Courtrai, p. 149: "coniunctio disiunctiva, in quantum coniunctio est, coniungit aliqua invicem ratione modi significandi proportionalis".

[69]   Siger de Courtrai, p. 149: "in quantum disiunctiva, disiungit significata illorum respectu tertii per modum significandi similiter proportionalem".

[70]   Siger de Courtrai, p. 149: "per modum significandi proportionalem hoc quod est 'Socrates' et 'Plato' significant per modum disponibilis et unibilis, et ideo haec coniunctio 'vel', ut coniunctio est, significans per modum unitatis et disponentis, constructionem habet congruam cum eis".

[71]   Siger de Courtrai, pp. 149-150: "hoc quod est Socrates et Plato significant per modum disiungibilis respectu alicuius tertii; ista coniunctio 'vel' de suo modo significandi accidentali significat per modum disiungentis respectu tertii et ideo constructionem congruam habet ...".

[72]   Michel de Marbais: "coniunctio disiunctiva, unde coniunctio est, significat per modum coniungentis ... Ipsa tamen ... supra modum istum addit suum modum disiungentis ... Nec isti sibi ad invicem repugnant, quia ipsa coniungit aliqua inter se et disiungit ea in respectu alicuius tertii ... Dicendo 'Sor vel Plato currit", hec coniunctio 'vel' coniungit le 'Sor' et le 'Plato' ... disiungit tamen respectu del 'currit' " (Thurot, p. 192).

[73]   Thomas of Erfurt, #172: "secundus modus est modus significandi per modum coniungentis duo extrema inter se, distinguendo ea respectu tertii".

Modus significandi essentialis

It has already been explained that Siger insisted on two general modes for the conjunction as for the other indeclinable partes, *i.e.* general and specific; we find, therefore, that the general mode is the same as in the other indeclinables and expresses its general syntactic function, while the specific mode is used to particularise this function, and this is to signify by means of the mode of uniting. Siger explains that he has been able to make such a definition as a result of Priscian's definition,[74] in that Priscian's use of the term coniunctiva (connecting) he equates to his own term of modus disponentis, which is clearly true to the extent that 'disponere' expresses the general syntactic function just as 'coniungere' does in the case of the conjunction, and Priscian's use of 'added meaning and exhibiting their mutual relationship' (vim vel ordinem demonstrans) Siger equates to his own specific mode which, as we have said, is the more particular syntactic function, peculiar to the conjunction.

Thomas, as we have already explained, cannot use the matter-form contrast in the indeclinable partes, and his modus generalissimus tends to say very much the same as Siger's specific mode. In the case of the conjunction, Thomas is uncharacteristically brief, and all he has to say about the modus generalissimus is that it is the mode of signifying by means of the mode of joining two members;[75] this he explains briefly by non-linguistic means, *i.e.* that this mode is derived by reference to the external world, from that property of joining to be found in things in the external world of realities.[76]

Modus subalternus

This mode, peculiar to Thomas, is his means of developing in detail the definition made of the essential mode in his modus generalissimus.

---

[74] Siger de Courtrai, p. 148: "hoc quod dicit 'coniunctiva' tangit modum disponentis quia coniungere disponere est, vel per hoc quod dicit 'vim vel ordinem demonstrans' circumloquitur modum significandi specificum ad illa duo, scilicet, modum unitatis, et hoc modo in diffinitione verbi circumloquitur modum fieri esse vel motus peragendi vel patiendi".

[75] Thomas of Erfurt, #170: "modus significandi essentialis generalissimus coniunctionis est modus significandi per modum coniungentis duo extrema".

[76] Thomas of Erfurt, #170: "sumitur iste modus significandi a proprietate coniungentis, et unientis in rebus extra".

Donatus   described three accidents in the conjunction, *i.e.* potestas, figura and ordo: we saw in the adverb, to which Donatus had attributed three accidents, namely significatio, comparatio and figura, that one accident, significatio, became for Thomas the material from which he created his two subaltern modes and their modi specialissimi. Similarly, we find that Thomas's treatment of Donatus's accidents in the conjunction is very similar, *i.e.* two accidents, figura and ordo, to which Thomas adds species, become his accidental modes, and the third, *i.e.* potestas, he uses to furnish the material for his modi subalterni and specialissimi. It was also seen in dealing with the adverb that Donatus used significatio to enumerate the different types of adverb without listing them exhaustively, and in the case of the conjunction, we find that Donatus used potestas to enumerate the different types of conjunction, which he divides into five, namely disjunctive, copulative, expletive, causal and rational,[77] all of which reappear in Thomas as modi specialissimi of the conjunction. A further feature of Thomas's organisation reveals the great consistency in their procedure, whatever our criticisms may be of their criteria; we saw that significatio in the subaltern modes of the adverb was constituted as a special mode of determining the verb or participle by virtue of its own meaning or of the modes of signifying of the verb or participle. Similarly the subaltern modes of the conjunction are divided by means of their meaning or by means of the mutual relationship between the members that the conjunction is used to link, and as such 'potestas' becomes a special mode of joining.[78] Like significatio 'potestas' is not an accidental mode but becomes an essential mode to classify the different types of adverb.[79] There are therefore two subaltern modes of the conjunction, the first of which is the mode of joining by way of meaning and the second is the mode of joining by way of the relationship between the members.[80]

The first subaltern mode is the mode of joining two members which

---

[77]   Donatus (*Ars Minor*): "potestas coniunctionum quot species habet? Quinque. Copulativas, disiunctivas, expletivas, causales, rationales".

[78]   Thomas of Erfurt, #171: "potestas in coniunctione consistit in speciali modo coniungendi".

[79]   Michel de Marbais: "potestas est quidam modus significandi datus coniunctioni ad designandum rem sub modo essendi vel ratione coniungentis in ratione copulantis vel disiungentis vel explentis vel in ratione cause vel effectus vel antecendentis et consequentis" (Thurot, p. 193).

[80]   Thomas of Erfurt, #171: "dividitur iste modus coniungentis duo extrema in modum coniungentis duo extrema per vim, et in modum coniungentis duo extrema per ordinem".

have no dependence[81] on each other, such as two substantives, two adjectives or even two sentences, which have no necessary mutual relationship.[82] This subaltern mode is divided into two modi specialissimi, the first one of which is the mode of signifying by means of the mode of joining two members together with regard to a third member of a construction,[83] and these constitute the copulative conjunctions: the second modus specialissimus is the mode of joining two members together but by distinguishing them from the third member of the construction,[84] and these constitute the disjunctive conjunctions.

The second subaltern mode is the mode of joining two members which are drawn together by virtue of their mutual relationship,[85] and this mode is divided into two modi specialissimi; the first modus specialissimus is the mode of joining two members according to the relationship they derive from the first member,[86] and this mode constitutes the causal conjunctions which expresses the relationship of cause and effect, e.g. "Socrates currit, ergo movetur"; the second modus specialissimus is the mode of joining two members according to the relationship they derive from the second member[87] and this mode constitutes the rational conjunctions, which express the relationship of antecedent and consequence, e.g. "terra inter ponitur inter solem et lunam; ergo luna eclipsatur".

Traditional grammar divides the conjunction into coordinating and subordinating: the conjunctions outlined in Thomas's modi subalterni and specialissimi are all of the coordinating type: Thomas's account of

---

[81] Thomas of Erfurt, #172: "modus significandi per modum coniungentis duo extrema per vim est modus significandi, uniendi duo extrema, quae inter se dependentiam non habent".
[82] Thomas of Erfurt, #172: "duo substantiva, vel duo adiectiva, vel duas orationes, inter se ordinem non habentes".
[83] Thomas of Erfurt, #172: "primus est modus significandi per modum coniungentis duo extrema inter se, et respectu alicuius tertii. Et iste modus constituit coniunctiones copulativas".
[84] Thomas of Erfurt, #172: "secundus modus est modus significandi per modum coniungentis duo extrema inter se, distinguendo ea respectu tertii. Et hic modus constituit coniunctiones disiunctivas".
[85] Thomas of Erfurt, #173: "modus significandi per modum coniungentis duo extrema secundum ordinem est modus unientis duo extrema per ordinem inclinata."
[86] Thomas of Erfurt, #173: "primus est modus significandi per modum coniungentis duo extrema secundum ordinem ex parte ante se tenentia. Et hic modus constituit coniunctiones causales".
[87] Thomas of Erfurt, #173: "secundus est modus significandi per modum coniungentis duo extrema secundum ordinem ex parte consequentis se habentia. Et hic modus constituit coniunctiones rationales".

the conjunction, in so far as a normative and even more so as a descriptive grammar of Latin is concerned, is very incomplete since he says nothing of the subordinating conjunctions, nor does he say anything at all of those conjunctions which require a certain mood.[88]

We can summarise the essential modes of the conjunction thus:[89] every conjunction which is used to join two elements[90] does so in one of two ways, *i.e.* by virtue either of its meaning or of the relationship between the two elements. If it joins by virtue of its meaning, the conjunction joins the two elements with regard to a third member of the construction, *e.g.* "Socrates et Plato currunt", or else it joins the two elements but distinguishes them with regard to a third member, *e.g.* "Socrates vel Plato currit". If, however, the conjunction joins by virtue of the mutual relationship between the words it joins, it does so either by stating the relationship which derives either from the first and is transferred to the second, or from the second to the first. Thus, just as the modus generalissimus is divided into the modi subalterni and the modi specialissimi, so the conjunction is divided according to its meaning or the relationship between the words it joins: the conjunction according to its meaning is divided into the copulative and disjunctive conjunctions, and the conjunction according to the mutual relationships may be considered as the causal and rational conjunctions.

Modus significandi accidentalis

At the very end of his description of the adverb, Thomas had stated, almost as an afterthought, that the accidental modes of the adverb, comparatio, species and figura, were the same as in the nomen. Similarly, in the conjunction, Thomas posits three accidental modes, *i.e.* species, figura and ordo; Donatus had posited potestas, figura and ordo as accidents of the conjunction, but of these, Thomas included potestas as a feature of the subaltern essential mode. Of the three accidental modes, of the conjunction as described by Thomas, species and figura are derived from the same properties as are the same features in the

---

[88]   It is interesting to see the influence of logic on sentence structure in the Modistic scheme: the subordinating conjunction, for instance, is omitted since it plays very little part in logic.

[89]   *Cf.* Appendix B, pp. 378-379: the diagram explains the structure of the Modistic conception of the coniunctio.

[90]   Thomas of Erfurt, #174: "omnis coniunctio aut coniungit duo extrema, aut duo extrema coniuncta ornat. Si coniungit, hoc est dupliciter; aut per vim, aut per ordinem".

nomen.[91] Thomas takes, therefore, these same features in the nomen as his yardstick and describes the derivational aspects of the adverb and conjunction according to the same pattern in the nomen[92] – they are, however, absolute modes and the pars in question can therefore have no part in any syntagm by virtue of the accidental modes of species and figura.

Donatus's third accident, ordo,[93] is included by Thomas as an accidental mode of the conjunction; this is an active mode of signifying by means of which the conjunction *consignifies* the order of the members that it is joining together[94] – this refers to the word order of the conjunction in relation of these members, and it is by virtue of 'ordo' that the conjunction is pre-posed, post-posed or either pre-posed or post-posed to the members it is used to link together.[95] There are two possible explanations for the inclusion of 'ordo' as an accidental mode – unfortunately Thomas does not expatiate on this aspect of the conjunction, and we are perforce compelled to speculate ourselves. Donatus, we must remember, described ordo as an accident, though it does not necessarily follow that whatever Donatus called an accident will constitute for the Modistae an accidental mode. A much more likely explanation, and one hinted at by Thomas,[96] is a reference to the external world of things, *i.e.* just as things can be linked together, so can words and sentences be linked together. We have already seen that Thomas is prepared to make word order a relevant feature in grammar; we are, however, no longer dealing with the signification of the conjunction, but with the *consignification,* which we have elsewhere described as functional or syntactic meaning, therefore if word order is a relevant syntactic feature, it will be so by means of consignification, and therefore ordo will be an accidental mode, (a) because it cannot be a subaltern essential mode since it does not create any type

---

[91]   Thomas of Erfurt, #175: "de specie et figura in coniunctione idem sicut in nomine dicendum est; ab eisdem enim proprietatibus sumuntur utrobique".
[92]   Thomas does not, however, give us any examples of species or figura as accidental modes of the conjunction.
[93]   Donatus (*Ars Minor*): "ordo coniunctionum in quo est? Quia aut praepositivae coniunctiones sunt, ut: ac, ast; aut subiunctivae, ut: que, autem; aut communes, ut: et, igitur, ergo".
[94]   Thomas of Erfurt, #175: "est ordo in coniunctione modus significandi activus, quo mediante coniunctio ordinem extremorum consignificat".
[95]   Thomas of Erfurt, #175: "ratione cuius ordinis aut coniunctio praeponitur tantum, aut postponitur, aut indifferenter praeponitur et postponitur extremis coniunctis".
[96]   Thomas of Erfurt, #175: "ordo in coniunctione sumitur ab ordine in rebus ab extra".

of conjunction, and (b) if it is syntactically functional, it must be a respective mode, and in Thomas's scheme only accidental modes can be respective; so ordo, which establishes the syntactic valence of the relative word order of the conjunction in relation to the partes orationis that it joins together, must be an accidental mode.[97] This fits it well into the Modistic descriptive scheme in that an accidental mode expresses variations additional to the 'essence' of the pars which occur from without; the essence of the conjunction (though this stretches the whole concept of 'essence' to a very flimsy length) is to join words or sentences together and this, i.e. ordo, is the one permitted variation to this essence apart from the derivational items previously mentioned.

C. PRAEPOSITIO

The Modistae were quite clearly dissatisfied with the definition of the preposition handed down from the Greek and Latin grammarians. Thrax had defined the preposition as "a part of speech placed before other parts of speech in syntactical combinations and in word formation";[98] this is echoed almost exactly by Priscian in his definition.[99]

This definition was unsatisfactory to the Modistae because of its confusion of syntax and word-formation which was unacceptable to the Modistae as a result of their theory that each and every word must have its own meaning. Donatus's definition of the preposition[100] was even more unacceptable to the Modistae, since it too does not take into consideration the meaning of the preposition considered as a word, but tends to treat the preposition more as a separable and inseparable prefix.

The preposition was conceived by the Modistae as the means of designating the relationship which certain substantial properties have towards the act, some being used to express the fact that the substance

---

[97]   Priscian's reasons for ordo being considered an accident of the conjunction should be noted in this context, cf.: Priscian (XVI, 15-16): "ordo accidere dicitur coniunctionibus, qui communis est paene omnibus dictionibus. Quaedam enim naturaliter praeponuntur, ut praepositiones casualibus et adverbia peraque verbis ... Est tamen quando auctoritas praepostere his utitur ... similiter igitur coniunctiones pleraeque tam praeponi quam supponi possunt. Sunt tamen quaedam quae semper praeponuntur, ut 'at, ac, vel' ... aliae quae semper supponuntur, ut 'que, ne' ... aliae paene omnes indifferenter et praeponi et supponi possunt, ut 'et, atque'".

[98]   R. H. Robins, A. and M., p. 40.

[99]   Priscian (XIV.1):" est praepositio pars orationis indeclinabilis, quae praeponitur aliis partibus vel appositione vel compositione".

[100]   Donatus (Ars Minor): "praepositio ... est ... pars orationis quae praeposita aliis partibus orationis significationem earum aut complet aut mutat aut minuit".

is undergoing an action and others to express the limit of the action.[101] Siger pointed out in his introductory remarks to the preposition that the preposition was used with the accusative, dative, *etc.* to express the relationship between the nominal, *i.e.* nominal form and the act, *i.e.* the verbal form. The nominative and vocative do not require such a link since their relationship to the act is quite different;[102] the preposition was devised to designate transitivity, but the nominative and vocative must be intransitive.[103] The terms 'transitive' and 'intransitive' have already been discussed, but it must be pointed out once more that these terms were used by Thomas in particular to describe the fundamental types of constructions and the relationships between the *two* constituent members. An intransitive construction is of the type NV, *e.g.* "Socrates currit", in which the relationship between the nomen 'Socrates' and the verb 'currit' is realised by means of 'compositio' which is an accidental mode of the verb; a transitive construction is of the type VN, *e.g.* "legit librum", but it would be possible to have a transitive construction of the type VpN, *e.g.* "currit ad campum", which could be used to illustrate Siger's argument of verbs being either unaidedly or aidedly transitive, but in both cases the relationship between the verb and the post-posed oblique nominal form is realised by means of 'significatio', an accidental mode of the verb and the counter-balance to 'compositio'. Thomas recognises the feasibility of such a construction[104] and includes it, without illustration or further discussion, among his transitive constructions 'actuum'.[105] Siger also explains that some verbs which are unaidedly (vehementer) transitive do not require a preposition to link them to the case form, *e.g.* 'amo', but there are other verbs which are not unaidedly (non vehementer) transitive, *e.g.* 'venio', and require a preposition to link them to the case-form and for this purpose prepositions were invented.[106] Siger

---

[101]   G. Wallerand, *Op. cit.*, p. (55).
[102]   Siger de Courtrai, p. 150: "non autem nominativo nec vocativo, quia actus de se unit se ex parte ante nominativo et vocativo".
[103]   Siger de Courtrai, p. 150: "praepositiones sunt ad retorquendum casualem ad actum et iterum quia omnes praepositiones inventae sunt propter habitudines transitivas denotandas ... nunc nominativus et vocativus sunt intransitivi".
[104]   Thomas of Erfurt, #214: "principia propria congruitatis huius constructionis 'percutio Socratem' sunt duo modi conformes, scilicet: modus dependentis vel transeuntis, sub modo ut alterum et modus terminantis sub modo ut quem. Si ille modus ut quem sit praepositione contractus, tunc similiter modus transeuntis sub modo ut alterum proportionabiliter est contrahendus".
[105]   These constructions and technical terms are discussed at greater length in Chapter VII.
[106]   Siger de Courtrai, p. 150: "unde quaedam sunt verba quae sunt ita vehementis

admits, in saying all this, that he is following Priscian, a fact which explains perhaps the more formal nature of his statement of Latin syntax.

Thomas denies that the preposition was devised just to express transitivity, since there are some verbs which require the preposition but which express no transitiveness,[107] e.g. "sum in domo", and indeed in an example such as "annulus ex auro", a non-classical construct, the nomen 'annulus' requires a preposition and yet cannot express any transition. The preposition was devised, Thomas argues, to provide the link between the act and the case-forms, i.e. accusative and ablative; it will be remembered that when Thomas discussed the accidental mode of case in the nomen he defined the accusative as analogous to 'quem' and the ablative as analogous to 'quo', but these cases are both referable to the act by means of a preposition,[108] and such a union is made by means of prepositions which govern the accusative or ablative.[109] Therefore, Thomas argues, the preposition was created in the first place to link up with the case-form and then to restrict the case-form to its relation with the act, i.e. the verbs.[110]

The preposition for the Modistae is therefore a pars orationis which signifies by means of the mode of turning the substance back to the act[111] which is a semantic restatement of the more formal definition that preposition and a nomen can create adverbial phrases and combine with a verb to make an endocentric construction with the verb as the head of such a construction. Siger admits that Priscian perceived many similarities between the adverb and preposition[112] which Siger agreed

---

transitus quod se et immediate possunt transire in casuale, ut: amo . . ., et quaedam sunt quae non sunt vehementis transitus, quod etiam possunt de se et immediate transire in casuale, ut: venio . . ., propter quod praepositiones adinventae fuerunt ut, ipsis mediantibus, casuale retorquatur ad actus tales".

[107] Thomas of Erfurt, #176: "quaedam verba praepositiones exigunt, quae tamen nullam habent transitionem, nec velocem, nec tardam, ut dicendo, 'sum in domo' ".

[108] Thomas of Erfurt, #176: "accusativus est modus significandi ut quem, contrahibilis per modum ut ad quem . . . similiter ablativus est modus significandi per modum ut quo, contrahibilis ut a quo".

[109] Thomas of Erfurt, #176: "talis coarctatio casualis fit per praepositiones accusativo casui, vel ablativo deservientes".

[110] Thomas of Erfurt, #176: "praepositio inventa est, ut primo modum casualem contrahat et coarctet; et deinde casualem ad actum reducat".

[111] Michel de Marbais: "prepositio est pars orationis significans per modum retorquentis substantiam ad actum" (Thurot, p. 195).

[112] Priscian (XVI.31): "adverbia quidem et sine casibus et cum casibus proferri possunt . . . praepositiones vero suam significationem servantes semper casibus adiunguntur, ut 'per', . . . quando adverbium est, mutat significationem et pro 'valde' accipitur".

would be possible as a result of the general essential mode of the pre-position.[113] Both Siger and Thomas are more specific than Michel in their definition of the preposition.[114] Thomas defines it as the pars orationis which signifies by means of the mode of being adjoined or next to another case-form but referring it back to the act;[115] Siger echoes this[116] in his specific mode but states more specifically in his definition the case-forms to be considered. Siger's habit of following Priscian closely, as far as the indeclinable partes are concerned, stands him in good stead, because he is able to make a much more economic statement than either Thomas or Priscian by means of his specific mode, which states succinctly what was Priscian's intention in saying that the prepositions are next to case-forms only and in particular only to the accusative and ablative – as far as Latin is concerned.

As a result of their theory that every word must have its own indi-vidual meaning, the Modistae took strong 'exception' to the statement of their predecessors that one of the functions of the prepositions was to be used as a prefix in word-formation. Michel states categorically that such words are not prepositions.[117] This is clearly a false identi-fication of the bound morpheme with free word-classes and although the Modistae did not express it so formally, they denied the status of word to such forms because they signify nothing and are therefore not words nor do they possess modes of signifying.[118] According to the predecessors of the Modistae, a preposition could be such in one of two ways, i.e. by apposition or by composition; the Modistae argued, rightly so, that the first type represents the genuine preposition since it retains its modus generalissimus of expressing the relationship between the sub-

---

[113] Siger de Courtrai, p. 151: "iste modus significandi (generalis) potest haberi per Priscianum qui vult quod praepositiones disponant aliquo modo actum sicut adverbia, unde plurimas ponit convenientias Priscianus ... inter praepositiones et adverbia".

[114] Martin of Dacia is similarly quite specific, e.g. #175: "praepositio significat per modum retorquentis casuale ad actum vel prout illud casuale se habet in ratione principii respectu illius actus vel in ratione termini respectu illius actus".

[115] Thomas of Erfurt, #176: "est praepositio pars orationis, significans per mo-dum adiacentis alteri casuali, ipsum contrahens, et ad actum reducens".

[116] Siger de Courtrai, p. 151: "modus specificus est modus significandi per mo-dum retorquentis casuale ad actum casuale inquam se habens ut 'quem' vel ut 'quo' ".

[117] Michel de Marbais: "omnis prepositio addita parti per compositionem non est vere prepositio" (Thurot, p. 195).

[118] Thomas of Erfurt, #180: "praepositiones in compositione non sunt verae prae-positiones, quia per se nihil significant, cum non sint per se dictiones, nec etiam per se modum significandi habent".

stantial element and the act,[119] but the second kind cannot be a preposition since it merely completes, changes or reduces the meaning of the word with which it is compounded and loses its real function as a preposition[120] by acting as a prefix.[121] Siger comes to the support of Priscian arguing that Priscian did not really mean to suggest that such prefixes were prepositions, because as prefixes they lose their meaning as words, and cannot therefore be partes orationis, but Siger argues that Priscian merely suggested the similarity between two forms, one of which is a preposition and the other a bound morpheme used as a prefix.[122]

Modus significandi essentialis

In the preceding section, it was seen by the definitions of Siger and Thomas that for Siger the essential modes of the preposition, hidden beneath Modistic semanticisation of the formal definitions the Modistae inherited from Thrax and Priscian, consist of a general mode, which, as in the other indeclinable partes, represents a common feature of syntactic relationship by means of the mode of disposition and a specific mode which is the mode of signifying by means of the mode of uniting the case-form with the act, *i.e.* the verb.This is substantially the same as Thomas's modus generalissimus which is defined as the mode of signifying by means of the mode of adjacency to some case-form and referring it back to the act.[123] As in the case of the other indeclinable partes, Thomas justifies his definition of the modus generalissimus by reference to the world of reality, and the source of such a modus generalissimus is to be found in the property of determination and limitation present

[119]   Thomas of Erfurt, #179: "per appositionem, cum praepositio servat sibi vim divionis, et manet praepositio per eius modum significandi essentialem generalissimum. Et haec est vera praepositio, et ab aliis partibus orationis distincta".
[120]   Thomas of Erfurt, #179: "praepositio (in compositione) non retrahit, nec retorquet, sed complet, aut mutat, aut minuit".
[121]   Thomas of Erfurt, #180: "sed adduntur aliis dictionibus tamquam syllabicae adiectiones, ut 'met', 'pte', et huiusmodi".
[122]   Siger de Courtrai, p. 151: "manifestum est quod non est pars secundum intentionem Prisciani, et si non est pars, non est praepositio, propter quod manifeste patet quod talia addita aliquibus non sunt praepositiones secundum intentionem Prisciani, tamen talia quae sunt praepositiones, si cadunt cum eadem parte cum illis cum quibus componuntur, habent aliquam similitudinem cum praepositionibus veris".
[123]   Thomas of Erfurt, #176: "modus significandi essentialis generalissimus praepositionis est modus significandi per modum adiacentis alteri casuali ipsum contrahens, et ad actum retorquens".

in the external world.[124] This relationship between the case-form and the act can be described by means of the following diagram:

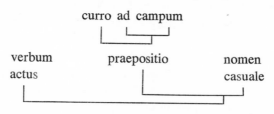

Modus subalternus

Donatus ascribed only one accident to the preposition,[125] *i.e.* casus, by means of which he stated the different kinds of preposition, *i.e.* those prepositions which are used with the accusative, those with the ablative and those with both cases; Thomas used this accident of casus[126] as he had used Donatus's accidents in the other declinable and indeclinable partes to establish his subaltern modes, and so casus comes to constitute a special mode of referring and junction.[127] There are, therefore, three subaltern modes of the preposition, the first of which is the mode of signifying by means of the mode of contracting and joining the accusative,[128] the second by means of the mode of contracting and joining the ablative[129] and the third by means of the mode of contracting and joining either the accusative or ablative.[130]

The subaltern modes are divided into their modi specialissimi; once more Thomas resorts to an exhaustive inventory in order to compensate for his inability to semanticise, and we find as elsewhere that Thomas tends to provide a more detailed list of a pars orationis whenever he is

---

[124] Thomas of Erfurt, #176: "iste modus praepositionis sumitur a proprietate determinationis et coarctationis in rebus".
[125] Donatus (*Ars Minor*): "praepositioni quod accidunt? Unum ... Casus tantum ... Accusativus et ablativus".
[126] *Cf.* Appendix B, pp. 380-381 for a diagram of the structure of the Praepositio.
[127] Thomas of Erfurt, #177: "casus in praepositione consistit in speciali modo contrahendi et retorquendi. Michel de Marbais: modus significandi accidentalis (casus) dicitur modus significandi retorquentis casuale ad actum in ratione termini terminantis vel in ratione principii initiantis". (Thurot, p. 197).
[128] Thomas of Erfurt, #177: "primus est modus significandi per modum contrahentis et retorquentis accusativum tantum".
[129] Thomas of Erfurt, #177: "secundus modus est modus significandi per modum contrahentis et retorquentis ablativum tantum".
[130] Thomas of Erfurt, #177: "tertius modus est modus significandi per modum contrahentis et retorquentis accusativum et ablativum, scilicet utrumque indifferenter".

unable to provide a semanticised formal statement – formal definitions take a back seat in the declinable partes but are resorted to in syntactic form much more frequently in the indeclinable partes, when semantics can clearly offer no satisfactory explanation of a feature or when the various species of a pars cannot be described in terms of meaning. The first subaltern mode, *i.e.* the mode by means of contracting the accusative, is divided into thirty modi specialissimi which constitute thirty different types of preposition, *e.g.* 'apud', 'ante', *etc.*, all of which have their different modes of contraction with the case-form;[131] the second subaltern mode is divided into fifteen different types of preposition, *e.g.* 'a', 'ab', 'absque', *etc.*;[132] the third subaltern mode is divided into four modi specialissimi which constitute four types of preposition which can contract with either the accusative or ablative, *e.g.* 'in', 'sub', 'super', 'subter'.

We see then that just as the modus generalissimus of the preposition is divided into three subaltern modes which themselves are divided into various modi specialissimi, so the preposition is divided into three groups each of which contains an exhaustive list of its constituents, *i.e.* into prepositions which are used with the accusative, into prepositions which are used with the ablative, and into prepositions which are used with both the accusative and ablative.[133] Further the prepositions used with the accusative are divided into thirty types of prepositions, the prepositions with the ablative into fifteen different types, and the prepositions with both the accusative and ablative into four different types.

D. INTERIECTIO

An important change made by Latin grammarians in the list of word-classes was the separation of the interjection from the adverb;[134] the Greeks had included the interjection as a sub-class of the adverb,[135] since they both determine the verb, even if the verb is understood. The

---

131   Thomas of Erfurt, #177: "quae diversos habent modos contrahendi casuale".
132   This means that there is one mode, one modus specialissimus for each preposition.
133   Thomas of Erfurt, #178: "praepositio simpliciter sumpta dividitur in praepositiones deservientes accusativo tantum, et in praepositiones deservientes utrique".
134   Siger de Courtrai, p. 152: "quia interiectiones habent significationem verbi et non adverbia, ideo Latini separant eam ab adverbio et ab aliis partibus orationis".
135   Siger de Courtrai, p. 152: "Graeci ponebant interiectionem sub adverbio quia interiectiones determinant ipsa verba expressa sive subintellecta".

first grammarian, we are told,[136] to make of the interjection a separate pars orationis was Remmius Palaemon, and this change was also made by Donatus and Priscian; Priscian established that the interjection required no syntactic union necessarily with any part of the sentence, and so it came to be defined as a pars orationis which signifies a state of mind.[137]

The Modistae retained Priscian's and Donatus's[138] definition, and Michel de Marbais indeed reproduced Donatus's definition almost word for word.[139] Donatus had ascribed to the interjection only one accident, significatio, which creates the different types of interjection to express the different emotions, i.e. joy, fear, admiration, etc. and we shall see that Thomas uses significatio, as he had used other accidents in the other indeclinable partes, as a device to create different types of interjection – the interesting thing being that this time he bypasses the modus subalternus completely, and uses Donatus's significatio directly as the source of the modi specialissimi which are the modes of signifying for the different kinds of interjection.[140]

The Modistae mark, however, a retrograde step from Donatus and Priscian – at least Martin and Thomas do, by insisting on the intimate relationship between the verb and interjection. It has already been stated that one of the reasons for the Greeks including the interjection as a sub-class of the adverb was its relationship with the verb; Priscian freed the interjection from such a restricted function on the formal grounds of syntactic freedom, but in the Middle Ages we find grammarians such as Martin of Dacia and Thomas of Erfurt insisting once more on its close association with the verb.[141] Thomas defined the interjection as a pars orationis which signifies by means of the mode of determining something, i.e. verb or participle by representing an attitude or change

---

[136]   R. H. Robins, A. and M., p. 58.
[137]   Priscian (XV.40): "romanarum artium scriptores separatim hanc partem ab adverbiis accipere, quia videtur affectum habere in se verbi et plenam motus animi significationem, etiamsi non addatur verbum, demonstrare".
[138]   Donatus (Ars Minor): "interiectio ... est pars orationis significans mentis affectum voce incondita".
[139]   Michel de Marbais: "interiectio est pars orationis significans rem suam per modum animam afficientis" (Thurot, p. 197).
[140]   This refers to the different allocations of features to the subaltern and accidental modes by the Modistae in contrast to Donatus's allocation of the same features.
[141]   Martin of Dacia: "modus significandi essentialis generalis interiectionis est modus adiacentis alteri, significantis per modum fieri, afficientis subiectum in quo est ille actus".

of mind;[142] he justifies this by recourse to Donatus's definition of the interjection,[143] but it seems much more likely that he was led to stress its affiliation to the verb as a result of the argument, that 'every sentence must have a verb'. Siger has been accused of conservatism,[144] of being too faithful to his classical models, but in the case of the interjection he has provided us with a definition which is much more satisfactory, if we can accept any semantic definition of a grammatical category as satisfactory – at least he has not stepped out of character, and so we find that, as in the other indeclinable partes, his general mode postulates the syntactic function which the interjection shares with the other indeclinables, and his specific mode becomes the defini- of the particular pars. We can say of the interjection that its general mode functions by means of the modus disponentis and that it fulfils its specific function by means of the modus specificus, i.e. by signifying by means of the mode of affecting the mind;[145] therefore, as Siger points out,[146] the interjection signifies a concept of the mind because speech cannot express what has not first been conceived by the mind – but it does not do this by determining the verb or participle in particular.

Modus significandi essentialis

There is little need to dwell at any length on the essential modes of the interjection; as has just been pointed out, Siger, as in all the other partes orationis, divides the essential mode into general and specific – the general mode signifies by means of the mode of disposition and the specific mode signifies, i.e. functions syntactically, as postulated in the general mode, by means of the mode of affecting the mind.[147] Siger's specific mode is normally the equivalent to Thomas's modus generalissimus in the indeclinables, but it has been suggested that in the inter-

---

[142]   Thomas of Erfurt, #181: "interiectio est pars orationis significans per modum determinantis alterum quod est verbum vel participium, affectus vel motus animae repraesentans".

[143]   Thomas of Erfurt, #181: "hoc voluit Donatus significare, cum dixit quod 'interiectio est pars orationis significans mentis affectum voce incognita', id est, conceptum mentis sub voce non deliberata, sed quasi abrupte prolata".

[144]   G. Wallerand, Op. cit., p. (72).

[145]   Siger de Courtrai, p. 152: "generalis est significare per modum disponentis ... specialis est significare per modum afficientis animam".

[146]   Siger de Courtrai, p. 152: "licet interiectio significet mentis conceptum quia nihil est per vocem significatum nisi prius fuerit conceptus ab intellectu, tamen illum conceptum significat interiectio per modum afficientis animam".

[147]   Siger de Courtrai, p. 152: "specialis est significare per modum afficientis animam".

jection there is a divergence of opinion, and Thomas defines his modus generalissimus as the mode of determining the verb or participle and representing different states of mind;[148] the mind is affected by different emotions, *e.g.* sorrow, fear, joy, *etc.*, and the interjections serve to express these different states of mind.

Modus specialissimus

Donatus ascribed one accident to the interjection, *i.e.* significatio,[149] by means of which he established the various types of interjection. In the other indeclinables Thomas had used Donatus's accidents as the source of his subaltern modes, which were the general types of the pars in question to be refined into the different types by means of the modi specialissimi. In the interjection, however, Thomas dispenses with the subaltern modes, and divides the modus generalissimus directly into four modi specialissimi, which constitute four different types of interjection; once more, Thomas falls back on a purely semantic analysis of the Latin interjection, rather than develop the theory of the interjection (if this is indeed possible) as a feature of general grammar, and little is, therefore, to be achieved by a detailed analysis of Thomas's modi specialissimi. There are four modi specialissimi, which represent four types of interjection, all of which signify by means of the mode of determining the verb or participle, and each expresses a different state of mind,[150] *i.e.* sorrow, *e.g.* 'heu'; joy, *e.g.* 'evax'; admiration, *e.g.* 'papae'; and fear, *e.g.* 'deeh'. All of these are derived from the same property as Donatus's accident of significatio, and the significatio of the interjection becomes a special mode of determining the verb or participle by representing some special state of mind.[151]

---

[148] Thomas of Erfurt, #181: "modus significandi essentialis generalissimus interiectionis est modus significandi per modum determinantis alterum, quod est verbum, vel participium, affectiones animi repraesentans".
[149] Donatus (*Ars Minor*): "interiectioni quid accidit? Tantum significatio".
[150] Thomas of Erfurt, #182: "primus est modus significandi interiectionis per modum determinantis alterum, motum doloris vel tristitiae in anima repraesentans ... secundus modus est modus significandi per modum determinantis alterum, motum gaudii vel laetitiae in animam repraesentans ... tertius modus est modus significandi per modum determinantis alterum, motum admirationis in anima repraesentans ... quartus modus est modus significandi per modum determinantis alterum, motum terroris, vel metum repraesentans".
[151] Thomas of Erfurt, #182: "significatio interiectionis consistit in speciali modo determinandi, specialem motum in anima repraesentans".

VII

SYNTAX

A. DIASYNTHETICA

The Modistae used only two of the traditional divisions of grammar, *i.e.* Etymologia and Diasynthetica, in their descriptive process; Siger and Martin of Dacia did not in fact use these terms, but Martin certainly, and Siger (it seems reasonable to say) might well have (if his work had been complete) divided his material according to this dichotomy, Etymologia being the analysis of the partes orationis in terms of their modes of signifying, and Diasynthetica the theory of the syntax of these partes orationis.

There is a curious division and also association between these two parts of Modistic grammar; the two parts are actually kept strictly apart – indeed Roos points out[1] that the separation is so severe that, of the extant manuscripts of Martin's grammatical treatise, some contain no section on syntax. On the other hand the whole Modistic theory of syntax is based on the modes of signifying, which were in the first place created as a device for describing the partes orationis alone, so that grammatical concord, a purely syntactical feature, is expressed in terms of the inter-relationships between the accidental modes of the partes involved and the other major syntactical relationship too, *i.e.* government is expressed by means of the modes of signifying.

Scholars have maintained that syntax was the main object of mediaeval grammatical writings, but it does seem that the wish was often stronger than the deed.[2] As in modern linguistic theory, syntax was not

---

[1] H. Roos, *Die Modi Significandi*, p. 139.

[2] Roos has defined the treatises on the modes of signifying as 'Lehre der Wortklassen', and it does seem that the Modistae were for the most part content with their analysis of the partes orationis: a similar gap can be found in the work of many modern linguists who rarely venture beyond their phonological studies. It is also quite clear that mediaeval syntactic theories do merit careful and detailed study, and contain much of interest to the modern linguist, and Thurot is there-

entirely satisfactorily handled by the Modistae if the lacunae in their work are any guide, but obviously for different reasons; it may well have been that semantics produced, by Modistic standards, satisfactory criteria in defining the partes orationis, but semantics alone are clearly unsatisfactory for syntax, so that if logic is excluded, the only criteria left to the grammarian are formal criteria, and the Modistae did not make any systematic use of these in describing their syntax. Mention has just been made of the association between Etymologia and Diasynthetica despite their actual physical separation; this is in fact a very important achievement, since the interpenetration of levels, though not practised by all modern schools of linguistics, is looked upon by many scholars [3] as an important and very necessary feature of linguistic description.

If we take Thomas's section on Diasynthetica as typical of Modistic syntactic description, we would find that it can be, for purposes of analysis, divided into four parts, *e.g.* the principles of construing (principia construendi), construction (constructio), congruity (congruitas) and completion (perfectio); the principles of construing are clearly based on Aristotle's four causes of material, formal, efficient and final.[4] Thomas uses these principles in the analysis of the three stages of syntax, *i.e.* constructio, congruitas, and perfectio, so that we have two interrelated processes, *i.e.* (i) constructio represents the combinations of constructibles, congruitas the proper congruence of such combinations, and perfectio completes the process of expressing a mental concept, because perfectio, in addition to the requirements of the constructio, calls for a complete construction to contain a suppositum and appo-

---

fore quite wrong in his assessment of mediaeval syntactic theories, *cf.* Ch. Thurot, *Op. cit.*, p. 237.

[3]   *Cf.* the work of scholars such as K. L. Pike, W. S. Allen, J. R. Firth, M. A. K. Halliday, N. A. Chomsky.

[4]   Martin's section on syntax is quite different from Thomas's but this is much more a matter of organisation than grammatical doctrine; indeed we find in Thomas's section on syntax too that his work shows the refinements of time. Martin's syntactic theory can be divided roughly into the same four parts, though he refers to the first part not as 'principia construendi', which is Thomas's term, but as 'principia constructionis', and similarly he does not speak of 'passiones sermonis', which is Thomas's term, but rather of 'passiones grammaticales'. He does not dwell at any great length on the transitive constructions but goes into some detail on the intransitive constructions. He does not however establish the actuum and personarum sub-type of constructions, except once in an Appendix in which he refers to a construction such as "similis tibi" as a transitive personarum construction. It should be understood that he does describe these types of construction, but not in these terms.

situm, *i.e.* subject and predicate, and (ii) each construction is subject to analysis in terms of the four principles of construing, *i.e.* the material represents the members of the potential construction, the formal represents the construction itself, the efficient represents the 'congruity', *i.e.* the mutual appropriateness (congruitas)[5] of the construction, and the final the completed construction which has satisfied all the requirements for the expression of a compound concept of the mind. Thomas completes his section on syntax by a more detailed description of the different types of construction and then by an explanation of congruitas and perfectio as features in linguistic description rather than their application to any particular type of sentence.

This type of syntactical theory represents a great change from the work of the predecessors of the Modistae; Peter Helias, Robert Kilwardby, *etc.* wrote their grammars in the form of commentaries on Priscian, which means that they were, of necessity, much more restricted to Latin syntax, whereas the Modistae, whatever their failings and inability to escape their environment, did attempt to create something quite new in the form of a syntactic theory of their own in which we can see the burgeonings of a syntactical theory which contains features to be found in the analytical procedures of certain modern linguists.[6] In this, they are much more original than in their analyses of the partes orationis which were mere semanticisations of the formal categories of Priscian's grammar.

B. SYNTAX IN THE MIDDLE AGES

Scholars are agreed that there was, in the Middle Ages, a considerable increase in the study of syntax[7] since it is a part of grammar which is susceptible to rules and principles; it would be quite wrong to suggest[8] that, apart from commentaries on Priscian by grammarians such as Peter Helias and Robert Kilwardby, there were few[9] systematic treatises

---

[5] 'Congruitas' seems to have been a general relational term used by the Modistae to state the relations of concord, governmental concord, government (or rection), collocation, colligation and context of situation.

[6] *Cf.* K. L. Pike, re the interpenetration of levels, and R. S. Wells and other Americans linguists for the theory of Immediate Constituents.

[7] Ch. Thurot, *Op. cit.*, p. 213.

[8] *Cf.* Ch. Thurot, *Op. cit.*, p. 237.

[9] A closer examination of the manuscript tradition is in process; this will undoubtedly compel us to alter our views about the extent of systematic treatments of syntax since it has already revealed a large number of independent treatises on syntax.

on syntax [10] – teaching manuals such as Alexander de Villedieu's [11] are not considered in this context since they can hardly be said to be theories of syntax.

It would be quite wrong to say that the mediaeval grammarians made no progress in their syntactical theories; they, *i.e.* Peter Helias, Robert Kilwardby, *etc.*,[12] are, it is true, largely content to follow Priscian, but we do find in their work improvements on the theories of their predecessors, though always of course within the framework imposed on their conception of grammar by the structure of the languages they knew and also in terms of the syntactic systems expounded by their predecessors. Wackernagel [13] noted, inter alia, that mediaeval grammarians consolidated the use of the concept of suppositum and appositum, that they learned to distinguish between government (regimen) and congruity (congruitas) and that the copula was introduced as a syntactic element; in addition to this, we can see in Thomas of Erfurt the first signs of an Immediate Constituent analysis. But in all this, their analysis never goes beyond nominal constructions, *e.g.* 'homo albus', exocentric constructions, *e.g.* 'Socrates currit', the formalised syllogism of Aristotelian and mediaeval logic, the use of the copula, *e.g.* 'vir est albus', all of which were imposed, without their realising it, on their theory by the requirements of the syntax of the classical language.

The use that mediaeval grammarians made of the opposition of suppositum-appositum is perhaps their most important achievement, though until more is known of syntactic theories of the 12th century it will not be possible to establish the details of its refinement; it does seem however that it was with the Modistae that the actual opposition received its most extensive use. Apollonius had taught that a complete sentence should consist of two words only, and his term 'syntaxis' Priscian interpreted as 'constructio';[14] Priscian therefore, considered only a construction consisting of a nomen and verbum to be complete (perfecta) and had, as a result, taught that a sentence without a nomen or pronomen

---

[10]   Reference has already been made to the importance and value of mediaeval syntactic theory; Thurot seems to have over-stated his case, and it is quite clear that he was unacquainted with much of the writings of the Modistae, not to mention the grammarians of the second half of the 12th century, *cf.* de Rijk, *Op. cit,* II, pp. 112-116.

[11]   Alexander de Villedieu, *Doctrinale* (ed. D. Reichling).

[12]   The speculative grammarians are not included in this group.

[13]   J. Wackernagel, *Vorlesungen über Syntax*, Vol. I, p. 23.

[14]   Ch. Thurot, *Op. cit.*, p. 214.

and a verb was incomplete.[15] Thurot claims[16] that the classical grammarians do not seem to have understood the distinction between subject (subiectum) and predicate (praedicatum), and yet it is beyond doubt that Priscian used the term suppositum in a purely grammatical sense and without any metaphysical implication.

Peter Helias used the terms supponi and apponi to describe the subject and predicate[17] and it is quite clear that his use of supponere must also be seen in a strictly grammatical sense. These terms were established in the form of suppositum and appositum as technical terms in mediaeval syntactic theory; the Modistae do make use of the terms subiectum and praedicatum but very infrequently,[18] but this is by no means a suggestion that they in anyway supersede suppositum and appositum as technical terms in their syntactic theory. These terms were also extensively used by the terminist logicians within their technical vocabulary;[19] this is yet a further example of the close interpenetration between logic and grammar in the Middle Ages.

Roos is, of course, quite right[20] to stress the difference between the prescriptive grammarian of the Middle Ages and the Modistae who sought to produce a theory of grammar rather than a teaching manual, and this is apparent in Modistic syntactic theories as well as in their analysis of the partes orationis. If we cannot subscribe to Roos's statement[21] that syntax was 'das Hauptziel' of mediaeval grammar, at least as far as the Modistae are concerned, who in some cases stopped short when they came to a consideration of syntax[22] and in others did not devote the same detailed attention to their analysis of syntax as they had done to the partes orationis, we must not on the other hand belittle

---

[15]   Priscian (XVII.12): "si tollas nomen aut verbum, imperfecta sit oratio".
[16]   Ch. Thurot, *Op. cit.*, pp. 216-217.
[17]   Peter Helias: "sicut enim nomen repertum est ad significandum de quo dicitur, ita et verbum ad significandum quid de aliquo dicitur. Unde nomen nunquam apponitur nisi auxilio verbi substantivi, nec verbum supponitur nisi auxilio nominis substantivi: sed quodlibet nomen per se supponitur et verbum per se apponitur" (Thurot, p. 217).
[18]   Thomas of Erfurt, #116: "licet hoc verbum 'est' non significet aliquid essentialiter ab ente distinctum, attamen in ista propositione subiectum accipitur ut materia, et praedicatum ut forma, quae essentialiter differunt".
[19]   *Cf.* de Rijk, *Op. cit. I*, pp. 20-22; *II*, Ch. 16.
[20]   H. Roos, *Op. cit.*, p. 151: "Martin de Dacia und seine Nachfolger wollten nicht so sehr eine empirische Grammatik als vielmehr 'Prolegomena zu einer Grammatik' schreiben. Sie geben eine Metaphysik der Grammatik oder die 'Theorie' der Grammatik überhaupt."
[21]   H. Roos, *Die Modi Significandi*, p. 140.
[22]   Siger de Courtrai and Michel de Marbais.

Modistic syntactical theory.[23] It is quite clear that, for instance, Martin's and Thomas's sections on syntax represent an attempt to break away from tradition and, despite their many shortcomings, become a concise, very systematic and as a result very original statement of syntactic theory. Even so, they were not able to rid themselves entirely of their past nor of their intellectual background, since the unconscious influence of the favourite sentence-type of Latin, and the restraints that logic placed on their concept of grammatical structure show through their syntactic theory, e.g. Thomas makes little attempt to describe the syntax of the subordinating conjunction.[24] Furthermore, their rudimentary IC type of analysis[25] is based entirely on the primary exocentric and endocentric constructions of Latin such as "Socrates currit" and "lego librum", and in the final analysis their 'perfect' construction must contain a suppositum and an appositum in the same sense that Priscian required a noun and a verb for a complete sentence.[26]

C. THEORIES OF THE MODISTAE

An important feature of Modistic syntactical theory was its development from being a normative grammar to an attempt to become a theory of syntax. It is not possible, however, to say with any absolute degree of certainty whether the Modistae would have produced a syntactical theory as uniform as their description, despite variations in presentation, of the partes orationis had been. Roos says that the Etymologia is orientated in terms of its syntax, which is confirmed by Thomas,[27] but we have no means of confirming this by reference to Siger or Michel since their work is incomplete.

[23] J. Wackernagel, *Op. cit.*, p. 22: "von der Sprachwissenschaft des Mittelalters darf man nicht mit Verachtung sprechen. Wir verdanken ihr gerade auf dem Gebiet der Syntax wertvolle Erkenntnis und Termini, die für uns schlechterdings unentbehrlich sind".
[24] He refers in fact to one example only of the use of a subordinating conjunction (and had not indeed listed this type of conjunction at all in his consideration of this pars orationis), since mediaeval logic made little use of this type of conjunction.
[25] This term is used here as a form of shorthand to suggest the kind of analysis Thomas proposed.
[26] Priscian (XVII.13): "si tollas nomen aut verbum, deficiet oratio, desiderans vel nomen vel verbum".
[27] Thomas of Erfurt, #22: "primo prout sunt principium formale partis orationis absolute, secundum quem modum pertinent ad Etymologiam: deinde prout sunt principium intrinsecum constructionis unitis partis cum alia, secundum quem pertinent ad Diasyntheticam".

Thomas and Martin follow closely the order of Priscian,[28] *i.e.* they describe the partes orationis as such in the section on 'Etymologia' and then discuss the partes orationis at another, *i.e.* syntactic level, in the section on 'Diasynthetica'. Throughout the discussion of the partes orationis there is an unconscious division between Thomas and Martin on the one hand and Siger and Michel on the other as a result of their presentations of the essential modes of signifying of the eight partes orationis; furthermore, Thomas and Martin have complete sections on syntax, and although Siger does make a reference at the end of his discussion of the nomen[29] to a projected section on syntax and Michel also refers to his "Questiones supra Priscianum" in which he would presumably deal with matters of syntax,[30] it is not easy to conjecture on the nature of their syntactical theory.

The only real information we have of the syntactic theories of Michel and Siger indeed rests in their discussions of the various modes of signifying as 'principia constructionis'. It is possible, however, to suggest a number of similarities between Thomas's and Siger's syntactical procedure, which does reinforce the impression that the closeness in their syntax might well have been as close as their analysis of the partes orationis. Siger defines the construction as a combination of constructibles[31] which is analogous to Martin's and Thomas's definition.[32] Siger, without saying so specifically, seems to have followed Priscian (as indeed Thomas did in the final analysis) in considering the construction as made up of two constructibles, but which can however combine in one of two ways. As a result of this last requirement, Siger's theory seems to depart from Priscian and to correspond to Thomas's theory which divided the construction into intransitive or transitive, each of which was divided into 'constructio actuum' (which corresponds to the favourite S P and verb-oblique[33] types of sentence respectively) and 'constructio personarum' (which consists of

---

[28] Boethius of Dacia: "Nam Priscianus in minori volumine docet congruam iuncturam dictionum et quidquid docet est propter ipsam sicut litteram, sillabam, dictionem et species et alia. Unde maius volumen ordinatur in minus volumen. Quod et Priscianus ostendit, cum secundum incipiens dicit: Quoniam in ante expositis libris . . ." (quoted by Roos, p. 140).

[29] Siger de Courtrai, p. 108: "de constructione et regimine casuum cum aliis partibus orationis, post dicetur".

[30] This work is not available – indeed Thurot makes no reference to it whatsoever.

[31] Siger de Courtrai, p. 131: "constructio est constructibilium unio".

[32] Martin of Dacia #197: "constructio nihil aliud est quam passio constructibilium. Est enim constructio constructibilium unio".

[33] Both Siger and Thomas use sentences such as "Socrates currit" and "lego librum" as examples of this type of construction.

N N clusters,[34] in which one member will be the dependent determinator of the other). It is quite clear that Siger had in mind a similar analysis of his material[35] but without making use of Thomas's terminology or without presenting his theory in as systematic a manner as Thomas did.

Siger and Michel have, however, an additional feature in their descriptions of the partes orationis, which is absent from Thomas;[36] both Siger and Michel call this 'principium constructionis', and it consists of an additional statement made about each mode of signifying to the effect that the pars in question could or could not function syntactically by virtue of this or that mode of signifying. It seems to have been a descriptive device used by Siger and Michel to classify the various modes of signifying, not only in terms of their semantic, but also in terms of their syntactic qualities, prior to giving a more detailed exposition of syntactic theory.[37] It does not, however, amount to a theory of syntax, and the phenomenon should be considered as a preliminary or introductory aspect of a theory of syntax which we are unfortunately in no position to describe. It seems, however, safe to say that the 'principia constructionis' are only a convenient way of stating in advance which modes of signifying can be used syntactically and which Siger includes as part of the description of the pars in question; Thomas

[34] N = Nomen: again, both Siger and Thomas use examples such as "homo albus" and "cappa Socratis" to illustrate these constructions.
[35] Siger reaches a point which is very close to Thomas's perfectio though he does not reach this point as the result of any systematic analysis: this is something which has to be deduced from ideas culled from his descriptions of the partes orationis and his grammatical Sophismata, e.g. p. 130: "constructio causatur ex modis significandi"; p. 132: "ad constructionem supposito cum apposito exigitur ex parte supposito modus significandi per modum habitus et per modum per se entis; quia in quolibet apposito sunt duo istis proportionales, scilicet, modus significandi per modum fieri, qui modo habitus proportionatur in supposito, et modum significandi per modum dependentis, qui proportionatur modo per se stantis in supposito"; p. 153: "omnis constructio congrua est per modos significandi proportionales".
[36] Thurot tells us that Michel and the other Modistae (he actually says: "Michel de Marbais et tous ceux qui ont traité de Modis significandi") classified as 'principia constructionis' some of the accidental modes of signifying of the partes orationis; this is not strictly true, since Siger describes the general essential modes of the declinable partes as 'principia constructionis' in addition to certain of the accidental modes of these partes, and furthermore, Thomas makes no use at all of the term in his analysis and description of the partes orationis in the section on Etymologia.
[37] Martin of Dacia is quite positive about the principium constructionis; he states that all the accidental modes are principia constructionis, viz. #66 "alii sunt modi significandi posteriores omnibus modis essentalibus ... et ipsi dicuntur modi significandi accidentales, et hi sunt maxime principia constructionis sive construendi".

scrupulously avoided doing this, though this does not mean that Thomas did not have recourse to syntactic material in his descriptions of the partes orationis.[38] Siger provides many illustrations of the 'principia constructionis',[39] but little of any value is obtained for a general theoretical approach to the problem of word-classes and the description of their syntax, since Siger's examples refer to Latin syntax only. The real innovation consists of Siger's including the 'principia constructionis', *i.e.* syntactic criteria – which is much more formal than the semantic[40] analysis so characteristic of the Modistae – as an integral and deliberate part of his descriptive analysis of the partes orationis.[41]

An interesting feature of Siger's description – and in this sense he seems to score over Thomas – is his general use of the modes of signifying to introduce aspects of the various partes which are clearly fundamental to his syntactic theory, *e.g.* he describes the general essential mode of the nomen as a 'principium constructionis' since it will be the suppositum[42] in opposition to the general essential mode of the verb; the verb, by virtue of its modus dependentis, will be the appositum,[43] and this makes the general mode of the verb a 'principium constructionis' since it can combine with the suppositum to create a construction, but by definition, *i.e.* by virtue of the modus dependentis,

---

[38]   *E.g.* his use of compositio as an accidental mode of the verb.
[39]   *E.g.* the comparative with the nominative – "Achilles est fortior quam Achilles"; the genitive – 'mulier egregiae formae'; the dative – 'amabilis mihi': disjunctive conjunction – 'Socrates vel Plato currit', *etc.*
[40]   It has been pointed out on several occasions that the Modistae restated the quasi-formal categories of Priscian in more semantic terms; this does not mean that they were deliberately non-formal in their grammatical procedure, and indeed there are instances, *e.g.* in their treatment of the indeclinable partes orationis, when they have recourse, unconsciously it would seem, to formal criteria in their statements, and in their own eyes the Modistae were not very far removed from the more formal Priscian.
[41]   A clear distinction must be made between 'derivation' in an historical sense and a technical term in descriptive grammar. 'Synchronic derivation' would be a better term in descriptive grammar since it is a way of "describing the relationship of one word to another", B. Bloch and G. L. Trager, *Outline of Linguistic Analysis*, p. 55, and it is in the sense of 'synchronic derivation' that derivation is used with reference to the absolute and respective modes.
[42]   Siger de Courtrai, pp. 95-96: "iste modus significandi [nominis] est principium constructionis suppositi cum apposito, quia modus significandi per modum fieri seu motus seu esse in apposito proportionatur modo significandi per modum substantiae, permanentis habitus seu entis".
[43]   Siger de Courtrai, p. 108: "omne verbum significat rem suam per modum significandi dependentis et per consequens nullum verbum, in quantum tale, poterit supponere verbo, immo, omne verbum requirit aliquid in ratione suppositi quod dependentiam eius sustentat".

the verb must always be the dependent constructible, as in "Socrates currit" and in "lego librum".

Much of Siger's syntax has perforce to be deduced from a knowledge of Thomas's syntax in view of Siger's haphazard presentation of these syntactic details,[44] but this should not detract from the value of the 'principium constructionis'[45] as a marker (at the pre-syntactic level) of a mode of signifying, by virtue of which a pars orationis may become the member of a potential construction. Its exact relationship and function within the construction will be decided by the proportionality of the 'principia constructionis' of the pars to the 'principia constructionis' (expressed by means of the respective modes of signifying) of the other members of the construction.[46]

Thomas deals with the partes orationis and their modes of signifying, purely and simply, before beginning his section on syntax; he does in fact warn us at a very early stage[47] that this will be his procedure. Thomas's syntactic theory is quite different from that of his predecessors;[48] furthermore, (and it may be this fact which induced Thurot to say[49] that no grammarian of the Middle Ages appears to have made a systematic and a priori division of syntax),[50] Thomas's syntactic theory is not normative, nor does it seem to have been made even with grammatical instruction in Latin in mind.[51] This, of course, is entirely in keeping with Modistic theory and practice; they may have been teachers but they were teachers of grammar, not teachers of Latin,[52] and their purpose was to speculate on the nature of grammar. Thomas, therefore, sets out a description of the partes orationis with an occasional remark in the direction of syntax, viz. his description of 'compositio' in the verb, and then a section on syntax which he divides into four parts, i.e.

---

[44] These are scattered throughout his 'Summa' and his 'Sophismata'.

[45] This is very similar to Bloomfield's division of grammatical forms and lexical forms, cf. L. Bloomfield, Language, p. 166, and the function of the principium constructionis seems to be to act as a marker of a grammatical form.

[46] Siger de Courtrai, p. 131: "modi significandi respectivi ... sunt principium constructionis quia sunt principium unionis constructibilis cum constructibili".

[47] In fact at the end of his preamble before he begins his description of Etymologia and the partes orationis.

[48] I.e. grammarians prior to the Modistae.

[49] Ch. Thurot, Op. cit., p. 237.

[50] Cf. p. 108, n. 7.

[51] Cf. H. Roos, Die Modi significandi, p. 151.

[52] There is a modern ring to this, because the structural linguist and the teacher of languages, though they are both dealing with language, do not by any means have always the same end in view.

principia construendi, constructio, congruitas, and perfectio;[53] this is
much the same method of analysis adopted by Martin of Dacia.[54]

D. PRINCIPIA CONSTRUENDI

Thomas analyses syntax as a series of stages (passiones sermonis) which
are necessary before any complete statement can be made. With this in
mind, Thomas produces a most important section as a preamble to his
description of a syntax, a section which is full of interesting implications
for the analysis of any construction and of any complete statement
(constructio perfecta), since it contains procedures which can be applied to the analysis either of any construction or the members of any
construction (constructibilia) or of the complete sentence.

This section he calls the principles of constructing (principia construendi), which are based clearly enough on Aristotle's four causes,
i.e. material, formal, efficient, and final. It will be seen[55] that these four
causes can be applied to the analysis of any construction and also to the
analysis of the process of construction (constructio), congruity (congruitas), and completion (perfectio); it also means that the first two
causes refer acutely to the nature of the partes orationis which make up
the constructible elements of a construction. It must be remembered
that the dictio and the pars orationis are the same materially but differ
formally;[56] the dictio and the pars orationis refer to the same thing
materially, but differ formally since the pars orationis possesses the
mode of signifying, and it is potential consignification, predicated as it
is to the material, which gives the pars orationis its grammatical power.
Similarly but on a different level the constructible is a prior constituent
of a construction, but in itself has no syntactic function, *i.e.* it is the
potentiality of the actuality of a construction.[57]

---

[53]   The remainder of this chapter is based on Thomas who, of all the Modistae,
has left us with the most complete account of Modistic syntactic theory.
[54]   A separate study of Martin of Dacia and his syntactic theory is being prepared.
[55]   Thomas of Erfurt, #184: "applicare eos ad constructionem, congruitatem, et
perfectionem, ostendendo qui modi significandi, quarum constructionum, con-
gruitatum, perfectionum, sunt principia".
[56]   Thomas of Erfurt, #4: "rationem significandi ... per quam efficitur signum
... et sic formaliter est dictio; et rationem consignificandi ... et sic formaliter est
pars orationis".
[57]   Various grammatical constituents can be stated in terms parallel to the dichotomy of matter and form:

The principium materiale thus refers to the dictio and the principium formale to the pars orationis, *i.e.* the material refers to the constructibles, but this is meaningless except that any dictio can have the potentiality of consignification, which brings us to the various forms of a pars orationis which result from the totality of its essence and accidents. We are still pre-syntactic, and a further process of selection is necessary before we can be said to be dealing with syntactic units; and this is done by the principium efficiens which represents those modes of signifying which, along with the proper concord, *i.e.* by means of 'similitudo' and 'proportio', fuse the two constituent members into a congruent construction, though the process is not complete until the construction can express a compound concept of the mind.

This is the procedure for any construction, but it is also the procedure for the whole of syntax as set out by Thomas. The principium materiale refers to the individual constructibles which have no syntactic functions in that they have as yet no being, no syntactic existence; it is the purpose of the principium formale to give form to the construction which means therefore the combination of the two constructibles. The principium efficiens corresponds to those respective modes of signifying of the constructibles which will become the modus dependentis and the modus terminantis and 'effect' the construction by preparing and arranging the constructibles (to which they belong as modes of signifying [58]) in the construction so that the combination may become concordant. Lastly, the principium finale represents the last stage, since its purpose is the expression of a compound concept of the mind which can be achieved only by a proper combination of constructibles.

We can thus see a three-fold relationship between the four causes, the members of the construction and the different speech levels:

	materia	*forma*
dictio	vox	ratio significandi
pars orationis	vox	ratio consignificandi
modus essentialis	generalis	specificus
nomen	modus entis	determinata apprehensio
verbum	modus esse	distantia
participium	modus esse	indistantia
adverbium	modus disponentis	modus determinantis actum
principia construendi	principium materiale	principium formale
constructio	constructibilia	unio constructibilium

This list does not, however, exhaust the number of oppositions based on the matter-form contrast.

[58] Thomas of Erfurt, #187: "dicuntur modi significandi principium intrinsecum, quasi inter constructibilia manentes".

principium materiale	– constructibilia	– Etymologia
principium formale	– unio constructibilium	– Constructio
principium efficiens	– unio congrua constructibilium	– Congruitas
principium finale	– expressio mentis conceptus compositi	– Perfectio

Principium materiale

The principium materiale represents the constructibles, the relationship between the constructible and the constructio being identical to that of substance and accident; an accident exists as a modification of a substance or thing and is predicated of a substance, and so the constructibles will be the substance of the constructio; or stated otherwise, the constructio represents an accidental change in the constructible.[59] This means that the constructio, which consists of two constructibles, will consist largely of the subject-predicate type, which is caused by the dependence of one constructible on the other; the member of a construction must be either a dependent, or a determinant, and so a constructio will be made up of a dependent and a terminant constructible.

Thomas makes an interesting observation, which is very revealing in terms of modern syntactic analysis, *i.e.* that it would be mistaken to consider the construction "homo albus currit bene" to be just one construction, the reason being the different dependences in it, *i.e.* (i) the dependence of the adiectivum on the substantivum, (ii) the verbum on the suppositum, (iii) the determinant on the determinable, so that we can analyse this construction into: –

homo   albus   currit   bene

This suggests, apart from anything else, that the term constructio can be used both to mean a construction in the modern sense of immediate constituent, and also to mean a construction, better described in Modistic terms as 'constructio perfecta'. Similarly, the construction "Socrates percutit Platonem" consists of more than one constructio in view of the dependence of the verb on the pre-posed suppositum and the dependence of the verb on the post-posed oblique form.

---

[59] Thomas of Erfurt, #185: "subiectum est materia accidentis, nam accidens non habet materiam ex qua, sed in qua; ergo constructibilia sunt materia constructionis".

Principium formale

This represents the form of the construction, *i.e.* the actual combination of the constructibles. Once more we find the dichotomy of form and matter being introduced as criteria for a grammatical definition.[60] The form gives existence or actuality to the matter of the thing under consideration, and similarly, therefore, the potential constructio, at its material stage (principium materiale), is actualised into a combination of constructibles by means of the form, *i.e.* the principium formale.[61] Form has nothing to do with outward shape, but is "an immanent constitutive principle of activity",[62] which informs or determines a thing, in this case the constructio, and thereby makes of the potential construction a particular type of construction. So then, the principium materiale might be said to be the potential constructio, upon which the principium formale bestows form and thereby represents the potentiality of a proper congruent construction which will then be realised by the other two principles. The mediaeval metaphysician conceived of reality as a hierarchy, the levels of which consist of the material element potentially informable as an act so as to become the matter of the next level;[63] the Modistae conceived of a similar hierarchy of grammar, which has already been suggested rather imperfectly.[64] The step from the prinpium formale to the principium efficiens represents an important step for the grammarian; the principium materiale, and the principium formale deal directly with the partes orationis, and more particularly, with the modes of signifying which constitute the partes orationis. So far, the grammarian has been dealing with features of language, which, in Modistic terms, have correlates in reality, but with the principium efficiens and the principium finale, the grammarian is handling the modes of signifying, not according to the dictates of reality, but according to the more grammatical requirements of 'congruitas' and 'perfectio'.

Principium efficiens

This is the realisation of the construction, and two factors are involved

---

[60] F. C. Copleston, *Aquinas*, p. 93: "first matter, considered in abstraction, is pure potentiality for successive actualisation by substantial forms, each of which stands to its matter as act to potentiality, actualising the matter's potentiality".
[61] Thomas of Erfurt, #186: "constructio habet esse per constructibilium unionem; ergo constructibilium unio est forma constructionis".
[62] F. C. Copleston, *Op. cit.*, p. 86.
[63] F. C. Copleston, *Op. cit.*, p. 95.
[64] By means of the diagram, p. 348.

which Thomas called 'intrinsecum' and 'extrinsecum', the first representing a permanent and internal relationship and the last being an external, *i.e.* mental factor. The principium intrinsecum represents the process of selection which started with the raw material of the principium materiale and continued with the potential nature of the principium formale; the principium intrinsecum represents the respective modes of signifying by virtue of which one constructible either depends on the other, or determines the dependence of the other.[65] As a result of these modes of signifying two general modes can be abstracted which serve to decide the internal relationships of every constructio; these are the mode of being dependent (modus dependendi) and the mode of terminating the dependence (modus dependentiam terminans). Every constructio contains two constructibles, one being the dependent and the other the determinant,[66] and the nature of the constructio, *i.e.* transitive or intransitive, will decide which will be the dependent or terminant, though by definition,[67] the transitive or intransitive nature of the construction is decided, in part at least, by means of the modes of signifying of the dependent constructible, and additional factors can often help to establish the dependent and terminant constructibles.[68] If the stage has been reached in the grammatical hierarchy when the dictates of reality no longer control the modes of signifying, this does not detract from the prime importance of the modes of signifying, and the control, so to speak, of the modes of signifying in the relationship between the dependent and the terminant constructibles is now ordered according to the requirements of the 'congruitas' of a 'constructio perfecta'.

These modes of signifying create in effect the constructio, since they prepare and arrange the constructibles for the actual combination, which will account for their internal relationships.[69] The act of combination is performed by the mind which is the external factor in any

[65] Thomas of Erfurt, #187: "intrinsecum sunt modi significandi respectivi, ratione quorum vel unum constructibile est ad alterum dependens, vel alterius dependentiam determinans".
[66] Thomas of Erfurt, #185: "unius constructionis non sunt nisi duo constructibilia principalia, scilicet: dependens, et terminans".
[67] Thomas of Erfurt, #192: "constructio intransitiva est constructio, inqua secundum constructibile, per suos modos significandi, *dependet* ad primum [my emphasis]".
[68] Thomas of Erfurt, #191: "illud constructibile est dependens, quod ratione alicuius modi significandi tantum petit vel exigit".
[69] Thomas of Erfurt, #187: "hi modi significandi dicuntur efficere constructionem, pro tanto, quia praeparant et disponunt constructibilia ad actualem unionem, quae fit per intellectum; ... est intellectus qui constructibilia per modos significandi disposita et praeparata actu unit in constructione et sermone".

constructio; this is the principium extrinsecum. The constructio has, with this stage, come into being, and there remains only the principium finale which states the end or result attained by the construction.

Principium finale

The aim of the constructio perfecta is to express a compound concept of the mind; the principium finale really represents then the sum total of the other principia which combine together to express a mental concept, *i.e.* it becomes a composite realisation of the constructibles, their combination, their modes of signifying, and the mind which fuses them together, and the mental concept which caused them and the mental concept they express.

E. PASSIONES SERMONIS

Hitherto, we have been dealing with individual partes orationis and their different modes of signifying; now we deal with the combinations of these partes orationis by virtue of selected modes of signifying, *i.e.* the respective modes of signifying. The constructio perfecta is achieved by a chain of factors, starting with the constructibles themselves; (it would seem that Siger had felt it very necessary to indicate separately, when describing the partes orationis and their modes of signifying, those aspects of a particular pars which would have the further function of being constructible at a higher level than that of the word).[70] Moving on from the word, we find three stages or levels (passiones) of language, which can be described as the combination of constructibles (constructio), the concord of such combinations (congruitas), and the final completed construction (perfectio); this last must, by definition,[71] contain a verb, since 'distantia' is a criterion for the essential mode of the verbum, which accounts perhaps for the insistance on the constructio being of the favourite sentence types of N V, *i.e.* Nomen Verbum (subject and predicate[72]) and V N, *i.e.* verb and oblique-nominal.

[70] *I.e.* by describing each mode of signifying which has this function as a 'principium constructionis'.
[71] Thomas of Erfurt, #225: "cum constructio perfecta sit ad exprimendum mentis conceptum compositum secundum distantiam ... haec distantia solum est inter suppositum et appositum, ex hoc quod solum verbum est appositum, quod per modum distantis se habet".
[72] The Noun-Verb (SP) is the traditional complete sentence and goes as far back in grammatical history as the Greek Grammarians.

We shall see that both these sentence types are described in terms which are to a very large extent formal, but, and this is of course entirely in keeping with the intellectual spirit of the age, they are based, for their very form, on criteria which are metaphysical rather than grammatical.

Constructio is quite clearly more important than congruitas, and the constructio must be established before any statement about its concord can be made. Both these stages must be passed before the final completed construction is achieved.

Thomas proceeds to describe, first of all, the constructio which he does first by means of definition, and then by analysing the different types of construction and their concords;[73] he then describes the feature of congruitas as such, and finally perfectio as the final stage of his syntax.

Constructio per definitionem

There are two ways of knowing a thing, *i.e.* by definition or by division, or the classification of the thing into its various species – in the case of the construction, into the various types of construction. By definition, a thing is known in accordance with its essence, and by division, a thing is known by its potentiality.[74] By definition, therefore, we know a thing as it is, and so by definition, a construction is the combination of constructibles created by the mind from the modes of signifying for the expression of a compound concept of the mind.[75]

Such a definition states in effect the four causes which, by definition, produce the object, in this case, the constructio; thus the constructibles refer to the principium materiale, and the combination of the constructibles to the principium formale; the modes of signifying refer to the principium efficiens intrinsecum and the action of the mind to the principium efficiens extrinsecum, and the expression of a compound concept refers to the principium finale.

---

[73] The Modistae use 'concord' much more extensively than modern grammarians; indeed, it has already been suggested that 'congruitas' is a general term for different kinds of linguistic relationships, *e.g.* government, concord, collocation, *etc.*

[74] Thomas of Erfurt, #189: "per definitionem, qua res cognoscitur secundum sui esse; et per divisionem, qua res cognoscitur secundum sui posse".

[75] Thomas of Erfurt, #189: "constructio est constructibilium unio, ex modis significandi, et intellectus causata, ad exprimendum mentis conceptum compositum finaliter adinventa".

Congruitas

Thomas's syntactic theory consists of three stages; the final stage, which he called 'perfectio', is the achievement of a complete construction (constructio perfecta).[76] The first stage, which has just been discussed, is the constructio, which takes the various partes orationis as they have been described in terms of their modes of signifying, and combines these partes orationis or constructibles together as a first step towards the complete construction. Thomas's method of exposition is to describe first the various types of construction and the concord of each construction, and then the theory of concord (congruitas) as it applies to the whole of syntax, since it is clearly not enough to throw together any two constructibles. There are three basic requirements for this concord, which Thomas describes in more detail; only then is the last stage, *i.e.* perfectio, reached – the expression of a complete construction by means of the proper combination of the modes of signifying, which will create perfect understanding in the mind of the hearer.[77]

Congruitas, therefore, is the next step beyond constructio; it is not enough to combine just any two constructibles, but it must be a combination which satisfies three requirements: (a) the conformity of all the modes of signifying involved,[78] (b) the collocation[79] of the constructibles as required by the context of the situation,[80] (c) the concord and government which must exist between the constructibles.[81] Congruitas is thus the proper combination of the constructibles by means of the conformity, *i.e.* mutual appropriateness, of the modes of signifying required for any kind of construction.

The first two requirements are very closely linked, since they are concerned with the proper combination of the constructibles, and this can be achieved by reason of the concord, or more negatively, the non-

[76] Thomas follows Priscian closely in his definition of a 'constructio perfecta'.
[77] Thomas of Erfurt, #223: "generare perfectum sensum in animo auditoris".
[78] Thomas of Erfurt, #218: "congruitas et incongruitas causantur ex conformitate vel disconformitate modorum significandi".
[79] Thomas of Erfurt, #218: "proprietas vel improprietas sermonis causatur ex convenientia vel repugnantia significatorum specialium". 'Collocation' and 'context of situation' are technical terms in J. R. Firth's and 'London' theory, *cf.* J. R. Firth, *Papers in Linguistics.*
[80] Thomas of Erfurt, #220: "conformitas modorum significandi sit principium constructionis et congruitatis, distinguendum est de conformitate, quia duplex est conformitas, scilicet: proportionis et similitudinis".
[81] Thomas of Erfurt, #221: "congruitas nihil aliud est, quam partium sermonis debita unio, ex modorum significandi conformitate ad aliquam speciem constructionis requisitorum derelicta".

discord of the meanings of the constructibles, or by reason of the symmetry, or more negatively, the non-dissimilarity of the modes of signifying.[82]
The meanings and the modes of signifying of the constructibles are
inextricably interwoven, though it would be a mistake, as Thomas
himself argues,[83] not to regard them as separate entities; otherwise it
would be enough, and this Thomas strenuously denies,[84] to say that a
construction is or is not 'congruent' by virtue of the accord or disaccord
of the meaning of the constructibles – this, Thomas maintains, comes
really within the province of the logician and in itself is not enough to
create the concord of a sentence.[85]

There are in fact two things involved here; one is the concord or
non-concord of a sentence,[86] and the other is the propriety or im-
propriety of the sentence which stems from the accord or non-accord of
the members of the sentence. In "cappa nigra" we have what Thomas
calls concord and propriety, but in "cappa categorica" we have what
he calls concord, but not propriety. Stated more linguistically, we can
say that we are dealing with concord at two levels; in the case of "cappa
categorica" we may have the internal concord of gender, number, etc.,
and Thomas might well describe this as an intransitive 'constructio
personarum'. But in such a construction, we have quite clearly not
taken into account the collocability of these constructibles, which requires that the context of situation be taken into account,[87] but rather
with reference purely and simply to the meanings of the two constituents; i.e. though there may be concord between them, there is no
propriety (proprietas) because of their meanings, and therefore we
require both concord (congruitas) and proper collocation (proprietas)
before we can say that the completed construction has been achieved.
It would be reasonable to maintain that this is why Thomas discusses

82 Thomas of Erfurt, #218: "debita unio potest contingere dupliciter: uno modo
ex convenientia significatorum specialium; et per oppositum unio indebita ex
repugnantia ipsorum. Alio modo ... ex conformitate modorum significandi, et
per oppositum indebita ex indebita modorum significandi discrepantia".
83 Thomas of Erfurt, #218: "quidam, non distinguentes inter significatorum specialium convenientiam vel repugnantiam, et modorum significandi conformitatem
vel discrepantiam".
84 Thomas of Erfurt, #218: "quidam ... dixerunt omnem constructionem esse
congruam vel incongruam, in qua est significatorum specialium convenientia vel
repugnantia. Sed hoc non valet".
85 Thomas of Erfurt, #218: "congruitas sit de consideratione grammatici per se.
Sed convenientia vel repugnantia significatorum specialium a grammatico per se
non consideratur, sed magis a logico: ergo congruitas in sermone ab his non
causatur".
86 Thomas of Erfurt, #218: "haec est congrua et propria, 'cappa nigra' ".
87 Cf. J. R. Firth, Papers in Linguistics, for the use of these terms.

under his general consideration of the different types of construction the 'congruitas' as an independent syntactic feature, *i.e.* by reason of this feature we have first internal concord and then the external concord of the sentence as a whole which controls the collocations of its members. It seems that 'proprietas' acts here as an indirect structural marker at a different level which congruitas serves to complement and thereby to complete the construction.

The requirement of conformity of all the modes of signifying, which is closely connected to the collocations of the members of a construction, raises the problem of the terminant member of a transitive construction, since this terminant constructible may itself be potentially the dependent member of another construction,[88] *viz.* the function of 'librum' in the constructions "lego librum" and "lego librum Virgilii". In a case such as this, it is not necessary for the constructible which is the terminant in the first construction, *i.e.* 'librum' in "lego librum', to be considered in terms of its possible dependence on another terminant constructible of another construction which, though it may stand outside the first construction, is in effect an expansion of the first construction. In the construction "lego librum", 'lego' is the dependent and 'librum' the terminant constructible, but in the case of "lego librum" and "librum Virgilii" in which 'librum', which was the terminant of 'lego', has also become the dependent of 'Virgilii', Thomas states that as far as the congruence of "lego librum" is concerned, no notice need be taken of the possible relationship between 'librum' and 'Virgilii'.[89]

The third requirement is a very important one and represents one of the features that Wackernagel noted[90] as one of the valuable contributions of mediaeval grammatical technique to the theory of syntax. There are two kinds of grammatical agreement, *i.e.* government and concord; the Modistae and other mediaeval grammarians recognised this, and as a result the Modistae stipulated that the conformity of the modes of signifying, which has just been discussed, will be one of two kinds, *i.e.* complementary syntactical arrangement (proportio) or modal uniformity (similitudo),[91] which are discrete and mutually exclusive. This division

---

[88]   Thomas of Erfurt, #219: "constructibile dependens sit terminatum per constructibile terminans".

[89]   Thomas of Erfurt, #219: "si habeat dependentiam ad diversas constructiones, non requisitur quod omnes dependentiae sint semper actu terminatae, sed sufficit quod secundum unam constructionem terminentur, ut ... 'lego librum', haec est congrua, licet non addatur Virgilii, vel aliquid aliud, quod terminet dependentiam huius, quod est 'librum', secundum quam dependet a parte post".

[90]   J. Wackernagel, *Op. cit.*, p. 23.

[91]   Thomas of Erfurt, #220: "quandoque utraque ad constructionem requiritur,

derives from the nature of the relationship between the modes of signifying of the constructibles. It will happen that the dependent constructible may possess certain modes of signifying which do not belong to it, *i.e.* which do not derive from its own properties but which derive from the properties of the terminant constructible of which it is the dependent; in such a case the conformity will be one of 'similitudo', what we would call concord, as in a construction consisting of an adjective and a substantive or in a construction consisting of a suppositum in the nominative case with a personal verb.[92] The adjective acquires gender, number, person, *etc.* not from its own properties, but from the properties of the substantive to which it is attributed in an endocentric phrase,[93] so that the substantive requires the modes of concord and not of government in order to produce a congruent construction,[94] *i.e.* one in which one constructible will show the same features as the other constructible; similarly the personal verb acquires its number and person from its suppositum,[95] so that the relationship between them will, in this instance, be one of 'similitudo' and not 'proportio'.

If, on the other hand, the constituent members of a construction possess certain modes of signifying which derive from their own properties and are *not* acquired from the properties of the other member, *i.e.* the dependent constructible possesses these properties in and of itself and does not derive them from the terminant constructible,[96] the relationship will be one of proportionality (proportio), as in the case of the adjective which possesses in its own right and from its own proper-

---

quandoque autem sufficit proportionis tantum, quandoque autem sufficit similitudinis conformitas tantum".

[92] Thomas of Erfurt, #220: "constructibile terminans debet habere modos significandi constructibilis dependentis, ut patet de constructione adiectivi cum substantivo, et in constructione suppositi nominativi casus cum verbo personali".

[93] Thomas of Erfurt, #220: "adiectivum habet tam genus, quam numerum, quam personam ex proprietatibus rei subiectae ... unde ex parte substantivi non requirit modos proportionabiles sed similes".

[94] Thomas of Erfurt, #220: "constructibile dependens habet aliquos modos significandi, non ex proprietatibus suae rei per se, sed ex proprietatibus rei constructibilis terminantis: et tunc inter illos modos significandi exigitur similitudo, et non proportio".

[95] Thomas of Erfurt, #220: "verbum personale habet numerum, et personam, ex proprietatibus rei suppositae; ideo hos modos requirit in supposito, non proportionabiles, sed similes".

[96] Thomas of Erfurt, #220: "si constructibile dependens habet aliquos modos significandi ex proprietatibus suae rei per se, et non ex proprietatibus rei constructibilis terminantis, tunc exigitur in illis modis significandi proportio, et non similitudo".

ties the modus adiacentis; it will therefore demand the modus per se
stantis in the substantive,[97] with which it will combine to form a construction, *i.e.* they will thus be syntactically related in any construction.
Such a relationship in this particular instance is not so much one of
government, but represents in fact the constituent class of the constructibles.

Congruitas is thus achieved by means of the conformity of the modes
of signifying of the constituents of a construction, and by the collocations of the constituents; the conformity of the modes of signifying is
closely linked to the collocations of the partes which make up the construction, since there will clearly be no collocation in an instance such
as "cappa categorica". The congruitas of a construction requires colligation as well as semantic collocation in addition to concord between
the members of a construction. In Modistic terms, we can say that
congruitas demands the proper combination (unio debita) of constructibles, propriety of meaning, and mutual appropriateness of the modes
of signifying; congruitas becomes, therefore, a combination, in effect,
of the 'similitudo' and 'proportio' of the modes of signifying of the
constructible members of a construction.

Perfectio

This is the third stage in Modistic syntax; to complete the process,
'perfectio' represents the last stage which produces the complete construction or sentence by means of a proper, *i.e.* 'congruent' combination
of constructibles which will express a mental concept in the form of a
favourite sentence-type of Latin and create perfect understanding in the
mind of the hearer.[98] Thomas states as the first requirement for a complete construction the presence of a suppositum and appositum;[99] this
means that separation (distantia)[100] becomes an essential ingredient in
the expression of a complete mental concept, which can therefore be
done only by means of an S P construction. This is, of course, a tradi-

---

[97] Thomas of Erfurt, #220: "quia adiectivum habet modum adiacentis proprie et
de proprietatibus suae rei, ideo per huiusmodi modum adiacentis requirit in
subiecto modum per se stantis, qui est sibi proportionabilis".

[98] Thomas of Erfurt, #227: "passio sermonis tertia et ultima, ex debita constructibilium unione derelicta, cum sufficientia exprimendi mentis conceptum compositum secundum distantiam et generandi perfectam sententiam in animo auditoris".

[99] Thomas of Erfurt, #224: "perfectio acquiritur ex constructibilium unione
debita, non quorumcumque, sed suppositi cum apposito".

[100] One of the principal and most characteristic features of the verb was 'distantia',
which both Thomas and Siger defined as an essential mode of the verb.

tion which goes back at least as far as Apollonius, but it is interesting
to see that the philosophical and logical training of the Modistae made
them, without realising it, create a syntax which is in actual fact based
on the favourite sentence-type of Latin; their motive was the expression
of substance which must somehow be in a state of flux,[101] hence the
requirement of suppositum and appositum, and yet it was ultimately
the structure of their language which forced them to this.

There are, therefore, two aims to every complete construction –
Thomas expressed them by means of 'propinquus' and 'remotus'; the
primary one (finis propinquus) is the expression of a composite mental
concept by means of a verb.[102] It is not enough to state it as the expression of a mental concept since this can be done without the verb
(secundum indistantiam) as in the case of 'homo albus", but this is incomplete; therefore the mental concept must be expressed by means of
a construction containing a verb as in "homo est albus",[103] since the
secondary aim (finis remotus) of any construction is to create perfect
understanding in the mind of the hearer which can be done only by
means of the proper combination of constructibles,[104] which must by
definition contain a verb.[105]

It means, then, that in any complete construction there are three
necessary conditions before the construction can be said to be complete, and this shows clearly the progression involved in these stages of
constructio, congruitas and perfectio. Constructio stipulates two constructibles as necessary members should show not only grammatical but
collocational concord; perfectio demands, when these requirements
have been satisfied, that the two members must be the suppositum and
appositum, otherwise the construction is not perfect.[106] In other words,

[101] Thomas of Erfurt, #113: "huic modo verbi, qui est modus esse et successionis,
proportionatur in supposito et in obliquo modus entis, id est, modus habitus permanentis".
[102] Thomas of Erfurt, #223: "finis propinquus est expressio mentis conceptus
compositi, secundum distantiam".
[103] Thomas of Erfurt, #223: "alioquin conceptus mentis est compositus secundum
distantiam, ut componendo 'hominem' cum 'albo', mediante copula dicendo, 'homo
est albus' ".
[104] Thomas of Erfurt, #223: "finis remotus constructionis est generare perfectum
sensum in animo auditoris, ex constructibilium debita unione".
[105] Thomas of Erfurt, #225: "haec distantia solum est inter suppositum et appositum, ex hoc quod solum verbum est appositum, quod per modum distantis
se habet".
[106] Thomas of Erfurt, #225: "constructio perfecta sit ad exprimendum mentis
conceptum compositum secundum distantiam finaliter ordinata, oportet, quod
sicut est distantia inter conceptus mentis compositos, sic etiam sit distantia in
constructibilium unione".

a construction such as "homo albus" demonstrates the proper concords but is incomplete since it does not contain a verb. We have thus two of the conditions necessary for a complete construction, *i.e.* conformity and congruence of all the modes of signifying and a combination of suppositum and appositum.

The third condition is a very necessary addition to the other two conditions. It is not enough, if we are to achieve the aim of every complete construction, to have concord of the combination of suppositum and appositum; in addition, every dependence must be completed. In every construction, one member will be a dependent constructible and the other will be the terminant, so that if we are to complete the construction, the dependence of the dependent constructible must be completed, since otherwise the complete expression of the mental concept will not be possible.[107] A construction such as "si Socrates currit", is incomplete,[108] because the constructible 'si', added to the construction "Socrates currit", introduces a new dependence, *i.e.* its own dependence on something outside this particular construction which will remain incomplete, until this dependence is completed by something which is, presumably, consequential to this incomplete construction.[109] Perfectio becomes thus the expression, in purely notional terms, of the possibility of silence and the end of a grammatical structure, *i.e.* one with no external syntactic relations and therefore a complete sentence.

F. CONSTRUCTIO PER DIVISIONEM

The *definition* of constructio (as already given in a previous section[110]) refers to the totality of a construction; in fact, constructio, as defined by Thomas, seems to imply a second definition, *i.e.* as a "significant group of words", whereas the *division* of constructio points to the

---

[107] Thomas of Erfurt, #225: "requiritur ex parte constructionis, quod nulla dependentia sit non terminata, quae retrohat ipsam ab eius fine, qui est mentis conceptum compositum exprimere, et perfectum sensum in animo auditoris generare".

[108] In this 'constructio imperfecta', *i.e.* "si Socrates currit", 'si' is a subordinating conjunction; this is the only example that Thomas gives of a subordinating conjunction – indeed he does not state specifically that it is either a subordinating construction or conjunction; reasons have been given elsewhere why Thomas, for extra-linguistic reasons, did not include the subordinating constructions and conjunctions in his grammatical statement.

[109] Thomas of Erfurt, #227: "ista coniunctio, 'si', huic constructioni addita, 'Socrates currit', facit in ea novam dependentiam ad aliquid extra se, ut ad aliquid consequens, quod si non exprimatur, semper imperfecta manebit".

[110] *Cf.* p. 302.

classification of each construction as an Immediate Constituent made up of two constructibles. Constructio can be divided in the first place into transitive and intransitive,[111] each of these constructions being further divided into 'actuum' and 'personarum', which can perhaps best be described as major and minor colligations.[112]

Every construction consists of two constructibles; such a scheme inherited from a representation of Scholastic dualism, coupled with the syntactic theories the Modistae inherited from their Greek and Roman predecessors, has been projected, particularly by Thomas,[113] into a conception of syntax as a series of favourite sentence type propositions such as subject-predicate and verb-nominal oblique, or as a series of minor combinations consisting of the determinable element and its determination. In each of these constructions one member will be the dependent member and the other the terminant. This establishes the first essential division in his system of constructions; if the first constructible is the terminant and the second member therefore the dependent, we have an *intransitive* construction,[114] and a *transitive* construction will have the first member as the dependent and the second as the terminant member.[115]

Each basic type of construction can be divided into two kinds, actuum and personarum, *i.e.* major and minor colligations. In any construction there are two constituents or constructibles only; in all constructions, one constructible will be the terminant and the other the dependent,[116] and in the case of the minor intransitive construction this relationship is more specific and consists of determinant and determinable. The first

---

[111] Thomas's definitions of transitive and intransitive are quite different from those given in traditional and normative grammars.

[112] *Cf.* J. R. Firth, H. F. Simon, for the use of this term.

[113] This whole discussion of 'constructio' is based entirely on Thomas's work.

[114] Thomas of Erfurt, #192: "constructio intransitiva est constructio, in qua secundum constructibile, per suos modos significandi, dependet a primum; ut dicendo, Socrates currit".

[115] Thomas of Erfurt, #192: "constructio transitiva est in qua primum constructibile, per suos modos significandi, dependet ad secundum, secundo per eius dependentiam a primo recedente, si dependens fuerit . . . ut dicendo, percutio Socratem".

[116] Thomas insists on the importance and function of the order of the constructibles, *i.e.* an intransitive construction consists of a first member which will be the terminant and a second which will be the dependent, and a transitive construction consists of a first member which will be the dependent and a second which will be the terminant. Word order must therefore be considered as fairly fixed and to be used in syntactic analysis. This applies in the 'major' *i.e.* NV and VN constructions, but in the minor construction of 'intransitiva personarum' word order is not at issue, for, as was explained above, 'second' in this context means 'logically second' and carries no suggestion of word order.

constructible is defined as the one that depends on the oblique, and the
second as the one that depends on the suppositum;[117] in a determinant-
determinable relationship, however, the determinant is always the
second constructible[118] but this is *not* a matter of word-order – the
determinant is *logically* the second constructible, *i.e.* in "homo albus"
or "omnis homo", 'albus' and 'omnis' are the determinant constructibles
and are the 'second' constructible since there must be a 'man' before
he can be described as a 'white' (*etc.*) man. The constructible that
depends on the suppositum depends on the principium and the constructible that depends on the oblique is said to depend on the terminus.[119] The use of the terms 'principium' and 'terminus' refers clearly
to the use of the terms as criteria in the cases of the nomen, and confirms that word order was looked upon by Thomas as fundamentally
functional. These relationships of first and second constructible, principium and terminus, *etc.*, can be represented schematically thus:

Constructibile primum			*Constructibile secundum*	
Intransitiva actuum	Socrates	(principium) (terminant)	currit	(dependent)
Intransitiva personarum	Socrates	(determinable) (terminant)	albus	(determinant) (dependent)
Intransitiva personarum	currit	(determinable) (terminant)	bene	(determinant) (dependent)
Transitiva actuum	lego	(dependent)	librum	(terminus) (terminant)
Transitiva personarum	filius	(dependent)	Socratis	(terminant)

The question is which will be the terminant and which the dependent,
since we cannot have two of either in any construction; once more,
Thomas refers to a metaphysical correlate to explain a grammatical
feature. Substance in nature is a combination of matter and form, one
of which is act and the other potentiality, and so in grammar a construction is made up of dependent and terminant.[120] Thomas defines

[117] Thomas of Erfurt, #191: "constructibile primum, quod post se dependet ad
obliquum; illud vero secundum, quod ante se dependet ad suppositum".
[118] Thomas of Erfurt, #191: "illud est secundum, quod dependet ad deter-
minabile".
[119] Thomas of Erfurt, #191: "quod post se dependet ad obliquum, dependet ad
ipsum ut ad terminum et ultimum; quod ante se dependet ad suppositum dependet
ad ipsum ut ad principium et ad primum".
[120] Thomas of Erfurt, #191: "sicut ex materia et forma, quorum unum est in
actum alterum in potentia, fit per se compositum in natura; sic ex ratione dependendi et terminandi fit per se constructio in sermone".

these by means of not very satisfactory notional criteria, *i.e.* that a constructible which, by reason of any mode of signifying 'seeks' or 'looks forward' is the dependent, and the constructible which, by reason of any mode of signifying, 'gives' or 'satisfies' is the terminant.[121] In actual fact, the description of these constructibles can be made much more economically, *i.e.* in a transitive construction the first constructible is the dependent and the second the terminant, *e.g.* lego librum, and in an intransitive construction the first constructible is the terminant and the second the dependent, *e.g.* "Socrates currit"; in other words, in any transitive construction the sequence is dependent-terminant and in any intransitive construction the sequence is terminant-dependent.

Each basic construction type can be divided into *actuum* (major) and *personarum* (minor) colligations; in the actuum construction,[122] the dependent member will always be the verb signifying by means of the modus actus the mode of action, and the terminant member will be a nominal form. We have thus a system of N V and V N constructions which can be described as the favourite construction types of Latin and are imposed on the Modistae by their own grammatical tradition and traditional logic. The intransitive personarum type of construction[123] represents various kinds of expansion by means of a modification of the N or the V element of the actuum construction; this modification can in effect be made by any type of word-class (pars orationis), since by definition, the dependent constructible in a personarum construction can signify by means of the mode of substance (modus substantiae) or any other pars orationis, except that the preposition cannot determine the verbal members. In the transitive personarum construction we have a purely nominal piece in which the terminant constructible, which can be one of four cases, *i.e.* genitive, dative, accusative or ablative, will represent the variation in this type of construction. This division of transitive and intransitive, actuum and personarum does not, however, fall equally under the modern exocentric-endocentric type of construction; only one, *i.e.* the S P or N V intransitive *actuum* construction is an exocentric construction, all the others being endocentric. An additional qualification is imposed on the

---

[121] Thomas of Erfurt, #191: "illud constructibile est dependens, quod ratione alicuius modi significandi tantum petit vel exigit; illud constructibile est terminans, quod ratione alicuius modi significandi tantum dat, vel concedit, etc.".

[122] Thomas of Erfurt, #195: "constructio intransitiva actuum est in qua constructibile dependens per modum actus significat".

[123] Thomas of Erfurt, #195: "constructio intransitiva personarum est in qua constructibile dependens significat per modum substantiae vel quomodolibet aliter".

two members of the constructio intransitiva personarum in that one member will be the determinant and the other will be the determinable constructible – and this additional qualification can be applied to either member of the intransitive actuum construction. We can, therefore, present the various constructions according to the following scheme:

Intransitive *Actuum*   *Personarum*
            N V : exocentric N determination: endocentric
                               V determination: endocentric
Transitive   V N : endocentric N N : endocentric

There are, in Thomas's scheme, two key concepts of inter-word relationships, *i.e.* dependentia and determinatio. Dependentia is a quasi-formal term used to express any relationship between two constructibles; it should not be interpreted as a head-subordinate relationship but more like the modern use of rection.[124] The terminant constructible must state the specific nature of the relationship, whereas the dependent constructible merely specifies the type of relationship, *i.e.* N V, V N, or N N without further specification, *i.e.* in "Socrates currit",[125] 'Socrates' is the terminant and 'currit' is the dependent, and in "Socratis interest", 'Socratis', though in the genitive case, is nevertheless the terminant and 'interest' the dependent; it is undoubtedly the dependent constructible which actually creates the relationship. Determinatio is used to describe the relationship between the member, either N or V, of the intransitive construction which has acquired an additional qualification or modification; in such cases we *can* talk about subordinate and head, the subordinate being the determinant constructible used to specify or qualify the head members of the construction, *e.g.* 'albus' is the subordinate in "homo albus" just as 'bene' is the subordinate in "currit bene".

There are five types of the N V type, *i.e.* the intransitive type of construction; these vary according to the case-form of the N element. Of the six cases of the nomen, all with the exception of the vocative, which can never be the first element of a construction,[126] can be the N and therefore act as the suppositum of these constructions, which can be exemplified thus, and according to the following diagram:

[124] L. Hjelmslev, *Principes de grammaire générale*, pp. 127-162.
[125] It would, of course, be more accurate to describe "*Socrates currit*" as a non-basic exocentric construction.
[126] As long ago as the Stoics and as recently as Hjelmslev, there has been dispute about the 'casual' nature of the vocative; *cf.* L. Hjelmslev, *La Catégorie des cas*, pp. 1-22.

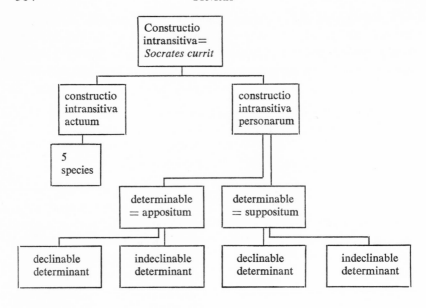

(a) nominative   – Socrates currit.
(b) genitive   – Socratis interest.
(c) dative   – Socrati accidit.
(d) accusative   – Socratem legere oportet.
(e) ablative   – a Socrate legitur.

There are four species of the V N type, *i.e.* the transitive actuum (signati) type of construction,[127] varying according to the N element; the nominative and vocative cannot function as the N element in these constructions which can be exemplified thus:

(a) genitive   – misereor Socratis
(b) dative   – faveo Socrati
(c) accusative   – lego librum
(d) ablative   – utor toga
and also by means of the following diagram:

---

[127] Thomas of Erfurt, #213: "constructio transitiva actuum dividitur in constructionem transitivam actus signati, et in constructionem transitivam actus exerciti ..." (#214); "constructio transitiva actus signati dividitur secundum diversitatem constructibilis terminantis".

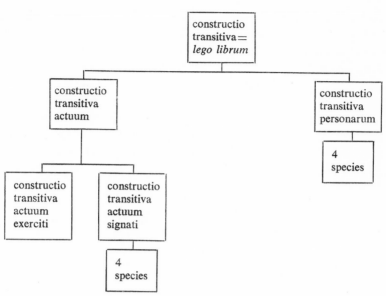

The intransitive personarum constructions represent expansions of either the N or the V element, in which the N or the V will be the determinable element; the determinant member can be either a declinable or an indeclinable pars orationis. If the determinable element is the N, then there are four possible constructions, by making the determinant a declinable pars which will therefore be one of four possible types of adjective, *e.g.* denominativum, relativum, interrogativum, distributivum, *e.g.* "homo albus", "omnis homo"; this type can be symbolised [A1].

If the determinable element is the N and the determinant an indeclinable pars, there will be four possible constructions according to the different indeclinable partes; this can be exemplified thus, and symbolised [A2]:

(a) Adverbium – Tantum Socrates legit
(b) Coniunctio – Socrates et Plato currunt
(c) Praepositio – A Socrate legitur
(d) Interiectio – Heu mortuus est.

If the determinable element is the V member, the determinant can be either a declinable or an indeclinable pars. If it is a declinable pars, we can have constructions such as: "sum albus" or "vocor Adrianus", in which we have either a copula, *i.e.* verbum substantivum, or a verbum vocativum, in which the dependence is 'backwards', and this type can be symbolised [B1]. If the determinant is an indeclinable pars, there will be only three possible types of construction depending on the type of indeclinable pars involved, since the preposition does not by definition construct with the verb; this type can be symbolised [B2]. Unfortunately, Thomas does not provide us with specific examples of this type of construction; however, the construction he used to exemplify the intransitive personarum, *e.g.* "Socrates albus currit bene" can be analysed into an intransitive construction of the [A1] type and an intransitive construction of the [B2] type, both of them being 'personarum' constructions, so that the whole construction can be analysed thus:

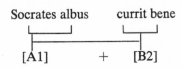

The transitive personarum constructions are the N N type only, and there are four species of this type of construction according to the case of the terminant constructible, *i.e.* the second N, and can be exemplified thus:

(a) **genitive** – filius Socratis
(b) **dative**   – simili Socrati
(c) **ablative** – celer pedibus.

G. CONSTRUCTIO INTRANSITIVA

An intransitive construction is one in which the second constructible depends on the first,[128] *e.g.* "Socrates currit"; in such constructions the first constructible is the terminant and the second the dependent. This type of construction is divided into two sub-types, *i.e.* actuum and personarum, the actuum exhibiting the basic pattern of suppositum and appositum which is the favourite S P sentence type of Latin; the personarum consists of a combination of determinable and determinant which is a modification applicable to either the suppositum or appositum. There are thus two types of intransitive constructions, which we can call major and minor, the major type being the intransitive actuum of the N V type and the minor the intransitive personarum made up of a determinable and a determinant and used to modify either the sup-

---

[128]   Thomas of Erfurt, #192: "constructio intransitiva est constructio, in qua secundum constructibile, per suos modos significandi, dependet ad primum".

positum or the appositum; although the minor type forms a grammatical syntagm, it will not form a complete sentence. "Socrates currit" is a constructio actuum, in which Socrates is the suppositum and also the terminant constructible, and 'currit' is the appositum and the constructible dependent on the suppositum. "Socrates albus" is a constructio personarum consisting of the determinable 'Socrates' which must be the terminant constructible and the determinant 'albus' which must be the dependent. The construction "Socrates albus currit bene" is in fact made up of two *lesser* intransitive constructions, *i.e.* the constructio personarum 'Socrates albus' and the intransitive constructio personarum 'currit bene', of which the first is an expansion of the suppositum 'Socrates' and the second an expansion of the appositum 'currit'.

Constructio intransitiva actuum

This type is a construction in which the dependent constructible signifies by means of the mode of action,[129] *e.g.* "Socrates currit"; the basic pattern is the N V type and represents the favourite S P sentence type of Latin, a different suppositum being used as a means of varying the type of construction. The appositum signifies by means of the modus distantis and is thereby separate from the suppositum, except that the accidental mode of 'compositio' renews the connection between the suppositum and the appositum, and offsets the separability of 'distantia';[130] the verb must be in grammatical proportionality (proportio), a term which, as we have seen, represents syntactic linkage and complementation, to the suppositum, and it will be the case form of the suppositum which will be the only means of varying this type of construction. It may be any case with the exception of the vocative, since this case, as was shown in the section of case in the accidental modes of the nomen, can never be the first member of a construction.

Congruitas constructionis intransitivae actuum

The congruence of this type of construction will consist of six modes of signifying in the dependent appositum which must be congruent to six

---

[129] Thomas of Erfurt, #195: "constructio intransitiva actuum est in qua constructibile dependens per modum actus significat".
[130] Thomas of Erfurt, #196: "cum appositum significet per modum distantis a supposito secundum situm, ideo supposito addi non potest sine medio. Tale medium est ipsa compositio ... et ideo compositio in huiusmodi dependentia maxime est verbo necessaria".

modes of signifying in the terminant suppositum. There is an association, for the Modistae, between word-order and the function of the
case-form; in an intransitive actuum construction, any case-form, except the vocative, can be the first, *i.e.* the terminant constructible, and
therefore it can act as the suppositum; similarly in a transitive construction, any case-form, except the nominative and vocative, will be
the second or oblique constructible.

The congruity (congruitas) between the terminant and dependent
members of an intransitive actuum construction derives from six factors
which are the same in every construction, except for one factor, for all
the cases of the suppositum, *i.e.* for the suppositum, the modus entis,
the modus per se stantis, the ratio principii, numerus, persona, and the
sixth represents a different criterion for each case, *e.g.* modus ut quod
est alterum which is one of the semi-formal criteria for the nominative
case. This will vary therefore according to the case of the nomen acting
as the suppositum; for the appositum, its criteria for the congruence of
the construction are the modus esse, compositio and mood (which are
accidental modes of the verb) which create the N V relationship between the suppositum and the verb, numerus, persona, and the modus
ut ipsum est alterum which corresponds to the modus ut quod est
alterum in the suppositum and represents the proportionality of the
verb to the appropriate case of the suppositum; the element which
changes in the suppositum and the appositum will be the 'modus ut
quod est alterum' and the 'modus ut illud est alterum', and will change
in accordance with the case of the nomen-suppositum.

Constructio intransitiva personarum

The characteristic feature of the constructio actuum was the suppositum-
appositum relationship, in which the variable element was the terminant
constructible, *i.e.* the suppositum. The intransitive personarum represents a very different type of construction, in which the dependent constructible signifies by means of the mode of substance or any other
pars.[131] It must be classed as a minor construction since it does not
represent a favourite sentence type and is made up of the determinable
and determinant elements. This type of construction is variegated by
means of the difference in the determining constructible.

The constructio personarum can be used to modify the suppositum

---

[131]   Thomas of Erfurt, #195: "constructio intransitiva personarum est in qua
constructibile dependens significat per modum substantiae, vel quomodolibet aliter".

or the appositum of an intransitive actuum construction; if it modifies the suppositum, it can do so by means of a determinant which can be either a declinable or an indeclinable pars orationis. The declinable determinant will be one of four kinds of adjective, *i.e.* denominativum, relativum, interrogativum, or distributivum, *e.g.* 'equus albus', 'omnis homo'.

If the determinant of the suppositum is an indeclinable pars orationis, it will be either an adverb, conjunction, preposition, or interjection, and in each case the indeclinable pars represents a different determination of the suppositum. The adverb acting as the determination of the suppositum can be explained by analogy to the construction "currere velociter est bonum", in which the infinitive acts as the suppositum by becoming a nominal element and the adverb 'velociter' acts as the determinant constructible by virtue of the verbality of the suppositum.[132] Similarly, the participle can act as the suppositum because the participle possesses the qualities[133] of an adjective which is a sub-species of nomen in the Modistic system, *e.g.* "heu mortuus est", and in this particular instance, the interjection will act as its determinant.

The determinant can also be added to the appositum and in such a construction, as in the previous types of constructio personarum, the determinant can be either declinable or indeclinable. If the determinant is declinable, it will produce a construction in which the determinant becomes the predicate of the copula or of the verbum vocativum, in which the dependence will be 'backwards', *e.g.* "sum albus", "vocor Adrianus", *i.e.* 'albus' is the determinant of the determinable 'sum'.

If the determinant is indeclinable, then it is possible to have one of three types of construction according to the dependent constructible, *i.e.* conjunction, adverb or interjection; the preposition cannot, of course, be a member of this type of construction since it must be the determinant in a construction in which the determinable will be a substantive.

Congruitas constructionis intransitivae personarum

The congruity (congruitas)[134] pattern of a construction, in which the

---

[132] Thomas of Erfurt, #208: "in ista oratione infinitivus non supponit per se, sed gratia nominis".

[133] Thomas of Erfurt, #208: "participium per accidens est suppositum cum omne participium sit adiectivum".

[134] Congruity is used as a translation equivalent of 'congruitas' but it should not be taken as 'concord' in the modern sense.

determinant is a declinable pars and is being used to determine the suppositum, consists of seven criteria, six of which are the same in every instance and the seventh refers more directly to the type of adjective used and its relationship to the constructible it will determine. These seven items of congruity show an interesting structural pattern. The first criterion establishes the general nature of the relationship between the two constructibles, *i.e.* the mode of determining (modus determinantis) on the part of the determinant and the mode of determinability (modus determinabilis) on the part of the determinable; the second refers to the basic and essential relationship between the two constructibles by means of their essential modes of signifying, *i.e.* the modus adiacentis, the characteristic feature of the adjective, and the modus per se stantis, the mark of the nomen substantivum. The other four criteria, common to all the constructions made up of this type of constructible, refer to the necessary congruity, *i.e.* of gender, number, case, and person, which must exist between two constructibles which share a common essence but which are, however, derived from the other;[135] the final item represents the particular type of constructible which is the determinant member and will vary in every instance according to the determinant constructible involved.

The congruity (congruitas) of a construction in which the determinant constructible is an indeclinable pars can be described by means of two criteria. The general criterion is the same in all these constructions and serves to establish the general nature of the relationship between the constructibles; the relationship of the determinant is expressed by the mode of determining (modus determinantis) and the determinable is expressed by the mode of determinability (modus determinabilis) as in the case when the determinant constructible was a declinable pars orationis. The second criterion, the particular, will be decided by and will vary according to the different indeclinable pars acting as the determinant in each of these constructions, *e.g.* the modus coniungentis in the construction with the conjunction as the determinant and the modus coniungibilis for the determinable, *i.e.* the suppositum; the correlative modes will similarly be required for the other indeclinable determinants.

In a construction when the determinant is applied to the appositum, the congruity is defined according to the same criteria as in those constructions when these indeclinable partes were the determinant of the

---

[135] Thomas of Erfurt, #71: "adiectivis, quae genus non habent ex proprietate suae rei subiectae, sed ex proprietate rei substantivi nominis".

suppositum;[136] therefore, in the construction "currit bene", we shall require the general criterion of the modus determinantis on the part of 'bene' and the modus determinabilis on the part of 'currit' and also the specific criterion required of the adverb together with the corresponding criteria required of the verb which is to be determined by the adverb.[137]

H. CONSTRUCTIO TRANSITIVA

A construction, in which the first constructible depends on the second, and the second constructible, if it has any dependence at all, will be the dependent of something which is quite different from the first constructible and will not immediately be part of this particular construction, is a transitive construction.[138] If we take as an example, "percutio Socratem", we see that the first constructible, *i.e.* 'percutio', is the first and dependent constructible, while 'Socratem' is the second and terminant constructible: this is, of course, a complete contrast to the intransitive construction. In this particular example, the terminant 'Socratem' is the dependent of no other constructible but serves merely to complete the dependence of the first constructible. In the case of "video legentem librum", we have two transitive constructions, *i.e.* 'video legentem' and 'legentem librum'; the first 'legentem' is the terminant of the dependent 'video' but becomes, with the addition of 'librum' the dependent of the oblique form, so that we have a constructible being at one and the same time the terminant of a construction and the dependent of a constructible which is quite different from the first.

---

[136] This section, *i.e.* the construction of the appositum and its determinant constructible, is one of the least satisfactory of Thomas's theory of the construction; the criteria are vague, and the dearth of illustration suggests that Thomas was aware of the flimsiness of this section and the lacunae in its argument in sharp contrast to his analysis of other types of construction. On the whole, his system of syntactic analysis is surprisingly modern in its attempt, despite all the drawbacks and restrictions implicit in an analysis of favourite sentence types established by means of non-linguistic criteria, to produce an analysis which might well be described as one of rudimentary Immediate Constituent analysis.

[137] The specific criterion will be, on the part of the adverb the modus determinantis ratione significati, and on the part of the verb the modus determinabilis; it should be noted that the modus determinantis and the modus determinabilis that are required as the *general* criterion refer to the relationship of the constructibles in this type of construction, while the modus determinantis ratione significati refers to the definition of the subaltern mode of the adverb to which 'bene' belongs.

[138] Thomas of Erfurt, #192: "constructio transitiva est in qua primum constructibile, per suos modos significandi, dependet ad secundum, secundo per eius dependentiam a primo recedente, si dependens fuerit".

The transitive construction, like the intransitive,[139] is divided into actuum and personarum – the dependent member of the actuum signifies by means of the mode of action (modus actus), and will be the verb; the dependent member of the personarum signifies by means of the mode of substance (modus substantiae) and will be a nomen; the general pattern of the actuum is V N and of the personarum N N.

Constructio transitiva actuum

This construction is one in which the dependent constructible signifies by means of the mode of action,[140] *e.g.* "lego librum". It is divided into two types, *i.e.* the actus signati and the actus exerciti.

The transitive construction actuum signati is divided and classified by means of the different terminant constructibles, which will be done in a four-fold manner according to the case of the terminant constructible, *i.e.* genitive = 'misereor Socratis', dative = 'faveo Socrati', accusative = 'percutio Socratem', and ablative = 'utor toga'.

The 'exerciti' type of transitive construction is not divided into different species but into individuals, and consists of the vocative with the adverb 'o'.

Congruitas constructionis transitivae actuum

As in the case of the intransitive constructions, the congruity of transitive constructions of the actus signati type stems from three general and specific criteria on the part of both constructibles. On the part of the dependent, *i.e.* the verb, the general criteria are (i) the modus esse,

---

[139] Thomas points out that the terms transitive and intransitive are related to the verb 'transire', the transitive referring to something which 'transit' from one place to another quite different place, whereas the intransitive does not 'transire' but remains in the same place; the result is that in the intransitive construction the dependence of the second constructible belongs to the first, whereas in a transitive construction the 'dependence' of the second constructible, if there is any further dependence, does not belong to the first but may 'transit' to something quite different from the first, *viz.* Thomas of Erfurt, #194: "constructionem intransitivam esse illam in qua constructibilia pertinent ad idem, vel tanquam ad idem videntur pertinere; constructionem transitivam esse illam, in qua constructibilia pertinent ad diversa, vel videntur pertinere ad diversa". This means that in the intransitive construction the second constructible which depends on the first will be identified with the first constructible, whereas in the transitive construction, the second constructible does not depend on the first, but tends to move away from the first constructible by virtue of its own potential dependence.

[140] Thomas of Erfurt, #212: "constructio transitiva actuum est in qua constructibile dependens per modum actus significat".

which is its essential feature, (ii) the significatio, *i.e.* the accidental mode of the verb which creates the relationship of dependence by the verb on a post-posed oblique nominal form, and (iii) the accidental mode of genus which signifies the quality of the relationship created by the "significatio' between the verb and the post-posed oblique. On the part of the terminant constructible, *i.e.* the nominal oblique, there must be, corresponding to those of the dependent verb, (i) the modus entis which is the essential feature of the nomen, (ii) the modus per se stantis which represents the nomen substantivum (because it would be wrong to say "percutio album"), and (iii) the mode of absolute final which will also include those instances of absolute final, though a preposition may have been used to create the actual V N relationship [141] – this produces a relationship rather like that of verb and object, *e.g.* the accusative without the preposition being the object of the verb in such an instance.

The special criteria vary in every instance, since a different congruity will be required according to the case of the oblique nominal; the congruity between the dependent, *i.e.* the verb, and the terminant, *i.e.* the substantive, in an oblique form, is based on the criteria for the different cases of the nomen, so that in "miseror Socratis", the congruity of the dependent and the terminant will be 'ut alterius' and 'ut cuius', which are, as we have seen, the semi-formal criteria for the genitive case.

The congruity of an 'exerciti' type of construction consists of the general modes and requires on the part of the terminant constructible the modus per se stantis and also the position of absolute final for the terminant; two special elements are also required, *i.e.* the modus excitantis or vocantis on the part of the adverb 'o' and the modus excitati on the part of the vocative.

Constructio transitiva personarum

This is the construction in which the dependent constructible signifies by means of the mode of substance,[142] and there are four species of this type of construction according to the differences of the terminant constructible; in each case the terminant consists of a nomen in a different case, *i.e.* genitive = 'filius Socratis', dative = 'similes Socrati', and

---

[141] Thomas of Erfurt, #214: "ex parte dependentis est modus generis, qui est quasi qualitas significationis accidentalis; cui correspondet in obliquo modus significandi per modum termini absolute modo conformi casuum contrahibilis".
[142] Thomas of Erfurt, #212: "constructio transitiva personarum est in qua constructibile dependens per modum substantiae significat".

ablative = 'celer pedibus';[143] it must be pointed out, however, that 'dependent' in this type of construction does not imply a relationship of subordinate to head.

Congruitas constructionis transitivae personarum

In this type of construction, the congruity consists of the modus entis in both constructibles, but as the mode of transitivity (modus transeuntis) in the dependent and the modus per se stantis in the terminant. The terminant must be a nomen substantivum; therefore it is incongruous to say "misereor albi" and equally so to say "cappa albi"; therefore on the model of the congruent construction "misereor Socratis", it is possible to create the congruent construction of "cappa Socratis". The special criterion for the congruity of these constructions consists of the congruence based on the translation equivalents, *i.e.* 'ut alterius/cuius', *etc.* for the dependent and 'ut cuius' *etc.* for the terminant, which are also the semi-formal criteria of case as an accidental mode of the nomen.

Three stages make up Thomas's theory of syntax; of these the constructio perfecta presupposes the concord (congruitas) of the constructibles and this in turn presupposes the constructio, a binary combination of constructibles made up from the similarity of their modes of signifying. To Thomas at least,[144] the construction was clearly by far the most important of these stages, and he therefore concentrates on a lengthy exposition of the various types of construction, being content to expound briefly afterwards the general principles of congruity (congruitas) and completion (perfectio), having already described in much more detail the congruity of the various constructions along with an analysis and exposition of the constructions themselves.

I. CONCLUSION

The analysis and description of the partes orationis were clearly the most important aspect of Modistic grammatical theory, but in any ex-

---

[143] Thomas also listed the accusative as one of the possible cases which can act as the terminant in this type of construction, and gives as an instance "Petrus albus percutit pedem". His criteria seem to be confused, to say the least, since in the same paragraph he says: #215: "constructio quae est adiectivi cum accusativo, non est incongrua, sed figurativa. Accusativus solus construitur congrue cum verbis significantibus actum; quia accusativus est terminus actus signati".

[144] It is fair to say that this is also true of Martin of Dacia.

amination of this theory, it is impossible to avoid reference to their syntactic theories, since it is quite evident that their theories of syntax were evolved, apart from certain (perhaps) unconscious influences, in terms of the modes of signifying of the partes orationis and cannot, therefore, be considered as separate from their theories of the modes of signifying.

The partes orationis were described by the Modistae according to the following plan:[145] the partes were divided into declinable and indeclinable, the declinables being then separated according to their essential modes of signifying. Each pars orationis was described separately in terms of its essential modes and then its accidental modes. Some of these accidental modes are familiar to traditional and modern grammar, e.g. gender, number, case, person, mood, etc., but others are peculiar to the Modistae, e.g. compositio in the verb. These accidental modes are an important part of Modistic procedure – so much so, that Siger tends to neglect the essential modes and concentrate on the accidental modes,[146] – they represent variations imposed on the essence of the pars and together with the essential modes they combine to make up the totality of the pars. The accidental modes (and in the case of Siger the essential modes too) are subjected to a further classification, i.e. that of absolute or respective mode, which describes the mode in terms of its syntactic potentiality.[147] Certain modes have in themselves no syntactical function, e.g. figura which can be described in modern terms as 'morphemic base structure',[148] and are therefore absolute modes, but other modes are respective, since they may realise a syntactic relationship either of concord or government with other partes or other members of the same pars, e.g. gender between the substantive and adjective, or case between the substantive and verb.[149]

All these modes of signifying were expressed in morpho-semantic

---

[145] The diagrams in Appendix C, pp. 387-389 attempt to show the inter-relationships between the declinable and indeclinable partes by means of their essential modes of signifying.

[146] This is certainly true, if the amount of space devoted to his description of the essential and accidental modes of the nomen and verbum is any guide.

[147] In Thomas's scheme, the accidental modes only are respective or absolute; Thomas, furthermore, was not averse to using syntactic criteria in his definitions of the partes orationis and the modes of signifying (cf. his discussion of persona and tempus as accidental modes of the verb), but he did not make systematic use of syntax in the way that Siger used 'principium constructionis' to classify the different modes in terms of their syntactic or non-syntactic functions.

[148] Cf. R. H. Robins, Thrax, p. 99.

[149] Thomas of Erfurt, #149: "tempus non est accidens respectivum verbi, cum secundum ipsum non dependeat ante se ad suppositum, nec post se ad obliquum".

terms, some of which are perhaps more formal than others; it must be remembered that they are the formulations by the Modistae of the same formal features of Latin that the modern linguist would have to describe in an analysis of Latin, and however much we may criticise the Modistae for their non-formal grammar, they were remarkably consistent in their procedure and did achieve a coherent grammatical system, even though their very consistency may have left them at times with the necessity of justifying themselves by means of lengthy and subtle explanations. Once the analysis of the modes of signifying of the partes orationis was complete, then and only then could the syntax of these partes in terms of their modes of signifying be described. Thus, we see the whole grammatical process of the Modistae, starting with 'vox' and ending with the completed sentence.

VIII

CONCLUSION:
THE MODISTAE AND MODERN LINGUISTIC THEORY

A. INTRODUCTION

Since the days of the ancient Greeks, one method of describing and classifying the words of a language has been by means of the method traditionally known as 'part-of-speech analysis'. Modern linguists have continued to use this type of analysis, – except that they substitute 'word' or 'form-class' for 'part of speech', and of course they attach much less importance to this type of analysis than did, for instance, the grammarians of the Middle Ages. Such a procedure cannot constitute a method for stating the facts about the grammar of any language, but for the mediaeval grammarian, the description of the 'parts of speech' of a language was grammatical analysis par excellence.[1]

What are, insofar as word-class theory is concerned, the great changes between the methods of the modern structuralist linguist and the traditional grammarian? These have often been described in great detail, but it is possible to suggest two major differences between them, *i.e.* the changes (a) in the criteria used in descriptive and analytical procedures and (b) in the attitude towards language universals. The former change may be characterised as the substitution by the structuralist, in a statement of the primary linguistic data, of strictly formal linguistic criteria[2] for the logical, philosophical, semantic, or mixture of semi-formal and notional criteria of the traditional grammarian.[3] It is no part of this study to contribute to the controversy between structuralist and traditional grammarians, so that in fairness to both sides it can be said that recent linguistics has been attempting a rehabilitation of the

---

[1] Roos describes the 'modi significandi' as "Lehre der Wortklassen".
[2] L. Hjelmslev, *Principes de grammaire générale*, p. 298: "pour qu'une catégorie ait une existence réelle du point de vue grammatical, il faut qu'elle se définisse par des critériums de forme, et non pas par des critériums purement sémantiques".
[3] R. H. Robins, *A. and M.*, p. 67, where he describes Priscian's criteria, *i.e.* "criteria of formal structure and behaviour, alleged 'meanings' and philosophical abstractions".

goals of traditional grammatical work but retaining all the while the rigour of the formal methods developed by the structuralist linguist.

Traditional grammar has often claimed (with some justification, it might be added) to be a universal grammar, but there are today many linguists who would question the feasibility of a universal grammar, by which is meant, in this instance, nothing more than a system of word-classes which can be expressed in terms of a natural language and in theory applied to other natural languages.[4] The flaw in such an approach is that consideration of the properties of this kind of universal grammar will be restricted to surface structures, but there is no reason to look for uniformity of surface structures.[5] Chomsky has proposed[6] the classification of universals as substantive or formal; he also points out that consideration of substantive universals has been the traditional concern of linguistic theory. It can be argued that any theory of universals which restricts itself to a consideration of substantive universals will obviously not satisfy the condition of explanatory adequacy, since it cannot provide for connection between levels nor for connection between deep and surface structure. The position is further complicated by the fact that the criteria for these substantive universals have rarely, if ever, been the same for the structuralist, the transformational, or the traditional grammarian; certainly the structuralist and the traditionalist grammarian have never really come to grips with the problem of formal universals. It can be said that the Modistae intuitively recognised that preoccupation with surface structure was inadequate; this is revealed by the fact that in their attempt to create a universal grammar they ignored almost totally features of surface structure and restricted themselves largely to problems of deep structure. It can also be said that they were intuitively conscious of both substantive and formal universals.[7] That they failed to achieve an adequate univer-

---

[4] C. E. Bazell, *Linguistic Form*, p. 78, insists on the need for the existence and analysis of the lexical categories of a language, but denies quite categorically that it is possible to draw up categories which will apply to all languages: "definitions intended for application to all languages can never be complete. The supposition that they might be gave rise to that most ridiculous of pseudo-problems, the question 'whether there are categories common to all languages'! Do all languages have a category of nouns? It is possible to define the noun in opposition to the verb, to the pronoun, or to any other part of speech. But it is not possible to define it in opposition to all possible parts of speech, for there is no limit to the possibilities. Hence the question cannot be answered".

[5] N. A. Chomsky, *Aspects*, p. 118.

[6] N. A. Chomsky, *Aspects*, pp. 27-30.

[7] I have simply used the terms that Chomsky has listed: this does not mean that I am using them as he does, nor am I implying that the Modistae applied criteria

sal grammar can be attributed to the limitations of their epistemology.

Despite these claims on behalf of the Modistae, there remain important differences between their theories and those of the modern linguist, and these represent a fundamental change in approach to the whole problem of linguistic description and ipso facto to the problem of the parts of speech. The Modistae, guided as they were by the metaphysical theories of their contemporaries, believed that their system of word-classes, constructed as they imagined them to be on the universality of the world of reality and exemplified by means of the idealised language of learning of the Middle Ages, i.e. Latin, was genuinely universal. Modern linguistic scholarship has shown that the analysis of a language by means of the parts of speech cannot alone constitute a universal grammar, since the parts of speech themselves are by no means universal.[8]

To say that traditional grammar does not constitute a universal grammar in no way invalidates the idea of universals in language, and in recent years linguistics has recognised the need for a means of representing the signals and the related semantics of languages. We must, however, be careful to distinguish between general and universal grammar.[9] Sapir[10] maintained that each language has its own scheme of form-classes but added that it is becoming increasingly clear that most languages use, for instance, the categories of 'noun' and 'verb'. It may be possible to proclaim the universality of grammatical categories such as 'noun' and 'verb', but the criteria for them, as for the other form-classes, although formal, will be different in the case of every language. This is in keeping with Hjelmslev's definition of general grammar.[11]

---

which would render their universals substantive or formal in the sense that Chomsky uses these terms.

[8] B. L. Whorf, "Science and Linguistics", *Language, Thought and Reality*, pp. 215-216, suggests that in Nootka "all words seem to us to be verbs ... we have, as it were, a monistic view of nature that gives us only one class of word for all kinds of event".

[9] J. R. Firth, "A Synopsis of Linguistic Theory, 1930-1955", *Studies in Linguistic Analysis*, p. 31: "a general linguistic theory applicable to particular linguistic descriptions, *not* a theory of universals for general linguistic description".

[10] E. Sapir, *Language*, pp. 118-119.

[11] L. Hjelmslev, *La structure morphologique*, p. 92: "la grammaire générale n'est pas une grammaire universelle, mais la théorie des réalisables et de leurs conditions". Roos is mistaken when he compares de Saussure and Hjelmslev to Martin of Dacia and by implication to the other Modistae by suggesting that the Modistae were attempting a prolegomena of language; the Modistae were in fact seeking a universal grammatical theory.

B. THE MODISTAE

There is a regrettable tendency among modern linguists to ignore altogether the work of their predecessors or else to refer to it disparagingly as 'traditional' and dismiss it therefore as useless.[12] Certainly, it would be easy to dismiss the theories of the Modistae as irrelevant to any modern theory and yet there are, in the Modistic system, features which are not unlike some of the ideas expressed by modern linguists. This must not be interpreted as a suggestion that modern linguists have derived these ideas from the Modistae but merely that modern theorists, who are after all dealing with the same type of raw material as the Modistae, have introduced concepts which do show a degree of similarity to those of the Modistae.[13]

It is questionable, to say the least, whether a theory of the past can be properly compared to one or more theories of the twentieth century, and indeed one of the problems is that there is no single theory current today; this is putting aside as non-pertinent the matter of the power of a linguistic theory, and similarly to attempt such a comparison is to ignore the predilection that any one linguist may have for any one theory. We are in fact trying to compare two intellectual trends which, for myriad reasons, cannot be properly compared. If any attempt were to be made to compare these trends, it could be said to imply an ignorance of all intellectual history and certainly of the intellectual processes on which any linguistic theory will be predicated. Furthermore, there is always the danger of seeing another theory, particularly one of the past, through the filter of one's own theory; many of the exaggerated claims on behalf of theoretical power arise from such a distorted view. It is, however, useful and enlightening, even if the whole of a linguistic theory cannot be subjected to comparative scrutiny, to observe that there are certain perennial problems in grammatical theory and that there may be modern developments which may have their origin in earlier work.

There are of course other problems involved when we attempt to compare the theories of the Modistae to modern linguistic theory. The

---

[12] Cf. L. Bloomfield, Language, Chapter I, in which he discusses pre-20th century grammatical work. Chomsky makes some very pertinent remarks in the introduction to his Cartesian Linguistics.

[13] There is a danger that over-enthusiasm may lead one to imagine that these resemblances amount almost to renewals in modern theories of ideas put forward by the Modistae and then forgotten. To do this would be to suggest that the Modistae were much better grammarians than they were in actual fact, and it would also minimise the very important advances that modern linguistics has made during the past 60 years.

first is that a mere matter of 600 years at least separates them, and any grammatical theory, if it is to be considered a complete theory, must take some account of its intellectual background. It is trite to say that these factors were quite different in the Middle Ages from those of today, and some of the inadequacies of the Modistic scheme can be attributed to the imperfections of the scholarly world in which they lived, *e.g.* the fact that their theories were conceived and worked out in terms of one language only, *i.e.* Latin, and that their own grammatical theory was derived from previous work carried out in terms of one other language, *i.e.* Greek, of very similar structure.

Another problem which is closely connected with the previous problem and which renders comparison very difficult is that the mediaeval view of man in his environment and the metaphysical theories of the world are entirely different from those of today;[14] grammar was looked upon by the Modistae as dependent on the structure of reality, whereas today language is considered by most linguists as "part of human co-operation, part of social action".[15] These conflicting views of grammar and grammatical analysis must be reconciled if any comparison is to be made.

One major contribution of modern linguistics has been the provision of criteria to assess the power of a linguistic theory. We have already discussed Modistic theory in terms of Hjelmslev's criteria of self-sufficiency, exhaustiveness and simplicity;[16] Chomsky has also proposed[17] criteria for the assessment of a linguistic theory which have also been referred to in terms of possible application to Modistic grammar.[18] In

---

[14] Throughout the discussion of their grammatical theories, a great deal was made of the fact that the Modistae created their grammatical doctrine from contemporary logical and metaphysical theories of reality. It is also perhaps worth repeating that this is really a case of putting the cart before the horse and that in fact their conception of substance, the principles of their logic, *etc.* were dictated by the structure of the language they were using to express these concepts.

[15] R. H. Robins, *A. and M.*, p. 89. Another factor which separates the Modistae from the linguist of today is what might be called the need for 'total' description, *cf.* J. R. Firth, "The Technique of Semantics", *Papers in Linguistics*.

[16] *Cf.* pp. 41-42.

[17] N. Chomsky, *Current Issues in Linguistic Theory*, Chap. 2.

[18] *Cf.* p. 19. It is also worth noting that the Modistae were very much concerned for the explanatory adequacy of their theory. It would seem that they, of all the mediaeval grammarians, had recognised the need, as verbalised by William of Conches, to supplement Priscian's bare description by greater explanatory adequacy of theory, *i.e.* "Quod ergo ab istis minus dictum est, dicere proposuimus, quod obscure exponere, ut ex nostro opere aliquis causas inventionis predictorum querat et diffinitionum Prisciani expositiones, ex antiquis vero glossis continuationem et expositionem littere eiusdem et exceptones regularum et fere et plerumque

terms of theoretical power, there are two further factors which must be considered in the process of evaluating: one is the extent that a theory will yield an explanation of the deep structure and it is reasonable to say that the Modistae, by the very nature of their theoretical criteria, were concerned with deep structure almost to the total exclusion of surface grammar;[19] the second is the 'creative' aspect of language use. Here again it can be claimed that Modistic grammar does have the power to form a new sentence, but only of a limited kind, and in a sense this is imposed by the very restrictions made by the Modistae on the choice of sentences which formed the corpus of their grammars.

Chomsky has insisted on the creative aspect of language use,[20] stressing the relationship between linguistic and mental processes, and this relationship was very much present in the creation of the word-classes by the Modistae. This is particularly apparent in Siger de Courtrai's definitions of the general modes of the noun and verb.

Chomsky has also stressed the difference and at the same time the necessary relationship between the underlying semantic interpretation of a form or sentence and its actual linguistic exponencies. The Modistae were not perhaps so much aware as the modern linguist is of the distinction between deep and surface grammar, probably because they were really concerned with deep grammar, and the superficial organisation of linguistic units was a matter of only secondary importance to them. This could account for their attitude to vernaculars and for some of their strange etymologies. Modistic definition of noun and verb is clearly a matter of deep grammar; there is no formal definition given but an appeal to what might be called deep grammar permitted them to distinguish between the modus entis which is the general mode of signifying of the noun and the modus esse which is the general mode of the verb.[21] A similar type of rationalization permitted them to include forms such as 'nihil', 'caecitas' in the category of noun.

Their intuitive recognition of deep grammar is much more clearly

---

petat" (Thurot, p. 17). This suggests an interesting point of contact between the Modistae and the modern generative grammarian.

[19] There is a wealth of literature on this subject, in particular N. Chomsky, *Cartesian Linguistics*, also his *Aspects of the Theory of Syntax*.

[20] N. Chomsky, *Cartesian Linguistics*, pp. 3-31. N. Chomsky, *Topics in the Theory of Generative Grammar*. Chapter I.

[21] Thomas of Erfurt, #24: "in rebus invenimus quasdam proprietates communissimas, sive modos essendi communissimos, scilicet modum entis, et modum esse. Modus entis est modus habitus, et permanentis, rei inhaerens, ex hoc quod habet esse. Modus esse est modus fluxus et successionis, rei inhaerens, ex hoc quod habet fieri".

revealed in certain aspects of their syntactic theory. In the section on syntax, it was pointed out that Modistic syntax depended on a three-stage progression of constructio, congruitas, and perfectio, and the realisation of perfectio which renders any construction complete calls for a reference to the underlying organisation of the sentence in terms of its semantic interpretation. However, a much more obvious reference to deep structure is their analysis of the intransitive construction: pieces such as "Socrates currit", "Socratis interest", "Socrati accidit" are all analysed similarly as intransitive constructions consisting of suppositum (subject) and appositum (predicate). There is some recognition by the Modistae of a formal distinction in the cases of the suppositum but in reality the Modistae were making, it would seem, an analysis of these constructions in terms of their deep structure.[22]

In assessing a grammar one has to take into account the purpose of the model. One may accuse the Modistae of providing an inadequate grammar and it is quite true that they restricted themselves to declarative sentences, but they did not set themselves the task of writing a complete grammar of Latin. Like their immediate predecessors, they were making commentaries on Priscian, not as teachers of Latin but rather of grammar, which to them was clearly independent of any didactic function. It has been stated repeatedly in the course of this study that the interrelationships between grammar and logic were constantly in view and the Modistae were in their own minds quite clear on the distinction.

Like Chomsky today, they sought to postulate a universal theory of grammar[23] but, unlike Chomsky, their theory of grammar did not aim to provide a grammar for individual languages;[24] their object was to produce a grammar that was universal, the grammar of the human

---

[22] Thomas of Erfurt, #196: "quod cum constructio intransitiva actuum sit constructio suppositi cum apposito: et cum nihil supponat, nisi casus, vel habens casum: ideo secundum diversitatem casus supponentis, diversificatur constructio intransitiva actuum. Aut ergo Nominativus casus supponit, ut dicendo, *Socrates currit*, aut Genitivus supponit, ut dicendo, *Socratis interest*; aut Dativus casus supponit, ut dicendo, *Socrati accidit*; aut Accusativus supponit, ut dicendo, *Socratem legere oportet*; aut Ablativus casus supponit, ut dicendo, *a Socrate legitur*. Vocativus autem supponere non potest, cum sibi ratio principii repugnet".

The division of suppositum/appositum could also be said to represent the basic IC cut; problems such as these also suggest solutions of the type proposed by Halliday, *viz.* M. A. K. Halliday, "Some notes on 'deep' grammar", *Journal of Linguistics* 2 (1966), 57-67.

[23] R. G. Godfrey, "Late Mediaeval Linguistic Meta-Theory and Chomsky's Syntactic Structures", *Word* 21 (1965), 251-256.

[24] N. Chomsky, *Topics in the Theory of Generative Grammar*, Chapter I.

mind. That they were indifferent to the problems of linguistic description and to contemporary vernaculars can be accounted for by means of an extension of their own criteria; the relationship of act and potentiality, which, as was pointed out earlier,[25] was a concept taken from contemporary metaphysics, allowed them to suppose that the language they were discussing, Latin, was higher on the scale of perfection and therefore statements made about Latin would not necessarily be applicable to languages lower on the scale. The Modistae were unaware, it would seem, of formal (substantive) distinctions, and hence structured their grammatical categories in semantic terms. It is reasonable to say that they were operating in terms of a restricted language but their purpose was explanatory; one might say that they bypassed the observational level by virtue of the fact that they accepted Priscian's corpus as the basis for their work, and similarly they ignored the descriptive level since they were not concerned with linguistic intuition.[26] Indeed they specified quite clearly the form of their grammar which was universal in intent and had as its object a complete and congruent expression of a mental concept.

It has been stated that the Modistae made little or no contributions to linguistic theory,[27] but this is putting the cart before the horse. To say that they contributed nothing comes from viewing their approach to linguistic theory through the filter of our own, though it would be equally wrong to exaggerate the power of their grammar. Our earlier apologia on behalf of the Modistae should not be taken as a justification for their theories: we reject Modistic grammar, as indeed we must, because we reject the whole intellectual system which engendered their theories.[28]

The framework of Modistic linguistics established a grammar which was concerned essentially with meaning: there was no phonological component for the simple reason that phonology has no part of grammar since it is essentially pre-linguistic. It is not that they were unaware of the presence of sound features, but these were simply not needed as part of their grammatical statement. However, the most obvious weakness of their grammar was their complete rejection of formal criteria; this becomes most noticeable by virtue of the fact that so much effort was expended on the description of parts of speech. It is almost as if they went

[25]   Cf. p. 52.
[26]   Cf. N. Chomsky, Current Issues in Linguistic Theory, p. 29.
[27]   F. P. Dinneen, An Introduction to General Linguistics, pp. 141-147: 402.
[28]   G. L. Bursill-Hall, "Notes on the Semantics of Linguistic Description", p. 41.

out of their way to reject formal criteria, but again it is important for the historian to state why this was so, and that they would do this becomes clear, when once we realise the purpose of their grammar. But their contributions were real in that the rigour of their methods created a method for looking at language, and grammatical theory depends to a large extent on the way that the theoretician looks at language. It is to little purpose to mention that they were criticised by Renaissance scholars for their rigour;[29] the recent history of linguistics provides excellent examples of theories which claimed considerable rigour and which have nonetheless been refuted. The Modistae did demand rigour in their methods but rigour in and of itself cannot create a successful theory; a theory requires rigorous descriptive procedures, but ones which are based on formal criteria, and these the Modistae failed utterly to provide. These were by no means the only weaknesses of Modistic theory, and even a cursory examination of their work will soon reveal serious lacunae in their whole approach to the problem of linguistic description.

It would be quite mistaken if we were to exaggerate the power of Modistic grammar or the value of its contributions to linguistic theory. In one sense, however, the Modistae appear to have been innovators, or at least to have completed a movement which is of some significance in the history of linguistics and which can be regarded as a positive contribution. The Greek and Latin, and for that matter, the earlier Mediaeval grammarians had been essentially descriptive grammarians; in other words, the predecessors of the Modistae had all written grammars as native speakers of their language and with this very much as a motive for their mode of grammatical explanation, a fact which may in part account for the absence of explanatory adequacy in their grammars. Grammarians after Peter Helias, and especially the Modistae, were concerned with the formulation of a general theory of grammar; that they should have done this in terms of a commentary on Priscian's grammar and in terms af Latin is no animadversion of their aims. Nor should their shortcomings be allowed to belittle their aims or their achievements. For the first time in the history of linguistics in Europe, we can point to what appears to have been a genuine attempt to create a universal theory of grammar. This does not prevent us from observing that the Modistae failed to do this, and indeed they could not have succeeded, but this was because the formulation of such a theory was

---

[29] F. P. Dinneen, *Op. cit.,* p. 147.

impossible in terms of the intellectual plinth on which they sought to construct such a theory.[30]

C. MODISTIC AND MODERN THEORIES

It has been no part of this study to analyse the work of the Modistae in relation to current work, but rather to characterise Modistic linguistics as it saw itself; inevitably, however, comparisons do arise. However, the danger of wholesale comparison – if indeed such is even possible – is surely obvious, and conversely any scissors-and-paste feature analysis can serve little purpose. What does emerge from even chance comparisons is the realisation that grammarians of the Middle Ages were probably just as much exercised by problems of grammatical theory as the modern theoretican, and it is possible that some of their attempts may have some bearing on the solution of problems that face the modern linguist.

Despite the caveats just made, it is possible to point to similarities between Modistic and grammatical theories, but we would be wise to do nothing more than to recognise in certain instances a fortuitous similarity, in others a potential development, and in others it may well be the re-emergence of ideas, but in all cases it can safely be said that the likenesses are never deliberately achieved.[31] The interest of these likenesses lies in the fact that we can find similar features in modern work, but in a much more developed form and stated in a much more systematic manner. It is interesting to note that the Modistae introduced features into their analysis of real interest to the modern linguist whenever they abandoned their notional, semantic criteria and started thinking about language in a purely linguistic manner. Rather than judge the Modistae too harshly, it would be more appropriate if we were to realise that the Modistae, products of their environment though they may have been, suggested certain analytical procedures which were well in advance of their time.

---

[30] Butterfield suggests that "the lack of mathematics, or the failure to think of mathematical ways of formulating things, was partly responsible for what appeared to be verbal subleties and an excessive straining of language", cf. H. Butterfield, *The Origins of Modern Science*, p. 15. Butterfield is of course talking about the mediaeval scientist but it is a statement which could very easily be applied to the Modistae.

[31] "In other words, the modern world is in a certain sense a continuation of the mediaeval one – it is not to be regarded as merely a reaction against it", cf. H. Butterfield, *Op. cit.*, p. 28. This remark applies very appropriately to linguistics.

Reference has already been made by at least one modern scholar[32] to the similarity between de Saussure's theory of 'le signe linguistique' and Modistic use of 'signum' and the 'modus signandi'. Modistic use of 'vox' is also part of their 'sign' theory, and although phonetics was excluded from their linguistic theory, vox cannot be dismissed as an element of 'expression'; in the Modistic scheme, a state of affairs is found not unlike de Saussure's 'phonème',[33] although 'vox' bears no resemblance whatsoever to the Bloomfieldian 'phoneme'. We must, however, counsel caution because this similarity between 'vox' and the Saussurean 'phonème' is only relative, if for no other reason than that de Saussure did not exclude phonic criteria from his theory whereas the Modistae avoid all reference to 'le mot parlé' and exclude 'action vocale' from their sphere of activity. But "la réalisation de l'image intérieure dans le discours" is surely very close to the part played by the 'vox' in the change from the modus intelligendi to the modus significandi and in the realisation of the 'dictio' and the 'pars orationis'. There remains the one gap – and this is, on this topic, surely unbridgeable – between the Modistae and the moderns, *i.e.* that the Modistae did exclude sound altogether from grammar, whereas modern linguists insist on sound as part of language study even if they do not agree on the part that phonetics and phonology play in a total description.

It is at the level of syntax[34] that we find more solid ground for arguing on behalf of some relevance between Modistic theories, but it is once more imperative to stress the need for caution. Modistic syntactic procedures, at least in so far as Thomas and Martin described them – Siger had nothing to offer at this level – were full of lacunae, and it would be doing modern theories of syntax a grave injustice to suggest that they are in any way really similar to the theories of the Modistae. The fact is that there are one or two features in their syntax which can be discussed in terms of comparable features in modern theories, and it is this likeness which brings a real interest and a further importance (in addition to their intrinsic value) to the study of the syntactical and grammatical theories of the Modistae.

In the section on syntax, we saw that Thomas, by means of his

[32] R. H. Robins, *A. and M.*, pp. 82-83.
[33] F. de Saussure, *Cours de linguistique générale*, p. 98: "ce terme, impliquant une idée d'action vocale, ne peut convenir qu'au mot parlé, à la réalisation de l'image intérieure dans le discours".
[34] A condensed version of Modistic syntax can be found in my paper, "Aspects of Modistic Grammar", *Monograph Series on Languages and Linguistics* 19 (1966), 133-148.

various types of constructions, created a very elementary form of Immediate Constituent analysis of sentence structures. It would be wrong to make anything more of this than a fortuitous similarity between this type of syntactic analysis and Modistic syntactic theory and practice, since Thomas uses only four types of simple construction, and does not discuss more complex types of sentences. It is not possible, therefore, to envisage any construction in Thomas's scheme any more complicated than a sentence of the type NVN with expansions of these three elements to produce a sentence of the type Nd Vd Nd (d = determinant), which could therefore be thought of the following ICs:

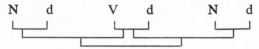

The Modistae expressed these relations by means of the various dependences between the constructibles, so that in an NV or a VN construction, the V element is the dependent of the N element, whereas in an Nd or a Vd construction, the d element is both the dependent and also the determinant of the N or V determinable.

This shows a more definite similarity to the theories of dependences and fundamental relations found in the work of Hjelmslev[35] and Bazell.[36] Bazell has evolved a much more sophisticated and at the same time a much more concise and economic scheme of relationships by means of his relationships of determinant-determinatum and superordinate-subordinate, the superordinate-subordinate relationship being a means of stating more specifically the relationship of the determinant to the determinatum. This is, of course a much more economical way of stating the relationships, *i.e.* by means of one binary opposition, one member of which will be either the superordinate or the subordinate member, in contrast to the four constructions described by Thomas,[37]

[35] L. Hjelmslev, "La structure morphologique"; "Structural Analysis of Language"; "La notion de rection". These papers are part of the collection *Essais linguistique, TCLC* 12 (1959).

[36] C. E. Bazell, "On the Neutralisation of Syntactic Oppositions", *TCLC* 5 (1949), 77-86. C. E. Bazell, "Syntactic Relations and Linguistic Typology", *C.F.S.* 8 (1940), 5-20. C. E. Bazell, "The Fundamental Syntactic Relations". *Časopis pro Moderní Filologii* 33 (1949), 9-15. C. E. Bazell, *Linguistic Form*, 1953.

[37] In Bazell's scheme, an attributive adjective and noun would be a dD (d = determinant, D = determinatum) relationship, the d being the subordinate; in Thomas's scheme, this would be a constructio intransitiva personarum with the noun as the determinable and the adjective as the determinant. In Bazell's scheme, a subject-predicate construction and a verb-object construction would be dD in the case of the SP construction and Dd in the case of the verb-object construction.

i.e. the basic NV construction in which both the N and the V elements may have determinants, so that this construction may be either NV, or NdV, or NVd, or NdVd, and we have in addition the other constructions of VN and NN.

Similarly, Hjelmslev, by means of his relationships of solidarity, selection, and combination,[38] has suggested a type of analysis which Thomas, with his relationships of principium-dependent (NV) and terminus-dependent (VN), had suggested but in an obviously primitive form, and to make any more of this would be to attach an undue and exaggerated importance to the theories of the Modistae in relation to these modern theories.

It would however be unfair to the Modistae to fail to point out how full of promise their syntactic theory was. Hjelmslev suggests in his *Prolegomena* that syntax is concerned with the relations between categories only and described traditional syntax as the relations between 'variants' but glossematics as the relations between 'invariants'. Without seeking to exaggerate the originality of Modistic syntax, it is possible to see the burgeonings of a somewhat similar theory, if we consider the fundamental relations of principium-dependent or terminus-dependent of Thomas's scheme to be the 'invariants' since his syntactic theory is built around these basic relationships.

D. CONCLUSION

The history of linguistics in the 20th century is largely an account of the division between traditional and structuralist grammar; it is no part of this work to contribute to the controversy. In recent years, however, there have been signs of a revival of interest in the theories of our predecessors and there are a number of advantages to this. Linguistics is both a cumulative and interpretative science; the history of linguistics allows us to view the study of language in the context of its history and successive intellectual and cultural developments within a more general theme of the history of science. This is particularly true if we accept, as we must, that just as language must be studied as part of the social

---

though in both constructions the verb would be the 'dependent' constructible. One of the additional advantages of Bazell's system is that the terms 'transitive' and 'intransitive' are now free to be used in the sense that convention and tradition have given them.

[38]   L. Hjelmslev, *Prolegomena*, pp. 15-25.

process and activity, so too the study of linguistic theory and ipso facto the history of linguistic theory must be carried on within their contexts of situation.[39]

Much of recent work in the history of linguistics has been concerned with a reassessment of traditional grammar; this has been very much, for example, the purpose of Chomsky's recent incursions into earlier ideas,[40] but it would be quite mistaken to regard this merely as an attempt to rehabilitate traditional grammar. There is much in traditional work which must be discarded, but to discard it all in one fell swoop is to throw out the baby with the bath. Descriptive techniques are no substitute for theory and yet it serves little to construct a theory which does not take into consideration the strength and value of previous work.

The value for the modern linguist of a study of the Modistae (or indeed for any established theory of the past) and the importance of their theories in relation to twentieth-century linguistic theories do not lie in their intrinsic value as contributions to general grammatical theory. Apart from certain isolated features, Modistic grammatical theories and descriptive techniques would be discarded by most modern linguists, no matter what 'school' of linguistic doctrine they profess to belong to, since Modistic criteria are essentially semantic and they never used formal linguistic criteria in any systematic manner.

The real value of a study by the modern linguist of any group of grammarians of the past is that it affords an excellent picture of a grammatical theory established against a different intellectual and academic background. The justification of such a study by a linguist must be that the synchrony and diachrony of language is reflected in the synchrony and diachrony of grammatical theory.[41] To ignore one's past is an act of arrogance,[42] and we must respect our predecessors and their contributions to linguistic science even if we do discard so much of their work. It is particularly appropriate to study the Modistae in this context, since they found themselves in an academic atmosphere not

[39] For these terms, cf. J. R. Firth, *Papers in Linguistics 1934-1951*.

[40] N. Chomsky, *Cartesian Linguistics*, 1966.

[41] Linguists such as Jakobson and Martinet have refused to accept the rigid distinctions suggested by de Saussure between synchronic and diachronic linguistics; similarly the criteria for the assessment of a theory should be the same, whether we are dealing with a theory current today or with one of the past.

[42] Firth was even more outspoken: "to dismiss two thousand years of linguistic study in Asia as well as in Europe as negligible in so far as it contributed to comparative grammar is just plain stupid", cf. "The Semantics of Linguistic Science", *Papers in Linguistics*, p. 139.

unlike our own today. Grammatical study in the 13th century, after many generations of association (and often subordination) to literary studies, enjoyed an independence it had never known before. If it did not achieve the autonomy which linguists today claim for linguistic science,[43] the Modistae did nonetheless succeed in making the study of grammar an independent discipline. Linguistics today has renewed itself and incorporated many ideas from its past; it is therefore proper that we should study the attempts of grammarians of another age to create a theory of grammar and descriptive procedure against an intellectual and academic background and as part of a body of knowledge which are so different from those of the modern linguist.

---

[43] This can be ascribed to the general inadequacies of the intellectual life of the period rather than to the grammatical theorists in particular.

APPENDICES

APPENDIX A

DEFINITIONS OF THE MODES USED BY MARTIN OF DACIA, SIGER DE COURTRAI AND THOMAS OF ERFURT

	Martin of Dacia	Siger de Courtrai	Thomas of Erfurt
Modus essendi	modi essendi sunt proprietates rei, secundum quod res est extra intellectum.	proprietates rerum seu entium.	rei proprietas absolute.
modus intelligendi activus	modi intelligendi sunt eadem proprietates rei secundum quod res est in intellectu et ut eaedem proprietates cum re sunt intellectae.	modus quo intellectus comprehendit modum essendi seu proprietatem ipsius rei.	ratio concipiendi, qua mediante intellectus rei proprietas significat, concipit vel apprehendit.
modus intelligendi passivus		ipse modus essendi ab ipso intellectu apprehensus seu modus intelligendi relatus ad modum essendi.	modus, sive proprietas rei, prout est per vocem significata.
modus signandi activus		ratio quaedam seu ens rationis concessum voci ab intellectu secundum quod talis vox talem rem signat per quam rationem signandi vox formaliter dicitur dictio.	
modus signandi passivus		ipsa res mediante ratione signandi passiva per vocem signata seu ratio signandi relata ad ipsam rem.	
modus significandi	modus significandi est proprietas rei consignificata per vocem. modus significandi est forma partis orationis quia dat sibi esse et distinguit eam ab omni parte orationis alia a se.		

	Martin of Dacia	Siger de Courtrai	Thomas of Erfurt
modus significandi activus		ratio concessa voci ab intellectu secundum quod talis vox talem modum essendi significat.	modus, sive proprietas vocis ab intellectu sibi concessa, mediante qua vox proprietatem rei significat.
modus significandi passivus		ipse modus essendi per vocem, mediante modo significandi active significatus, seu modus significandi relatus ad modum essendi.	modus, sive proprietas rei, prout est per vocem significata.
modus significandi essentialis	dicitur essentialis pro tanto, quia est de essentia cuiuslibet sub se contenti.	modus significandi conferens ad essentiam partis vel aliquorum ipsius partis.	per quem pars orationis habet simpliciter esse, vel secundum genus, vel secundum speciem.
modus significandi essentialis generalis		modus significandi pertinens ad essentiam plurium partium orationis sicut substantia ad nomen et ad pronomen.	
modus significandi essentialis specialis	sub unoquoque modorum significandi essentialium generalium contingit reperiri modos significandi speciales immediatos et mediatos, quia contingit ibi reperiri modos immediatos qui naturam sui modi significandi generalis maxime participant et modos mediatos qui naturam sui modi significandi generalis minus participant. Unde modi immediati magis essentiales sunt modis mediatis.		
modus significandi essentialis generalissimus.			qui est de essentia partis orationis et cuiuslibet suppositi sub se contenti.

	Martin of Dacia	Siger de Courtrai	Thomas of Erfurt
modus significandi essentialis specificus		modus significandi qui additus modo significandi generali constituit speciem, ut qualitas in nomine.	
modus significandi essentialis subalternus.			qui est de essentia suppositorum illius partis, nec generalissime, nec specialissime, sed medio modo se habens.
modus significandi essentialis specialissimus.			qui est de essentia quorumdam suppositorum illius partis.
modus significandi accidentalis	alii sunt modi significandi posteriores omnibus modis essentialibus qui iam dicti sunt, et ipsi dicuntur modi significandi essentiales, et hi sunt maxime principia constructionis sive construendi.	modus significandi adveniens alicui post suum completum esse.	qui advenit parti post esse completum, non dans esse simpliciter parti, secundum gnus, nec secundum speciem.
modus significandi absolutus		qui non conceduntur dictioni in comparatione ad modum significandi alterius dictionis sed magis ut vox mediantibus illis designet talem modum essendi circa rem. Isti modi non sunt principium unionis dictionis cum dictione.	per quem unum constructibile non habet respectum ad alterum, sed solum ad rei proprietatem.
modus significandi respectivus		qui conceduntur dictioni in comparatione ad modum significandi alterius dictionis eis proportionalem et tales sunt principium constructionis quia sunt principium unionis constructibilis cum constructibili.	per quem unum constructibile habet respectum non solum ad rei proprietatem, sed etiam per quem unum constructibile habet respectum ad alterum.

APPENDIX B

DIAGRAMMATIC EXPOSITIONS OF THE METALANGUAGE, THE DIFFERENT PARTES ORATIONIS, AND THE SYNTACTIC THEORIES OF SIGER DE COURTRAI AND THOMAS OF ERFURT.

Siger de Courtrai and Thomas of Erfurt:
Metalanguage

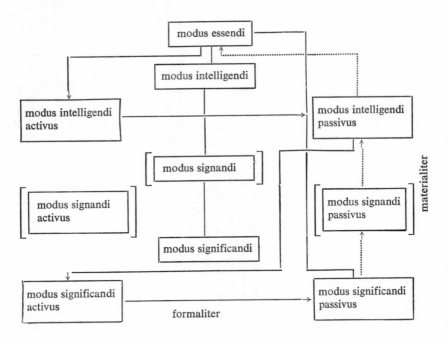

Siger de Courtrai:
Metalanguage

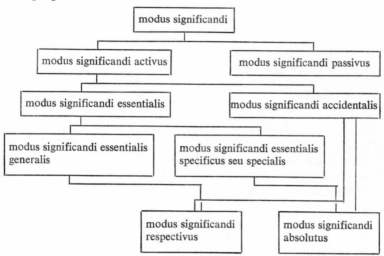

Siger de Courtrai:
Metalanguage

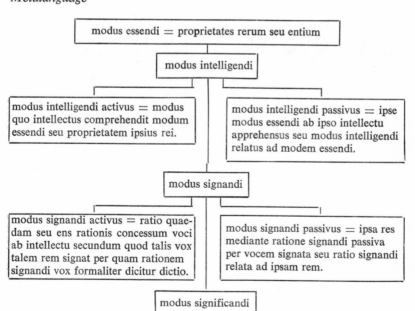

Siger de Courtrai:
Metalanguage

```
                    ┌─────────────────────┐
                    │ modus significandi  │
                    └─────────────────────┘
```

| modus significandi activus = ratio concessa voci ab intellectu secundum quod talis vox talem modum essendi significat. | modus significandi passivus = ipse modus essendi per vocem, mediante modo significandi activo significatus, seu modus significandi relatus ad modum essendi. |

| modus significandi essentialis = modus significandi conferens ad essentiam partis vel aliquorum ipsius partis. | modus significandi accidentalis = modus significandi adveniens alicui post suum completum esse. |

| modus significandi essentialis generalis = modus significandi pertinens ad essentiam plurium partium orationis sicut substantia ad nomen et ad pronomen. | modus significandi essentialis specificus = modus significandi qui additus modo significandi generali constituit speciem, ut qualitas in nomine. |

| modus significandi respectivus = qui conceduntur dictioni in comparatione ad modum significandi alterius dictionis eis proportionalem et tales sunt principium constructionis quia sunt principium unionis constructibilis cum constructibili. | modus significandi absolutus = qui non conceduntur dictioni in comparatione ad modum significandi alterius dictionis sed magis ut vox mediantibus illis designet talem modum modum essendi circa rem. Isti modi non sunt principium constructionis quia non principium unionis dictionis cum dictione. |

Siger de Courtrai:
Metalanguage –
Modus significandi

Modus significandi			
Modus significandi activus			Modus signi-ficandi passivus
modus significandi essentialis		modus significandi accidentalis	
modus significandi respectivus	modus significandi generalis		casus tempus genus modus gradus numerus persona coniugatio qualitas
modus significandi absolutus		modus significandi specificus	species figura

Thomas of Erfurt:
Metalanguage

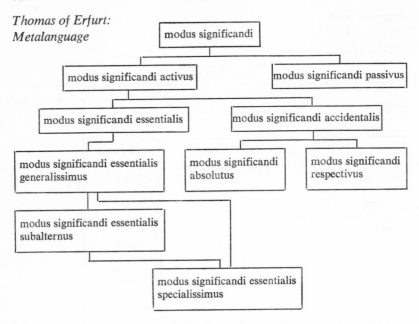

Thomas of Erfurt:
Metalanguage

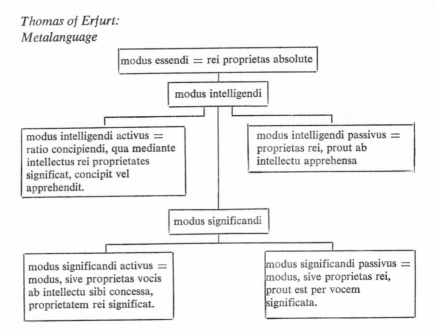

Thomas of Erfurt:
Metalanguage

modus significandi activus

modus significandi essentialis = per quem pars orationis habet simpliciter esse vel secundum genus, vel secundum speciem.	modus significandi accidentalis = qui advenit parti post eius esse completum.	
modus significandi essentialis generalissimus = qui est de essentia partis orationis et cuiuslibet suppositi sub se contenti.	modus significandi absolutus = dicitur ille, per quem unum constructibile non habet respectum ad alterum, sed solum ad rei proprietatem.	modus significandi respectivus = est per quem unum constructibile habet respectum non solum ad rei proprietatem, sed etiam per quem unum constructibile habet respectum ad alterum.
modus significandi essentialis subalternus = qui est de essentia suppositorum illius partis, nec generalissime, nec specialissime, sed medio modo habens.		
modus significandi essentialis specialissimus = qui est de essentia quorumdam suppositorum illius partis.		

Thomas of Erfurt:
Metalanguage-
Modus significandi

Modus significandi					
Modus significandi activus					Modus significandi passivus
modus significandi essentialis			modus significandi accidentalis		
modus significandi generalissimus	modus significandi subalternus	modus significandi specialissimus	modus significandi absolutus	modus significandi respectivus	
			species figura	casus tempus genus modus numerus persona coniugatio compositio significatio	

Siger de Courtrai:
Modus significandi
essentialis nominis

```
                          ┌─────────────────────────────┐
                          │ modus significandi essentialis│
                          │ generalis nominis = modus     │
                          │ significandi substantiae      │
                          │ permanentis habitus seu entis.│
                          └─────────────────────────────┘
┌──────────────────┐
│ modus significandi│
│ essentialis       │
│ nominis           │
└──────────────────┘
                          ┌─────────────────────────────┐
                          │ modus significandi essentialis│
                          │ specialis nominis = modus     │
                          │ qualitatis seu distinctae     │
                          │ apprehensionis a quolibet alio,│
                          │ quia qualitatis seu formae est │
                          │ distinguere, in quo modo       │
                          │ significandi nomen differt a   │
                          │ pronomine.                     │
                          └─────────────────────────────┘
```

Siger de Courtrai:
Modus significandi
accidentalis nominis

	species — designans proprietatem determinandi ab aliquo vel a nullo.
	qualitas — designans circa rem modum essendi vel quod ei repugnat reperiri in pluribus vel prout rei non repugnat reperiri in pluribus.
	adiectivum — designans circa rem modum essendi adiacentis.
modus significandi accidentalis nominis	*substantivum* — designans circa rem modum per se entis et abstracti sive sit proprie ens per se, sicut substantiae, sive sint entia per se distincta ab illo in quo sunt, et ut sic significata, ut in accidentibus abstractis.
	gradus — designans circa rem modum essendi prout est in excessu vel cum excessu.
	genus — designans circa rem modum essendi indifferentem se habentem quodammodo ad modos essendi speciales generum.
	numerus — designans circa rem modum essendi unius aut multi.
	figura — designans circa rem modum essendi indivisionis vel compositionis.
	casus — designans circa rem modum essendi cadentis, inquam rei, intellectus, et vocis, seu eiusdem nominis.

Siger de Courtrai:
Modus significandi
accidentalis nominis

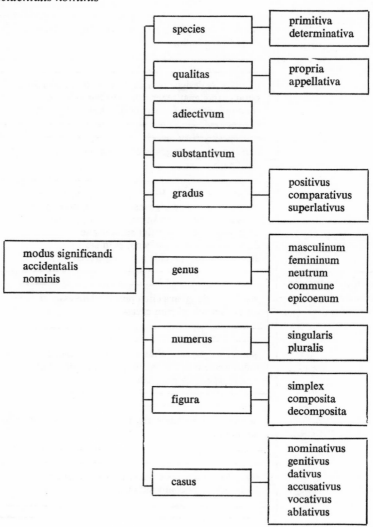

Thomas of Erfurt:
Nomen

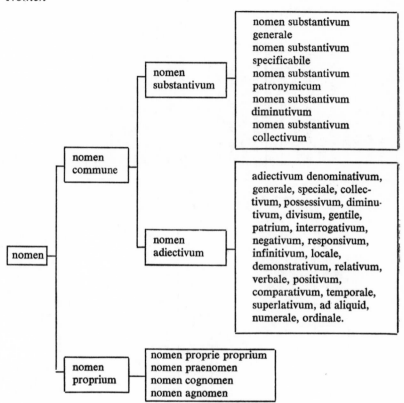

nomen substantivum
generale
nomen substantivum
specificabile
nomen substantivum
patronymicum
nomen substantivum
diminutivum
nomen substantivum
collectivum

adiectivum denominativum,
generale, speciale, collectivum, possessivum, diminutivum, divisum, gentile,
patrium, interrogativum,
negativum, responsivum,
infinitivum, locale,
demonstrativum, relativum,
verbale, positivum,
comparativum, temporale,
superlativum, ad aliquid,
numerale, ordinale.

nomen substantivum

nomen adiectivum

nomen commune

nomen

nomen proprie proprium
nomen praenomen
nomen cognomen
nomen agnomen

nomen proprium

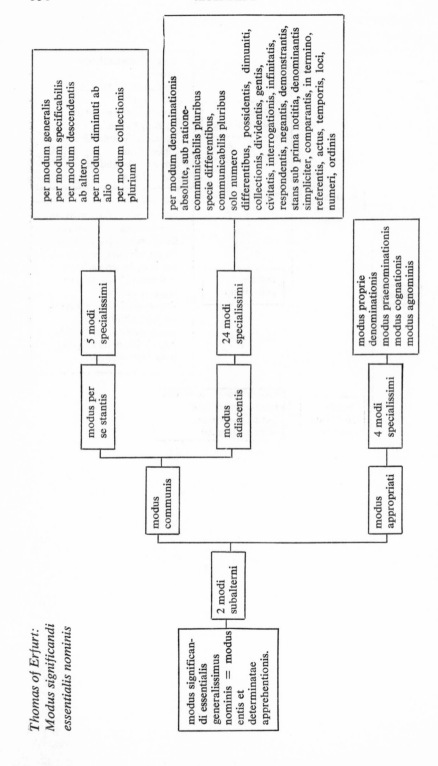

Thomas of Erfurt:
Modus significandi
essentialis nominis

Thomas of Erfurt:
Modus significandi
accidentalis nominis

modus significandi accidentalis nominis	*species* — mediante quo modum significandi primarium vel secundarium significat.
	genus — sumptus a proprietate activa, vel passiva, quae in rebus separatis magis prompte et determinate invenitur.
	numerus — mediante quo nomen proprietatem indivisibilitatis, quae est proprietas unius, vel proprietatem divisibilitatis, quae est proprietas multitudinis, significat.
	figura — mediante quo nomen proprietatem simplicis, compositi, vel decompositi significat.
	casus — mediante quo nomen proprietatem principii vel termini consignificat.
	persona — mediante quo nomen proprietatem loquendi consignificat.

Thomas of Erfurt:
Modus significandi
accidentalis nominis

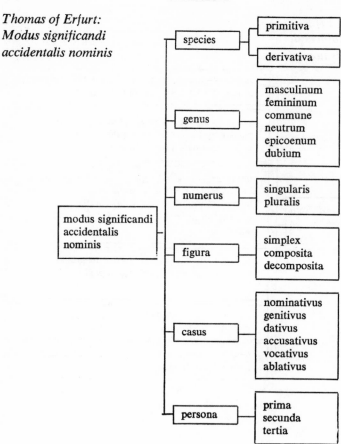

Siger de Courtrai:
Modus significandi
essentialis verbi

modus significandi
essentialis verbi

modus significandi essentialis
generalis = modus significandi
per modum fluxus, fieri seu
motus, seu esse.

modus significandi essentialis
specificus = modus significandi
essentialis de aliquo seu
significare per modum distantis
vel facientis alterum extremum
orationis, in quo differt a
participio quod significat rem
suam per modum distantis et
facientis unum extremum
orationis cum supposito.

Siger de Courtrai:
Modus significandi
accidentalis verbi

```
                              ┌─────────────────────────────────────────────┐
                              │ genus — dividitur in activum, passivum,     │
                              │ neutrum, deponens et commune.                │
                              └─────────────────────────────────────────────┘

                              ┌─────────────────────────────────────────────┐
                              │ tempus — designans circa rem modum essendi  │
                              │ praesentialitatis vel praeteritionis vel     │
                              │ futuritionis, et dicitur in praesens,        │
                              │ praeteritum et futurum.                      │
                              └─────────────────────────────────────────────┘

                              ┌─────────────────────────────────────────────┐
                              │ modus — designans circa rem modum essendi   │
                              │ variae inclinationis animi, varios eius      │
                              │ affectus demonstrans et dicitur in           │
                              │ indicativum, imperativum, optativum,         │
                              │ coniunctivum, infinitivum.                   │
                              └─────────────────────────────────────────────┘

 ┌──────────────────────┐     ┌─────────────────────────────────────────────┐
 │ modus significandi   │     │ species — sicut in nomine, scilicet         │
 │ accidentalis verbi   │     │ primitiva et derivativa.                     │
 └──────────────────────┘     └─────────────────────────────────────────────┘

                              ┌─────────────────────────────────────────────┐
                              │ figura — sicut in nomine.                    │
                              └─────────────────────────────────────────────┘

                              ┌─────────────────────────────────────────────┐
                              │ numerus — sicut in nomine.                   │
                              └─────────────────────────────────────────────┘

                              ┌─────────────────────────────────────────────┐
                              │ coniugatio — quasi una eademque ratione     │
                              │ declinationis plurima verba coniunguntur.    │
                              └─────────────────────────────────────────────┘

                              ┌─────────────────────────────────────────────┐
                              │ persona — designans circa rem modum essendi │
                              │ prout convenit alicui sub aliquo modo        │
                              │ loquendi et in hoc convenit cum prima        │
                              │ significatione; dicitur in primam,           │
                              │ secundam et tertiam et in hoc                │
                              │ convenit cum secunda significatione.         │
                              └─────────────────────────────────────────────┘
```

Siger de Courtrai:
Modus significandi
accidentalis verbi

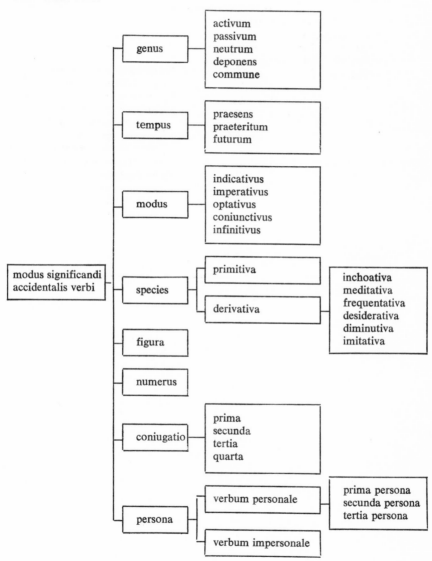

Thomas of Erfurt:
Verbum

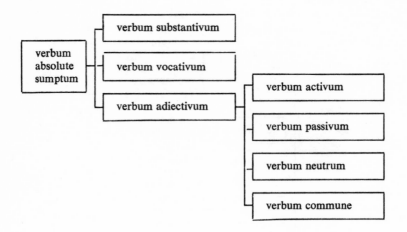

*Thomas of Erfurt:
Modus significandi
essentialis verbi*

modus significandi essentialis generalissimus = modus esse et distantis a substantia.

3 modi subalterni

modus esse cum distantia sumitur generaliter, aliquid specificabile per esse speciale.

modus esse cum distantia sumitur generaliter respectu rei propriae nominationis tantum.

modus esse cum distantia sumitur generaliter specialiter, prout stat in speciali pro esse actionis vel passionis.

4 modi specialissimi

modus esse distantis sub modo actionis tantum.

modus esse distantis per modum passionis tantum.

modus esse distantis sub modo neutri sive sub privatione utriusque.

modus esse distantis sub modo utriusque, scilicet actionis et passionis.

Thomas of Erfurt:
Modus significandi
accidentalis verbi

```
                    ┌──────────────────────────────────────────────────┐
                    │ compositio — mediante quo verbum consignificat    │
                    │ proprietatem inhaerentis secundum esse, et quo    │
                    │ mediante verbum distans a supposito, primo et     │
                    │ principaliter ad suppositum inclinatur.           │
                    └──────────────────────────────────────────────────┘

                    ┌──────────────────────────────────────────────────┐
                    │ qualitas — modus — mediante quo proprietatem verbi│
                    │ per modum indicii, imperii, voti, dubii, vel      │
                    │ infiniti circa verbi dependentiam ad suppositum   │
                    │ consignificat: et forma — mediante quo verbum     │
                    │ modum existendi primarium vel secundarium         │
                    │ significat.                                       │
                    └──────────────────────────────────────────────────┘

                    ┌──────────────────────────────────────────────────┐
                    │ coniugatio — modus significandi rem verbi prout   │
                    │ inflectitur per diversas proprietates temporum,   │
                    │ numerorum, modorum et personarum.                 │
                    └──────────────────────────────────────────────────┘

                    ┌──────────────────────────────────────────────────┐
 modus signifi-     │ significatio — mediante quo verbum significat     │
 candi acciden-  ───│ proprietatem dependentiae ad quemlibet obliquum   │
 talis verbi        │ post se.                                          │
                    └──────────────────────────────────────────────────┘

                    ┌──────────────────────────────────────────────────┐
                    │ genus — mediante quo proprietatem dependentiae rei│
                    │ verbi post se ad obliquum, sub ratione termini,   │
                    │ significat.                                       │
                    └──────────────────────────────────────────────────┘

                    ┌──────────────────────────────────────────────────┐
                    │ persona — quo mediante verbum proprietatem loquendi│
                    │ consignificat non inhaerentem de se,              │
                    │ sed ut res verbi applicabilis est                 │
                    │ rei suppositi subsistentis                        │
                    │ per se secundum proprietates loquendi.            │
                    └──────────────────────────────────────────────────┘

                    ┌──────────────────────────────────────────────────┐
                    │ numerus — sicut in nomine.                        │
                    └──────────────────────────────────────────────────┘

                    ┌──────────────────────────────────────────────────┐
                    │ figura — sicut in nomine.                         │
                    └──────────────────────────────────────────────────┘

                    ┌──────────────────────────────────────────────────┐
                    │ tempus — quo mediante verbum, citra rem, modum    │
                    │ temporis consignificat.                           │
                    └──────────────────────────────────────────────────┘
```

Thomas of Erfurt:
Modus significandi
accidentalis verbi

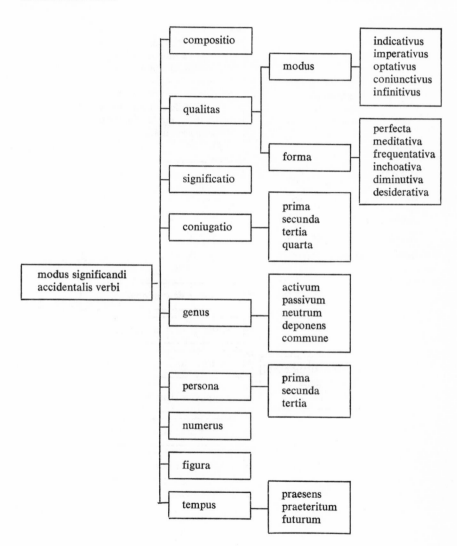

Siger de Courtrai:
Modus significandi
essentialis participii

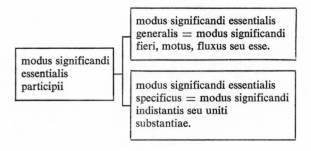

Siger de Courtrai:
Modus significandi
accidentalis participii

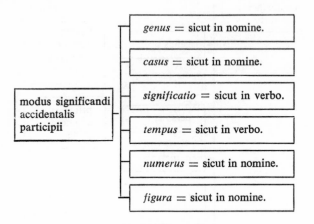

Thomas of Erfurt:
Participium

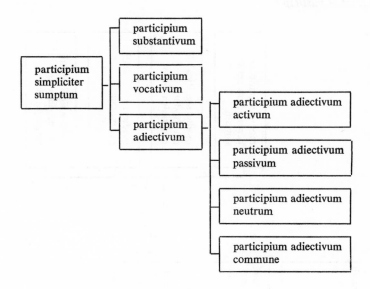

Thomas of Erfurt:
Modus significandi
essentialis participii

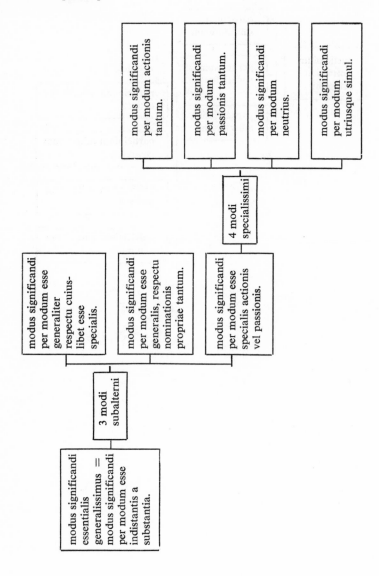

Thomas of Erfurt:
Modus significandi
accidentalis participii

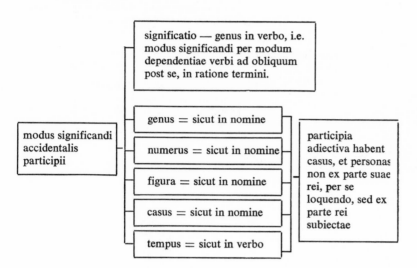

modus significandi accidentalis participii

significatio — genus in verbo, i.e. modus significandi per modum dependentiae verbi ad obliquum post se, in ratione termini.

genus = sicut in nomine

numerus = sicut in nomine

figura = sicut in nomine

casus = sicut in nomine

tempus = sicut in verbo

participia adiectiva habent casus, et personas non ex parte suae rei, per se loquendo, sed ex parte rei subiectae

Siger de Courtrai:
Modus significandi
essentialis pronominis

| modus significandi essentialis pronominis | modus significandi essentialis generalis = modus significandi substantiae, habitus permanentis, seu entis. |
| | modus significandi essentialis specialis = modus significandi indeterminati, confusi, substantiae mere seu sine qualitate. |

Thomas of Erfurt:
Pronomen

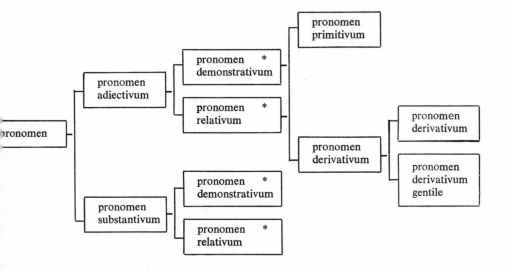

* *Demonstratio* and *relatio* do not create different types of pronoun, but re-present different aspects of the same pronoun, and are present or absent according to the degree of concreteness present in a particular pronoun.

Thomas of Erfurt:
Modus significandi
accidentalis pronominis

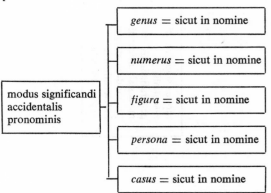

Thomas of Erfurt:
Modus significandi
essentialis pronominius

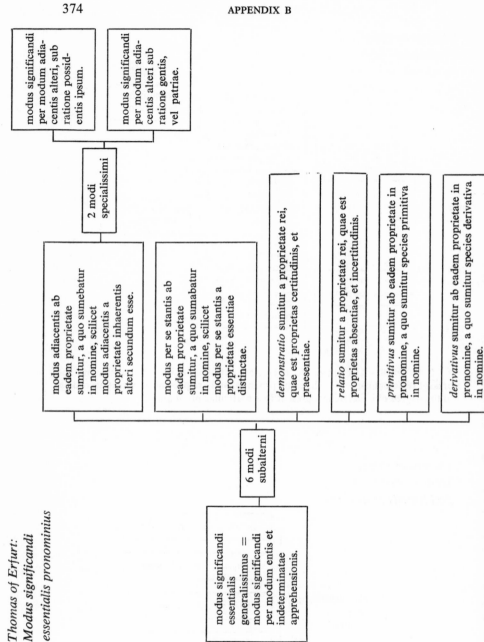

modus significandi
per modum adia-
centis alteri, sub
ratione possid-
entis ipsum.

modus significandi
per modum adia-
centis alteri sub
ratione gentis,
vel patriae.

2 modi
specialissimi

modus adiacentis ab
eadem proprietate
sumitur, a quo sumebatur
in nomine, scilicet
modus adiacentis a
proprietate inhaerentis
alteri secundum esse.

modus per se stantis ab
eadem proprietate
sumitur, a quo sumabatur
in nomine, scilicet
modus per se stantis a
proprietate essentiae
distinctae.

demonstratio sumitur a proprietate rei,
quae est proprietas certitudinis, et
praesentiae.

relatio sumitur a proprietate rei, quae est
proprietas absentiae, et incertitudinis.

primitivus sumitur ab eadem proprietate in
pronomine, a quo sumitur species primitiva
in nomine.

derivativus sumitur ab eadem proprietate in
pronomine, a quo sumitur species derivativa
in nomine.

6 modi
subalterni

modus significandi
essentialis
generalissimus =
modus significandi
per modum entis et
indeterminatae
apprehensionis.

Siger de Courtrai:
Modus significandi
essentialis adverbii

```
                              ┌─────────────────────────────┐
                              │ modus significandi essentialis│
                              │ generalis = significare per  │
                     ┌────────│ modum disponentis.           │
┌──────────────────┐ │        └─────────────────────────────┘
│ modus significandi│─┤
│ essentialis adverbii│        ┌─────────────────────────────┐
└──────────────────┘ │        │ modus significandi essentialis│
                     │        │ specificus = significare per │
                     └────────│ modum determinantis actum vel│
                              │ aliquid quod rem suam significat│
                              │ per modum esse, fieri, motus │
                              │ vel actus.                   │
                              └─────────────────────────────┘
```

Thomas of Erfurt:
Adverbium

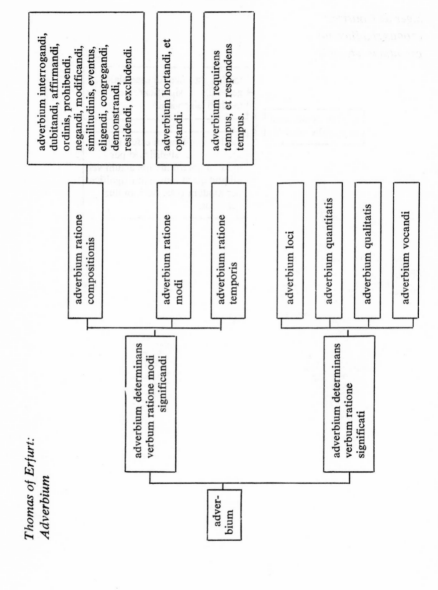

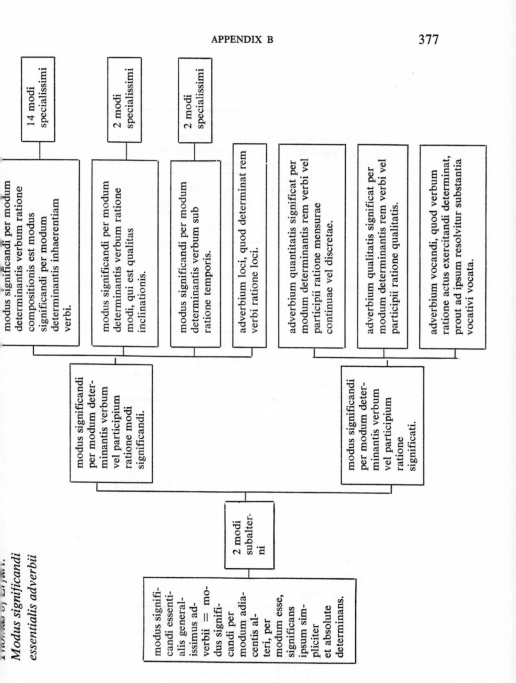

Modus significandi
essentialis adverbii

modus significandi essentialis generalissimus adverbii = modus significandi per modum adiacentis alteri, per modum esse, significans ipsum simpliciter et absolute determinans.

2 modi subalterni

modus significandi per modum determinantis verbum vel participium ratione modi significandi.

modus significandi per modum determinantis verbum vel participium ratione significati.

modus significandi per modum determinantis verbum ratione compositionis est modus significandi per modum determinantis inhaerentiam verbi.

14 modi specialissimi

modus significandi per modum determinantis verbum ratione modi, qui est qualitas inclinationis.

2 modi specialissimi

modus significandi per modum determinantis verbum sub ratione temporis.

2 modi specialissimi

adverbium loci, quod determinat rem verbi ratione loci.

adverbium quantitatis significat per modum determinantis rem verbi vel participii ratione mensurae continuae vel discretae.

adverbium qualitatis significat per modum determinantis rem verbi vel participii ratione qualitatis.

adverbium vocandi, quod verbum ratione actus exercitandi determinat, prout ad ipsum resolvitur substantia vocativi vocata.

Siger de Courtrai:
Modus significandi
essentialis coniunctionis

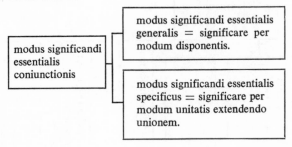

Thomas of Erfurt:
Coniunctio

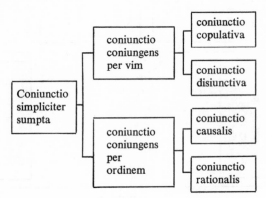

Thomas of Erfurt:
Modus significandi
accidentalis coniunctionis

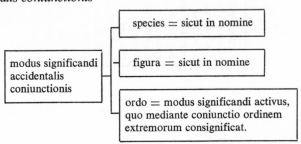

Thomas of Erfurt:
Modus significandi
essentialis coniunctionis

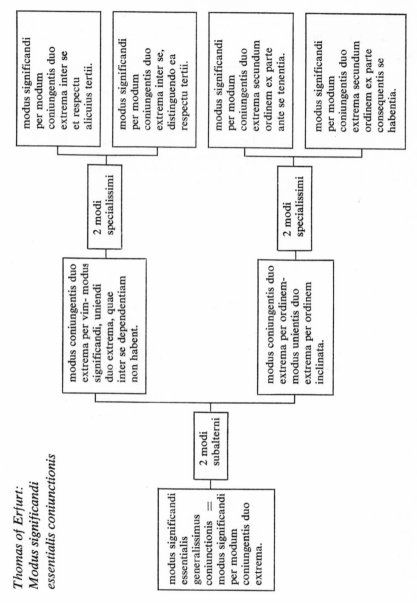

Siger de Courtrai:
Modus significandi
essentialis praepositionis

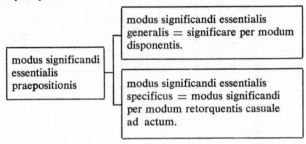

Thomas of Erfurt:
Praepositio

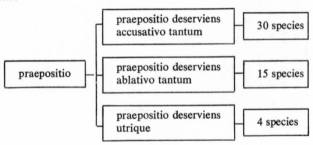

Thomas of Erfurt:
Modus significandi
essentialis praepositionis

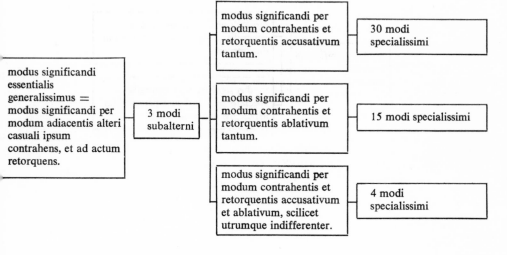

modus significandi essentialis generalissimus = modus significandi per modum adiacentis alteri casuali ipsum contrahens, et ad actum retorquens.

3 modi subalterni

modus significandi per modum contrahentis et retorquentis accusativum tantum.

30 modi specialissimi

modus significandi per modum contrahentis et retorquentis ablativum tantum.

15 modi specialissimi

modus significandi per modum contrahentis et retorquentis accusativum et ablativum, scilicet utrumque indifferenter.

4 modi specialissimi

Siger de Courtrai:
Modus significandi
essentialis interiectionis

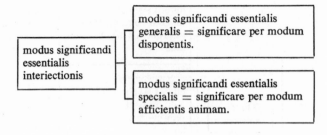

Thomas of Erfurt:
Interiectio

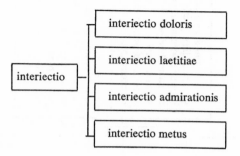

Thomas of Erfurt:
Modus significandi
essentialis interiectionis

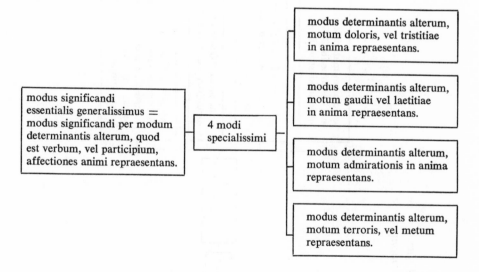

Thomas of Erfurt:
Passiones sermonis

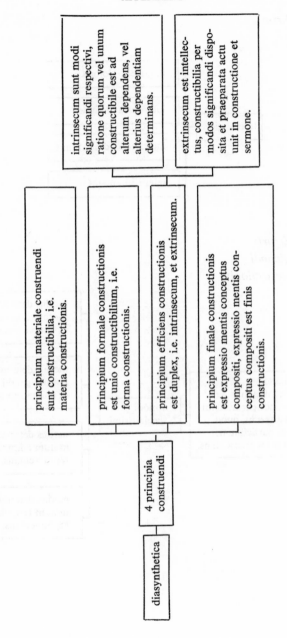

Thomas of Erfurt:
Constructio

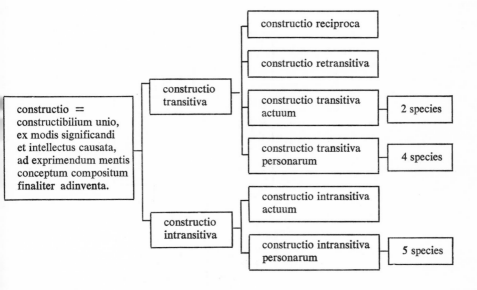

Thomas of Erfurt:
Constructio intransitiva

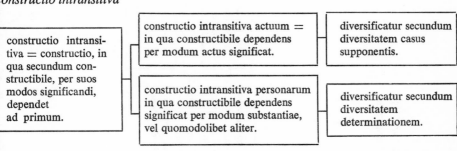

Thomas of Erfurt
Constructio transitiva

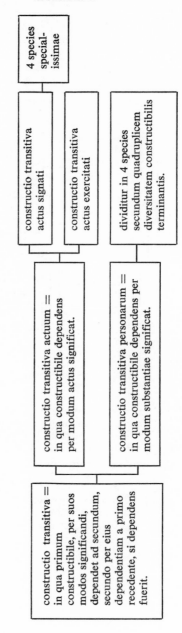

APPENDIX C

DIAGRAM OF THE DECLINABLE AND INDECLINABLE PARTES ORATIONES

	Partes orationis						
Partes declinabiles				**Partes indeclinabiles**			
Modus entis		Modus esse		Modus disponentis			
modus determinatae apprehensionis	modus indeterminatae apprehensionis	modus distantis	modus indistantis	modus determinantis actum	modus coniungentis duo extrema	modus retorquentis casuale ad actum	modus afficientis animam
Nomen	Pronomen	Verbum	Participium	Adverbium	Coniunctio	Praepositio	Interiectio.

Appendix C
Partes declinabiles

Partes declinabiles						
Modus entis					**Modus esse**	
modus determinativae apprehensionis			modus indeterminativae apprehensionis		modus distantis	modus indistantis
nomen commune		nomen proprium				
nomen substantivum	nomen adiectivum		pronomen: substantivum, demonstrativum	pronomen: adiectivum, relativum, derivativum	verbum: substantivum, vocativum, adiectivum	participium substantivum vocativum adiectivum
				pronomen derivativum: gentile possessivum	verbum adiectivum: activum passivum neutrum commune	participium adiectivum activum passivum neutrum commune
5 species	24 species	4 species				

Appendix C
Partes indeclinabiles

Partes indeclinabiles			
Modus disponentis			
Adverbium	**Coniunctio**	**Praepositio**	**Interiectio**
modus determinantis actum	modus coniungentis duo extrema	modus retorquentis casuale	modus afficientis animam

Adverbium				Coniunctio		Praepositio	Interiectio
ratione significati	ratione modi significandi			coniunctio per vim	coniunctio per ordinem	praepositio deserviens: (1) accusativo = 30 species (2) ablativo = 15 species (3) utrique = 4 species	Interiectio (1) doloris (2) gaudii (3) admirationis (4) terroris
	ratione compositionis	ratione modi	ratione temporis				
adverbium loci, quantitatis, qualitatis, vocandi.	14 species	2 species	2 species				

Appendix C
Modus entis

Modus entis				
Modus determinatae apprehensionis				Modus indeterminat apprehension
Nomen				Pronomen
modus significandi essentialis		modus significandi accidentalis		
modus communis		modus appropriati	modus absolutus	modus respectivus	
modus per se stantis Nomen substantivum generale, speciale, patronymicum, collectivum, dimimutivum.	*modus adiacentis* Nomen adiectivum: generale, speciale denominativum, collectivum, possessivum, diminutivum, divisivum, gentile, patrium, infinitum, interrogativum, responsivum, negativum, ordinale, demonstrativum, relativum, numerale, positivum, locale, comparativum, superlativum, ad aliquid, temporale, verbale.	Nomen: proprium praenomen cognomen agnomen	species figura	casus genus gradus numerus persona qualitas	

APPENDIX D   ACCIDENTS AND ACCIDENTAL MODES

Pars	Feature	Donatus	Priscian	Martin	Siger	Thomas
Nomen	casus	accident	accident	accidental	accidental	accidental
	genus	,,	,,	,,	,,	,,
	numerus	,,	,,	,,	,,	,,
	figura	,,	,,	,,	,,	,,
	species	,,	,,	,,	,,	,,
	gradus				,,	
	persona			,,		,,
	qualitas	,,		essential	,,	essential
	comparatio	,,		,,	,,	,,
Verbum	tempus	accident	accident	accidental	accidental	accidental
	coniugatio	,,	,,	,,	,,	,,
	genus	,,	,,	,,	,,	,,
	numerus	,,	,,	,,	,,	,,
	figura	,,	,,	,,	,,	,,
	persona	,,	,,	,,	,,	,,
	qualitas	,,				,,
	modus	(,,)	,,	,,	,,	(,,)
	species	(,,)	,,	,,	,,	(forma)
	compositio			,,		,,
	significatio			,,		,,
Participium	genus	accident	accident	accidental	accidental	accidental
	significatio	,,	,,	,,		,,
	casus	,,	,,	,,		,,
	persona	,,				,,
	tempus	,,	,,	,,		,,
	numerus	,,	,,	,,		,,
	figura	,,	,,	,,		,,
Pronomen	genus	accident	accident	accidental		accidental
	persona	,,	,,	(,,)		(,,)
	numerus	,,	,,	,,		,,
	figura	,,	,,	,,		,,
	casus	,,	,,	,,		,,
	species		,,	,,		,,
	qualitas	,,		essential		essential
Adverbium	comparatio	accident	accident	accidental		essential
	figura	,,	,,	,,		,,
	species				(essential)	,,
	significatio	,,	,,	essential		essential
Coniunctio	figura	accident	accident	accidental		accidental
	ordo	,,	,,	,,		,,
	species					,,
	potestas	,,	,,	essential	(essential)	essential
Praepositio	casus	accident	accident	essential	(essential)	essential
Interiectio	significatio	accident	accident	essential		essential

APPENDIX E GLOSSARY

	Martin of Dacia	Siger de Courtrai	Thomas of Erfurt
Adverbium:	significat per modum determinantis sive per modum adiacentis alteri quod significat per modum fieri.	significare per modum determinantis actum vel aliquid quod rem suam significat per modum esse, fieri, motus vel actus.	adverbium est pars orationis significans per modum esse significat ipsum esse absolute determinans.
Casus (nomen):	casus accipitur a quadam proprietate sive dispositione rei quae est si habere in ratione principii vel in ratione termini.	casus est modus significandi accidentalis designans circa rem modum essendi cadentis, inquam rei, intellectus et vocis, seu eiusdem nominis.	casus est modus significandi accidentalis nominis, mediante quo nomen proprietatem principii, vel termini consignificat.
Casus (praepositio):	casus in praepositione est habitudo casualis ad actum.		casus in praepositione consistit in speciali modo contrahendi et retorquendi.
Compositio:	modus significandi sive intelligendi uniens extremum distans cum altero extremo.		compositio est modus significandi accidentalis verbi, mediante quo verbum consignificat proprietatem inhaerentis secundum esse, et quo mediante verbum distans a supposito, primo et principaliter ad suppositum inclinatur.
Congruitas:	congruitas in grammatica non est aliud quam passio grammatice ex proportione seu conformitate modorum significandi causata.		congruitas..est..partium sermonis debita unio ex modorum significandi conformitate ad aliquam speciem constructionis requisitorum derelicta.
Coniugatio:	modus intelligendi rem sive fieri secundum quod cadit sub diversis inflexionibus temporum.	nominatur coniugatio quasi una eademque ratione declinationis plurima verba coniunguntur.	coniugatio est modus significandi rem verbi prout inflectitur per diversas proprietates temporum, numerorum, modorum et personarum.
Coniunctio:	significat per modum connectentis sive unientis duas substantias res-	significare per modum unitatis extendendo unionem.	coniunctio est pars orationis, per modum coniungentis duo extrema

Constructio:	duos actus respectu duarum substantiarum vel etiam duas substantias respectu duorum actuum. constructio est passio constructibilium sive constructibilium unio.	constructio est constructibilium unio.	constructio est constructibilium unio, ex modis significandi, et intellectus causata, ad exprimendum mentis conceptum compositum finaliter adinventa.
Declinatio:	declinatio in nomine est modus intelligendi rem ut cadit sub diversis inflexionibus casuum.	casus est declinatio nominum vel aliarum casualium dictionum, quae maxime fit in fine.	declinatio est modus significandi rem nominis, per quem inflectitur.
Dictio:	dictio est vox habens rationem significandi aliquid.	per rationem signandi rem formaliter dicitur dictio.	dictio dicitur formaliter per rationem signandi voci superadditam, quia dictio est vox significativa.
Figura:	figura non accipitur a parte vocis, cum vox non sit de consideratione grammatici, sed a parte rei.. figura accepta est a modo intelligendi rem simplicis conceptus vel compositi vel collecti. cf. species (verbum).	figura est modus significandi accidentalis nominis designans circa rem modum essendi indivisionis vel compositionis.	figura est modus significandi accidentalis nominis, mediante quo, nomen proprietatem simplicis, compositi, vel decompositi significat.
Forma:			forma est modus significandi accidentalis verbi, mediante quo verbum modum existendi primarium vel secundarium significat.
Genus (nomen):	genus in nomine accipitur a discretione sexus.. genus est discretio sexus vel similitudo cum dictionibus discernentibus sexum. genus in nomine acceptum est a proprietate agentis vel patientis vel utriusque vel neutrius.	genus est modus significandi accidentalis nominis designans circa rem modum essendi indifferentem, se habentem quodammodo ad modos essendi speciales generum.	genus est modus significandi accidentalis nominis, sumptus a proprietate activa, vel passiva, quae in rebus separatis magis prompte et determinate invenitur.
Genus (verbum):	genus in verbo variatur penes hos modos significandi, scilicet penes modum significandi qui facit actionem et passionem et cetera.	genus seu significatio dividitur in activum, passivum, neutrum, deponens, et commune.	genus est modus significandi accidentalis verbi, mediante quo proprietatem dependentiae rei verbi post se ad obliquum, sub ratione

	Martin of Dacia	Siger de Courtrai	Thomas of Erfurt
Genus (verbum): (continued)	unde modus significandi qui facit genus in verbo simpliciter est modus intelligendi rem sub actione vel passione vel utroque vel neutro.		termini, significat.
Gradus:		gradus est modus significandi accidentalis nominis designans circa rem modum essendi prout est in excessu vel cum excessu, et dividitur in positivum, comparativum, et superlativum.	
Interiectio:	significat per modum afficientis animam in qua est actus.	significare per modum afficientis animam.	interiectio est pars orationis significans per modum determinantis alterum, quod est verbum, vel participium, affectus vel motus animae repraesentans.
Modus (verbum):	modus est inclinatio animi varios eius affectus demonstrans.	modus in verbo est modus significandi accidentalis verbi designans circa rem modum essendi variae inclinationis animi, varios eius affectus demonstrans.	modus verbi..est..modus significandi accidentalis verbi, mediante quo proprietatem verbi per modum indicii, imperii, voti, dubii, vel infiniti circa verbi dependentiam ad suppositum consignificat.
Nomen:	significat per modum habitus et quietis et determinatae apprehensionis.	modus significandi essentialis generalis nominis est modus significandi substantiae, permanentis habitus seu entis .. modus significandi specialis est modus qualitatis seu distinctae apprehensionis a quolibet alio, quia qualitatis seu formae est distinguere.	nomen est pars orationis significans per modum entis, vel determinatae apprehensionis.
Nomen substantivum:		substantivum est modus significandi accidentalis designans circa rem modum per se entis et abstracti sive sit proprie ens per se .. sive sint entia per se distinc-te ob illo in quo sunt	nomen substantivum significat per modum determinati secundum essentiam.

Numerus:

ipsum est quiescens in altero et ita utrumque significat per modum quietis.

numerus a modo intelligendi rem per modum unius vel plurium acceptus est.. modus significandi qui facit numerum singularem est modus significandi per modum unius sive per modum singularis sive per modum indivisi.. modus significandi qui facit numerum pluralem est modus significandi per modum plurium sive per modum pluralis sive per modum divisi.

modus significandi qui facit numerum est modus significandi sive intelligendi rem per modum numerati sive prout est numerata. unire per ordinem est quando uniuntur aliqua quae prius inclinabantur ad se invicem.

accidentalis nominis designans circa rem modum essendi adiacentis.

numerus est modus significandi accidentalis nominis designans circa rem modum essendi unius aut multi.

modum inhaerentis alteri secundum esse.

numerus est modus significandi accidentaliter nominis, mediante quo nomen proprietatem divisibilitatis, quae est proprietas unius, vel proprietatem divisibilitatis, quae est proprietas multitudinis significat.

Ordo:

ordo est in coniunctione modus significandi activus, quo mediante coniunctio ordinem extremorum consignificat.

Pars orationis:

omnis pars orationis est pars per suum modum significandi. omnis pars orationis est pars per suum modum significandi essentialem generalem.

pars est dictio, et vox, ideo modus consignificandi per quem pars est pars praesupponit rationem significandi, vocem et significatum.. vox formaliter dicitur pars orationis per modum significandi activum.

pars est pars secundum se per hanc rationem consignificandi seu modum significandi activum, tanquam per principium formale… pars orationis est dictio, ut habet modum significandi activum.

Participium:

significat per modum fieri indistantis.

est modus significandi generalis participii, modus significandi fieri, motus, fluxus seu esse.. modus significandi specificus participii est modus significandi indistantis seu uniti distantiae.

participium est pars orationis significans per modum esse indistantis a substantia, sive uniti cum substantia.

	Martin of Dacia	Siger de Courtrai	Thomas of Erfurt
Perfectio:	finis perfectae orationis est perfectus sensus in animo auditoris, qui haberi non potest sine supposito et apposito quare et cetera. Unde oratio dicitur perfecta, quand anima quiescit semper ipsam.		perfectio .. est .. passio sermonis tertia et ultima, ex debita constructibilium unione derelicta, cum sufficientia exprimendi mentis conceptum compositum secundum distantiam, et generandi perfectam sententiam in animo auditoris.
Persona (nomen):	persona accipitur a quadam proprietate quae est modus loquendi.		est persona modus significandi nominis, mediante quo nomen proprietatem loquendi consignificat.
Persona (verbum):	modus significandi qui facit personam in verbo, est modus intelligendi rem verbi prout attribuitur alteri secundum quod habet modum loquendi, et secundum hanc variam attributionem variatur verbum per varias personas.	persona est modus significandi accidentalis verbi designans circa rem modum essendi prout convenit alicui sub aliquo modo loquendi.	persona est modus significandi, quo mediante verbum proprietatem loquendi consignificat non inhaerentem de se, sed ut res verbi applicabilis est rei suppositi subsistentis per se secundum proprietates loquendi.
Potestas:	potestas est quidam modus significandi qui est modus unientis duo extrema vel per vim vel per ordinem .. potestas est essentialis coniunctioni.		potestas in coniunctione consistit in speciali modo coniungendi. Et istius modi modus est modus coniungendi per vim, et per ordinem.
Praepositio:	significat per modum retorquentis casuale ad actum vel prout illud casuale se habet in ratione principii respectu illius actus vel in ratione termini respectu illius actus.	modus specificus est modus significandi per modum retorquentis casuale ad actum.	praepositio est pars orationis significans per modum adiacentis alteri casuali, ipsum contrahens, et ad actum reducens.
Pronomen:	significat per modum habitus et quietis, id est per modum substantiae merae.	modus significandi per quem pronomen est pronomen est modus significandi substantiae, habitus permanentis, seu entis .. modus significandi indeterminati, confusi, substantiae mere seu sine qualitate, accidit pronomini,	pronomen est pars orationis significans per modum entis, et indeterminatae apprehensionis.

strativum:

monstrantis rem sub maxima certitudine scilicet ut praesens est. demonstrativum semper facit primam notitiam de re et semper demonstrat rem ut praesens est. est modus notificantis rem semper ut absens est.. relatio semper refert rem secundum quod ipsa est absens, id est sub absentia.

ficat rem sub ratione vel proprietate praesentiae seu notitiae primae.

Pronomen relativum:

relativum semper refert suum antecedens ut ipsum absens est, sive illa res quam refert sit praesens vel absens.

pronomen relativum significat rem sub proprietate absentiae, et incertitudinis, seu notitiae secundae.

Qualitas:

dividitur in duos modos significandi qui totam eius naturam evacuant scilicet in modum significandi per modum communis et in modum significandi per modum appropriati.

qualitas propria est modus significandi accidentalis nominis designans circa rem modum essendi vel quod ei repugnat reperiri in pluribus ... qualitas appellativa est modus significandi accidentalis nominis designans circa rem modum essendi prout rei non repugnat reperiri in pluribus.

qualitas, quam assignat Donatus pro accidente nominis, dividens eam in qualitatem propriam et appellativam, nominat duos modos essentialis nominis subalternos, scilicet modum communis, et appropriati.

Significatio: (adverbium)

modus significandi qui est significatio dividitur in multas species quae adverbia specialia constituunt.. cum adverbium ex sua inventione debeat determinare verbum, aut ergo determinat verbum ratione rei significatae aut ratione modorum significandi.

significatio in adverbio est modus significandi, quo mediante adverbium repraesentat specialem modum determinandi verbum, vel participium, aut ratione significati, aut ratione modi significandi.

Significatio: (interiectio)

significatio interiectionis est specialis modus determinationis circa actum afficientis subiectum in quo est actus iste.

significatio interiectionis consistit in speciali modo determinandi specialem motum in anima repraesentans.

	Martin of Dacia	Siger de Courtrai	Thomas of Erfurt
Significatio: *(verbum)*	significatio accidentalis est modus transeundi in aliud et hoc solum in accusativum.		significatio accidentalis est modus significandi accidentalis verbi, mediante quo verbum significat proprietatem dependentiae ad quemlibet obliquum post se. quia dicitur signum per rationem signandi.
Signum:	signum est quod habet rationem significandi aliquid . . signum in plus se habet quam dictio, quia omnis dictio potest dici signum, sed non e converso, quia signum potest dici de nutu corporeo, de voce et de aliis; dictio autem tantum de voce dicitur.		
Species: *(nomen)*	modus significandi rem, prout ipsa est sive intelligitur sub modo essendi priori vel posteriori vel prout imponitur sub esse primitivo vel derivativo . . Unde species est per primitivam et derivativam dividitur tamquam per differentias oppositas. species est primaria vel secundaria dictionis origo. Unde primitivum significat rem sub esse primo . . derivativum est quod significat rem sub esse secundario, sive prout est sub esse posteriori sive prout imponitur secundario vel posterius.	species est modus significandi accidentalis nominis designans proprietatem determinandi **ab** aliquo vel a nullo.	species est modus significandi accidentalis nominis, mediante quo modum significandi primarium vel secundarium significat.
Species: *(verbum)*	quod per formas verborum secundum quas aliquid dicitur perfectae formae vel meditativae vel frequentativae.	species in verbo sicut in nomine duae sunt scilicet primitiva et derivativa.	cf. forma
Tempus:	tempus in verbo est modus intelligendi fieri sub instanti vel sub continuo tempore, et secun-	tempus est modus significandi accidentalis verbi designans circa rem modum essendi praesentiali- t̲a̲t̲i̲s̲ vel p̲r̲a̲e̲t̲e̲r̲i̲t̲i̲o̲n̲i̲s̲ vel f̲u̲t̲u̲r̲i̲-	tempus est modus significandi accidentalis verbi, quo mediante verbum, citra rem, modum tem- p̲o̲r̲i̲s̲ c̲o̲n̲s̲i̲g̲n̲i̲f̲i̲c̲a̲t̲.

Verbum:

variatur tempus per triplicem sui differentiam, scilicet praesens, praeteritum et futurum. significat per modum fieri distantis a substantia.

modus significandi generalis essentialis verbi est modus significandi per modum fluxus, fieri seu motus, seu esse .. modus specificus verbi est modus significandi essentialis de aliquo seu significare per modum distantis vel facientis alterum extremum orationis.

verbum est pars orationis significans per modum esse distantis a substantia.

Vox:

vox significat rem et consignificat proprietates rei. vox per accidens consideratur a grammatico.

vox non est vox propter modum proferendi: vox est percussio aeris respirati ad arteriam vocalem ab iis partibus cum imagine significandi.

vox, inquantum vox, non consideratur a grammatico, sed inquantum signum, quia grammatica est de signis rerum.

BIBLIOGRAPHY

TEXTS

Donatus, *Ars Grammatica*, ed. H. Keil, *Grammatici Latini*, Vol. IV (Leipzig, 1864).
Priscian, *Institutionum Grammaticarum Libri XVIII*, ed. H. Keil, *Grammatici Latini*, II-III (Leipzig, 1864).
Petrus Abaelardus, *Dialectica*, ed. L. M. de Rijk (Assen, 1956).
Alexander de Villadei, *Doctrinale*, ed. D. Reichling (= *Monumenta Germaniae Paedagogica*, Bd. 12) (Berlin, 1893).
Eberhardus Bethuniensis, *Graecismus*, ed. J. Wrobel, *Corpus Grammaticorum Medii Aevi*, I (Breslau, 1887).
Robert Kilwardby, "Super Priscianum de Constructionibus" (MS. Corpus Christi College, Oxford, 119).[1]
De Grammatica (Oxford, Bodleian Library, MS. Digby 55).[1]
Roger Bacon, *Summa Grammatica*, ed. R. Steele, Fasc. 15, *Opera Hactenus Inedita Rogeri Baconi* (Oxford, 1909).
Thurot, Ch., "Notices et extraits de divers manuscrits latins pour servir à l'histoire des doctrines grammaticales au moyen âge", *Notices et Extraits des manuscrits de la Bibliothèque Impériale XXII* (Paris, 1868).[2]
John of Dacia, *Summa Gramatica*, ed. A. Otto, *Corpus philosophorum danicorum Medii Aevi* (Copenhagen, 1955).
Martin of Dacia, *De Modis Significandi*, ed. H. Roos, *Corpus Philosophorum Danicorum Medii Aevi*, II (Copenhagen, 1961).
Michel de Marbais, *De Modus Significandi*, extracts published in Ch. Thurot, *Op. cit.*
Siger de Courtrai, *Summa Modorum Significandi*, ed. G. Wallerand, *Les Œuvres de Siger de Courtrai. Les Philosophes belges*, VIII (Louvain, 1913).
Simon of Dacia, *Opera*, ed. A. Otto, *Corpus Philosophorum Danicorum Medii Aevi III* (Copenhagen, 1963).
Thomas of Erfurt, *De Modis Significandi sive Gramatica Speculativa*, ed. Fr. M. Fernandez Garcia (Florence, 1902).

[1] I am indebted to Dr. R. W. Hunt of the Bodleian Library for the loan of his transcriptions of these manuscripts.
[2] Thurot's work has been used in particular as the source for the quotations from Michel de Marbais and Peter Helias.

THE MEDIAEVAL BACKGROUND

Abelson, P., *The Seven Liberal Arts* (New York, 1906).
Artz, F. B., *The Mind of the Middle Ages* (New York, 1953).

Barrett, H. M., *Boethius. Some Aspects of his Time and Work* (Cambridge, 1940).
Bocheński, I. M., *Summulae Logicales Petri Hispani* (Rome, 1947).
Boehner, P., *Mediaeval Logic* (Manchester, 1952).
Bolgar, R. R., *The Classical Heritage* (Cambridge, 1954).
Bréhier, E., *La philosophie du Moyen Age, L'Evolution de l'humanité*, Vol. 45 (Paris, 1937).
Buchanan, S., "An Introduction to the 'De Modis Significandi' of Thomas of Erfurt", *Philosophical Essays for A. N. Whitehead* (London, 1936).
Carré, M. H., *Realists and Nominalists* (Oxford, 1946).
Chenu, M. D., "Grammaire et théologie aux XII et XIIIe siècles", *Archives d'histoire doctrinale et littéraire du moyen âge* (Paris, 1935-1936).
Copleston, F. C., *Aquinas* (London, 1955).
——, *A History of Philosophy: Vol. II, Augustine to Scotus* (London, 1950).
Curtius, E. R., "Das mittelalterliche Bildungswesen und die Grammatik", *Romanische Forschungen* 40 (1947), 1-26.
——, *European Literature and the Latin Middle Ages* (London, 1953).
Delhaye, P., "L'Organisation scolaire au XIIe siècle", *Traditio* 5 (1947), 211-263.
Denifle, H., *Die Entstehung der Universitäten des Mittelalters bis 1400* (Berlin, 1956).
Forest, A., Steenberghen, F. van, Gandillac, M. de, *Le mouvement doctrinal du XIe au XIVe siècle* (Paris, 1951).
Geyer, B., "Peter Abelards philosophische Schriften", *Beiträge zur Geschichte der Philosophie des Mittelalters*. Band 21, Heft 1 (Münster, 1919).
Ghellinck, J. de, *L'Essor de la littérature latine au XIIe siècle* (Paris, 1946).
Gilson, E., *La philosophie au moyen âge* (Paris, 1944).
——, *History of Christian Philosophy in the Middle Ages* (London, 1955).
Grabmann, M., *Die Geschichte der Scholastischen Methode* (Freiburg, 1900-1910).
——, *Forschungen über die lateinischen Aristotelesübersetzungen des 13ten. Jahrhunderts* (Münster, 1916).
——, "De Thoma Erfordiensi auctore Grammaticae quae Joanni Duns Scoto adscribitur speculativae", *Archivum Francisanum Historicum* 15 (1922), 273-277.
——, "Die Entwicklung der mittelalterlichen Sprachlogik", *Philosophisches Jahrbuch der Görresgesellschaft* 35 (1922), 122-135, 199-214.
——, *Mittelalterliches Geistesleben*, Vols. 1-3 (München, 1916).
——, "Eine für Examinazwecke abgefasste Questionensammlung der Pariser Artistenfakultät aus der ersten Hälfte des 13ten Jahrhunderts", *Revue néoscolastique* 36 (1934), 211-229.
——, "Handschriftliche Forschungen und Funde zu den philosophischen Schriften des Petrus Hispanus, des späteren Papsten Johannes XXI", *Sitzungsbericht der Bayerischen Akademie der Wissenschaften* (München, 1936).
——, "Die Introductiones in Logicam des Wilhelm von Shyreswood", *Sitzungsbericht der Bayerischen Akademie der Wissenschaften* (München, 1937).
——, "Auslegung der Aristotelischen Logik aus der Zeit von Boethius bis Petrus Hispanus", *Abhandlungen der Preussischen Akademie der Wissenschaft* (Berlin, 1937).
——, *Die Sophismataliteratur des 12ten und 13ten Jahrhunderts mit Textausgabe eines Sophisma des Boethius von Dacien* (Münster, 1940).
——, "Gentile da Cingoli, ein italienisches Aristoteleserklärer aus der Zeit Dantes", *Sitzungsbericht der Bayerischen Akademie der Wissenschaften* (München, 1941).
——, "Thomas von Erfurt und die Sprachlogik des mittelalterlichen Aristotelismus", *Sitzungsbericht der Bayerischen Akademie der Wissenschaften* (München, 1943).

——, "Ein Tractatus de Universalibus." *Mediaeval Studies* 9 (1947), 56-70.

——, "Aristoteles im zwölften Jahrhundert", *Mediaeval Studies* 12 (1950), 123-162.

——, "Die geschichtliche Entwicklung der mittelalterlichen Sprachphilosophie und Sprachlogik. Ein Überblick." *Mélanges Joseph de Ghellinck, S.J.* (Gembloux, 1951).

Haskins, C. H., *The Rise of the Universities* (New York, 1923).

——, *The Renaissance of the Twelfth Century* (Cambridge, Mass., 1927).

——, *Studies in Mediaeval Culture* (New York, 1929).

Hauréau, B., *Histoire de la philosophie scolastique* (Paris, 1872-1880).

Heinimann, S., "Zur Geschichte der grammatischen Terminologie im Mittelalter", *Zeitschrift für Romanische Philologie* 79 (1963), 23-37.

Heidegger, M., *Die Kategorien- und Bedeutungslehre des Duns Scotus* (Tübingen, 1916).

Hunt, R. W., "The Introduction to the 'Artes' in the Twelfth Century", *Studia Mediaevalia* (= *Miscellanea Martin*) (Bruges, 1948), 85-112.

——, "Hugutio and Petrus Helias", *Mediaeval and Renaissance Studies* 2 (1950), 174-178.

Jeauneau, E., "Deux rédactions des gloses de Guillaume de Conches sur Priscien". *Recherches de théologie ancienne et médiévale* 27 (1960), 212-247.

Jourdain, A. *Recherches critiques sur l'âge et l'origine des traductions latines d'Aristote et sur des commentaires grecs ou arabes employés par les docteurs scolastiques* (New York (revised edition), 1960).

Kneale, W. and M., *The Development of Logic* (Oxford, 1962).

Knowles, D., *The Evolution of Mediaeval Thought* (New York, 1962).

Lacombe, G., *Aristoteles Latinus. Pars prior. Corpus Philosophorum Medii Aevi* (Rome, 1939).

Leff, G., *Mediaeval Thought from Saint Augustine to Ockham* (London, 1958).

Lehmann, P., "Mitteilungen aus Handschriften VIII", *Sitzungsbericht der Bayerischen Akademie der Wissenschaften* (München, 1944).

Manitius, M., *Geschichte der lateinischen Literatur des Mittelalters. Handbuch der Klassischen Altertumswissenschaft*. Band 9 (München, 1911).

Manthey, F., *Die Sprachphilosophie des hl. Thomas von Aquin und ihre Anwendung auf Probleme der Theologie* (Pederborn, 1937).

Martinelli, L., p.s.s., *Thomas d'Aquin et l'analyse linguistique* (Montréal, 1963).

McKeon, R. P., "Rhetoric in the Middle Ages", *Speculum* 17 (1942), 1-32.

Mullally, J. P., *The 'Summulae Logicales' of Peter of Spain. University of Notre Dame Publications in Mediaeval Studies*, No. 8 (Notre Dame, 1945).

Norden, E., *Die antike Kunstprosa vom VIten Jahrhundert vor Christ bis in die Zeit der Renaissance* (Leipzig, 1898).

——, "Die lateinische Literatur im Übergang vom Altertum zum Mittelalter", *Kultur der Gegenwart* 8 (1901), 373-411.

O'Donnell, J. R., "The Syncategoremata of William of Sherwood", *Mediaeval Studies* 3 (1941), 46-93.

O'Mahony, B. E., "A Mediaeval Semantic. The scholastic 'Tractatus de modus significandi' ", *Laurentianum* 5 (1964), 448-486.

Paetow, L. J., *The Arts Course at Mediaeval Universities with Special Reference to Grammar and Rhetoric* (= *The University of Illinois Studies, Vol. 3, No. 7*) (Urbana, 1909).

——, *The Battle of the Seven Arts* (*Memoirs of the University of California, Vol. 4, No. 1*) (Berkeley, 1914).

Patch, H. R., *The Tradition of Boethius* (New York, 1935).

Prantl, C., *Geschichte der Logik im Abendlande* (Leipzig, 1855-1870).

Rashdall, H., *The Universities of Europe in the Middle Ages* (Oxford, 1894).

Rijk, L. M. de, *Logica Modernorum. A Contribution to the History of Early Terminist Logic*. Vols. 1-2 (Assen, 1967).

Sandys, J. E., *A History of Classical Scholarship* (Cambridge, 1903).

Sikes, J. G., *Peter Abelard* (Cambridge, 1932).

Southern, R. W., *The Making of the Middle Ages* (London, 1953).

Steenberghen, F. van, *Aristotle in the West* (Louvain, 1955).

——, *La Philosophie au xiiie siècle* (Louvain, 1966).

——, *The Philosophical Movement in the 13th Century* (Edinburgh, 1955).

Strecker, K., *Introduction to Mediaeval Latin*. Translated and revised, R. B. Palmer (Berlin, 1957).

Taylor, H. O., *The Classical Heritage of the Middle Ages* (New York, 1903).

——, *The Mediaeval Mind* (New York, 1925).

Thomson, S. Harrison, "Robert Kilwardby's Commentaries in Priscianum and in Barbarismum Donati", *The New Scholasticism* 12 (1938), 52-65.

Vignaux, P., *La philosophie au moyen âge* (Paris, 1938).

Webb, C. C. J., *John of Salisbury* (London, 1932).

Werner, K., *Die Scholastik des späteren Mittelalters* (Vienna, 1881).

——, "Die Sprachlogik des Johannes Duns Scotus", *Sitzungsberichte der Oesterreichischen Akademie der Wissenschaften*. Band 85 (Vienna, 1877).

Wulf, M. de, *Philosophy and Civilisation in the Middle Ages* (New York, 1922).

——, *History of Mediaeval Philosophy* (London, 1926).

——, *An Introduction to Scholastic Philosophy* (New York, 1953).

THE HISTORY OF LINGUISTICS

Arens, H., *Sprachwissenschaft* (München, 1955).

Baebler, J. B., *Beiträge zu einer Geschichte der lateinischen Grammatik im Mittelalter* (Halle, 1885).

Bursill-Hall, G. L., "Mediaeval grammatical theories", *Canadian Journal of Linguistics* 9 (1963), 39-54.

——, "Notes on the Semantics of Linguistic Description", *In Memory of J. R. Firth* (London, 1966), 40-51.

——, Aspects of Modistic Grammar. (*Georgetown University Monograph Series on Languages and Linguistics* 17) (1966), 133-148.

Cassirer, E., *Die Philosophie der symbolischen Formen. Vol. 1. Die Sprache* (Berlin, 1923).

Chase, W. J., *The Ars Minor of Donatus. University of Wisconsin Studies in the Social Sciences and History*, No. 11 (Madison, 1926).

Chomsky, N. A., *Cartesian Linguistics* (New York, 1966).

Collart, J., *Varron, Grammairien Latin* (Paris, 1954).

Dinneen, F. P., s.j., *An Introduction to General Linguistics* (New York, 1967).

Dixon, R. M. W., *What is Language? A New Approach to Linguistic Description* (London, 1965).

Funke, O., *Studien zur Geschichte der Sprachphilosophie* (Berne, 1927).

Godfrey, R. G., "The Language Theory of Thomas of Erfurt", *Studies in Philology* 57 (1960), 22-29.

——, "Late Mediaeval Linguistic Meta-Theory and Chomsky's Syntactic Structures", *Word* 21 (1966), 251-266.

Henry, D. P., *The De Grammatico of St Anselm. The Theory of Paronymi* (*Notre Dame Publications in Mediaeval Studies* 18) (Notre Dame, 1964).

Hoenigswald, H. M., Review: R. H. Robins, *Ancient and Mediaeval Grammatical Theory in Europe. Language* 29 (1953), 180-182.

Hunt, R. W., "Studies in Priscian in the 11th and 12th Centuries", *Mediaeval and Renaissance Studies* 1-2 (1941-1943: 1950), 194-231: 1-56.

Ivić, M., *Trends in Linguistics* (The Hague, 1965).
Jeep, L., *Zur Geschichte der Lehre von den Redeteilen bei den lateinischen Grammatikern* (Leipzig, 1893).
Kukenheim, L., *Contributions à l'histoire de la grammaire grecque, latine et hébraïque* (Leiden, 1951).
——, *Esquisse historique de la linguistique française et de ses rapports avec la linguistique générale* (Leiden, 1962).
Langendoen, T., "A Note on the Linguistic Theory of Varro", *Foundations of Language* 2 (1966), 33-36.
Leclerc, V., "Michel de Roubaix ou de Brabant, Grammairien", *Histoire littéraire de la France* 21 (1847), 267-271.
Lersch, L., *Die Sprachphilosophie der Alten* (Bonn, 1838-1841).
McCanles, M., "Peter of Spain and William of Ockham: From Metaphysics to Grammar", *The Modern Schoolman* 43 (1965-1966), 133-141.
Mounin, G., *Histoire de la linguistique des origines au XXe siècle* (Paris, 1967).
Nehring, A., "A Note on Functional Linguistics in the Middle Ages", *Traditio* 9 (1953), 430-434.
Otto, A., "Magister Johannes Dacus und seine Schriften", *Classica et Mediaevalia* 13 (1952), 73-86.
Pedersen, H., *The Discovery of Language* (Bloomington, 1962).
Pinborg, J., "Mittelalterliche Sprachtheorien. Was heisst modus significandi", *Fides quaerens intellectum* (1964), 66-84.
——, *Die Entwicklung der Sprachtheorie im Mittelalter. Beiträge zur Geschichte der Philosophie und Theologie des Mittelalters.* Band 42, Heft 2 (Münster/ Copenhagen, 1967).
Reichling, A., "What is General Linguistics?" *Lingua* 1 (1948), 8-24.
Robins, R. H., *Ancient and Mediaeval Grammatical Theory in Europe* (London, 1951).
——, "Dionysius Thrax and the Western Grammatical Tradition", *TPS* 9 (1957), 67-106.
——, "The Development of the Word Class System of the European Grammatical Tradition", *Foundations of Language* 2 (1966), 3-19.
——, *A Short History of Linguistics* (London, 1967).
Roos, H., s.j., "Martinus de Dacia und seine Schrift 'De Modis Significandi' ", *Classica et Mediaevalia* 8 (1946), 87-115.
——, "Sprachdenken im Mittelalter", *Classica et Mediaevalia* 9 (1948), 200-215.
——, *Die Modi Significandi des Martinus de Dacia. Forschungen zur Geschichte der Sprachlogik im Mittelalter. Beiträge zur Geschichte der Philosophie und Theologie des Mittelalters*, Band 37 (Copenhagen, 1952).
Rotta, P., *La Filosofia del Linguaggio nella Patristica e nella Scholastica* (Turin, 1909).
Steinthal, H., *Geschichte der Sprachwissenschaft bei den Griechen und Römern* (Berlin, 1863-1891).
Teeter, K. V., "New Lamps for Old", (*Georgetown University Monograph Series on Languages and Linguistics* 19) (1966), 83-95.
Watermann, J. T., *Perspectives in Linguistics* (Chicago, 1963).

MODERN LINGUISTICS

Bazell, C. E., "On the Neutralisation of Syntactic Oppositions", *TCLC* 5 (1949), 77-86.
——, "On the Problem of the Morpheme", *Archivum Linguisticum* 1 (1949), 1-15.
——, "Syntactic Relations and Linguistic Typology", *CFS* 8 (1949), 5-20.

——, "The Fundamental Syntactic Relations", *Časopis pro Moderní Filologii* 33 (1949), 9-15.
——, *Linguistic Form* (Istanbul, 1953).
——, "Meaning and the Morpheme", *Word* 18 (1962), 132-142.
Bloomfield, L., *Language* (New York, 1933).
Brøndal, V., *Les parties du discours* (Copenhagen, 1928).
Chomsky, N. A., *Syntactic Structures* (The Hague, 1957).
——, "Formal Properties of Grammars", *Handbook of Mathematical Psychology*, Vol. 2 (eds. R. Luce, R. Bush, E. Galantar) (New York, 1963), 323-418.
——, *Current Issues in Linguistic Theory* (The Hague, 1964).
——, "A Transformational Approach to Syntax", *The Structure of Language*, eds. J. A. Fodor and J. J. Katz (Englewood Cliffs, N.J., 1964), 211-245.
——, *Aspects of the Theory of Syntax* (Cambridge, Mass., 1965).
——, *Topics in the Theory of Generative Grammar* (The Hague, 1966).
Coseriu, E., *Logicismo y Antilogicismo en la Gramatica* (Montevideo, 1957).
Dingwall, W. O., "Transformational Grammar: Form and Theory", *Lingua* 12 (1963), 233-275.
Dixon, R. M. W., *Linguistic Science and Logic* (The Hague, 1963).
——, "A Trend in Semantics", *Linguistics* 1 (1963), 30-57.
Firth, J. R., *Papers in Linguistics 1934-1951* (London, 1957).
——, "A Synopsis of Linguistic Theory 1930-1955", *Studies in Linguistic Analysis* (1967), 1-32.
Garvin, P. L., Review: L. Hjelmslev, *Prolegomena to a Theory of Language*, *Language* 30 (1954), 69-96.
de Groot, A. W., "Les oppositions dans les systèmes de la syntaxe des cas", *Mélanges Bally* (1939), 107-127.
——, "Structural Linguistics and Word Classes", *Lingua* 1 (1948), 427-500.
——, "Classification of Cases and Use of Cases", *For Roman Jakobson* (The Hague, 1956), 187-196.
Haas, W., "Linguistic Relevance", *In Memory of J. R. Firth* (London, 1966), 116-142.
Halliday, M. A. K., "Categories of the Theory of Grammar", *Word* 17 (1961), 241-292.
——, "Class in Relation to the Axes of Chain and Choice", *Linguistics* 2 (1963), 5-15.
——, "Some Notes on 'Deep' Grammar", *Journal of Linguistics* 2 (1966), 57-67.
——, "Lexis as a Linguistic Level", *In Memory of J. R. Firth* (London, 1966), 148-162.
Hjelmslev, L., *Principes de grammaire générale* (Copenhagen, 1928).
——, *La catégorie des cas. Étude de grammaire générale* (Aarhus, 1935-1937).
——, "La structure morphologique", *Essais linguistiques, TCLC* 12 (1959), 113-138.
——, "La notion de rection", *Ibid.*, 139-151.
——, "Le verbe et la phrase nominale", *Ibid.*, 165-191.
——, "Structural Analysis of Language", *Ibid.*, 27-35.
——, "Pour une sémantique structurale", *Ibid.*, 96-112.
——, *Prolegomena to a Theory of Language*, trans. F. J. Whitfield (Madison, 1961).
Hockett, C. F., "Two Models of Grammatical Description", *Word* 10 (1954), 210-234.
——, "Linguistic Elements and their Relations", *Language* 37 (1961), 29-54.
——, "Sound Change", *Language* 41 (1965), 185-204.
Jakobson, R., "Beitrag zur allgemeinen Kasuslehre", *TCLP* 6 (1936), 240-288.
——, "Implications of Language Universals for Linguistics", *Universals of Language* (ed. J. H. Greenberg, 1963), 208-219.

Jespersen, O., *Philosophy of Grammar* (London, 1924).
Katz, J. J. and Fodor, J. A., "The Structure of a Semantic Theory", *Language* 39 (1963), 170-210.
Katz, J. J. and Postal, P. M., *An Integrated Theory of Linguistic Description* (Cambridge, Mass., 1964).
Kuryłowicz, J., "Dérivation lexicale et dérivation syntaxique", *BSLP* 37 (1936), 79-93.
——, "Le problème du classement des cas". *Bulletin de la société polonaise de linguistique* 9 (1949), 20-43.
Lyons, J., *Structural Semantics* (Oxford, 1963).
Martinet, A., *A Functional View of Language* (Oxford, 1962).
——, *Elements of General Linguistics* (London, 1964).
McIntosh, A., "Patterns and Ranges", *Language* 37 (1961), 325-337.
Nida, E. A., "The Analysis of Grammatical Constituents", *Language* 24 (1948), 168-177.
Otto, W., "Grundlagen der Sprachwissenschaft gesehen von der Wortlehre aus", *Zeitschrift für romanische Philologie* 71 (1955), 161-171.
Paul, H., *Prinzipien der Sprachgeschichte* (Halle, 1909).
Postal, P. M., "Underlying and Superficial Linguistic Structure", *Harvard Educational Review* 34 (1964), 246-266.
Robins, R. H., "A Problem in the Statement of Meaning", *Lingua* 3 (1952), 121-137.
——, "Noun and Verb in Universal Grammar", *Language* 28 (1952), 289-298.
——, "In Defence of WP", *TPS* (1959), 116-144.
——, "Some Considerations on the Status of Grammar in Linguistics", *Archivum Linguisticum* 11 (1959), 91-114.
——, "Grammar, Meaning, and the Study of Language", *Canadian Journal of Linguistics* 9 (1964), 98-114.
——, *General Linguistics* (London, 1964).
Saporta, S., "Morph, Morpheme, Archimorpheme", *Word* 12 (1956), 9-14.
Saussure, F. de, *Cours de linguistique générale* (Paris, 1931).
Spang-Hanssen, H., *Recent Theories on the Nature of the Linguistic Sign, TCLC* 9 (Copenhagen, 1954).
Tesnière, L., *Éléments d'une syntaxe structurale* (Paris, 1954).
Trager, G. L., "The Field of Linguistics", *Studies in Linguistics, Occasional Papers* 1 (Norman, Oklahoma, 1949).
Wackernagel, J., *Vorlesungen über Syntax* (Basle, 1920-1924).
Weinrich, U., "On the Semantic Structure of Language", *Universals of Language* (ed. J. H. Greenberg, 1963), 114-171.
Wells, R. S., "Immediate Constituents", *Language* 23 (1947), 81-117.
Whorf, B. L., *Language, Thought, and Reality* (New York, 1956).

INDEX AUCTORUM

Thomas of Erfurt

Grammatica Speculativa

(ed. Garcia),

INDEX EXEMPLORUM CITATORUM

INDEX NOMINUM

(The names of Siger de Coutrai and Thomas of Erfurt do not appear in this index since they occur on almost every page of the text).

Abercrombie, D., 14.
Aelfric, 22, 198.
Albertus Magnus, 29, 34.
Alcuin, 198.
Alexander de Villa-Dei, 26, 27, 36, 233, 289.
Alexandria (Alexandrian school), 16-19, 21, 26, 115, 197.
Allen, W. S., 287.
Apollonius Dyscolus, 16, 19, 171, 178, 180, 197, 242, 289.
Aristotle, 14-18, 23-29, 31, 37, 46, 90, 120, 125, 126, 128, 135, 136, 196, 197, 198, 200, 202, 215, 218, 235, 287, 289, 296.

Bazell, C. E., 328, 338, 339.
Bede, 198.
Bloch, B., 150, 294.
Bloomfield, L., 46, 47, 65, 98, 121, 139, 192, 295, 330, 337.
Bocheński, I. M., 14.
Boethius, 15, 16, 22, 167, 197.
Boethius of Dacia, 14, 32, 33, 53, 292.
Butterfield, H., 336.

Cassiodorus, 22, 198.
Chomsky, N. A., 12-14, 18, 27, 75, 287, 328, 330-334, 340.
Copleston, F. C., 47, 52, 92-95, 138, 183, 185, 299.

Dingwall, W. O., 12, 14.
Dinneen, F. P., 334, 335.
Dionysius Thrax, 12, 16, 19, 21, 58, 115, 127, 162, 163, 170, 177, 178, 180, 197, 198, 214, 215, 223, 242-244, 258, 267, 276, 280.
Donatus, 16, 17, 20, 21, 23, 24, 35, 40, 45, 46, 53, 114, 117, 122, 124, 133, 141, 142, 147-149, 155, 160, 162, 163, 165, 172, 180-184, 186-188, 192, 194, 195, 198, 214-216, 220, 224, 228, 229, 231, 233, 234, 241-243, 250, 256, 259, 262, 263, 267-269, 272, 274-276, 281, 283-285.

Eberhardus Bethuniensis, 26.
Erhardus Knab von Zwiefalten, 32.

Firth, J. R., 15, 37, 46-48, 57, 63, 73, 74, 267, 287, 303, 304, 310, 329, 331, 340.

Gilson, E., 25, 26, 30, 31.
Godfrey, R. G., 13, 333.
Grabmann, M., 31-34, 39.

Halliday, M. A. K., 12, 287, 333.
Haskins, C. H., 23, 25, 26, 31.
Heidegger, M., 118-120, 173.
Hjelmslev, L., 35, 41, 47, 79, 96, 110, 171, 176, 178, 179, 313, 327, 329, 331, 338, 339.
Hockett, C. F., 12, 61, 119, 218, 254, 256.
Hoenigswald, H., 11.
Humboldt, W. von, 13.
Hunt, R. W., 16, 22, 27, 28, 199.

Isidore of Seville, 22, 198.

Jean Josse de Marvilla, 32.
Jespersen, O., 200, 256, 261.
Johannes Aurifaber, 32.

INDEX RERUM